FAA AIRMEN KNOWLEDGE
COMMERCIAL PILOT
TEST GUIDE

Cover Photo: Piper aircraft in flight courtesy of Piper Aircraft, Inc.

ISBN 978-0-88487-061-6

Jeppesen
55 Inverness Drive East
Englewood, CO 80112-5498
Web Site: www.jeppesen.com
Email: Captain@jeppesen.com
Copyright © Jeppesen
All Rights Reserved. Published 1993-2008, 2011, 2015, 2021

Preface

Thank you for purchasing the *FAA Airman Knowledge — Commercial Pilot Test Guide*. This test guide helps you understand the learning objectives that apply to questions on the FAA Commercial Pilot Airplane — Airman Knowledge Test so you can take the test with confidence. This test guide contains examples of the types of questions that appear on the FAA knowledge test along with correct answers, explanations, and study references. Explanations of why the other choices are wrong are included where appropriate. Questions are organized by topic, with explanations located to the right side of each question. You can use the sliding mask to cover up the answers and test yourself. Full-color legends and figures identical to the figures on the FAA test are included in Appendix 1 and 2 in the back of the book. This test guide is a component of the Guided Flight Discovery Pilot Training System and is not intended as a stand-alone learning tool but as a supplement to your instructor-led flight and ground training.

GUIDED FLIGHT DISCOVERY PILOT TRAINING SYSTEM

The Guided Flight Discovery Pilot Training System provides the finest pilot training available. Rather than just teaching facts, Guided Flight Discovery concentrates on an application-oriented approach to pilot training. The comprehensive and complete system emphasizes the why and how of aeronautical concepts when they are presented. As you progress through your training, you will find that the revolutionary Guided Flight Discovery system leads you through essential aeronautical knowledge and exposes you to a variety of interesting and useful information that will enhance and expand your understanding of the world of aviation.

Although you can use each element of the Guided Flight Discovery Pilot Training System separately, the effectiveness of the materials is maximized by using all of the individual components in a systems approach. In addition to this test guide, the primary components of the Instrument Training Program are described below.

INSTRUMENT/COMMERCIAL TEXTBOOK/E-BOOK

This *Instrument Commercial* textbook/e-Book is your primary source for initial study and review. The text contains complete and concise explanations of the fundamental concepts and ideas that every pilot needs to know to effectively operate in the instrument and commercial flight environments. The subjects are organized in a logical manner to build upon previously introduced topics. Subjects are often expanded upon through the use of Discovery Insets, which are strategically placed throughout the chapters. The Summary Checklists, Key Terms, and Questions are designed to help you review and prepare for both the knowledge and practical tests.

Jeppesen e-Books are electronic versions of traditional textbooks and reference materials that you can view on computers and other devices. Jeppesen e-Books are available on iOS or Android devices and PC or Mac computers. Jeppesen e-Books provide valuable features, including the ability to quickly jump to specific information, bookmark pages, and take notes. Direct linking to chapters in each book is provided through the table of contents.

INSTRUMENT/COMMERCIAL SYLLABUS

The syllabus is an outline of the Instrument Rating Course, Commercial Pilot Certification Course, and Multi-Engine Rating Course. The syllabus provides a basic framework for your training in a logical sequence and assigns appropriate study material for each lesson. Ground and flight lessons are coordinated to ensure that your training progresses smoothly and that you are consistently introduced to topics on the ground prior to being required to apply that knowledge in the airplane. The syllabus is available in print and e-Book versions.

FAR/AIM

The Jeppesen FAR/AIM includes the current *Federal Aviation Regulations* (FARs) and the *Aeronautical Information Manual* (AIM) in one publication available in printed form or as an e-Book. The FAR/AIM includes FAR Parts 1, 3, 11, 43, 48, 61, 67, 68, 71, 73, 91, 97, 103, 105, 107, 110, 119, 135, 136, 137, 141, 142, NTSB 830, and TSRs 1552 and 1562. The AIM is a complete reproduction of the FAA publication with full-color graphics and the Pilot/Controller Glossary. The AIM contains basic flight information and ATC procedures to operate effectively in the U.S. National Airspace System.

Table of Contents

Introduction

The *FAA Airman Knowledge — Commercial Pilot Test Guide* is designed to help you prepare for the FAA Commercial Pilot—Airplane Airman Knowledge Test. This test guide contains examples of the types of questions that appear on the FAA knowledge test that applies to airplanes. To ensure comprehensive preparation for the knowledge test, one or more questions apply to each knowledge subject code in the Commercial Pilot — Airplane Airman Certification Standards. Questions about rotorcraft are not included. We recommend that you use this test guide as part of the Guided Flight Discovery (GFD) Pilot Training System.

USING THE TEST GUIDE

The test guide is organized like the GFD *Instrument/Commercial* textbook. Ten numbered chapters and lettered sections within each chapter correspond to the chapters and sections that apply to the commercial pilot content in the textbook. Within the chapters of this test guide, each section contains a content summary followed by sample knowledge test questions that typically appear in the same sequence as the textbook material. The question is shown in the left column with the applicable Airman Certification Standards (ACS) code(s). Answers and explanations are in the right column with references to applicable sections in the textbook and to FAA publications. The following is an example of the information that appears with each question and explanation.

[1]	[2]	[3]	[4]	[5]	[6]
9-4	**CA.I.C.K3b**	**9-4.**	**Answer C.**	**GFDIC 9A**	**AW**
(FAA Question)		*(Explanation of FAA Question)*			

[1] Jeppesen designated test guide question number. The first number is the chapter where the question is located in the test guide, which corresponds to the chapter in the GFD textbook. The second number is the question number within the chapter. In this example, the question is the 4th question in Chapter 9 of the test guide.

[2] The airman certification standards (ACS) code(s). These codes are associated with Knowledge subject areas in the FAA Commercial Pilot — Airplane Airman Certification Standards (ACS), which provides the standards that you must meet for your commercial pilot practical test (checkride). In some cases, codes that apply to Risk and Skills subject areas of the ACS are also included as applicable. As revisions to the ACS are released, the FAA might modify these codes slightly so some codes in this knowledge test guide might not match the most recent version of the ACS.

[3] The Jeppesen designated test guide number. This number is repeated in the right-hand column above the explanation.

[4] The correct answer to the question. In this example, answer C is correct.

[5] The location of content in the GFD *Instrument/Commercial* textbook that applies to the question. In this case, the question is covered in Chapter 9, Section A in the textbook.

[6] Abbreviation for the FAA or other authoritative source document. In this example, the reference is the *Aeronautical Information Manual* (AIM).

REFERENCE ABBREVIATIONS

The following abbreviations for references are used in Jeppesen airman knowledge test guides.

AC	—	Advisory Circular
A/FD	—	Airport/Facility Directory (section in Chart Supplement)
AFH	—	Airplane Flying Handbook, FAA-H-8083-3
AIM	—	Aeronautical Information Manual
ASI-SA##	—	Air Safety Institute (AOPA) Safety Advisor (by number ##)
AW	—	Aviation Weather, AC 00-6
AWS	—	Aviation Weather Services, AC 00-45
FAR	—	Federal Aviation Regulation (14 CFR)
GFDIC	—	Guided Flight Discovery Instrument/Commercial Textbook
GFDPP	—	Guided Flight Discovery Private Pilot Textbook
GFDPPM	—	Guided Flight Discovery Private Pilot Maneuvers
IAP	—	Instrument Approach Procedure
IFH	—	Instrument Flying Handbook, FAA-H-8083-15
IPG	—	Instrument Procedures Guide (Jeppesen)
IPH	—	Instrument Procedures Handbook, FAA·H-8083-16
NAVWEPS	—	Aerodynamics for Naval Aviators
PHB	—	Pilot's Handbook of Aeronautical Knowledge, FAA-H-8083-25
RMH	—	Risk Management Handbook, FAA-H-8083-2
WBH	—	Aircraft Weight and Balance Handbook, FAA-H-8083-1
TERPS	—	U.S. Standard for Terminal Instrument Procedures
TSA	—	Transportation Security Administration

QUESTION ANSWERS AND EXPLANATIONS

To the right of the question, an explanation of the correct answer and why the other answers are wrong, (if needed) is included. Wrong answers are not explained for calculated answers, unless a common error in the calculations leads to one of the wrong answers. The correct answers have been determined by Jeppesen to be the best choice of the available answers based on official reference documents. Some questions that were valid when the FAA test was developed might no longer be appropriate due to ongoing changes in regulations or official operating procedures. The knowledge test that you take can be updated at any time. Therefore, when taking the FAA test, be sure to answer the questions according to the latest regulations or official operating procedures.

APPENDICES

Three appendices are included in the back of the test guide:

- Appendix 1—FAA Legends: the legends from the FAA *Airman Knowledge Testing Supplement for Commercial Pilot* are an important resource for answering questions about charts and information included in the Chart Supplement. For example, if you do not know the answer to a chart-related question or how to interpret an Airport/Facility Directory excerpt, refer to the legends and remember that they are available during your test.

- Appendix 2—FAA Figures: refer to these figures from the FAA *Airman Knowledge Testing Supplement for Commercial Pilot* when required to answer questions about information in a figure. A copy of this supplement is available during your test.

PREPARING FOR THE FAA TEST

To become a safe and competent instrument-rated pilot, you need more than just the academic knowledge required to pass a test. For a comprehensive ground training program, a structured ground school with a qualified flight or ground instructor is essential. An organized course of instruction covers the content more quickly, and enables you to obtain answers to questions you think of as you learn the material. The additional instruction is beneficial in your flight training.

Use this test guide in conjunction with the GFD *Instrument/Commercial* textbook. Follow these steps to get the most benefit from your study:

1. After reading a section of the textbook, review the summary checklist and answer the questions at end of the section to reinforce the material.

2. Refer to the corresponding section in this study guide and test your knowledge of the subject area by answering the sample FAA questions. Cover the answers in the right-hand column, read each question, and choose what you consider the best answer. A sliding mask is provided for this purpose.

3. Move down the sliding mask and read the answer and explanation for that question.

4. Mark the questions you miss for further study and review before taking the knowledge test.

5. After you complete your study, schedule your knowledge test right away, while the information is fresh in your mind.

FAA TRACKING NUMBER

Prior to taking the FAA airman knowledge test, you must establish an FAA tracking number (FTN) within the Integrated Airman Certification and Rating Application (IACRA) system. IACRA is the web-based certification/rating application that guides the user through the FAA's airman application process. IACRA helps ensure applicants meet regulatory and policy requirements through the use of extensive data validation.

To register for an FTN in IACRA, you must visit the IACRA website and follow the instructions provided. The FTN is a number assigned to you by the FAA that stays with you throughout the course of your aviation career. If you have been issued an airman certificate in the past, then you already have an FTN. Record your FTN as it will be required later by your instructor when recommending you for the practical test and by the FAA examiner/evaluator when you take the practical test. You may also need to reference this number to inquire about your application.

SCHEDULING THE TEST

After you have your FTN, you can register to take your FAA Airman Knowledge Test by going to the registration and scheduling website operated by PSI Services LLC at: https://faa.psiexams.com/FAA/login. After the PSI system verifies your FTN, you will be able to create a user profile in the PSI system and schedule your knowledge test. When you create your account in PSI's system, choose a username and password. You will use those credentials to access your account in PSI's system and register or check the status of your knowledge test.

ELIGIBILITY

When you arrive to the testing center, you must show that you have completed the appropriate ground instruction or home study course by presenting a:

- Certificate of graduation or a statement of accomplishment certifying the satisfactory completion of the ground school portion of a course from a FAA certificated pilot school. (FAR 61.71(a))

OR

- Written statement or logbook endorsement from an FAA authorized ground or flight instructor certifying that you are prepared to take the required knowledge test. (FAR 61.65(a)(4))

You must provide:

- Your federal training number (FTN).
- Identification that includes a photo, date of birth, signature, and physical, residential address. If you are a U.S. citizen or resident alien, you must provide one or more of the following:
    - Identification card issued by an U.S. state, territory, or government entity, such as a driver permit or license, government ID card or military ID card.
    - Passport
    - Alien residency (green) card.

    Non-U.S. citizens must provide a passport *and* a U.S. driver permit or license or government ID card.

TAKING THE KNOWLEDGE TEST

The Commercial Pilot—Airplane (CAX) test contains 100 multiple-choice questions, and you have 2 hours and 30 minutes to complete it. Each test question is independent of other questions—a correct response to one question does not depend on, or influence, the correct response to another. The minimum passing score is 70 percent.

TEST MATERIALS, REFERENCE MATERIALS, AND AIDS

You are allowed to use aids, reference materials, and test materials within specified guidelines, provided the actual test questions or answers are not revealed. The following guidelines apply:

- Aviation-oriented calculators — You may use any model of aviation-oriented calculator, including small electronic calculators that perform arithmetic functions (add, subtract, multiply and divide). Simple programmable memories, which allow addition to, subtraction from, or retrieval of one number from the memory and simple functions, such as square root and percent keys are permissible.

- Calculators — Testing centers may provide calculators to applicants and/or deny applicants' use of their personal calculators based on the following limitations.
    - Before and upon completion of the test, while in the presence of the unit member (proctor), you must actuate the "ON/OFF" switch or "RESET" button and perform any other function that ensures the erasure of any data stored in memory circuits.
    - The use of electronic calculators incorporating permanent or continuous type memory circuits without erasure capability is prohibited. The unit member (proctor) may refuse the use of your calculator when unable to determine the calculator's erasure capability.
    - If you calculator has a printer, you must surrender any printouts of data at the completion of the test.
    - You may not use magnetic cards, magnetic tapes, modules, computer chips, or any other device that can store pre-written programs or information related to the test.
    - You may not use any booklet or manual containing instructions related to the use of test aids.

- Written materials — You may not take any written materials (either handwritten, printed, or electronic) other than the supplement book provided by the unit member (proctor) into the testing area.

- Test materials — You may use scales, straightedges, protractors, plotters, navigation computers, blank log sheets, and electronic or mechanical calculators that are directly related to the test.

- Manufacturer's aids — Permanently inscribed instructions on the front and back of such aids, such as formulas, conversions, regulations, signals, weather data, holding pattern diagrams, frequencies, weight and balance formulas, and air traffic control (ATC) procedures) are permissible.

- Dictionaries — You are not allowed to have a dictionary in the testing area.

- Final decision — The unit member (proctor) makes the final determination of which test materials and personal possessions you may take into the testing area.

TEST-TAKING TIPS

Before starting the actual test, the testing software gives you a few sample questions so that you can practice navigating through the test. The sample questions in your practice session have no relation to the content of the test. This "practice test" familiarizes you with the look and feel of the system screens, including how to select answers, mark questions for later review, view the time remaining in the test, and use other features of the testing software.

After you start the actual test, you answer the questions that appear on the screen. If you are prepared, you will likely have plenty of time to complete the test. After you begin the test, the screen will show you the time remaining for completion. When taking the test, keep the following points in mind:

1. Answer each question in accordance with the latest regulations and procedures. If a recent change invalidates a question, you receive credit if you answer it. However, the FAA normally deletes or updates these questions.

2. Read each question carefully before looking at the possible answers. Make sure you clearly understand the problem before attempting to solve it.

3. After formulating an answer, determine which of the alternatives most nearly corresponds with that answer. The answer chosen should completely resolve the problem.

4. A question might appear to have more than one possible answer; however, only one answer is correct and complete. The other answers are either incomplete or are derived from popular misconceptions.

5. Make sure that you select an answer for each question. Questions left unanswered are counted as incorrect.

6. If you find a certain question difficult, mark it for review and proceed to the next question. After you answer the less difficult questions, return to the questions you marked for review and answer them. The review marking procedure is explained before you start the test. Although the testing software alerts you to unanswered questions, make sure that every question has an answer recorded before submitting the test for grading.

7. After solving a calculation problem, select the answer nearest to your solution. The problem has been checked with various calculators. If you solve it correctly, your result will be closer to the correct answer than the other choices.

8. For graph type questions, you may request a printed copy of the graph on which you may draw and write to compute the answer. You must turn in all paper work when you complete the test.

YOUR TEST RESULTS

All knowledge test data will be sent electronically to IACRA immediately after you complete the knowledge test. The testing center also provides your airman knowledge test report (AKTR) with your score and FTN. The AKTR lists the ACS codes that apply to the subject areas of the questions that you answered incorrectly. Prior to taking the practical test, compare the codes on the AKTR to the ACS codes in the *Commercial Pilot—Airplane Airman Certification Standards* to determine the specific subjects that you should study and the areas in which you should obtain additional training.

You present the AKTR to the examiner before taking your practical test to prove you have completed the appropriate knowledge test within the required time frame. During the oral portion of the practical test, the examiner is required to evaluate the noted areas of deficiency based on the codes shown on the AKTR. The airman knowledge test report includes ACS codes for incorrect answers. The AKTR is valid for 24 calendar months. If the AKTR expires before you complete the practical test, you must retake the knowledge test.

RETESTING AFTER FAILURE

If you receive a score less than 70%, you may apply for retesting after an authorized instructor provides additional training and an endorsement that states you are competent to pass the test. Before retesting, you must surrender the previous test report to the unit member (proctor), who will destroy that test report after administering the retest. The results from the latest test taken are the official score.

CHAPTER 1

Building Professional Experience

NOTE: No FAA Commercial questions apply to GFD Instrument Commercial textbook Chapter 1, Section A — Instrument Rating Requirements.

SECTION A
Instrument Rating Requirements

Chapter 1, Section A, of the *Commercial Pilot FAA Airman Knowledge Test Guide* corresponds to the same chapter and section of the *GFD Instrument/Commercial* textbook: Instrument Rating Requirements. Because this section is specific to instrument training, no FAA commercial pilot knowledge test questions apply.

SECTION B
Commercial Pilot Requirements

COMMERCIAL PILOT TRAINING

- For you to be eligible for a commercial pilot certificate, you must be at least 18 years of age, hold a private pilot certificate, be able to read, write, speak, and understand the English language, and meet specific training and flight time requirements described in the FARs, as well as pass a knowledge and practical test. Under FAR Part 141, you must hold an instrument rating or be concurrently enrolled in an instrument rating course.

- As part of the commercial pilot training requirements, you must receive 10 hours of flight training in a turbine-powered airplane, a complex airplane, or a technically advanced airplane (TAA).

- A complex airplane is an airplane that has:
    - Retractable landing gear;
    - Flaps;
    - Controllable pitch propeller or a full authority digital engine control (FADEC) system.

- A technically advanced airplane (TAA) is an airplane that has:
    - A primary flight display (PFD) with an airspeed indicator, turn coordinator, attitude indicator, heading indicator, altimeter, and vertical speed indicator;
    - A multifunction display (MFD) with a moving map using GPS navigation to display the aircraft position;
    - A two-axis autopilot integrated with the navigation and heading guidance system.

- A high performance airplane is defined as an airplane having an engine of more than 200 horsepower.

- To operate as pilot in command of either a complex or high performance airplane, you must receive training and an endorsement from your instructor. The training required to receive a high performance or complex airplane endorsement will focus on the operation of advanced airplane systems.

COMMERCIAL PILOT PRIVILEGES

- With respect to pilot certification, aircraft are organized into category, class, and type.
    - Category—airplane, rotorcraft, glider, lighter-than-air, and powered-lift.
    - Class—single-engine land, single-engine sea, multi-engine land, multi-engine sea, helicopter, gyroplane, airship, and balloon.
    - Type—make and model.

- A type rating is required to act as pilot in command of a:
    - Large aircraft (except lighter-than-air). According to FAR Part 1, "large aircraft" means an aircraft of more than 12,500 pounds, maximum certificated takeoff weight.
    - Turbojet-powered airplanes.
    - Other aircraft specified by the Administrator through aircraft type certificate procedures.

- According the FARs, to "operate" is to use, cause to use, or authorize to use aircraft, for the purpose of air navigation including the piloting of aircraft, with or without the right of legal control (as owner, lessee, or otherwise).

- A "commercial operator" is a person who, for compensation or hire, engages in the carriage by aircraft in air commerce of persons or property, other than as an air carrier or foreign air carrier and "operational control" means the exercise of authority over initiating, conducting, or terminating a flight.

- FAR 61.133 states that as a commercial pilot, you may act as pilot in command of an aircraft for compensation or hire and you may carry persons or property for compensation or hire provided you meet the qualifications that apply to the specific operation.

- Although some commercial operations are governed by FAR Part 91, many others, such as common carriage, on-demand, flag, and commuter operations must meet additional requirements described in FAR Parts 117, 119, 121, 125, 129, 135, 136, and 137.

- Under FAR Part 91, you may not engage in common carriage, which involves holding out, or advertising your services to furnish transportation for any member of the public.

- FAR Part 119 — *Certification: Air Carriers and Commercial Operators* describes the certification requirements an operator must meet in order to obtain and hold a certificate authorizing operations under FAR Parts 121, 125, or 135.

- FAR 119.1 lists specific operations not governed by FAR Parts 121, 125, or 135 for which the holder of a commercial pilot certificate may be paid. These operations include:

    ◦ Student instruction.

    ◦ Nonstop commercial air tours with specific restrictions listed in FAR 119.1.

    ◦ Ferry or training flights.

    ◦ Aerial work operations, including crop dusting, seeding, spraying, bird chasing, banner towing, aerial photography or survey, fire fighting, and powerline or pipeline patrol.

    ◦ Nonstop parachute operations within a 25 statute mile radius of the airport.

- You may conduct nonstop commercial air tours not governed by FAR Parts 121, 125, or 135 in an airplane with a passenger-seat configuration of 30 seats or fewer and a maximum payload capacity of 7,500 pounds or less; within a 25 statute mile radius of the departure airport; and with a letter of authorization (LOA) issued under FAR 91.147.

- If you do not hold an instrument rating, your commercial certificate will be issued with the limitation: "The carriage of passengers for hire in airplanes on cross-country flights in excess of 50 nautical miles or at night is prohibited."

- As a commercial pilot, you may not operate restricted, limited, primary, or experimental categories of aircraft for compensation or hire.

CURRENCY REQUIREMENTS

- You are required to document and record the training time and aeronautical experience used to meet the requirements for a certificate, rating, or flight review and the aeronautical experience required for meeting the recent flight experience requirements.

- According to FAR 61.65, to act as pilot in command, you must have accomplished a flight review and received a logbook endorsement from an authorized instructor within the previous 24 calendar months.

- You do not need to accomplish the flight review if, within the previous 24 calendar month, you have passed a pilot proficiency check or practical test for a pilot certificate, rating or operating privilege or for a flight instructor certificate, rating, renewal, or reinstatement.

- To act as pilot in command of an aircraft carrying passengers, you must have performed at least 3 takeoffs and landings in an aircraft of the same category and class (and type, if a type rating is required) within the preceding 90 days. To carry passengers at night—the period from 1 hour after sunset to 1 hour before sunrise as defined by FAR 61.57—the takeoffs and landings must have been during that time period and to a full stop.

- To act as PIC of a tailwheel airplane, you must have received flight training and an endorsement from an authorized instructor and the 3 landings required to carry passengers also must be to a full stop.

FAA WINGS—PILOT PROFICIENCY PROGRAM

- If you satisfactorily complete a current phase of the FAA WINGS—Pilot Proficiency Program within the previous 24 calendar months, you will not have to complete the flight review required by FAR 61.56.

- At faasafety.gov, you can find detailed information regarding the WINGS Program, including links to a WINGS Program User's Guide and to AC 61-91, *WINGS—Pilot Proficiency Program.*

SPECIFIC AIRCRAFT AND OPERATIONS

- According to FAR 61.58, to serve as PIC of an aircraft that is type certificated for more than one required pilot flight crewmember or is turbojet-powered, you must:
    - Within the preceding 12 calendar months, complete a PIC proficiency check in an aircraft that is type certificated for more than one required pilot flight crewmember or is turbojet-powered;
    - Within the preceding 24 calendar months, complete a PIC check in the particular type of aircraft in which you will serve as PIC that is type certificated for more than one required pilot flight crewmember or is turbojet-powered.

- FAR 61.55 outlines the requirements to serve as second-in-command (SIC) of an aircraft type certificated for more than one required pilot flight crewmember or in operations requiring an SIC. Among other requirements, within the previous 12 calendar months, you must:
    - Become familiar with the operating procedures, performance specifications and limitations, flight manual, placards, and markings for the specific type of aircraft;
    - Performed and logged pilot time in the type of aircraft or in a flight simulator that represents the specific type of aircraft.

- You may log second in command time:
    - If you are qualified in accordance with the SIC requirements of FAR 61.55, and you occupy a crewmember station in an aircraft that requires more than one pilot by the aircraft's type certificate or;
    - You hold the appropriate category, class, and instrument rating (if an instrument rating is required for the flight) for the aircraft being flown, and more than one pilot is required under the type certification of the aircraft or the regulations under which the flight is being conducted.

- According to FAR 61.31, to act as PIC of a tailwheel airplane, you must have received and logged flight training and received a logbook endorsement from an authorized instructor who found you proficient in the operation of a tailwheel airplane.

- As a private, commercial or ATP, you must meet specific requirements outlined in FAR 61.69 to tow a glider or unpowered ultralight vehicle. You must have:
    - Logged at least 100 hours of as PIC in the aircraft category, class and type that you are using for the tow.
    - A logbook endorsement from an authorized instructor that you have received ground and flight training towing gliders or unpowered ultralight vehicles.
    - Logged at least 3 flights while towing a glider or unpowered ultralight vehicle or have simulated towing flight procedures in an aircraft while accompanied by a qualified pilot and received a logbook endorsement.
    - Within 24 calendar months before the flight, made at least 3 actual or simulated tows of a glider or unpowered ultralight vehicle while accompanied by a qualified pilot or made at least 3 flights as pilot in command of a glider or unpowered ultralight vehicle towed by an aircraft.

MAINTAINING YOUR PRIVILEGES

- After changing your permanent mailing address, you may not exercise the privileges of a pilot or flight instructor certificate after 30 days unless the FAA Airman Certification Branch has been notified in writing.

- According to FAR 61.15, when a pilot is convicted of operating a motor vehicle while either intoxicated or impaired by alcohol or a drug, the pilot must notify the FAA Civil Aviation Security Division, in writing, not later than 60 days after the conviction.

SECTION B ■ **Commercial Pilot Requirements**

MEDICAL REQUIREMENTS

- Although you need at least a third-class medical certificate to be eligible for a commercial pilot certificate, you must have a second-class medical certificate to exercise commercial pilot privileges.
- A second-class medical certificate is valid for 12 calendar months for operations requiring a commercial certificate.

BASICMED

- The BasicMed rule allows you to act as pilot in command using a driver's license instead of a medical certificate if you meet BasicMed requirements and comply with certain limitations. One of the limitations is that you may not conduct flight operations for compensation or hire.
- To qualify for the BasicMed rule, you must:
    - Possess and carry a valid U.S. driver's license.
    - Have completed an approved medical education course—available online from the Aircraft Owners and Pilots Association (AOPA)—within the previous 24 calendar months.
    - Have received a comprehensive medical exam from a state-licensed physician within the previous 48 months.
    - Certify that you are under the care and treatment of a physician for any diagnosed medical condition that could impact your ability to fly and that you are medically fit to fly.
    - Agree to a National Driver Register check.
- Under the BasicMed rule, you may conduct flight operations:
    - In an aircraft certificated to carry no more than 6 occupants, including the pilot, and with a maximum certificated takeoff weight of no more than 6,000 pounds.
    - Below 18,000 feet MSL.
    - At a maximum airspeed of 250 knots.
    - That are entirely within the United States.
    - That are not for compensation or hire.

AIRWORTHINESS REQUIREMENTS

- The owner or operator is responsible for maintaining the aircraft in an airworthy condition. As pilot in command, you are responsible for making sure the airplane is airworthy before flying it.
- During preflight, you must verify that the required paperwork is on board the airplane and the required maintenance and inspections have been accomplished. Use the acronym ARROW to help you remember the required documents:
    - Airworthiness certificate (FAR 91.203).
    - Registration certificate (FAR 91.203).
    - Radio station class license (required by the Federal Communications Commission when transmitting to ground stations outside the United States).
    - Operating limitations, which may be in the form of an FAA-approved airplane flight manual and/or pilot's operating handbook (AFM/POH), placards, instrument markings, or any combination thereof. (FAR 91.9).
    - Weight and balance data, as well as an equipment list.
- The airworthiness certificate must be displayed at the cabin or flight deck entrance so that it is legible to passengers and crew. The airworthiness certificate means the aircraft met the design and manufacturing standards for safe flight and remains valid as long as the required maintenance and inspections are performed on the aircraft within the specified time periods.

- An appropriately certificated aviation maintenance technician (AMT) must perform the annual inspection, the 100-hour inspection, and additional required inspections and make aircraft maintenance logbook entries approving the aircraft for return to service.

- An AMT must have an inspection authorization (IA) designation to complete and endorse the annual inspection and an annual inspection may also fulfill the requirement for the 100-hour inspection.

- Required inspections include:
  - Every 12 calendar months (all aircraft): annual; emergency locator transmitter (ELT).
  - Every 24 calendar months: transponder (all aircraft); altimeter and static system (aircraft operated under IFR).
  - Every 100 hours: aircraft used for flight instruction for hire and provided by the flight instructor; aircraft that carry any person, other than a crewmember, for hire.

- Inspections are normally scheduled based on calendar months. For example, if an annual inspection is completed on October 6, 2017, the next annual inspection is due on October 31, 2018.

- The 100-hour inspection is based on time in service and must be completed within 100 hours after the previous inspection, even if that inspection was completed earlier than required.

- If you are enroute to an airport where the 100-hour inspection is to be performed, you may overfly the 100-hour time by up to 10 hours, but the next inspection is still due within 100 hours of the time the original inspection was due.

- The ELT battery must be replaced or recharged if the transmitter has been operated for a total of 1 hour or after 50 percent of useful battery life (or charge) has expired.

MAINTENANCE RECORDS

- Most aircraft maintenance and repairs are required to be performed by FAA-certificated aviation mechanics, but FAR 43.7 allows preventive maintenance to be performed by a person who holds at least a private pilot certificate. Examples of preventive maintenance are: replacing and servicing batteries, replacing spark plugs, and servicing wheel bearings and struts.

- According to FAR 43.9, any person who maintains, performs preventive maintenance, rebuilds, or alters an aircraft part shall make an entry in the maintenance record.

- Aircraft maintenance records must contain the current status of life-limited parts of each airframe, engine, propeller, rotor, and appliance.

- Records must include the description and completion date of any work performed and the signature and certificate number of the person approving the aircraft for return to service.

- You may not carry passengers in an aircraft that has been maintained, rebuilt, or altered in a manner that might have appreciably changed its flight characteristics or substantially affected its operation in flight until an appropriately rated pilot with at least a private pilot certificate flies the aircraft to make an operational check and logs the flight in the aircraft records.

AIRWORTHINESS DIRECTIVES

- Airworthiness directives (ADs) are legally enforceable rules governed by FAR Part 39.

- An AD could be a one-time fix for a defect, recurring maintenance or inspections to address a specific issue, or limitations on the operation of an aircraft. The aircraft owner or operator must maintain records in the maintenance logbooks that show compliance with all pertinent ADs.

- ADs are not flexible—their time interval may not be "overflown" unless a provision is included in the AD allowing it.

- A special airworthiness information bulletin (SAIB) contains non-regulatory information that does not meet the criteria for an AD but is issued to alert, educate, and make recommendations to the aviation community.

SECTION B ■ Commercial Pilot Requirements

AIRCRAFT EQUIPMENT REQUIRED FOR VFR

FAR 91.205 requires specific equipment to be installed and operational for day and night VFR flight, which includes flight instruments, engine and system monitoring indicators, and safety equipment.

SECTION B ■ Commercial Pilot Requirements

Flight Instruments

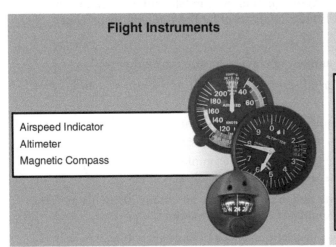

Airspeed Indicator
Altimeter
Magnetic Compass

Engine and System Monitoring Indicators

Tachometer
Manifold Pressure Gauge (in airplanes with a constant-speed propeller)
Fuel Gauge (for each tank)
Oil Temperature Gauge (air-cooled engine)
Oil Pressure Gauge
Temperature Gauge (liquid-cooled engine)
Landing Gear Position Indicator (in airplanes with retractable landing gear)

Safety Equipment

Red or White Anticollision Light System
Seat Belts
Front-Seat Shoulder Harnesses
Emergency Locator Transmitter (ELT)
For hire over water and beyond gliding distance from shore:
Flotation Gear (for each person on board)
Signaling Device

Additional Night Requirements

Position Lights
Adequate Source of Electrical Power
Spare Fuses (within reach of the pilot if the aircraft uses fuses)
Landing Light (if operated for hire)

INOPERATIVE INSTRUMENTS AND EQUIPMENT

- A minimum equipment list (MEL) takes into consideration the regulations and the specific requirements for your aircraft and flight operation and indicates the equipment that is allowed to be inoperative for a particular flight. MELs are not common for light single-engine piston-powered airplanes.

- If your airplane does not have an MEL, use the procedure described in FAR 91.213. Answer yes or no— do any of the following require the inoperative equipment?

  ○ The VFR-day type certificate requirements; FAR prescribed in the airworthiness certification regulations.

  ○ FAR 91.205 for the specific kind of flight operation (e.g. day or night VFR) or by other flight rules for the specific kind of flight to be conducted.

  ○ The aircraft's equipment list or the kinds of operations equipment list (KOEL).

  ○ An airworthiness directive (AD).

- If the answer is YES to ANY of the questions about required equipment, the airplane is not airworthy and maintenance is required. If the answer is NO to ALL of these questions, then you may fly the airplane after the inoperative equipment is:

  ○ Removed and the cockpit control placarded by an AMT.

  ○ Deactivated and placarded "inoperative" (by an AMT if deactivation involves maintenance).

- If you determine that the airworthiness requirements are not met, the FAA may permit the airplane to be flown to a location where the needed repairs can be made by issuing a special flight permit, sometimes called a ferry permit.

- To obtain a special flight permit, an application must be submitted to the nearest FAA flight standards district office (FSDO).

- If an AD prohibits further flight until the AD is satisfied, the FSDO may not issue a special flight permit and an AMT might have be transported to the aircraft's location to resolve the AD.

ADDITIONAL CERTIFICATES AND RATINGS

- The addition of a multi-engine rating to your private or commercial certificate does not require a minimum number of ground or flight instruction hours under FAR Part 61. Under FAR Part 141, a multi-engine rating course must include the ground and flight instruction hours in accordance with the applicable Part 141 appendices.

- To become a certificated flight instructor (CFI), you must pass two knowledge exams and a practical test. Under FAR Part 61, a specific number of ground or flight instruction hours is not required for CFI training. An FAR Part 141 flight instructor course must include the ground and flight instruction hours specified in Appendix F, Part 141.

- To apply for an airline transport pilot (ATP) certificate, you must be at least 23 years of age and hold a first-class medical. A total of 1,500 hours of flight time is required including 250 hours of pilot-in-command time, 500 hours of cross-country time, 100 hours of night flight, and 75 hours of instrument experience.

NOTE: An asterisk appearing after an ACS code (i.e. CA.IV.A.K2*) indicates that the question subject appears more than one time in the ACS. The code shown corresponds to the first instance of the subject in the ACS.

1-1   CA.I.A.K1

To act as PIC of a complex airplane, you must have

A – Received training in an airplane with an engine that is more than 200 horsepower and obtained a logbook endorsement.

B – Received training in an airplane with retractable landing gear, flaps, and a controllable-pitch propeller and obtained a logbook endorsement.

C – Passed a knowledge test on the appropriate airplane systems and passed a practical test in an airplane with retractable landing gear, flaps, and controllable-pitch propeller.

1-1. Answer B. GFDIC 1B, FAR 61.31

A high performance airplane is defined as an airplane having an engine of more than 200 horsepower. A complex airplane is an airplane with retractable landing gear, flaps, and a controllable pitch propeller or a full authority digital engine control (FADEC) system.

To operate as pilot in command of a either a complex or high performance airplane, you must receive training and an endorsement from your instructor. The training required to receive a high performance or complex airplane endorsement will focus on the operation of advanced airplane systems.

SECTION B ■ Commercial Pilot Requirements

1-2   CA.I.A.K1

To act as pilot in command of an airplane that is equipped with retractable landing gear, flaps, and controllable-pitch propeller, you must

A – make at least six takeoffs and landings in such an airplane within the preceding 6 months.

B – receive and log ground and flight training in such an airplane, and obtain a logbook endorsement certifying proficiency.

C – hold a multi-engine airplane class rating.

1-2. Answer B. GFDIC 1B, FAR 61.31

No person may act as pilot in command of a complex airplane—an airplane that has retractable landing gear, flaps, and a controllable pitch propeller or a full authority digital engine control (FADEC) system— unless that person has received and logged ground and flight training from an authorized instructor in a complex airplane, or flight simulator that is representative of a complex airplane, and has received a one-time endorsement in the logbook from the instructor who certifies that the person is proficient to operate a complex airplane.

1-3   CA.I.A.K1

To act as PIC of a high performance airplane, which training or experience would meet the additional requirements.

A – Logged at least five hours as SIC in a high performance or turbine-powered airplane in the last 12 calendar months.

B – Received and logged ground and flight training in an airplane with retractable landing gear, flaps, and controllable-pitch propeller.

C – Received and logged ground and flight training in a high performance airplane and a received a logbook endorsement.

1-3. Answer C. GFDIC 1B, FAR 61.31

A high performance airplane is defined as an airplane having an engine of more than 200 horsepower. A complex airplane is an airplane with retractable landing gear, flaps, and a controllable pitch propeller or a full authority digital engine control (FADEC) system.

To operate as pilot in command of a either a complex or high performance airplane, you must receive training and an endorsement from your instructor. The training required to receive a high performance or complex airplane endorsement will focus on the operation of advanced airplane systems.

1-4   CA.I.A.K1

To act as pilot in command of an airplane with more than 200 horsepower, you are required to

A – receive and log ground and flight training from a qualified pilot in such an airplane.

B – obtain an endorsement from a qualified pilot stating that you are proficient to operate such an airplane.

C – receive and log ground and flight training from an authorized instructor in such an airplane.

1-4. Answer C. GFDIC 1B, FAR 61.31

A high performance airplane is defined as an airplane having an engine of more than 200 horsepower. A complex airplane is an airplane with retractable landing gear, flaps, and a controllable pitch propeller or a full authority digital engine control (FADEC) system.

To operate as pilot in command of a either a complex or high performance airplane, you must receive training and an endorsement from your instructor. The training required to receive a high performance or complex airplane endorsement will focus on the operation of advanced airplane systems.

1-5   CA.I.A.K1

A technically advanced airplane (TAA) is defined as an airplane with

A – a PFD, an MFD with a moving map using GPS navigation, and a two-axis autopilot.

B – GPS equipment and ADS-B capability.

C – a PFD, an MFD with a moving map using GPS navigation, a two-axis autopilot, and an engine with more than 200 horsepower.

1-5. Answer A. GFDIC 1B, FAR 61.1

A technically advanced airplane (TAA) is an airplane that has:

- A primary flight display (PFD) with an airspeed indicator, turn coordinator, attitude indicator, heading indicator, altimeter, and vertical speed indicator;

- A multifunction display (MFD) with a moving map using GPS navigation to display the aircraft position;

- A two-axis autopilot integrated with the navigation and heading guidance system.

1-6   CA.I.A.K2

Which of the following are considered aircraft class ratings?

A – Transport, normal, utility, and acrobatic.

B – Airplane, rotorcraft, glider, and lighter-than-air.

C – Single-engine land, multi-engine land, single-engine sea, and multi-engine sea.

1-6. Answer C. GFDIC 1B, FAR 61.5

With respect to pilot certification, aircraft are organized into category, class, and type.

- Category—airplane, rotorcraft, glider, lighter-than-air, and powered-lift.

- Class—single-engine land, single-engine sea, multi-engine land, multi-engine sea, helicopter, gyroplane, airship, and balloon.

- Type—make and model required for any aircraft over 12,500 pounds and/or with a turbojet powerplant.

1-7   CA.I.A.K2

Unless otherwise authorized, the pilot in command is required to hold a type rating when operating any

A – aircraft that is certificated for more than one pilot.

B – multi-engine airplane having a gross weight of more than 12,000 pounds.

C – aircraft of more than 12,500 pounds maximum certificated takeoff weight.

1-7. Answer C. GFDIC 1B, FAR 1.1, FAR 61.31

A type rating is required to act as pilot in command of a:

- Large aircraft (except lighter-than-air). According to FAR Part 1, "large aircraft" means an aircraft of more than 12,500 pounds, maximum certificated takeoff weight.

- Turbojet-powered airplanes.

- Other aircraft specified by the Administrator through aircraft type certificate procedures.

1-8   CA.I.A.K2

Regulations which refer to "operate" relate to that person who

A – acts as pilot in command of the aircraft.

B – is the sole manipulator of the aircraft controls.

C – causes the aircraft to be used or authorizes its use.

1-8. Answer C. GFDIC 1B, FAR 1.1

"Operate," with respect to aircraft, means use, cause to use, or authorize to use aircraft, for the purpose of air navigation including the piloting of aircraft, with or without the right of legal control (as owner, lessee, or otherwise).

SECTION B ■ **Commercial Pilot Requirements**

1-9   CA.I.A.K2

Regulations which refer to "commercial operators" relate to that person who

A – is the owner of a small scheduled airline.

B – for compensation or hire, engages in the carriage by aircraft in air commerce of persons or property, as an air carrier.

C – for compensation or hire, engages in the carriage by aircraft in air commerce of persons or property, other than as an air carrier.

1-9. Answer C. GFDIC 1B, FAR 1.1

"Commercial operator," means a person who, for compensation or hire, engages in the carriage by aircraft in air commerce of persons or property, other than as an air carrier or foreign air carrier.

1-10   CA.I.A.K2

Regulations which refer to the "operational control" of a flight are in relation to

A – the specific duties of any required crewmember.

B – acting as the sole manipulator of the aircraft controls.

C – exercising authority over initiating, conducting, or terminating a flight.

1-10. Answer C. GFDIC 1B, FAR 1.1

"Operational control," with respect to a flight, means the exercise of authority over initiating, conducting, or terminating a flight.

1-11   CA.I.A.K1

If you hold a commercial pilot certificate, you may act as pilot in command of an aircraft for compensation or hire, if you

A – are qualified in accordance with 14 CFR part 61 and with the applicable parts that apply to the operation.

B – are qualified in accordance with 14 CFR part 61 and have passed a pilot competency check given by an authorized check pilot.

C – hold appropriate category, class ratings, and meet the recent flight experience requirements of 14 CFR part 61.

1-11. Answer A. GFDIC 1B, FAR 61.133

FAR 61.133 states that as a commercial pilot, you may act as pilot in command of an aircraft for compensation or hire and you may carry persons or property for compensation or hire provided you meet the qualifications that apply to the specific operation.

Although some commercial operations are governed by FAR Part 91, many others, such as common carriage, on-demand, flag, and commuter operations must meet additional requirements described in FAR Parts 117, 119, 121, 125, 129, 135, 136, and 137.

1-12   CA.I.A.K2

What limitation is imposed on a newly certificated commercial pilot – airplane, if that person does not hold an instrument rating? The carriage of passengers

A – for hire on cross-country flights is limited to 50 NM for night flights, but not limited for day flights.

B – or property for hire on cross-country flights at night is limited to a radius of 50 NM.

C – for hire on cross-country flights in excess of 50 NM, or for hire at night is prohibited.

1-12. Answer C. GFDIC 1B, FAR 61.133

If you do not hold an instrument rating, your commercial certificate will be issued with the limitation: "The carriage of passengers for hire in airplanes on cross-country flights in excess of 50 nautical miles or at night is prohibited."

1-13   CA.I.A.K2

As a commercial pilot, you decide to start a small business flying non-stop tours to look at Christmas lights during the holiday season. What authorizations, if any, are required to conduct Christmas light tours?

A – No authorizations or approvals are required if you hold the appropriate category and class rating for the aircraft that will be flown.

B – You must apply for and receive a Letter of Authorization from a Flight Standards District Office.

C – You must apply to the FAA to receive an exemption to carry passengers at night within a 50 mile radius of your departure airport.

1-13. Answer B. GFDIC 1B, FAR 119.1, FAR 91.147

You may conduct nonstop commercial air tours not governed by FAR Parts 121, 125, or 135 in an airplane with a passenger-seat configuration of 30 seats or fewer and a maximum payload capacity of 7,500 pounds or less; within a 25 statute mile radius of the departure airport; and with a letter of authorization (LOA) issued under FAR 91.147.

1-14   CA.I.A.K2

You are acting as a commercial pilot, but are not operating under the regulations of 14 CFR Part 119. Which of these operations are you authorized to conduct?

A – On-demand, passenger carrying flights of nine persons or less.

B – Aerial application and aerial photography.

C – On-demand cargo flights.

1-14. Answer B. GFDIC 1B, FAR 119.1

Common carriage, on-demand, flag, and commuter operations must meet additional requirements described in FAR Parts 117, 119, 121, 125, 129, 135, 136, and 137.

FAR 119.1 lists specific operations not governed by FAR Parts 121, 125, or 135 for which the holder of a commercial pilot certificate may be paid. These operations include:

- Student instruction.

- Nonstop commercial air tours with specific restrictions listed in FAR 119.1.

- Ferry or training flights.

- Aerial work operations, including crop dusting, seeding, spraying, bird chasing, banner towing, aerial photography or survey, fire fighting, and powerline or pipeline patrol.

- Nonstop parachute operations within a 25 statute mile radius of the airport.

SECTION B ■ Commercial Pilot Requirements

1-15   CA.I.A.K2

In what type of operation, not regulated by 14 CFR Part 119, may a commercial pilot act as pilot in command and receive compensation for services?

A – Part-time contract pilot.

B – Nonstop flights within a 25 SM radius of an airport to carry persons for intentional parachute jumps.

C – Nonstop flights within a 25 SM radius of an airport to carry cargo only.

1-15. Answer B. GFDIC 1B, FAR 119.1

Common carriage, on-demand, flag, and commuter operations must meet additional requirements described in FAR Parts 117, 119, 121, 125, 129, 135, 136, and 137.

FAR 119.1 lists specific operations not governed by FAR Parts 121, 125, or 135 for which the holder of a commercial pilot certificate may be paid. These operations include:

- Student instruction.

- Nonstop commercial air tours with specific restrictions listed in FAR 119.1.

- Ferry or training flights.

- Aerial work operations, including crop dusting, seeding, spraying, bird chasing, banner towing, aerial photography or survey, fire fighting, and powerline or pipeline patrol.

- Nonstop parachute operations within a 25 statute mile radius of the airport.

1-16   CA.I.A.K2

In what type of operation, not regulated by 14 CFR Part 119, may a commercial pilot act as pilot in command and receive compensation for services?

A – Crop dusting, spraying, and bird chasing.

B – On-demand, nine or less passengers, charter flights.

C – On-demand cargo flights.

1-16. Answer A. GFDIC 1B, FAR 119.1

Common carriage, on-demand, flag, and commuter operations must meet additional requirements described in FAR Parts 117, 119, 121, 125, 129, 135, 136, and 137.

FAR 119.1 lists specific operations not governed by FAR Parts 121, 125, or 135 for which the holder of a commercial pilot certificate may be paid. These operations include:

- Student instruction.

- Nonstop commercial air tours with specific restrictions listed in FAR 119.1.

- Ferry or training flights.

- Aerial work operations, including crop dusting, seeding, spraying, bird chasing, banner towing, aerial photography or survey, fire fighting, and powerline or pipeline patrol.

- Nonstop parachute operations within a 25 statute mile radius of the airport.

1-17 CA.I.A.K2

Which is required to operate an aircraft towing an advertising banner?

A – Approval from ATC to operate in Class E airspace.

B – A certificate of waiver issued by the Administrator.

C – A safety link at each end of the towline which has a breaking strength not less than 80 percent of the aircraft's gross weight.

1-17. Answer B. GFDIC 1B, FAR 91.311

According to FAR 91.311, no pilot of a civil aircraft may tow anything with that aircraft (other than gliders), except in accordance with the terms of a certificate of waiver issued by the Administrator.

1-18 CA.I.A.K2

Which is true with respect to operating limitations of a "restricted" category airplane?

A – No person may operate a "restricted" category airplane carrying passengers or property for compensation or hire.

B – A pilot of a "restricted" category airplane is required to hold a commercial pilot certificate.

C – A "restricted" category airplane is limited to an operating radius of 25 miles from its home base.

1-18. Answer A. GFDIC 1B, FAR 91.313

As a commercial pilot, you may not operate these categories of airplanes for compensation or hire:

- Restricted category—special-purpose aircraft, such as agricultural spray planes or slurry bombers used to fight forest fires.
- Limited category—military aircraft that are now allowed to be used only for limited purposes in civil aviation.
- Experimental category—a wide range of aircraft, such as amateur homebuilt and racing airplanes, as well as research and development aircraft used to test new design concepts.
- Primary category—aircraft of simple design that is intended exclusively for pleasure and personal use.

1-19 CA.I.A.K2

The carriage of passengers for hire by a commercial pilot is

A – not authorized in a "utility" category aircraft.

B – authorized in "restricted" category aircraft.

C – not authorized in a "limited" category aircraft.

1-19. Answer C. GFDIC 1B, FAR 91.315

As a commercial pilot, you may not operate these categories of airplanes for compensation or hire:

- Restricted category—special-purpose aircraft, such as agricultural spray planes or slurry bombers used to fight forest fires.
- Limited category—military aircraft that are now allowed to be used only for limited purposes in civil aviation.
- Experimental category—a wide range of aircraft, such as amateur homebuilt and racing airplanes, as well as research and development aircraft used to test new design concepts.
- Primary category—aircraft of simple design that is intended exclusively for pleasure and personal use.

SECTION B ■ Commercial Pilot Requirements

1-20   CA.I.B.K2

No person may operate an aircraft that has an experimental airworthiness certificate

A – under instrument flight rules (IFR).

B – when carrying property for hire.

C – when carrying persons or property for hire.

1-20. Answer C. GFDIC 1B, FAR 91.319

As a commercial pilot, you may not operate these categories of airplanes for compensation or hire:

- Restricted category—special-purpose aircraft, such as agricultural spray planes or slurry bombers used to fight forest fires.

- Limited category—military aircraft that are now allowed to be used only for limited purposes in civil aviation.

- Experimental category—a wide range of aircraft, such as amateur homebuilt and racing airplanes, as well as research and development aircraft used to test new design concepts.

- Primary category—aircraft of simple design that is intended exclusively for pleasure and personal use.

1-21   CA.I.B.K2

Which is true with respect to operating limitations of a "primary" category airplane?

A – No person may operate a "primary" category airplane carrying passengers or property for compensation or hire.

B – A "primary" category airplane is limited to a specified operating radius from its home base.

C – A pilot of a "primary" category airplane must hold a commercial pilot certificate when carrying passengers for compensation or hire.

1-21. Answer A. GFDIC 1B, FAR 91.325

As a commercial pilot, you may not operate these categories of airplanes for compensation or hire:

- Restricted category—special-purpose aircraft, such as agricultural spray planes or slurry bombers used to fight forest fires.

- Limited category—military aircraft that are now allowed to be used only for limited purposes in civil aviation.

- Experimental category—a wide range of aircraft, such as amateur homebuilt and racing airplanes, as well as research and development aircraft used to test new design concepts.

- Primary category—aircraft of simple design that is intended exclusively for pleasure and personal use.

1-22   CA.I.A.K4

Commercial pilots are required to have a valid and appropriate pilot certificate in their physical possession or readily accessible in the aircraft when

A – acting as pilot in command.

B – carrying passengers only.

C – piloting for hire only.

1-22. Answer A. GFDIC 1B, FAR 61.3

You must have a current pilot certificate, photo ID, and medical certificate in your physical possession or readily accessible in the aircraft any time you act as pilot in command (PIC). It makes no difference whether you are carrying passengers or flying for hire.

1-23   CA.I.A.K1

Does a commercial pilot certificate have a specific expiration date?

A – No, it is issued without a specific expiration date.

B – Yes, it expires at the end of the 24th month after the month in which it was issued.

C – No, but commercial privileges expire if a flight review is not satisfactorily completed each 12 months.

1-23. Answer A. GFDIC 1B, FAR 61.19

Any pilot certificate (other than a student pilot certificate) issued under FAR Part 61 is issued without a specific expiration date.

However, in addition to a flight review every 24 calendar months, to act as pilot in command of an aircraft carrying passengers, you must have performed at least 3 takeoffs and landings in an aircraft of the same category and class (and type, if a type rating is required) within the preceding 90 days.

1-24   CA.I.A.K1

What flight time must be documented and recorded by a pilot exercising the privileges of a commercial certificate?

A – Flight time showing training and aeronautical experience to meet requirements for a certificate, rating or flight review.

B – Only flight time for compensation or hire with passengers aboard which is necessary to meet the recent flight experience requirements.

C – All flight time flown for compensation or hire.

1-24. Answer A. GFDIC 1B, FAR 61.51

You are required to document and record the training time and aeronautical experiences used to meet the requirements for a certificate, rating, or flight review and the aeronautical experience required for meeting the recent flight experience requirements.

1-25   CA.I.A.K1

To act as pilot in command of an aircraft operated under 14 CFR part 91, a commercial pilot must have satisfactorily accomplished a flight review or completed a proficiency check within the preceding

A – 6 calendar months.

B – 12 calendar months.

C – 24 calendar months.

1-25. Answer C. GFDIC 1B, FAR 61.56

According to FAR 61.65, to act as pilot in command, you must have accomplished a flight review and received a logbook endorsement from an authorized instructor within the previous 24 calendar months.

You do not need to accomplish the flight review if, within the previous 24 calendar month, you have passed a pilot proficiency check or practical test or completed a current phase of the FAA WINGS—Pilot Proficiency Program.

SECTION B ■ Commercial Pilot Requirements

1-26   CA.I.A.K1

You have accomplished 25 takeoffs and landings in multi-engine land airplanes in the previous 45 days. For the flight you plan to conduct today, this meets the PIC recency of experience requirements to carry passengers in which airplanes?

A – Multi- or single-engine land.

B – Single-engine land airplane.

C – Multi-engine land airplane.

1-26. Answer C. GFDIC 1B, FAR 61.57

To act as pilot in command of an aircraft carrying passengers, you must have performed at least 3 takeoffs and landings in an aircraft of the same category and class (and type, if a type rating is required) within the preceding 90 days.

To carry passengers at night (at least 1 hour after sunset to 1 hour before sunrise), the takeoffs and landings must have been during that time period and to a full stop.

1-27   CA.I.A.K1

Prior to carrying passengers at night, as PIC, you must have accomplished the required takeoffs and landings in

A – the same category, class, and type of aircraft (if a type rating is required).

B – any category aircraft.

C – the same category and class of aircraft to be used.

1-27. Answer A. GFDIC 1B, FAR 61.57

To act as pilot in command of an aircraft carrying passengers, you must have performed at least 3 takeoffs and landings in an aircraft of the same category and class (and type, if a type rating is required) within the preceding 90 days.

To carry passengers at night—the period from 1 hour after sunset to 1 hour before sunrise as defined by FAR 61.57—the takeoffs and landings must have been during that time period and to a full stop.

1-28   CA.I.A.K1

If you do not meet the recency of experience requirements for night flight and official sunset is 1900 CST, the latest time passengers should be carried is

A – 1959 CST.

B – 1900 CST.

C – 1800 CST.

1-28. Answer A. GFDIC 1B, FAR 61.57

To act as pilot in command of an aircraft carrying passengers at night—the period from 1 hour after sunset to 1 hour before sunrise as defined by FAR 61.57—you must have performed at least 3 takeoffs and landings in an aircraft of the same category and class (and type, if a type rating is required) within the preceding 90 days.

1-29   CA.I.A.K1

To serve as pilot in command of an airplane that is type certificated for more than one pilot crew member, and operated under part 91, you must

A – complete a flight review within the preceding 24 calendar months.

B – receive and log ground and flight training from an authorized flight instructor.

C – complete a pilot-in-command proficiency check within the preceding 12 calendar months in an airplane that is type certificated for more than one pilot.

1-29. Answer C. GFDIC 1B, FAR 61.58

According to FAR 61.58, to serve as PIC of an aircraft that is type certificated for more than one required pilot flight crewmember or is turbojet-powered, you must:

- Within the preceding 12 calendar months, complete a PIC proficiency check in an aircraft that is type certificated for more than one required pilot flight crewmember or is turbojet- powered;

- Within the preceding 24 calendar months, complete a PIC check in the particular type of aircraft in which you will serve as PIC that is type certificated for more than one required pilot flight crewmember or is turbojet-powered.

1-30   CA.I.A.K1

To serve as second in command of an airplane that is certificated for more than one pilot crewmember, and operated under part 91, you must

A – receive and log flight training from an authorized flight instructor in the type of airplane for which privileges are requested.

B – hold at least a commercial pilot certificate with an airplane category rating.

C – within the last 12 months become familiar with the required information, and perform and log pilot time in the type of airplane for which privileges are requested.

1-30. Answer C. GFDIC 1B, FAR 61.55

FAR 61.55 outlines the requirements to serve as second-in-command (SIC) of an aircraft type certificated for more than one required pilot flight crewmember or in operations requiring an SIC. Among other requirements, within the previous 12 calendar months, you must:

- Become familiar with the operating procedures, performance specifications and limitations, flight manual, placards, and markings for the specific type of aircraft.

- Performed and logged pilot time in the type of aircraft or in a flight simulator that represents the specific type of aircraft.

1-31   CA.I.A.K1

What flight time may a pilot log as second in command?

A – Only that flight time during which the second in command is the sole manipulator of the controls.

B – All flight time while acting as second in command in aircraft configured for more than one pilot.

C – All flight time when qualified and occupying a crewmember station in an aircraft that requires more than one pilot.

1-31. Answer C. GFDIC 1B, FAR 61.51, FAR 61.55

You may log second in command time:

- If you are qualified in accordance with the second-in-command requirements of FAR 61.55, and you occupy a crewmember station in an aircraft that requires more than one pilot by the aircraft's type certificate or;

- You hold the appropriate category, class, and instrument rating (if an instrument rating is required for the flight) for the aircraft being flown, and more than one pilot is required under the type certification of the aircraft or the regulations under which the flight is being conducted.

1-32   CA.I.A.K1

To act as pilot in command of a tailwheel airplane, without prior experience, you must

A – log ground and flight training from an authorized instructor.

B – pass a competency check and receive an endorsement from an authorized instructor.

C – receive and log flight training from an authorized instructor as well as receive a logbook endorsement from an authorized instructor who finds you proficient in a tailwheel airplane.

1-32. Answer C. GFDIC 1B FAR 61.31

According to FAR 61.31, to act as PIC of a tailwheel airplane, you must have received and logged flight training and received a logbook endorsement from an authorized instructor who found you proficient in the operation of a tailwheel airplane.

SECTION B ■ Commercial Pilot Requirements

1-33   CA.I.A.K2

To act as pilot in command of an airplane towing a glider, the tow pilot is required to have

A – a logbook endorsement from an authorized glider instructor certifying receipt of ground and flight training in gliders, and be proficient with techniques and procedures for safe towing of gliders.

B – at least a private pilot certificate with a category rating for powered aircraft, and made and logged at least three flights as pilot or observer in a glider being towed by an airplane.

C – a logbook record of having made at least three flights as sole manipulator of the controls of a glider being towed by an airplane.

1-33. Answer A. GFDIC 1B, FAR 61.69

As a private pilot, commercial pilot, or ATP, you must meet specific requirements outlined in FAR 61.69 to tow a glider or unpowered ultralight vehicle. You must have:

- Logged at least 100 hours of as PIC in the aircraft category, class and type that you are using for the tow.

- A logbook endorsement from an authorized instructor that you have received ground and flight training towing gliders or unpowered ultralight vehicles.

- Logged at least 3 flights while towing a glider or unpowered ultralight vehicle or have simulated towing flight procedures in an aircraft while accompanied by a qualified pilot and received a logbook endorsement.

- Within 24 calendar months before the flight, made at least 3 actual or simulated tows of a glider or unpowered ultralight vehicle while accompanied by a qualified pilot or made at least 3 flights as pilot in command of a glider or unpowered ultralight vehicle towed by an aircraft.

1-34   CA.I.A.K2

To act as pilot in command of an airplane towing a glider, you must have accomplished, within the preceding 24 calendar months, at least

A – three actual glider tows under the supervision of a qualified tow pilot.

B – three actual or simulated glider tows while accompanied by a qualified tow pilot.

C – ten flights as pilot in command of an aircraft while towing a glider.

1-34. Answer B. GFDIC 1B, FAR 61.69

As a private pilot, commercial pilot, or ATP, you must meet specific requirements outlined in FAR 61.69 to tow a glider or unpowered ultralight vehicle. You must have:

- Logged at least 100 hours of as PIC in the aircraft category, class and type that you are using for the tow.

- A logbook endorsement from an authorized instructor that you have received ground and flight training towing gliders or unpowered ultralight vehicles.

- Logged at least 3 flights while towing a glider or unpowered ultralight vehicle or have simulated towing flight procedures in an aircraft while accompanied by a qualified pilot and received a logbook endorsement.

- Within 24 calendar months before the flight, made at least 3 actual or simulated tows of a glider or unpowered ultralight vehicle while accompanied by a qualified pilot or made at least 3 flights as pilot in command of a glider or unpowered ultralight vehicle towed by an aircraft.

1-35   CA.I.A.K2

If you change your permanent mailing address and fail to notify the FAA Airmen Certification Branch of this change, you are entitled to exercise the privileges of your pilot certificate for a period of

A – 30 days.

B – 60 days.

C – 90 days.

1-35. Answer A. GFDIC 1B, FAR 61.60

After changing your permanent mailing address, you may not exercise the privileges of a pilot or flight instructor certificate after 30 days unless the FAA Airman Certification Branch has been notified in writing.

1-36   CA.I.A.K2

A pilot convicted of operating a motor vehicle while either intoxicated by, impaired by, or under the influence of alcohol or a drug is required to provide a

A – written report to the FAA Civil Aeromedical Institute (CAMI) within 60 days after the motor vehicle action.

B – written report to the FAA Civil Aviation Security Division (AMC-700) not later than 60 days after the conviction.

C – notification of the conviction to an FAA Aviation Medical Examiner (AME) not later than 60 days after the motor vehicle action.

1-36. Answer B. GFDIC 1B, FAR 61.15

According to FAR 61.15, if you are convicted of operating a motor vehicle while either intoxicated or impaired by alcohol or a drug, you must notify the FAA Civil Aviation Security Division, in writing, not later than 60 days after the conviction.

1-37   CA.I.A.K2

A pilot convicted of a motor vehicle offense involving alcohol or drugs is required to provide a written report to the

A – FAA Civil Aeromedical Institute (CAMI) within 60 days after the conviction.

B – FAA Civil Aviation Security Division (AMC-700) within 60 days after the conviction.

C – nearest FAA Flight Standards District Office (FSDO) within 60 days after such action.

1-37. Answer B. GFDIC 1B, FAR 61.15

According to FAR 61.15, if you are convicted of operating a motor vehicle while either intoxicated or impaired by alcohol or a drug, you must notify the FAA Civil Aviation Security Division, in writing, not later than 60 days after the conviction.

SECTION B ■ Commercial Pilot Requirements

SECTION B ■ Commercial Pilot Requirements

1-38   CA.I.A.K3

A second-class medical certificate issued to a commercial pilot on April 10, this year, permits the pilot to exercise which of the following privileges?

A – Commercial pilot privileges through April 30, next year.

B – Commercial pilot privileges through April 10, 2 years later.

C – Private pilot privileges through, but not after, March 31, next year.

1-38. Answer A. GFDIC 1B, FAR 61.23

Although you need at least a third-class medical certificate to be eligible for a commercial pilot certificate, you must have a second-class medical certificate to exercise commercial pilot privileges. A second-class medical certificate is valid for 12 calendar months for operations requiring a commercial certificate.

1-39   CA.I.A.K5

To qualify for the BasicMed rule: within the previous 24 calendar months, you must have

A – received a medical exam from a state-licensed physician.

B – held at least a third class medical certificate.

C – completed an approved medical education course.

1-39. Answer C. GFDIC 1B, AC 68-1

If you have previously held a medical certificate that was not suspended, revoked or withdrawn, you might qualify to act as pilot in command under the BasicMed rule. To qualify for the BasicMed rule, you must:

- Possess and carry a valid U.S. driver's license.

- Have completed an approved medical education course—available online from the Aircraft Owners and Pilots Association (AOPA)—within the previous 24 calendar months.

- Have received a comprehensive medical exam from a state-licensed physician within the previous 48 months.

- Certify that you are under the care and treatment of a physician for any diagnosed medical condition that could impact your ability to fly and that you are medically fit to fly.

- Agree to a National Driver Register check.

1-40   CA.I.A.K5

When exercising the privileges of BasicMed, which conditions allow you to act as a PIC for compensation or hire?

A – A limitation of BasicMed is that you may not conduct flight operations for compensation or hire.

B – You are instrument rated and current.

C – You are operating an airplane certificated to carry no more than 6 occupants with a maximum takeoff weight or no more than 6,000 pounds.

1-40. Answer A. GFDIC 1B, AC 68-1

Under the BasicMed rule, you may conduct flight operations:

- In an aircraft certificated to carry no more than 6 occupants, including the pilot, and with a maximum certificated takeoff weight of no more than 6,000 pounds.

- Below 18,000 feet MSL.

- At a maximum airspeed of 250 knots.

- That are entirely within the United States.

- That are not for compensation or hire.

1-41　CA.I.A.K2

What person is directly responsible for the final authority as to the operation of the airplane?

A – Certificate holder.

B – Pilot in command.

C – Airplane owner/operator.

1-41. Answer B. GFDIC 1B, FAR 91.3

The pilot in command of an aircraft is directly responsible for, and is the final authority as to, the operation of that aircraft.

1-42　CA.I.B.K1a

Which list accurately reflects some of the documents required to be current and carried in a U.S. registered civil airplane flying in the United States under day visual flight rules (VFR)?

A – Proof of insurance certificate, VFR flight plan or flight itinerary, and the aircraft logbook.

B – Airworthiness certificate, approved airplane flight manual, and aircraft registration certificate.

C – VFR sectional(s) chart(s) for the area in which the flight occurs, aircraft logbook, and engine logbook.

1-42. Answer B. GFDIC 1B, FAR Part 91, PHB

Verify that all the required paperwork is on board the airplane. Use the acronym ARROW to help you remember the required documents.

- Airworthiness certificate (FAR 91.203).
- Registration certificate (FAR 91.203).
- Radio station class license (required by the Federal Communications Commission when transmitting to ground stations outside the United States).
- Operating limitations, which may be in the form of an FAA-approved airplane flight manual and/or pilot's operating handbook (AFM/POH), placards, instrument markings, or any combination thereof. (FAR 91.9).
- Weight and balance data, as well as an equipment list.

1-43　CA.I.B.K1a

Which of the following preflight actions is the pilot in command required to take in order to comply with the FARs regarding day visual flight rules (VFR)?

A – File a VFR flight plan with Flight Service.

B – Verify the airworthiness certificate is legible to passengers.

C – Verify approved position lights are not burned out.

1-43. Answer B. GFDIC 1B, FAR 91.203

According to FAR 91.203, you must ensure that the airworthiness certificate and registration certificate are in the airplane. The airworthiness certificate must be displayed at the cabin or cockpit entrance so that it is legible to passengers and crew.

Although not required for flight under VFR, filing a flight plan is strongly recommended so that you receive search and rescue protection. Position lights are not required for day VFR flight. However, if the aircraft has these lights and they are inoperative, you must follow the appropriate steps for flying with inoperative equipment or cancel the flight.

SECTION B ■ Commercial Pilot Requirements

1-44   CA.I.B.K1, CA.II.A.K2, 3

You are taking a 196 nautical mile VFR cross country flight in mountainous terrain. Which of the following actions must you take?

A – Verify the airworthiness certificate is legible to passengers.

B – File a VFR flight plan with Flight Service.

C – Ensure all items in the baggage area are strapped down.

1-44. Answer A. GFDIC 1B, FAR 91.203

According to FAR 91.203, you must ensure that the airworthiness certificate and registration certificate are in the airplane. The airworthiness certificate must be displayed at the cabin or cockpit entrance so that it is legible to passengers and crew.

Although not required for flight under VFR, filing a flight plan is strongly recommended so that you receive search and rescue protection. Properly securing baggage is good operating practice, but no specific requirements apply unless you are operating a large turbine-powered airplane.

1-45   CA.I.B.K1, CA.II.A.K2, 3

Who is primarily responsible for maintaining an aircraft in an airworthy condition?

A – The lead mechanic responsible for that aircraft.

B – Pilot in command or operator.

C – Owner or operator of the aircraft.

1-45. Answer C. GFDIC 1B, FAR 91.403

The owner or operator is responsible for maintaining the aircraft in an airworthy condition. As pilot in command, you are responsible for making sure the airplane is airworthy before flying it.

1-46   CA.I.B.K1b, CA.II.A.K2, 3

A standard airworthiness certificate remains in effect as long as the aircraft receives

A – required maintenance and inspections.

B – an annual inspection.

C – an annual inspection and a 100-hour inspection prior to their expiration dates.

1-46. Answer A. GFDIC 1B, FAR 91.407, 91.409

The airworthiness certificate means the aircraft met the design and manufacturing standards for safe flight and remains valid as long as the required maintenance and inspections are performed on the aircraft within the specified time periods.

1-47   CA.I.B.K1b, CA.II.A.K2, 3

After an annual inspection has been completed and the aircraft has been returned to service, an appropriate notation should be made

A – on the airworthiness certificate.

B – in the aircraft maintenance records.

C – in the FAA-approved flight manual.

1-47. Answer B. GFDIC 1B, FAR 91.407, FAR 91.409

An appropriately certificated aviation maintenance technician (AMT) must perform the annual inspection, the 100-hour inspection, and additional required inspections and make aircraft maintenance logbook entries approving the aircraft for return to service. An AMT must have an inspection authorization (IA) designation to complete and endorse the annual inspection.

1-48 CA.I.B.K1b, CA.II.A.K2, 3

You are conducting your preflight of an aircraft and notice that the last inspection of the emergency locator transmitter was 11 calendar months ago. You may

A – depart if you get a special flight permit.

B – depart because the ELT is within the inspection requirements.

C – not depart until a new inspection is conducted.

1-48. Answer B. GFDIC 1B, FAR 91.207

You may not fly an aircraft unless it has received an annual inspection and an emergency locator transmitter (ELT) inspection within the previous 12 calendar months. In addition, the ELT battery must be replaced or recharged if the transmitter has been operated for a total of 1 hour or after 50 percent of useful battery life (or charge) has expired.

1-49 CA.I.B.K1b

The maximum cumulative time that an emergency locator transmitter may be operated before the rechargeable battery must be recharged is

A – 30 minutes.

B – 45 minutes.

C – 60 minutes.

1-49. Answer C. GFDIC 1B, FAR 91.207

You may not fly an aircraft unless it has received an annual inspection and an emergency locator transmitter (ELT) inspection within the previous 12 calendar months. In addition, the ELT battery must be replaced or recharged if the transmitter has been operated for a total of 1 hour or after 50 percent of useful battery life (or charge) has expired.

1-50 CA.I.B.K1b, CA.II.A.K2, 3

Which is true concerning required maintenance inspections?

A – A 100-hour inspection may be substituted for an annual inspection.

B – An annual inspection may be substituted for a 100-hour inspection.

C – An annual inspection is required even if a progressive inspection system has been approved.

1-50. Answer B. GFDIC 1B, FAR 91.409

An appropriately certificated aviation maintenance technician (AMT) must perform the annual inspection, the 100-hour inspection, and additional required inspections and make aircraft maintenance logbook entries approving the aircraft for return to service. An AMT must have an inspection authorization (IA) designation to complete and endorse the annual inspection and an annual inspection may also fulfill the requirement for the 100-hour inspection.

1-51 CA.I.B.K1b, CA.II.A.K2, 3

An aircraft carrying passengers for hire has been on a schedule of inspection every 100 hours of time in service. Under which condition, if any, may that aircraft be operated beyond 100 hours out a new inspection?

A – The aircraft may be flown for any flight as long as the time in service has not exceeded 110 hours.

B – The aircraft may be dispatched for a flight of any duration as long as 100 hours has not been exceeded at the time it departs.

C – The 100-hour limitation may be exceeded by not more than 10 hours if necessary to reach a place at which the inspection can be done.

1-51. Answer C. GFDIC 1B, FAR 91.409

100-hour inspections are required on aircraft that are used for flight instruction for hire and provided by the flight instructor, or that carry any person, other than a crewmember, for hire.

The 100-hour inspection is based on time in service and must be completed within 100 hours after the previous inspection, even if that inspection was completed earlier than required. However, if you are enroute to an airport where the 100-hour inspection is to be performed, you may overfly the 100-hour time by up to 10 hours, but the next inspection is still due within 100 hours of the time the original inspection was due.

SECTION B ■ Commercial Pilot Requirements

1-52   CA.I.B.K1b, CA.II.A.K2, 3

A 100-hour inspection was due at 1402.5 hours on the tachometer. The 100-hour inspection was performed at 1409.5 hours. When is the next 100-hour inspection due?

A – 1502.5 hours

B – 1512.5 hours

C – 1509.5 hours

1-52. Answer A. GFDIC 1B, FAR 91.409

100-hour inspections are required on aircraft that are used for flight instruction for hire and provided by the flight instructor, or that carry any person, other than a crewmember, for hire.

The 100-hour inspection is based on time in service and must be completed within 100 hours after the previous inspection, even if that inspection was completed earlier than required. However, if you are enroute to an airport where the 100-hour inspection is to be performed, you may overfly the 100-hour time by up to 10 hours, but the next inspection is still due within 100 hours of the time the original inspection was due.

1-53   CA.I.B.K1b, CA.II.A.K2, 3

An ATC transponder is not to be used unless it has been tested, inspected, and found to comply with regulations within the preceding

A – 30 days.

B – 12 calendar months.

C – 24 calendar months.

1-53. Answer C. GFDIC 1B, FAR 91.413

You may not use an ATC transponder unless within the preceding 24 calendar months, that ATC transponder has been tested and inspected.

1-54   CA.I.B.K1b, CA.II.A.K2, 3

If an ATC transponder installed in an aircraft has not been tested, inspected, and found to comply with regulations within a specified period, what is the limitation on its use?

A – Its use is not permitted.

B – It may be used when in Class G airspace.

C – It may be used for VFR flight only.

1-54. Answer A. GFDIC 1B, FAR 91.413

You may not use an ATC transponder unless within the preceding 24 calendar months, that ATC transponder has been tested and inspected.

1-55   CA.I.B.K2

Which is correct concerning preventive maintenance, when accomplished by a pilot?

A – A record of preventive maintenance is not required.

B – A record of preventive maintenance must be entered in the maintenance records.

C – Records of preventive maintenance must be entered in the FAA-approved flight manual.

1-55. Answer B. GFDIC 1B, FAR 43.7, 43.9

FAR 43.7 allows preventive maintenance to be performed by a person who holds at least a private pilot certificate. Examples of preventive maintenance are: replacing and servicing batteries, replacing spark plugs, and servicing wheel bearings and struts. According to FAR 43.9, any person who maintains, performs preventive maintenance, rebuilds, or alters an aircraft part shall make an entry in the maintenance record.

1-56   CA.I.B.K1b

Aircraft maintenance records must include the current status of the

A – applicable airworthiness certificate.

B – life-limited parts of only the engine and airframe.

C – life-limited parts of each airframe, engine, propeller, rotor, and appliance.

1-56. Answer C. GFDIC 1B, FAR 91.417

Aircraft maintenance records must contain the current status of life-limited parts of each airframe, engine, propeller, rotor, and appliance. Records must include the description and completion date of any work performed and the signature, and certificate number of the person approving the aircraft for return to service.

1-57   CA.I.B.K1b

If an aircraft's operation in flight was substantially affected by an alteration or repair, the aircraft documents must show that it was test flown and approved for return to service by an appropriately-rated pilot prior to being operated

A – under VFR or IFR rules.

B – with passengers aboard.

C – for compensation or hire.

1-57. Answer B. GFDIC 1B, FAR 91.407

You may not carry passengers in an aircraft that has been maintained, rebuilt, or altered in a manner that might have appreciably changed its flight characteristics or substantially affected its operation in flight until an appropriately rated pilot with at least a private pilot certificate flies the aircraft to make an operational check and logs the flight in the aircraft records.

1-58   CA.I.B.K1c, CA.II.A.K2, 3

You are PIC of a flight and determine that the aircraft you planned to fly has an overdue airworthiness directive (AD). Which of the following is an appropriate decision?

A – No maintenance is available so you wait until after the trip to comply with the AD.

B – You make the flight because you can overfly an AD by 10 hours.

C – You cancel the flight and have the aircraft scheduled for maintenance.

1-58. Answer C. GFDIC 1B, FAR Part 39, FAR 91.403, FAR 91.417

ADs are legally enforceable rules governed by FAR Part 39. An AD could be a one-time fix for a defect, recurring maintenance or inspections to address a specific issue, or limitations on the operation of an aircraft. The aircraft owner or operator must maintain records in the maintenance logbooks that show compliance with all pertinent ADs.

Unlike regular inspections, which might include provisions for going over the time limit, ADs are not flexible—their time interval may not be "overflown" unless a provision is included in the AD allowing it.

1-59   CA.I.B.K1c

Assuring compliance with an airworthiness directive (AD) is the responsibility of the

A – owner or operator of that aircraft.

B – pilot in command of that aircraft.

C – pilot in command and the FAA certificated mechanic assigned to that aircraft.

1-59. Answer A. GFDIC 1B, FAR Part 39, FAR 91.403, FAR 91.417

ADs are legally enforceable rules governed by FAR Part 39. An AD could be a one-time fix for a defect, recurring maintenance or inspections to address a specific issue, or limitations on the operation of an aircraft. The aircraft owner or operator must maintain records in the maintenance logbooks that show compliance with all pertinent ADs.

SECTION B ■ **Commercial Pilot Requirements**

1-60   CA.I.B.K1c

Which is true relating to airworthiness directives (ADs)?

A – ADs are advisory in nature and are, generally, not addressed immediately.

B – Noncompliance with ADs renders an aircraft unairworthy.

C – Compliance with ADs is the responsibility of maintenance personnel.

1-60. Answer B. GFDIC 1B, FAR Part 39, FAR 91.403, FAR 91.417

ADs are legally enforceable rules governed by FAR Part 39. An AD could be a one-time fix for a defect, recurring maintenance or inspections to address a specific issue, or limitations on the operation of an aircraft. The aircraft owner or operator must maintain records in the maintenance logbooks that show compliance with all pertinent ADs.

Unlike regular inspections, which might include provisions for going over the time limit, ADs are not flexible—their time interval may not be "overflown" unless a provision is included in the AD allowing it.

1-61   CA.I.B.K1c

A new maintenance record being used for an aircraft engine rebuilt by the manufacturer must include previous

A – operating hours of the engine.

B – annual inspections performed on the engine.

C – changes as required by Airworthiness Directives.

1-61. Answer C. GFDIC 1B, FAR 91.421

ADs are legally enforceable rules governed by FAR Part 39. An AD could be a one-time fix for a defect, recurring maintenance or inspections to address a specific issue, or limitations on the operation of an aircraft. The aircraft owner or operator must maintain records in the maintenance logbooks that show compliance with all pertinent ADs.

Each manufacturer or agency that rebuilds an engine and grants zero time to an engine must enter in the new record, each change made as required by airworthiness directives.

1-62   CA.I.B.K2

Which is required equipment for powered aircraft during VFR night flights?

A – Anticollision light system.

B – Gyroscopic direction indicator.

C – Gyroscopic bank-and-pitch indicator.

1-62. Answer A. GFDIC 1B, FAR 91.205

The minimum equipment required by FAR 91.205 for VFR day and night operations includes flight instruments, engine and system monitoring indicators, and safety equipment. A red or white anticollision light system is listed by 91.205 for both day and night operations.

Instrument and equipment required for night VFR (in addition to that required for day VFR) includes position lights, a landing light (only during operations for hire), an adequate source of electrical energy, and a spare set of fuses when applicable.

1-63   CA.I.B.K3

Approved flotation gear, readily available to each occupant, is required on each airplane if it is being flown for hire over water,

A – beyond power-off gliding distance from shore.

B – more than 50 statute miles from shore.

C – in amphibious aircraft beyond 50 NM from shore.

1-63. Answer A. GFDIC 1B, FAR 91.205

If the aircraft is operated for hire over water and beyond power-off gliding distance from shore, approved flotation gear must be readily available to each occupant, and the aircraft must have at least one pyrotechnic signaling device on board.

1-64   CA.I.B.K3

Which is required equipment for powered aircraft during VFR night flights?

A – Sensitive altimeter adjustable for barometric pressure.

B – An electric landing light, if the flight is for hire.

C – Flashlight with red lens, if the flight is for hire.

1-64. Answer B. GFDIC 1B, FAR 91.205

The minimum equipment required by FAR 91.205 for VFR day and night operations includes flight instruments, engine and system monitoring indicators, and safety equipment. A red or white anticollision light system is listed by 91.205 for both day and night operations.

Instrument and equipment required for night VFR (in addition to that required for day VFR) includes position lights, a landing light (only during operations for hire), an adequate source of electrical energy, and a spare set of fuses when applicable.

1-65   CA.I.B.K2

If not equipped with required position lights, an aircraft must terminate flight

A – at sunset.

B – 30 minutes after sunset.

C – 1 hour after sunset.

1-65. Answer A. GFDIC 1B, FAR 91.205, FAR 91.209

Instrument and equipment required by 91.205 for night VFR (in addition to that required for day VFR) includes position lights, a landing light (only during operations for hire), an adequate source of electrical energy, and a spare set of fuses when applicable. In addition, FAR 91.209 states that no person may, during the period from sunset to sunrise, operate an aircraft unless it has lighted position lights.

1-66   CA.I.B.K1c

Special airworthiness information bulletins contain

A – legally enforceable rules that require mandatory compliance.

B – non-regulatory information that does not meet the criteria for an AD but is issued to alert, educate, and make recommendations to the aviation community.

C – one-time fixes for a defect, recurring maintenance or inspections to address a specific issue, or limitations on the operation of an aircraft.

1-66. Answer B. GFDIC 1B, FAA Document 8110.100

A special airworthiness information bulletin (SAIB) contains non-regulatory information that does not meet the criteria for an advisory circular (AD) but is issued to alert, educate, and make recommendations to the aviation community.

ADs are legally enforceable rules governed by FAR Part 39. An AD could be a one-time fix for a defect, recurring maintenance or inspections to address a specific issue, or limitations on the operation of an aircraft.

SECTION B ■ Commercial Pilot Requirements

1-67   CA.I.B.K3b

A minimum equipment list (MEL) is

A – based on the regulations and the specific requirements for your aircraft and flight operation and indicates the equipment that is allowed to be inoperative for a particular flight.

B – is a required document for all aircraft.

C – lists only the minimum equipment required by 91.205 for a specific flight operation.

1-67. Answer B. GFDIC 1B, FAR 91.213

If a minimum equipment list (MEL) exists for your aircraft, you must use it. The MEL takes into consideration the regulations and the specific requirements for your aircraft and flight operation and indicates the equipment that is allowed to be inoperative for a particular flight. MELs are not common for light single-engine piston-powered airplanes.

1-68   CA.I.B.K3a, b, c, d, CA.II.A.K2, 3

You discover inoperative equipment on an airplane that you are planning to fly. The airplane does not have an MEL. You must determine if the inoperative equipment is required by which four items?

A – VFR-day type certificate requirements; FAR 91.205; minimum equipment list; airworthiness directive.

B – VFR-day type certificate requirements; FAR 91.205; aircraft's equipment list or the kinds of operations equipment list; airworthiness directive.

C – VFR-day type certificate requirements; FAR 91.205; for the specific kind of flight operation; aircraft's equipment list or the kinds of operations equipment list; special airworthiness information bulletin.

1-68. Answer B. GFDIC 1B, FAR 91.213

If your airplane does not have an MEL, use the procedure described in FAR 91.213. Answer yes or no—do any of the following require the inoperative equipment?

• The VFR-day type certificate requirements; FAR prescribed in the airworthiness certification regulations.

• FAR 91.205 for the specific kind of flight operation (e.g. day or night VFR) or by other flight rules for the specific kind of flight to be conducted.

• The aircraft's equipment list or the kinds of operations equipment list (KOEL).

• An airworthiness directive (AD).

If the answer is YES to ANY of these questions, the airplane is not airworthy and maintenance is required. If the answer is NO to ALL of these questions, then you may fly the airplane after the inoperative equipment is:

• Removed and the cockpit control placarded by an AMT.

• Deactivated and placarded "inoperative" (by an AMT if deactivation involves maintenance).

1-69   CA.I.B.K3d, CA.II.A.K2, 3

You discover inoperative equipment on an airplane that you are planning to fly. The airplane does not have an MEL. You have determined that—according to the FARs—you may legally fly the airplane. What additional actions must be taken?

A – No further action is required.

B – You must obtain a special flight permit.

C – The equipment must be removed or deactivated and placarded "inoperative."

1-69. Answer C. GFDIC 1B, FAR 91.213

If your airplane does not have an MEL, use the procedure described in FAR 91.213. Answer yes or no—do any of the following require the inoperative equipment?

• The VFR-day type certificate requirements; FAR prescribed in the airworthiness certification regulations.

• FAR 91.205 for the specific kind of flight operation (e.g. day or night VFR) or by other flight rules for the specific kind of flight to be conducted.

• The aircraft's equipment list or the kinds of operations equipment list (KOEL).

• An airworthiness directive (AD).

If the answer is YES to ANY of these questions, the airplane is not airworthy and maintenance is required. If the answer is NO to ALL of these questions, then you may fly the airplane after the inoperative equipment is:

• Removed and the cockpit control placarded by an AMT.

• Deactivated and placarded "inoperative" (by an AMT if deactivation involves maintenance).

1-70   CA.I.B.K1d

If you determine that the airworthiness requirements are not met, a special flight permit

A – allows the aircraft to be flown to a location where the needed repairs can be made.

B – allows the aircraft to be flown with inoperative equipment until the next annual inspection.

C – can be issued by an AMT and allows the aircraft to be flown until scheduled repairs can be made.

1-70. Answer A. GFDIC 1B, FAR 91.213

If you determine that the airworthiness requirements are not met, the FAA may permit the airplane to be flown to a location where the needed repairs can be made by issuing a special flight permit, sometimes called a ferry permit. To obtain this permit, an application must be submitted to the nearest FAA flight standards district office (FSDO). However, if an airworthiness directive prohibits further flight until the AD is satisfied, the FSDO may not issue a ferry permit. In this case, an AMT might have to be transported to the aircraft's location to resolve the AD.

SECTION B ■ **Commercial Pilot Requirements**

SECTION C
Aviation Physiology

VISION IN FLIGHT

- Cones function well in bright light, are sensitive to colors, and enable you to see fine detail. Cones are concentrated in the center of the retina in a slight depression known as the fovea.

- The rods are your primary receptors for night vision and also are responsible for much of your peripheral vision.

DARK ADAPTATION

- Rods are able to detect images in the dark because they create a chemical called rhodopsin, also referred to as visual purple. As visual purple is formed, the rods can take up to 30 minutes to fully adapt to the dark.

- To preserve and improve your night vision:
    - Avoid looking directly at any bright light sources, such as landing lights, strobe light, or flashlights for 30 minutes before a night flight.
    - During flight, continually reduce the intensity of the instrument lights or the electronic flight display as your eyes adapt—keep the brightness at the minimum level for effective vision.
    - Reduce the level of cabin light or use dim white flashlight for reading paper charts and checklists. Keeping the interior lighting to a minimum level helps you to see outside visual references more clearly.

VISUAL ILLUSIONS

- The illusion of a false horizon occurs when the natural horizon is obscured or not readily apparent. For example, when flying over a sloping cloud deck, you might try to align the airplane with the cloud formation.

- At night, ground lights, stars, and reflections on the windscreen can lead to confusion regarding the position of the horizon.

- Rain, haze, or fog; and flying over water, at night, or over featureless terrain, such as snow, can cause you to fly a lower-than-normal approach.

- Narrow and upsloping runways can create the landing illusion of greater height causing you to fly a lower-than-normal approach.

- Wide and downsloping runways can create the landing illusion of less height causing you to fly a higher-than-normal approach.

SPATIAL DISORIENTATION

- Spatial disorientation is the lack of orientation with regard to the position, attitude, or movement of the airplane in space. You sense your body's position in relation to your environment using input from three primary sources:
    - Visual system.
    - Vestibular system—organs found in the inner ear that sense position by the way you are balanced.
    - Somatosensory system—nerves in the skin, muscles, and joints that, along with hearing, sense position based on gravity, feeling, and sound. (This system is sometimes referred to as your kinesthetic sense).

- In good weather and daylight, you obtain your orientation primarily through your vision. In IFR conditions or at night, fewer visual cues are available so your body relies upon the vestibular and kinesthetic senses to supplement your vision. Because these senses can provide false cues about your orientation, the risk of spatial disorientation occurring in IFR weather is quite high.

- In the absence of reliable visual information referenced to the natural horizon, you must rely on and properly interpret the indications of the flight instruments, and act accordingly.

- During prolonged constant-rate turns, abrupt head movements can set fluid in more than one semicircular canal in motion. This creates the strong sensation of turning or accelerating on an entirely different axis. The sensation, known as Coriolis illusion, causes serious disorientation.

- A rapid acceleration can produce the somatogravic illusion—the feeling that you are in a nose-high attitude although you are still in straight-and-level flight. This illusion can prompt you to lower the nose and enter a dive. A deceleration, such as rapidly retarding the throttle, produces the opposite effect.

- The inversion illusion, caused by an abrupt change from a climb to straight-and-level flight, creates the feeling that you are tumbling backward. The effect can cause you to lower the nose abruptly, which can intensify the illusion.

HYPOXIA

- Hypoxia occurs when the tissues in the body do not receive enough oxygen.

- An insidious characteristic of hypoxia is that its early symptoms include euphoria, which can prevent you from recognizing a potentially hazardous situation. Other symptoms include visual impairment (such as tunnel vision), cyanosis (blue fingernails and lips), headache, decreased response time, impaired judgment, drowsiness, dizziness, tingling fingers and toes, numbness, and limp muscles.

TYPES OF HYPOXIA

- Hypoxic hypoxia—not enough molecules of oxygen are available at sufficient pressure to pass between the membranes in your respiratory system. Hypoxic hypoxia can occur very suddenly at high altitudes during rapid decompression, or it can occur slowly at lower altitudes when you are exposed to insufficient oxygen over an extended period of time.

- The time of useful consciousness (TUC) is the maximum time you have to make a rational, life-saving decision and carry it out following a lack of oxygen at a given altitude. TUC varies from approximately 30 minutes at 20,000 feet MSL to 9 to 15 seconds at 45,000 feet MSL.

- Hypemic hypoxia—your blood is not able to carry a sufficient amount of oxygen to your body's cells caused by conditions, such as anemia, disease, blood loss, or deformed blood cells.

  - Hypemic hypoxia can be caused by carbon monoxide poisoning, which interferes with the attachment of oxygen to the blood's hemoglobin.

  - With most single-engine airplanes, ventilation air is heated by flowing through a shroud that surrounds the exterior of the exhaust muffler or manifold. If the exhaust system develops a crack or hole within the cavity, carbon monoxide can combine with the ventilation air and subsequently be delivered to the cabin.

- Stagnant hypoxia—your body has an oxygen deficiency in the body due to the poor circulation of the blood. During flight, stagnant hypoxia can be the result of pulling excessive positive Gs.

- Histotoxic hypoxia—the cells cannot effectively use oxygen. This impairment of cellular respiration can be caused by alcohol and other drugs such as narcotics and poisons.

SUPPLEMENTAL OXYGEN

When operating an unpressurized aircraft above:

- 12,500 feet MSL up to and including 14,000 feet MSL for more than 30 minutes, the flight crew must use supplemental oxygen.

SECTION C ■ Aviation Physiology

- 14,000 feet MSL, the minimum flight crew must be provided with, and use, supplemental oxygen the entire time.
- 15,000 feet MSL, passengers must be provided supplemental oxygen.

EAR AND SINUS BLOCK

- During a descent, the outside air pressure in the auditory canal will become higher than the pressure in the middle ear.
- Slow descent rates can help prevent or reduce the severity of ear problems and the eustachian tube can sometimes be opened by yawning, swallowing, or chewing.
- Pressure can be equalized by performing the Valsalva maneuver—holding the nose and mouth shut and forcibly exhaling to force air up the eustachian tube into the middle ear.

DECOMPRESSION SICKNESS

- Decompression sickness (DCS) is caused by a rapid reduction in the ambient pressure surrounding the body.
- Nitrogen and other inert gases expand to form bubbles that rise out of solution and produce symptoms that range from pain in the joints to seizures and unconsciousness.
- Scuba diving can cause DCS so the following wait times before ascending are recommended:
    - To 8,000 feet MSL—12 hours after a dive that did not require a controlled ascent (nondecompression stop diving); 24 hours after a dive that required a controlled ascent (decompression stop diving)
    - Above 8,000 feet MSL—24 hours after any dive.

HYPERVENTILATION

- Breathing too rapidly or too deeply can cause hyperventilation, a physiological disorder that develops when too much carbon dioxide (CO_2) is eliminated from the body.
- Symptoms of hyperventilation include drowsiness, dizziness, shortness of breath, feelings of suffocation, a pale, clammy appearance, muscle spasms, and a loss of consciousness.
- To overcome the symptoms of hyperventilation, you should slow your breathing rate, breathe into a paper bag, or talk aloud.

FITNESS FOR FLIGHT

- Because stress is cumulative, you bring into the flight varying degrees of stress left over from the other areas of your life. Excessive stress interferes with your ability to focus and cope with a given situation.
- Fatigue has been a major factor in many fatal accidents involving very experienced and highly qualified crews.
- Dehydration is a critical loss of water from the body. Although, dehydration can cause headaches, cramps, nausea, and dizziness, the first noticeable effect is typically fatigue.

ALCOHOL AND DRUGS

- The FARs specifically state that you must not fly within 8 hours of using alcohol, or when you have a blood alcohol level of .04% or greater.
- Alcohol and other depressants cause decreased mental processing, slow motor and reaction responses, and even small amounts of alcohol impair your judgment and decision-making abilities.
- The body requires about 3 hours to rid itself of all the alcohol contained in one mixed drink or one beer.

HYPOTHERMIA

- Hypothermia occurs when your body loses heat faster than it can produce heat, causing a dangerously low body temperature below 95°F (35°C).

- You might not be aware of your condition if you have hypothermia because the symptoms often begin gradually and the confused thinking associated with hypothermia prevents self-awareness.

NOTE: An asterisk appearing after an ACS code (i.e. CA.IV.A.K2*) indicates that the question subject appears more than one time in the ACS. The code shown corresponds to the first instance of the subject in the ACS.

1-71   CA.I.H.K1k

A sloping cloud formation, an obscured horizon, and a dark scene spread with ground lights and stars can create an illusion known as

A – elevator illusions.

B – autokinesis.

C – false horizons.

1-71. Answer C. GFDIC 1C, PHB

A false horizon occurs when the natural horizon is obscured or not readily apparent. For example, when flying over a sloping cloud deck, you might try to align the airplane with the cloud formation. At night, ground lights, stars, and reflections on the windscreen can lead to confusion regarding the position of the horizon.

1-72   CA.I.H.K1k

Which of these conditions can cause you to fly a higher-than-normal approach?

A – Rain, haze, or fog.

B – Narrow and upsloping runway.

C – Wide and downsloping runway.

1-72. Answer C. GFDIC 1C, PHB

Wide and downsloping runways can create the landing illusion of less height causing you to fly a higher-than-normal approach. Narrow and upsloping runways can create the landing illusion of greater height causing you to fly a lower-than-normal approach. Rain, haze, or fog; and flying over water, at night, or over featureless terrain, such as snow, can cause you to fly a lower-than-normal approach.

1-73   CA.I.H.K1k

Which of these conditions can cause you to fly a lower-than-normal approach?

A – Upsloping runway.

B – Wide runway.

C – Downsloping runway.

1-73. Answer A. GFDIC 1C, PHB

Narrow and upsloping runways can create the landing illusion of greater height causing you to fly a lower-than-normal approach. Wide and downsloping runways can create the landing illusion of less height causing you to fly a higher-than-normal approach.

SECTION C ■ **Aviation Physiology**

1-74   **CA.I.H.K1d**

You are most likely to experience somatogravic illusion during

A – a rapid descent.

B – deceleration upon landing.

C – rapid acceleration on takeoff.

1-74. Answer C. GFDIC 1C, PHB

A rapid acceleration can produce the somatogravic illusion—the feeling that you are in a nose-high attitude although you are still in straight-and-level flight. This illusion can prompt you to lower the nose and enter a dive. A deceleration, such as rapidly retarding the throttle, produces the opposite effect.

1-75   **CA.I.H.K1d**

To best overcome the effects of spatial disorientation, you should

A – rely on body sensations.

B – increase your breathing rate.

C – rely on aircraft instrument indications.

1-75. Answer C. GFDIC 1C, PHB

In good weather and daylight, you obtain your orientation primarily through your vision. In IFR conditions or at night, fewer visual cues are available so your body relies upon the vestibular and kinesthetic senses to supplement your vision. Because these senses can provide false cues about your orientation, the risk of spatial disorientation occurring in IFR weather is quite high.

In the absence of reliable visual information referenced to the natural horizon, you must rely on and properly interpret the indications of the flight instruments, and act accordingly.

1-76   **CA.I.H.K1d**

To cope with spatial disorientation, you should rely on

A – body sensations and outside visual references.

B – adequate food, rest, and night adaptation.

C – proficient use of the aircraft instruments.

1-76. Answer C. GFDIC 1C, PHB

In good weather and daylight, you obtain your orientation primarily through your vision. In IFR conditions or at night, fewer visual cues are available so your body relies upon the vestibular and kinesthetic senses to supplement your vision. Because these senses can provide false cues about your orientation, the risk of spatial disorientation occurring in IFR weather is quite high.

In the absence of reliable visual information referenced to the natural horizon, you must rely on and properly interpret the indications of the flight instruments, and act accordingly.

1-77   **CA.I.H.K1e**

Which is a correct action to recommend to a passenger to overcome motion sickness?

A – Breathe into a paper bag.

B – Focus on the instrument panel.

C – Focus on objects outside the airplane.

1-77. Answer C. GFDIC 1C, PHB

To prevent or alleviate motion sickness in passengers, suggest that they focus on objects outside the airplane. Breathing into a paper bag is a technique you can recommend to overcome hyperventilation.

1-78   CA.I.H.K1a

Hypoxia is the result of which of these conditions?

A – Excessive oxygen in the bloodstream.

B – Insufficient oxygen reaching the brain.

C – Excessive carbon dioxide in the bloodstream.

1-78. Answer B. GFDIC 1C, PHB

Hypoxia occurs when the tissues in your body do not receive enough oxygen.

1-79   CA.I.H.K1a, CA.VIII.A.K2a, b*

Which is a common symptom of hypoxia?

A – Increased breathing rate.

B – Increased response time.

C – Sense of well-being.

1-79. Answer C. GFDIC 1C, PHB

An insidious characteristic of hypoxia is that its early symptoms include euphoria, which can prevent you from recognizing a potentially hazardous situation. Remain alert for the other symptoms of hypoxia such as headache, increased response time, impaired judgment, drowsiness, dizziness, tingling fingers and toes, numbness, blue fingernails and lips (cyanosis), and limp muscles.

1-80   CA.VIII.A.K2c, CA.VIII.B.K2c

Which is true about the time of useful consciousness (TUC)?

A – TUC is the minimum amount of time you have to make decision following a lack of oxygen at a given altitude.

B – TUC is the maximum amount of time you have to make decision following a lack of oxygen at a given altitude.

C – TUC at 45,000 feet MSL is approximately 9 to 15 minutes.

1-80. Answer B. GFDIC 1C, PHB

The time of useful consciousness (TUC) is the maximum time you have to make a rational, life-saving decision and carry it out following a lack of oxygen at a given altitude. TUC varies from approximately 30 minutes at 20,000 feet MSL to 9 to 15 seconds at 45,000 feet MSL.

1-81   CA.I.G.R1, CA.I.H.K1f

Your aircraft has an exhaust manifold type heating system. The exhaust manifold isperiodically inspected to avoid

A – carbon monoxide poisoning.

B – overheating in the cockpit.

C – extremely cold temperatures in the cabin.

1-81. Answer A. GFDIC 1C, AC 91-59

Hypemic hypoxia can be caused by carbon monoxide poisoning, which interferes with the attachment of oxygen to the blood's hemoglobin. With most single-engine airplanes, ventilation air is heated by flowing through a shroud that surrounds the exterior of the exhaust muffler or manifold. If the exhaust system develops a crack or hole within the cavity, carbon monoxide can combine with the ventilation air and subsequently be delivered to the cabin.

SECTION C ■ **Aviation Physiology**

1-82 CA.I.G.R1, CA.I.H.K1f

Frequent inspections should be made of aircraft exhaust manifold-type heating systems to minimize the possibility of

A – exhaust gases leaking into the cockpit.

B – a power loss due to back pressure in the exhaust system.

C – a cold-running engine due to the heat withdrawn by the heater.

1-82. Answer A. GFDIC 1C, AC 91-59

Hypemic hypoxia can be caused by carbon monoxide poisoning, which interferes with the attachment of oxygen to the blood's hemoglobin. With most single-engine airplanes, ventilation air is heated by flowing through a shroud that surrounds the exterior of the exhaust muffler or manifold. If the exhaust system develops a crack or hole within the cavity, carbon monoxide can combine with the ventilation air and subsequently be delivered to the cabin.

1-83 CA.I.H.K1a, CA.VIII.A.K2a, b*, CA.I.H.K1f

Hypoxia susceptibility due to inhalation of carbon monoxide increases as

A – humidity decreases.

B – altitude increases.

C – oxygen demand increases.

1-83. Answer B. GFDIC 1C, PHB

As altitude increases, air pressure decreases and the body has difficulty getting enough oxygen. Add carbon monoxide, which further deprives the body of oxygen, and the situation can become critical.

1-84 CA.VIII.A.K1

In accordance with 14 CFR part 91, supplemental oxygen must be used by the required minimum flightcrew for that time exceeding 30 minutes while at cabin pressure altitudes of

A – 10,500 feet MSL up to and including 12,500 feet MSL.

B – 12,000 feet MSL up to and including 18,000 feet MSL.

C – 12,500 feet MSL up to and including 14,000 feet MSL.

1-84. Answer C. GFDIC 1C, FAR 91.211

When operating an unpressurized aircraft above:

- 12,500 feet MSL up to and including 14,000 feet MSL for more than 30 minutes, the flight crew must use supplemental oxygen.
- 14,000 feet MSL, the minimum flight crew must be provided with, and use, supplemental oxygen the entire time.
- 15,000 feet MSL, passengers must be provided supplemental oxygen.

1-85 CA.VIII.A.K1

What are the oxygen requirements when operating at cabin pressure altitudes above 15,000 feet MSL?

A – The flight crew must use supplemental oxygen after 30 minutes.

B – Both the flight crew and passengers must use supplemental oxygen the entire time.

C – The flight crew must use supplemental oxygen the entire time and the passengers must be provided with supplemental oxygen.

1-85. Answer C. GFDIC 1C, FAR 91.211

When operating an unpressurized aircraft above:

- 12,500 feet MSL up to and including 14,000 feet MSL for more than 30 minutes, the flight crew must use supplemental oxygen.
- 14,000 feet MSL, the minimum flight crew must be provided with, and use, supplemental oxygen the entire time.
- 15,000 feet MSL, passengers must be provided supplemental oxygen.

1-86 CA.I.H.K1c

Which is an action that you can take to help a passenger overcome ear pain due to higher pressure in the auditory canal in the middle ear?

A – Increase the aircraft's descent rate.

B – Recommend that your passenger perform the Valsalva maneuver prior to initiating a climb.

C – Decrease the aircraft's descent rate.

1-86. Answer C. GFDIC 1C, PHB

During a descent, the outside air pressure in the auditory canal will become higher than the pressure in the middle ear. Slow descent rates can help prevent or reduce the severity of ear problems and the eustachian tube can sometimes be opened by yawning, swallowing, or chewing. Pressure can be equalized by performing the Valsalva maneuver—holding the nose and mouth shut and forcibly exhaling to force air up the eustachian tube into the middle ear.

1-87 CA.I.H.K1l

What is the recommended waiting time before ascending to 8,000 feet MSL after scuba diving during which a controlled ascent was performed?

A – 12 hours.

B – 24 hours.

C – 48 hours.

1-87. Answer B. GFDIC 1C, PHB

Decompression sickness (DCS) is caused by a rapid reduction in the ambient pressure surrounding the body. Nitrogen and other inert gases expand to form bubbles that rise out of solution and produce symptoms that range from pain in the joints to seizures and unconsciousness. Scuba diving can cause DCS so the following wait times before ascending are recommended:

- To 8,000 feet MSL—12 hours after a dive that did not require a controlled ascent (nondecompression stop diving); 24 hours after a dive that required a controlled ascent (decompression stop diving)

- Above 8,000 feet MSL—24 hours after any dive.

1-88 CA.I.H.K1b

As hyperventilation progresses, you can experience

A – decreased breathing rate and depth.

B – heightened awareness and feeling of well-being.

C – symptoms of suffocation and drowsiness.

1-88. Answer C. GFDIC 1C, PHB

Breathing too rapidly or too deeply can cause hyperventilation, a physiological disorder that develops when too much carbon dioxide (CO_2) is eliminated from the body. Symptoms of hyperventilation include drowsiness, dizziness, shortness of breath, feelings of suffocation, a pale, clammy appearance, muscle spasms, and a loss of consciousness.

1-89 CA.I.H.K1b

Which is a common symptom of hyperventilation?

A – Drowsiness.

B – Decreased breathing rate.

C – A sense of well-being.

1-89. Answer A. GFDIC 1C, PHB

Breathing too rapidly or too deeply can cause hyperventilation, a physiological disorder that develops when too much carbon dioxide (CO_2) is eliminated from the body. Symptoms of hyperventilation include drowsiness, dizziness, shortness of breath, feelings of suffocation, a pale, clammy appearance, muscle spasms, and a loss of consciousness.

SECTION C ■ **Aviation Physiology**

1-90   CA.I.H.K1b

Which would most likely result in hyperventilation?

A – Insufficient oxygen.

B – Excessive carbon monoxide.

C – Insufficient carbon dioxide.

1-90. Answer C. GFDIC 1C, PHB

Breathing too rapidly or too deeply can cause hyperventilation, a physiological disorder that develops when too much carbon dioxide (CO_2) is eliminated from the body.

1-91   CA.I.H.K1b

To overcome the symptoms of hyperventilation, a pilot should

A – swallow or yawn.

B – slow the breathing rate.

C – increase the breathing rate.

1-91. Answer B. GFDIC 1C, PHB

Breathing too rapidly or too deeply can cause hyperventilation, a physiological disorder that develops when too much carbon dioxide (CO_2) is eliminated from the body. To overcome the symptoms of hyperventilation, you should slow your breathing rate, breathe into a paper bag, or talk aloud.

1-92   CA.I.H.K1g, h, i

What is true about the factors that affect fitness for flight?

A – Fatigue is not a factor in aircraft accidents.

B – The first noticeable effect of dehydration is typically fatigue.

C – Stress is not cumulative.

1-92. Answer B. GFDIC 1C, PHB

These factors affect your fitness for flight:

- Because stress is cumulative, you bring into the flight varying degrees of stress left over from the other areas of your life. Excessive stress interferes with your ability to focus and cope with a given situation.

- Fatigue has been a major factor in many fatal accidents involving very experienced and highly qualified crews.

- Dehydration is a critical loss of water from the body. Although, dehydration can cause headaches, cramps, nausea, and dizziness, the first noticeable effect is typically fatigue.

1-93   CA.I.H.K2

You attended a party last night and you consumed several glasses of wine. You are planning to fly your aircraft home and have been careful to make sure 8 hours have passed since your last alcoholic drink. You can make the flight now only if you are not under the influence of alcohol and your blood alcohol level is

A – below .04%.

B – below .08%.

C – 0.0%.

1-93. Answer A. GFDIC 1C, FAR 91.17

The FARs specifically state that you must not fly within 8 hours of using alcohol, or when you have a blood alcohol level of .04% or greater. The body requires about 3 hours to rid itself of all the alcohol contained in one mixed drink or one beer.

1-94   CA.I.H.K3

Which is true regarding the presence of alcohol within the human body?

A – A small amount of alcohol increases vision acuity.

B – An increase in altitude decreases the adverse effect of alcohol.

C – Judgment and decision-making abilities can be adversely affected by even small amounts of alcohol.

1-94. Answer C. GFDIC 1C, PHB, FAR 91.17

The FARs specifically state that you must not fly within 8 hours of using alcohol, or when you have a blood alcohol level of .04% or greater. Alcohol and other depressants cause decreased mental processing, slow motor and reaction responses, and even small amounts of alcohol impair your judgment and decision-making abilities.

1-95   CA.I.H.K3

To rid itself of all the alcohol contained in one mixed drink or one beer, the human body requires about

A – 1 hour.

B – 2 hours.

C – 3 hours.

1-95. Answer C. GFDIC 1C, PHB

The FARs specifically state that you must not fly within 8 hours of using alcohol, or when you have a blood alcohol level of .04% or greater. The body requires about 3 hours to rid itself of all the alcohol contained in one mixed drink or one beer.

1-96   CA.I.H.K1j

What is true about hypothermia?

A – Recognizing hypothermia is normally easy because symptoms occur rapidly.

B – A body temperature below 98° is considered hypothermia.

C – Hypothermia symptoms often begin gradually and can include confused thinking.

1-96. Answer C. GFDIC 1C

Hypothermia occurs when your body loses heat faster than it can produce heat, causing a dangerously low body temperature below 95°F (35°C). You might not be aware of your condition if you have hypothermia because the symptoms often begin gradually and the confused thinking associated with hypothermia prevents self-awareness.

SECTION C ■ Aviation Physiology

Section D
SRM Concepts

This section in the *Instrument/Commercial* textbook defines single-pilot resource management (SRM) concepts that you should be aware of as you begin your instrument training. Chapter 13, Section B — Commercial Pilot SRM provides a more extensive examination of SRM as it applies to operating in the commercial flight environment. The FAA questions associated with SRM concepts, such as aeronautical decision making, risk, task and automation management, situational awareness, and controlled flight into terrain awareness are presented in Chapter 13, Section B of this test guide.

CHAPTER 2

Principles of Instrument Flight

NOTE: No FAA Commercial Pilot questions apply to GFD Instrument/Commercial textbook Chapter 2, Section C — Attitude Instrument Flying.

SECTION A
Analog Flight Instruments

Chapter 2, Section A, of the *Commercial Pilot FAA Airman Knowledge Test Guide* corresponds to the same chapter and section of the *GFD Instrument/Commercial* textbook: Analog Flight Instruments. Although, the content of this section is a primary focus of instrument training, as a commercial pilot, you are required to understand aircraft systems, including the flight instrument systems. Typically, you will hold an instrument rating prior to obtaining a commercial certificate so you are most likely familiar with this content. However, you might wish to review this information and ensure you can answer knowledge test questions that apply to the analog flight instruments.

GYROSCOPIC INSTRUMENTS

- The gyroscopic instruments are the attitude indicator, heading indicator, and turn indicators (turn-and-slip indicator and turn coordinator).

- On many light airplanes, the vacuum system supplies power to the attitude and heading indicators, while the electrical system powers the turn coordinator. This configuration provides a backup in case one system fails.

- Gyroscopic instrument operation is based on rigidity in space and precession.

  - Rigidity in space refers to the principle that a wheel with a heavily weighted rim spun rapidly tends to remain fixed in the plane in which it is spinning. By mounting this wheel, or gyroscope, on a set of gimbals, the gyro is able to rotate freely in any plane. If the gimbals' base tilts, twists, or otherwise moves, the gyro remains in the plane in which it was originally spinning.

  - When an outside force tries to tilt a spinning gyro, the gyro responds as if the force had been applied at a point 90° further around in the direction of rotation. This effect is called precession, because the cause precedes the effect by 90°. Unwanted precession is caused by friction in the gimbals and bearings of the instrument, causing a slow drifting in the heading indicator and occasional small errors in the attitude indicator.

ATTITUDE INDICATOR

- The attitude indicator, or artificial horizon, is the only instrument that gives you an immediate and direct indication of the airplane's pitch and bank attitude.

- During a turn, the gyro in an attitude indicator can precess toward the inside of the turn, which might cause small bank angle pitch errors. For example, after you roll out of a 180-degree turn, the attitude indicator might briefly show a turn in the opposite direction and indicate a slight climb.

- In some attitude indicators, a skidding turn can precess the gyro to the inside of the turn, causing a slight bank error. For example, after you return to straight-and-level coordinated flight from a 180° skidding turn, the attitude indicator might show a turn in the opposite direction of the skid.

- Due to precession, some older attitude indicators will incorrectly indicate a climb when the aircraft accelerates and a descent when the airplane decelerates.

HEADING INDICATOR

- When properly set, the heading indicator is your main source of heading information.

- You must align the heading indicator with the magnetic compass before flight.

- Precession can cause the heading to drift from the proper setting, so you must check the heading indicator against the magnetic compass at approximately 15-minute intervals during flight.

TURN INDICATORS

- The turn indicator enables you to establish and maintain constant rate turns. A standard-rate turn is a turn at a rate of 3° per second. At this rate you complete a 360° turn in 2 minutes.

- Because a coordinated turn requires the aircraft to be banked, both the turn-and-slip indicator and the turn coordinator give you an indirect indication of bank.

- Both turn coordinators and turn-and-slip indicators indicate rate of turn. However, the gimbal in the turn coordinator is set at an angle, or canted, which allows its gyro to sense both rate of roll as you enter a turn and rate of turn. The turn coordinator has largely replaced the turn-and-slip indicator in modern training aircraft.

- The inclinometer is the part of the turn coordinator that contains the fluid and the ball. The position of the ball indicates the quality of the turn—whether you are using the correct angle of bank for the rate of turn. Apply rudder pressure on the side the ball is deflected (step on the ball) to correct a slipping or skidding condition.

    - Coordinated Turn — The correct amount of rudder pressure turns the airplane at the appropriate rate for the angle of bank. The horizontal component of lift exactly balances centrifugal force. The ball is centered.

    - Slip — Because of insufficient rudder pressure, the airplane is not turning fast enough for the angle of bank. The horizontal component of lift exceeds centrifugal force, which opposes the turn. The ball falls to the inside of the turn. To balance the force and coordinate the turn, increase the amount of rudder in the direction of the turn and/or decrease the amount of bank.

    - Skid — Excessive rudder pressure forces the airplane to turn faster than normal for the angle of bank. Centrifugal forces exceeds the horizontal component of lift. The ball swings to the outside of the turn. To balance the forces and coordinate the turn, decrease the amount of rudder in the direction of the turn, and/or increase the amount of bank.

- Slipping or skidding also alters the normal load factor because the wings must generate enough lift to support the weight of the airplane plus overcome centrifugal force. Because a skid generates a higher-than-normal centrifugal force, load factor is increased. In a slip, load factor decreases because centrifugal force is lower than normal.

INSTRUMENT CHECKS

- After engine start, the gyros normally reach full operating speed in approximately five minutes. During this time, you might see some vibration in the instruments.

- Before flight, perform the following instrument checks on gyroscopic instruments:

    - Attitude indicator—when the gyros have stabilized, ensure the horizon bar has stop vibrating and remains stable and level within 5° while the airplane is stopped or taxiing straight ahead on level ground. Ensure that the horizon bar tilts no more than 5° during taxi turns.

    - Heading indicator—after 5 minutes, set the indicator to the magnetic heading of the aircraft and check for proper alignment after taxi turns.

    - Turn coordinator or turn-and-slip indicator—prior to engine start, ensure the indicator airplane/needle is centered and the inclinometer is full of fluid. Turn on the master switch and listen for unusual noises from the electrically powered gyro. During taxi turns, verify that the ball moves to the outside of the turn, and the indicator airplane/needle deflects in the direction of the turn.

MAGNETIC COMPASS

- Magnetic dip is responsible for the most significant compass errors. This phenomenon makes it difficult to get an accurate compass indication when maneuvering on a north or south heading. Magnetic dip exists because the magnets in the compass try to point three dimensionally toward the earth's magnetic north pole, which is located deep inside the earth.

- In the northern hemisphere, compass turning errors are most apparent when turning from a heading of north or south. When turning from:

SECTION A ■ Analog Flight Instruments

- ◦ A northerly heading, the compass initially indicates a turn in the opposite direction, lagging behind the actual heading.

- ◦ A southerly heading, the compass indicates a turn in the correct direction, but leads the actual heading.

- ◦ An easterly or westerly heading, these turning errors are negligible.

- To compensate for northerly turning error in the northern hemisphere, you must roll out early on turns to the north, and turn past the compass-indicated heading on turns to the south. Remember the acronym, OSUN (Overshoot South, Undershoot North).

- The suspension of the compass card and magnetic dip cause acceleration and deceleration errors. In the northern hemisphere, the compass swings toward the north during acceleration and toward the south during deceleration. This error is greatest on east and west headings and decreases to zero on north and south headings.

- Remember the acronym, ANDS (Accelerate North, Decelerate South) to describe acceleration/deceleration error in the northern hemisphere.

- Deviation is error due to magnetic interference with metal components in the aircraft, as well as magnetic fields from aircraft electrical equipment. Deviation errors are recorded on a correction card mounted on or near the compass that tells you what direction to steer to get specific headings.

PITOT-STATIC INSTRUMENTS

AIRSPEED INDICATOR

- The airspeed indicator operates by comparing ram air (pitot) pressure to ambient (static) pressure. Indicated airspeed is the result of this raw measurement.

- Different types of airspeed are:

- ◦ Calibrated airspeed (CAS)—indicated airspeed corrected for installation and instrument errors.

- ◦ Equivalent airspeed (EAS)—calibrated airspeed corrected for compressibility.

- ◦ True airspeed (TAS)—the actual speed your airplane moves through undisturbed air. As atmospheric pressure decreases or air temperature increases, the density of the air decreases. As the air density decreases at a given indicated airspeed, true airspeed increases.

- ◦ Mach—the ratio of the aircraft's true airspeed to the speed of sound at the temperature and altitude in which the aircraft is flying.

- True airspeed is calibrated airspeed corrected for pressure altitude and non-standard temperature. At sea level on a standard day, CAS equals TAS.

- Many high performance aircraft have a Mach indicator incorporated with the airspeed indicator. A speed of Mach 0.85 means the aircraft is flying at 85% of the speed of sound at that temperature.

- The color-coded arcs on the airspeed indicator define speed ranges and the boundaries of these arcs identify airspeed limitations:

- ◦ White Arc—full-flap operating range

- ◦ Green Arc—normal operating range

- ◦ Yellow Arc—caution range: limit operations to smooth air

- ◦ V_{S0}—stalling speed, or minimum steady flight speed, in the landing configuration, at the maximum landing weight (bottom of white arc)

- ◦ V_{S1}—stalling speed, or minimum steady flight speed, obtained in a specified configuration. For light airplanes, this is normally power-off stall speed at maximum takeoff weight in a clean configuration—gear and flaps retracted. (bottom of green arc)

- ◦ V_{FE}—maximum speed with the flaps fully extended. Some aircraft allow partial flap extensions above this speed for approach operations. (top of white arc)

- ○ V$_{NO}$—maximum structural cruising speed (top of green arc)
- ○ V$_{NE}$—never-exceed speed (red line)

- Design maneuvering speed (V$_A$) is not marked on the airspeed indicator. During gusty or turbulent conditions, slow the aircraft below V$_A$, to ensure the load factor is within safe limits.

- At or below V$_A$, the airplane stalls before excessive G-forces can occur. V$_A$ decreases with the total weight of the aircraft and appears in your POH or on a placard.

- If you are flying in visible moisture, turn the pitot heat on to prevent pitot tube icing. Complete blockage of the pitot tube can cause the airspeed indicator to react opposite of normal, showing runaway airspeed as you climb, and extremely low airspeed in a descent.

ALTIMETER

- The altimeter indicates height in feet above the barometric pressure level set in the altimeter window. For example, if the altimeter is set to 30.00, it would indicate the height of the airplane above the pressure level of 30.00 in. Hg. If this is the correct local altimeter setting, then the 30.00 in. Hg. pressure level would be at sea level and the altimeter would indicate the true altitude above sea level (assuming standard temperature).

- The standard temperature and pressure at sea level are 15°C (59°F) and 29.92 inches of Hg. (1013.2 Mb.), respectively.

- When you change the altimeter setting, the indication changes in the same direction by approximately 1,000 feet for every inch of pressure.

- Setting your altimeter provides you with the means to correct your indicated altitude for pressure variations. Using the appropriate altimeter setting is necessary to ensure safe terrain clearance for instrument approaches and landings, and to maintain vertical separation between aircraft in the IFR environment.

- Types of altitude include:
    - ○ Indicated altitude—the altitude you read from the altimeter when it is set to the current altimeter setting.
    - ○ Calibrated altitude—indicated altitude corrected to compensate for instrument error.
    - ○ Pressure altitude—displayed on the altimeter when it is set to the standard sea level pressure of 29.92 in. Hg. Pressure altitude is the vertical distance above a theoretical plane, or standard datum plane, where atmospheric pressure is equal to 29.92 in. Hg.
    - ○ Density altitude—pressure altitude corrected for nonstandard temperature. Density altitude is a theoretical value used to determine airplane performance. When density altitude is high (temperatures are above standard), aircraft performance degrades.
    - ○ True altitude—the actual height of an object above mean sea level. The altimeter displays true altitude in flight only under standard conditions. Nonstandard temperature and pressure cause the indicated altitude to differ from true altitude.
    - ○ Absolute altitude—the actual height of the aircraft above the earth's surface.

- Regulations require that below 18,000 feet MSL, you must set your altimeter to the current reported altimeter setting of a station along the route and within 100 nautical miles of the aircraft.

- At or above 18,000 feet MSL, you must set your altimeter to 29.92 in. Hg. These high altitudes are referred to as flight levels (FL); 18,000 feet above the standard datum plane is FL180.

- If you are departing an airport where you cannot obtain a current altimeter setting, you should set the altimeter to the airport elevation. After departure, obtain the current altimeter setting as soon as possible from the appropriate ATC facility.

- A common altimeter error is failing to adjust the altimeter to the current altimeter setting as barometric pressure changes. If you do not reset your altimeter when you fly from:
    - ○ An area of higher pressure to an area of lower pressure, you could fly at a lower altitude than you had intended. True altitude is lower than indicated altitude. Remember, from high to low—look out below.

SECTION A ■ Analog Flight Instruments

- An area of lower pressure to an area of higher pressure, you could fly at a higher altitude than you had intended. True altitude is higher than indicated altitude. Remember, low to high—clear the sky.

- True altitude differs from indicated altitude when the air temperature is warmer or colder than standard. When the temperature is:

    - Warmer than standard, the altimeter indicates a lower altitude than that actually flown. True altitude is higher than indicated altitude.

    - Colder than standard, the altimeter indicates a higher altitude than that actually flown. True altitude is lower than indicated altitude.

INSTRUMENT CHECK

Before an IFR flight, verify that the altimeter indicates within 75 feet of the actual field elevation when set to the current altimeter setting.

VERTICAL SPEED INDICATOR

- The vertical speed indicator (VSI) measures how fast the static (ambient) pressure increases or decreases as the airplane climbs or descends. The VSI then displays this pressure change as a rate of climb or descent in feet per minute.

- If the VSI erroneously indicates a climb or descent during taxi, you can use the observed value as a zero indication during flight.

PITOT-STATIC SYSTEM BLOCKAGE

- The airspeed indicator is the only instrument affected by a pitot tube blockage. Two types of pitot blockage that can occur are:

    - The ram air inlet clogs but the drain hole remains open—the pressure in the line to the airspeed indicator vents out the drain hole, which causes the airspeed indication to drop to zero.

    - Both the ram air inlet and drain hole become clogged—air pressure is trapped in the line. If the static port remains open, the indicator reacts as an altimeter, showing an increase in airspeed when climbing and a decrease in airspeed when descending.

- A blocked static system affects all pitot-static instruments;

    - Airspeed indicator—when you are operating above the altitude where the static port became clogged, displays a slower airspeed than it should. When you are operating below the altitude where the static port became clogged, displays a faster airspeed than it should.

    - Altimeter—freezes in place and is unusable.

    - Vertical speed indicator—freezes at zero.

- The alternate static source can be located inside the aircraft cabin. Due to the slipstream, the pressure inside the cabin is usually less than that of outside air so normally when you select the alternate static source in an unpressurized airplane, the:

    - Altimeter reads a little higher than normal.

    - Airspeed reads a little faster than normal.

    - VSI momentarily shows a climb.

- Your airplane's POH might contain information regarding variations in airspeed and altimeter readings due to the use of the alternate static source.

NOTE: *An asterisk appearing after an ACS code (i.e. CA.IV.A.K2*) indicates that the question subject appears more than one time in the ACS. The code shown corresponds to the first instance of the subject in the ACS.*

2-1   CA.I.G.K1h

One characteristic that a properly functioning gyro depends upon for operation is the

A – ability to resist precession 90° to any applied force.

B – resistance to deflection of the spinning wheel or disc.

C – deflecting force developed from the angular velocity of the spinning wheel.

2-1. Answer B. GFDIC 2A, PHB

Gyroscopic instrument operation is based on rigidity in space and precession. Rigidity in space refers to the principle that a wheel with a heavily weighted rim spun rapidly tends to remain fixed in the plane in which it is spinning. By mounting this wheel, or gyroscope, on a set of gimbals, the gyro is able to rotate freely in any plane. If the gimbals' base tilts, twists, or otherwise moves, the gyro remains in the plane in which it was originally spinning.

2-2   CA.I.G.K1h

What is an operational difference between the turn coordinator and the turn-and-slip indicator? The turn coordinator

A – is always electric; the turn-and-slip indicator is always vacuum-driven.

B – indicates bank angle only; the turn-and-slip indicator indicates rate of turn and coordination.

C – indicates roll rate, rate of turn, and coordination; the turn-and-slip indicator indicates rate of turn and coordination.

2-2. Answer C. GFDIC 2A, PHB

Both turn coordinators and turn-and-slip indicators indicate rate of turn. However, the gimbal in the turn coordinator is set at an angle, or canted, which allows its gyro to sense both rate of roll as you enter a turn and rate of turn. The turn coordinator has largely replaced the turn-and-slip indicator in modern training aircraft. Both the turn coordinator and turn-and-slip indicator have inclinometers which indicate the quality (coordination) of a turn.

2-3   CA.I.G.K1f, h

What is an advantage of an electric turn coordinator if the airplane has a vacuum system for other gyroscopic instruments?

A – It is a backup in case of vacuum system failure.

B – It is more reliable than the vacuum-driven indicators.

C – It will not tumble as will vacuum-driven turn indicators.

2-3. Answer A. GFDIC 2A, PHB

On many light airplanes, the vacuum system supplies power to the attitude and heading indicators, while the electrical system powers the turn coordinator. This configuration provides a backup in case one system fails.

2-4   CA.I.G.K1h

If a standard rate turn is maintained, how long would it take to turn 360°?

A – 1 minute.

B – 2 minutes.

C – 3 minutes.

2-4. Answer B. GFDIC 2A, PHB

The turn indicator enables you to establish and maintain constant rate turns. A standard-rate turn is a turn at a rate of 3° per second. At this rate you complete a 360° turn in 2 minutes.

SECTION A ■ Analog Flight Instruments

2-5   CA.VI.A.K2

What causes the northerly turning error in a magnetic compass?

A – Coriolis force at the mid-latitudes.

B – Centrifugal force acting on the compass card.

C – The magnetic dip characteristic.

2-5. Answer C. GFDIC 2A, PHB

Magnetic dip is responsible for the most significant compass errors. This phenomenon makes it difficult to get an accurate compass indication when maneuvering on a north or south heading. Magnetic dip exists because the magnets in the compass try to point three dimensionally toward the earth's magnetic north pole, which is located deep inside the earth.

2-6   CA.VI.A.K2

What should be the indication on the magnetic compass as you roll into a standard rate turn to the right from an easterly heading in the Northern Hemisphere?

A – The compass will remain on east for a short time, then gradually catch up to the magnetic heading of the aircraft.

B – The compass will initially indicate a turn to the left.

C – The compass will indicate the approximate correct magnetic heading if the roll into the turn is smooth.

2-6. Answer C. GFDIC 2A, PHB

In the northern hemisphere, compass turning errors are most apparent when turning from a heading of north or south. When turning from:

- A northerly heading, the compass initially indicates a turn in the opposite direction, lagging behind the actual heading.

- A southerly heading, the compass indicates a turn in the correct direction, but leads the actual heading.

- An easterly or westerly heading, these turning errors are negligible and the compass with indicate the approximate correct heading.

2-7   CA.VI.A.K2

In the Northern Hemisphere, what should be the indication on the magnetic compass as the aircraft accelerates on a heading of 270°?

A – The compass swings toward a northerly heading.

B – The compass swings toward a southerly heading.

C – The compass remains on a heading of 270°.

2-7. Answer A. GFDIC 2A, PHB

The suspension of the compass card and magnetic dip cause acceleration and deceleration errors. In the northern hemisphere, the compass swings toward the north during acceleration and toward the south during deceleration. This error is greatest on east and west headings and decreases to zero on north and south headings.

Remember the acronym, ANDS (Accelerate North, Decelerate South) to describe acceleration/deceleration error in the northern hemisphere.

2-8   CA.VI.A.K2

Which statement is true about magnetic deviation of a compass? Deviation

A – varies over time as the agonic line shifts.

B – varies for different headings of the same aircraft.

C – is the same for all aircraft in the same locality.

2-8. Answer B. GFDIC 2A, PHB

Deviation is error due to magnetic interference with metal components in the aircraft, as well as magnetic fields from aircraft electrical equipment. Deviation errors are recorded on a correction card mounted on or near the compass that tells you what direction to steer to get specific headings.

2-9   CA.I.F.K1

Which is the V-speed for the stalling speed or the minimum steady flight speed in a specified configuration?

A – VS0.

B – VS.

C – VS1.

2-9. Answer C. GFDIC 2A, FAR 1.2, PHB

The color-coded arcs on the airspeed indicator define speed ranges and the boundaries of these arcs identify airspeed limitations, such as V_{S1}—stalling speed, or minimum steady flight speed, in a specific configuration. For light airplanes, this is normally power-off stall speed at maximum takeoff weight in a clean configuration—gear and flaps retracted (bottom of green arc).

2-10   CA.I.G.K1h

14 CFR Part 1 defines VNE as

A – maximum nose wheel extend speed.

B – never-exceed speed.

C – maximum landing gear extended speed.

2-10. Answer B. GFDIC 2A, FAR 1.2, PHB

The color-coded arcs on the airspeed indicator define speed ranges and the boundaries of these arcs identify airspeed limitations, such as V_{NE}—never-exceed speed (red line).

2-11   CA.I.G.K1h

14 CFR Part 1 defines VNO as

A – maximum operating limit speed.

B – maximum structural cruising speed.

C – never-exceed speed.

2-11. Answer B. GFDIC 2A, FAR 1.2, PHB

The color-coded arcs on the airspeed indicator define speed ranges and the boundaries of these arcs identify airspeed limitations, such as V_{NO}—maximum structural cruising speed (top of green arc).

2-12   CA.I.G.K1h

Which airspeed would you be unable to identify by the color coding of an airspeed indicator?

A – The never-exceed speed.

B – The power-off stall speed.

C – The maneuvering speed.

2-12. Answer C. GFDIC 2A, PHB

Design maneuvering speed (V_A) is not marked on the airspeed indicator. During gusty or turbulent conditions, slow the aircraft below V_A, to ensure the load factor is within safe limits. At or below V_A, the airplane stalls before excessive G-forces can occur. V_A decreases with the total weight of the aircraft and appears in your POH or on a placard.

2-13   CA.I.G.K1h

On final approach to a higher elevation airport, you should know that your indicated airspeed

A – should not change, but groundspeed will be faster.

B – should be higher, but groundspeed will be unchanged.

C – should be increased to compensate for the thinner air.

2-13. Answer A. GFDPP 2A, PHB

The airspeed indicator operates by comparing ram air (pitot) pressure to ambient (static) pressure. Indicated airspeed is the result of this raw measurement. When an indicated airspeed is specified by the manufacturer for a given situation, such as takeoff or landing, you normally should use that speed, regardless of the elevation.

Groundspeed is based on true airspeed (TAS). True airspeed is the actual speed your airplane moves through undisturbed air. As atmospheric pressure decreases or air temperature increases, the density of the air decreases. As the air density decreases at a given indicated airspeed, true airspeed increases.

SECTION A ■ Analog Flight Instruments

2-14   CA.I.G.K1h

Calibrated airspeed is best described as indicated airspeed corrected for

A – installation and instrument error.

B – instrument error.

C – non-standard temperature.

2-14. Answer A. GFDIC 2A, PHB

Calibrated airspeed (CAS) is indicated airspeed corrected for installation and instrument errors. True airspeed (TAS) is the actual speed your airplane moves through undisturbed air. At sea level on a standard day, CAS equals TAS.

2-15   CA.I.G.K1h

True airspeed is best described as calibrated airspeed corrected for

A – installation or instrument error.

B – non-standard temperature.

C – altitude and non-standard temperature.

2-15. Answer C. GFDIC 2A, PHB

True airspeed (TAS) is the actual speed your airplane moves through undisturbed air. Calibrated airspeed (CAS) is indicated airspeed corrected for installation and instrument errors. True airspeed is calibrated airspeed corrected for pressure altitude and non-standard temperature. At sea level on a standard day, CAS equals TAS.

2-16   CA.I.G.K1h

The ratio of an airplane's true airspeed to the speed of sound in the same atmospheric conditions is

A – equivalent airspeed.

B – transonic airflow.

C – Mach number.

2-16. Answer C. GFDIC 2A, PHB

Mach is the ratio of the aircraft's true airspeed to the speed of sound at the temperature and altitude in which the aircraft is flying. Many high performance aircraft have a Mach indicator incorporated with the airspeed indicator. A speed of Mach 0.85 means the aircraft is flying at 85% of the speed of sound at that temperature.

2-17   CA.I.G.K1h

What are the standard temperature and pressure values for sea level?

A – 15°C and 29.92 inches Hg.

B – 59°F and 1013.2 inches Hg.

C – 15°C and 29.92 Mb.

2-17. Answer A. GFDPP 2C, PHB

The standard temperature and pressure at sea level are 15°C (59°F) and 29.92 inches of Hg. (1013.2 Mb.), respectively.

2-18   CA.I.G.K1h

To determine pressure altitude prior to takeoff, the altimeter should be set to

A – the current altimeter setting.

B – 29.92 inches Hg and the altimeter indication noted.

C – the field elevation and the pressure reading in the altimeter setting window noted.

2-18. Answer B. GFDIC 2A, PHB

Pressure altitude is displayed on the altimeter when it is set to the standard sea level pressure of 29.92 in. Hg. Pressure altitude is the vertical distance above a theoretical plane, or standard datum plane, where atmospheric pressure is equal to 29.92 in. Hg.

2-19   CA.I.G.K1h

What altimeter setting is required when operating an aircraft at 18,000 feet MSL?

A – Altimeter setting at the departure or destination airport.

B – Current reported altimeter setting of a station along the route.

C – 29.92 inches Hg.

2-19. Answer C. GFDIC 2A, FAR 91.121

At or above 18,000 feet MSL, you must set your altimeter to 29.92 in. Hg. These high altitudes are referred to as flight levels (FL); 18,000 feet above the standard datum plane is FL180.

2-20   CA.I.G.K1h

When weather information indicates that abnormally high barometric pressure exists, or will be above _____ inches of mercury, flight operations will not be authorized contrary to the requirements published in NOTAMs.

A – 31.00

B – 32.00

C – 30.50

2-20. Answer A. GFDIC 2A, FAR 91.144

The standard altimeter is adjustable in the pressure range of 28.1 to 31.0 inches. When any information indicates that the barometric pressure on the route of flight currently exceeds or will exceed 31 inches of mercury, you may not operate an aircraft or initiate a flight contrary to any published NOTAM..

2-21   CA.I.G.K1h

If the pitot tube ram air pressure hole and drain hole become obstructed, the airspeed indicator will operate

A – like an altimeter as the aircraft climbs and descends.

B – like a very sluggish airspeed indicator lagging all changes by minutes.

C – normally due to the static port pressure changes.

2-21. Answer A. GFDIC 2A, PHB

The airspeed indicator is the only instrument affected by a pitot tube blockage. Two types of pitot blockage that can occur are:

- The ram air inlet clogs but the drain hole remains open—the pressure in the line to the airspeed indicator vents out the drain hole, which causes the airspeed indication to drop to zero.

- Both the ram air inlet and drain hole become clogged—air pressure is trapped in the line. If the static port remains open, the indicator reacts as an altimeter, showing an increase in airspeed when climbing and a decrease in airspeed when descending.

SECTION A ■ Analog Flight Instruments

SECTION B
Electronic Flight Displays

TECHNICALLY ADVANCED AIRPLANES

- Electronic flight displays are digital flight instrument that are integrated into a single display, as part of a glass cockpit (sometimes referred to as an integrated flight display).

- A general aviation airplane that has an electronic flight display and an autopilot is referred to as a technically advanced aircraft (TAA). A TAA is defined as an airplane equipped with an electronically advanced avionics system. At a minimum, this system must include:

  - A primary flight display (PFD) with an airspeed indicator, turn coordinator, attitude indicator, heading indicator, altimeter, and vertical speed indicator;

  - A multifunction display (MFD) with a moving map using GPS navigation to display the aircraft position;

  - A two-axis autopilot integrated with the navigation and heading guidance system.

- Although different manufacturers of electronic flight displays exist, these displays have similar features. The Garmin G1000 is a common display found in many general aviation airplanes and is used in the following discussion.

PRIMARY FLIGHT DISPLAY

ATTITUDE AND HEADING REFERENCE SYSTEM

- The attitude and heading reference system (AHRS) uses inertial sensors such as electronic gyroscopes, accelerometers, and a magnetometer to determine the aircraft's attitude relative to the horizon and heading.

- A magnetometer senses the earth's magnetic field to function as a magnetic compass, but without some of the errors associated with a conventional compass.

ATTITUDE INDICATOR

- A digital attitude indicator can have a virtual blue sky and brown ground with a white horizon line or can be displayed over a realistic representation of terrain features. The horizon line can extend the width of the PFD.

- Near the center of the attitude indicator display, a miniature aircraft symbol shows whether the nose is above or below the horizon and a pitch scale shows pitch angles of 5, 10, 15, and 20 degrees. Bank angle is shown with a roll scale with reference marks at 10, 20, 30, 45, and 60 degrees.

- A slip/skid indicator below the roll pointer helps you maintain coordinated flight.

HORIZONTAL SITUATION INDICATOR

- In addition to a compass card, the digital HSI displays the current airplane heading in a window, a course indicator arrow and CDI, and a turn rate indicator.

- The turn rate indicator displays index marks that are 18 degrees either side of center to provide a reference for making standard-rate turns.

- The end of the trend vector typically shows what the airplane's heading will be in six seconds if the turn continues at the same rate.

AHRS ERRORS

- The AHRS monitors itself constantly, comparing the data from different inputs and checking the integrity of its information.
- When the AHRS system detects a problem, it places a red X over the display of the affected instrument to alert you that the indications are unreliable.

AIR DATA COMPUTER

- The pitot tube, static source, and outside air temperature probe provide information to the air data computer (ADC), which uses these pressure and temperature inputs to determine the appropriate readings for the airspeed indicator, altimeter, and VSI.
- The ADC also provides information to display true airspeed and outside air temperature.

AIRSPEED INDICATOR

- On the digital airspeed indicator, a central window and a pointer on a moving vertical scale show the indicated airspeed. The vertical scale is called the airspeed tape, which has colored bars to indicate airspeed operating ranges.
- Many digital airspeed displays have a trend vector that shows the airspeed that the airplane will reach in six seconds if it continues to decelerate or accelerate at the same rate.

ALTIMETER

- Like the airspeed indicator, the digital altimeter provides a central window and a pointer on a moving tape to display the indicated altitude. The window at the bottom of the display shows the altimeter setting.
- When the airplane is climbing or descending, the altimeter typically displays a trend vector that shows the altitude that the airplane will reach in six seconds if it continues to climb or descend at the same rate.

VERTICAL SPEED INDICATOR

- On the digital VSI, you read vertical speed in feet per minute in a window that also serves as a pointer.
- The VSI tape remains motionless as the window moves up or down over the scale.

ADC SYSTEM ERRORS

- The ADC relies on inputs from sensors, such as the pitot tube, static source, and outside air temperature probe, to provide reliable instrument indications.
- If one or more of the sensors stops providing input, or if the computer determines that its own internal operations are not correct, it places a red X over the display of the affected instrument.

PFD FAILURE

- If the PFD goes black, integrated flight displays typically enable you to display PFD information on the MFD display in reversionary mode.
- If you have a catastrophic electrical failure and lose all electric power, you must use your backup instruments. The backup instruments are not electrically powered or are powered by a separate battery that is isolated from the main electrical system.

SECTION B ■ Electronic Flight Displays

MULTIFUNCTION DISPLAY

- The MFD typically enables you to program the GPS for navigation and displays navigation status, engine and systems data, a moving map, and navigation and communication frequencies.

- The MFD moving map can show data, such as your airplane's position, your route of flight, topography, terrain proximity/TAWS, weather information, and traffic.

- You can typically access MFD pages that provide elements such as airport information, instrument charts, GPS satellite status, checklists, trip planning calculations, and the nearest airports in the event you must divert.

AUTOMATION

- Take these steps to use an autopilot function:

    1. Specify the desired track by heading, course, series of waypoints, altitude, airspeed and/or vertical speed.

    2. Engage the desired autopilot functions.

    3. Verify that:

        ○   The selected modes appear on the annunciator panel.

        ○   You have selected the correct navigation source (if applicable).

        ○   The airplane is following the desired track.

    4. Continue to monitor the instruments and displays to ensure the autopilot is performing the correct actions.

    5. Be prepared to control the airplane manually in case of autopilot failure or programming errors.

- Advanced avionics equipment typically integrates the autopilot system with the flight director (FD) to perform tasks such as intercepting and tracking selected courses or changing altitude.

- The flight director (FD) communicates the information that you program to the autopilot, which controls the airplane.

NOTE: *An asterisk appearing after an ACS code (i.e. CA.IV.A.K2*) indicates that the question subject appears more than one time in the ACS. The code shown corresponds to the first instance of the subject in the ACS.*

2-22   CA.I.G.K1g

A technically advanced aircraft (TAA) is defined as an airplane equipped with an electronically advanced avionics system, which includes:

A – A multifunction display (MFD) with a moving map using VOR navigation to display the aircraft position.

B – A two-axis autopilot that contains it's own navigation and heading guidance system.

C – A primary flight display (PFD) with an airspeed indicator, turn coordinator, attitude indicator, heading indicator, altimeter, and vertical speed indicator.

2-22. Answer C. GFDIC 2B, PHB

A general aviation airplane that has an electronic flight display and an autopilot is referred to as a technically advanced aircraft (TAA). A TAA is defined as an airplane equipped with an electronically advanced avionics system. At a minimum, this system must include:

- A primary flight display (PFD) with an airspeed indicator, turn coordinator, attitude indicator, heading indicator, altimeter, and vertical speed indicator;

- A multifunction display (MFD) with a moving map using GPS navigation to display the aircraft position;

- A two-axis autopilot integrated with the navigation and heading guidance system.

2-23   CA.I.G.K1g

What is the function of the AHRS for the PFD of an electronic flight display?

A – To provide airspeed, altitude, and vertical speed information.

B – To provide attitude, heading, and airspeed information.

C – To provide attitude, heading, rate of turn, and slip/skid information.

2-23. Answer C. GFDIC 2B, PHB

To provide attitude, heading, rate of turn, and slip/skid information, electronic flight displays use an attitude and heading reference system (AHRS). The AHRS uses inertial sensors such as electronic gyroscopes and accelerometers to determine the aircraft's attitude relative to the horizon. An electronic magnetometer provides magnetic heading data.

2-24   CA.I.G.K1g

A digital attitude indicator typically displays a

A – roll scale with reference marks at 10, 25, 45, and 60 degrees.

B – a trapezoid slip/skid indicator located beneath the roll pointer.

C – turn-rate vector located on the roll scale to indicate standard-rate turns.

2-24. Answer B. GFDIC 2B, PHB

A digital attitude indicator typically bank angle with a roll scale with reference marks at 10, 20, 30, 45, and 60 degrees. A slip/skid indicator below the roll pointer helps you maintain coordinated flight. A turn rate indicator and trend vector are located on the HSI.

2-25   CA.I.G.K1g

What information is typically provided by the trend vector on the HSI of a PFD?

A – The end of the trend vector shows what the airplane's heading will be in six seconds if the turn continues as the same rate.

B – The trend vector shows the bank angle necessary for a standard-rate turn.

C – The end of the trend vector shows what the airplane's heading will be in 1 minute if the airplane is turning at a standard rate.

2-25. Answer A. GFDIC 2B, PHB

The end of the trend vector shows what the airplane's heading will be in six seconds if the turn continues at the same rate. Index marks 18 degrees either side of center on the turn-rate indicator provide a reference for standard-rate turns.

2-26   CA.I.G.K1g

If the AHRS or ADC detects a problem with the integrity of sensor information, what occurs?

A – The system reverts to reversionary mode and PFD information is displayed on the MFD.

B – A red X is placed over the display of the affected instrument.

C – An alert message appears and you must determine the affected instrument(s) by comparing the indications of all instruments.

2-26. Answer B. GFDIC 2B, PHB

The AHRS monitors itself constantly, comparing the data from different inputs and checking the integrity of its information. The ADC relies on inputs from sensors, such as the pitot tube, static source, and outside air temperature probe, to provide reliable instrument indications. If a source stops providing input or the AHRS or ADC system detects an integrity problem, a red X is displayed over the affected instrument to alert you that the indications are unreliable.

SECTION B ■ **Electronic Flight Displays**

2-27   CA.I.G.K1g

What is the function of the air data computer (ADC) for the PFD of an electronic flight display?

A – The ADC determines the readings for the airspeed indicator, attitude indicator, and altimeter.

B – The ADC determines the readings for the airspeed indicator, altimeter, and vertical speed indicator.

C – The ADC monitors all PFD instruments to compare the data from different inputs and check information integrity.

2-27. Answer B. GFDIC 2B, PHB

In an electronic flight display, the pitot tube, static source, and outside air temperature probe provide information to the air data computer (ADC). The ADC uses these pressure and temperature inputs to determine the appropriate readings for the airspeed indicator, altimeter, and vertical speed indicator. In addition, the ADC provides information to display true airspeed and outside air temperature on the PFD.

2-28   CA.I.G.K1g

The ADC displays readings for the

A – airspeed indicator, altimeter, and VSI.

B – attitude relative to the horizon and heading.

C – airspeed indicator, attitude indicator, and altimeter.

2-28. Answer A. GFDIC 2B, PHB

The pitot tube, static source, and outside air temperature probe provide information to the ADC, which then uses these pressure and temperature inputs to determine readings for the airspeed indicator, altimeter, and VSI.

2-29   CA.I.G.K1g

Which are features that can be provided by a multifunction display (MFD)?

A – A slip/skid indicator, instrument charts, and checklists.

B – Engine data, synthetic vision systems, and the vertical speed indicator.

C – A moving map, engine and systems data, and communication frequencies.

2-29. Answer C. GFDIC 2B, IPHB

The MFD displays navigation status, engine and systems data, a moving map, and navigation and communication frequencies. You can also typically access MFD pages that provide elements such as airport information, instrument charts, GPS satellite status, checklists, trip planning calculations, and the nearest airports.

2-30   CA.I.G.K1g

Which is an action you should take after engaging the autopilot?

A – Set the flight director command bars for the appropriate flight attitude.

B – Select the autopilot status page on the PFD to verify that the autopilot is receiving data from the AHRS and ADC.

C – Verify that the selected modes appear on the annunciator panel.

2-30. Answer C. GFDIC 2B, PHB

After engaging the autopilot, verify that:

- The selected modes appear on the annunciator panel.
- You have selected the correct navigation source (if applicable).
- The airplane is following the desired track.

SECTION C
Attitude Instrument Flying

Chapter 2, Section C, of the *Commercial Pilot FAA Airman Knowledge Test Guide* corresponds to the same chapter and section of the *GFD Instrument/Commercial* textbook: Attitude Instrument Flying. Because this section is specific to training for an instrument rating, no FAA commercial pilot knowledge test questions apply.

SECTION D

Instrument Navigation

VOR NAVIGATION

HORIZONTAL SITUATION INDICATOR

- The horizontal situation indicator (HSI) display combines a conventional VOR navigation indicator with a heading indicator.

- For VOR navigation, each dot on the course deviation scale of an HSI or a conventional VOR navigation indicator is 2°, or 200 feet per nautical mile.

- Reverse sensing—the CDI deflected away from the course you want to follow—occurs if you are flying a heading that is the reciprocal of the desired course when using a conventional VOR indicator. To avoid reverse sensing, your heading must generally agree with the course you select.

- An HSI cannot reverse sense when tuned to a VOR station, even if you set it opposite your intended course or heading.

STATION PASSAGE

- As you get close to a station, in an area called the cone of confusion, the CDI and TO/FROM indicators fluctuate.

- VOR station passage is indicated by the first positive, complete reversal of the TO/FROM indicator.

VOR OPERATIONAL CONSIDERATIONS

- VOR facilities are classified according to their usable range and altitude, or standard service volume (SSV). Depending on the altitude in feet AGL, VOR facilities have these usable ranges:

    - Terminal VOR (TVOR) : 25 NM—1,000 to 12,000.

    - Low altitude VORs (LVORs): 40 NM—1,000 to 18,000.

    - High altitude VORs (HVORs): 40 NM—1,000 to 14,500; 100 NM—14,500 to 18,000; 130 NM — 18,000 to 45,000; 100 NM—45,000 to 60,000.

- TVORs, which have only 50 watts of power and a usable range of 25 nautical miles, are normally placed in terminal areas to be used primarily for instrument approaches. HVORs and LVORs are used for navigation on most airways, and can also function as approach facilities when located on or near airports.

- You can find the SSV that applies to a particular VOR in the applicable Chart Supplement.

- To identify a facility before using it for navigation, check the Morse code identifier against your chart to make sure you are tuned to the correct facility.

- VOR facilities undergoing maintenance might transmit the word, TEST (_ . ... _), or they might transmit no audio at all.

VOR CHECKS

- To use a VOR for flight under IFR, the VOR system must have been tested for accuracy within the preceding 30 days.

- When conducting a VOR check, you must record the date and place where the check was done, as well as the bearing error indicated. In addition, you must sign the record indicating that you have completed the check.

- You can perform a VOR check, including using a VOT, ground and airborne checkpoints, or dual system check. VOT and checkpoint information is listed in the Associated Data section of the Chart Supplement. The location and frequency of VOTs are also included in the individual listings in the Airport/Facility Directory (A/FD) section. The following maximum tolerances are allowed:

    - VOR test facility (VOT)—180° TO or 360° FROM ±4°.
    - Ground checkpoint—published radial ±4°.
    - Airborne checkpoint—published radial ±6°.
    - Dual system check—difference between the two indicated bearings to the station is ±4°.

- VOR test facilities VOTs transmit only one radial—360°. Tune your VOR receiver and listen for a series of dots or a continuous tone that identifies the facility as a VOT. Determine that the needle centers, ±4° (ground or airborne), when the course selector is set to 180° with a TO indication, or 360° with a FROM indication.

- To use a ground checkpoint, taxi your aircraft to a designated point on the airport. After centering the CDI with a FROM indication, compare your VOR course selection to the published radial for that checkpoint. The maximum permissible error is ±4°.

- Airborne checkpoints usually are located over easily identifiable terrain or prominent features on the ground. After centering the CDI with a FROM indication, compare your VOR course selection to the published radial for that checkpoint. The maximum permissible error is ±6°.

- If neither a VOT or VOR checkpoint are available, you may conduct a VOR check by comparing the indications of two VOR systems that are independent of each other (except for the antenna). Set both systems to the same VOR facility and note the indicated bearing to that station. The maximum permissible variation between the two indicated bearings is 4°.

DISTANCE MEASURING EQUIPMENT

- Because the DME signal travels in a straight line to and from the ground station, the DME receiver displays slant-range, not horizontal, distance in nautical miles.

- Slant range error is negligible if the aircraft is 1 NM or more from the ground facility for every 1,000 feet of altitude above the station. DME is accurate to within ½ NM or 3% (whichever is greater), as long as you are at least 1 NM or more from the DME facility for every 1,000 feet of altitude above the station.

- Because VOR and DME are separate components, each transmits its own identification signal on a time sharing basis. The VOR transmits a 1,020 Hz Morse code identifier and possibly a voice identifier several times for each DME identifier, which is a 1,350 Hz tone at approximately 30 second intervals. If one of these tones is missing, do not use the associated portion of the facility for navigation.

DME ARCS

- Some instrument approach procedures incorporate DME arcs for transition from the enroute phase of flight to the approach course.

- You can perform a DME arc using a traditional VOR indicator, HSI, RMI, or GPS equipment. When using GPS equipment, DME is not required.

- Generally, you intercept the arc while flying to or from a VOR/DME or VORTAC. To join the arc, turn approximately 90° from your inbound or outbound course, making sure you begin your turn early enough so you do not overshoot the arc. For groundspeeds of 150 knots or less, a lead of about ½ mile is usually sufficient.

- As a guide in making range corrections if your aircraft drifts outside the arc, change the relative bearing 10°– 20° for each half-mile deviation from the desired arc. For example, in no-wind conditions, if the aircraft is ½ to 1 mile outside the arc, turn the aircraft 20° toward the facility to return to the arc.

- In practice, a DME arc is flown using a series of straight segments approximating the arc. As you complete the arc, plan to lead the turn to your inbound or outbound course.

SECTION D ■ Instrument Navigation

AREA NAVIGATION

REQUIRED NAVIGATION PERFORMANCE

- Required navigation performance (RNP) is a set of standards that apply to both airspace and navigation equipment.

- To comply with RNP standards, your navigation equipment must be able to keep the airplane within:

    ○ 2 NM for enroute operations.

    ○ 1 NM for terminal operations.

    ○ 0.3 NM for approach operations (the final approach course).

SATELLITE NAVIGATION — GPS

- GPS broadcasts a signal used by receivers to determine precise position, calculate time, distance, and bearings to waypoints, compute groundspeed, and provide course guidance.

- By calculating its distance from three satellites simultaneously, a GPS receiver can determine its general position with respect to latitude, longitude, and altitude. However, a fourth satellite is necessary to determine an accurate position.

WIDE AREA AUGMENTATION SYSTEM (WAAS)

- The accuracy of GPS is enhanced with the use of the wide area augmentation system (WAAS), a series of ground stations that generate a corrective message that is transmitted to the airplane by a geostationary satellite.

- The WAAS corrective message improves navigational accuracy by accounting for positional drift of the satellites and signal delays caused by the ionosphere and other atmospheric factors.

REQUIREMENTS FOR IFR GPS NAVIGATION

- GPS equipment without WAAS capability is approved for IFR operations by the most recent version of TSO-C129 or TSO-C196. VFR and hand-held GPS systems are not authorized for IFR navigation, instrument approaches, or as a principal instrument flight reference.

- VFR GPS panel mount receivers and hand-held units have no RAIM alerting capability so you will not be alerted to the loss of the required number of satellites in view, or the detection of a position error. Systematically cross-check your GPS position with other navigation sources to verify your position.

- You can determine if your equipment is approved for IFR enroute and approach operations and if it is WAAS-certified by referring to the airplane flight manual (AFM) or AFM supplements.

- If your GPS receiver is certified according to TSO-C129 or TSO-C196, your airplane must be equipped with the alternate avionics necessary to receive operational ground-based facilities appropriate for the route to the destination and to any required alternate.

- According to TSO-C129 or TSO-C196, a non-WAAS GPS receiver must continuously monitor and compare signals from multiple satellites to ensure an accurate signal through receiver autonomous integrity monitoring (RAIM).

- Prior to a flight under IFR with non-WAAS GPS equipment, you must confirm RAIM availability for the intended route and duration of the flight by checking NOTAMs, contacting Flight Service, accessing the FAA RAIM prediction website, or by using your GPS receiver's RAIM prediction function. If RAIM capability is lost during flight, you must begin to actively monitor an alternate means of navigation.

- WAAS-certified GPS receivers are approved for IFR operations by either TSO-C145 or TSO-C146.

- You can use a WAAS-certified GPS receiver as the sole navigation equipment for domestic enroute and terminal IFR flights without requiring alternate avionics for navigation and operating ground-based facilities.

- If you confirm WAAS coverage along the entire route of flight, you do not need to perform the RAIM prediction check prior to departure.

NAVIGATING WITH GPS

- Using GPS for IFR flight requires a current navigational database.
- When the navigation source is the GPS, the CDI displays the lateral distance from course, called the cross-track error.
- For GPS units, the CDI has three different sensitivities, one each for enroute, terminal, and approach phase of flight with the following cross-track errors for a full-scale deviation:
  - Enroute—2 NM (WAAS-certified GPS systems); 5 NM (non-WAAS systems).
  - Terminal (within 30 NM of the departure or destination airport)—1 NM cross-track error.
  - Approach (inside final approach)—0.3 NM.
- IFR random RNAV routes do not correspond with published courses and can only be authorized in a radar environment and with ATC approval.
- Plan any random routes to begin and end over arrival and departure transition fixes or navaids for your altitude, use preferred departure and arrival routes, and avoid prohibited and restricted airspace by three nautical miles.
- Define a random RNAV route with a minimum of one waypoint for each air route traffic control center area that you pass through and ensure that the first waypoint in each area is located within 200 nautical miles of the preceding center's boundary.

NOTE: *An asterisk appearing after an ACS code (i.e. CA.IV.A.K2*) indicates that the question subject appears more than one time in the ACS. The code shown corresponds to the first instance of the subject in the ACS.*

2-31   CA.VI.B.K1

Which situation would result in reverse sensing of a VOR receiver?

A – Flying a heading that is reciprocal to the bearing selected on the OBS.

B – Setting the OBS to a bearing that is 90° from the bearing on which the aircraft is located.

C – Failing to change the OBS from the selected inbound course to the outbound course after passing the station.

2-31. Answer A. GFDIC 2D, PHB
Reverse sensing—the CDI deflected away from the course you want to follow—occurs if you are flying a heading that is the reciprocal of the desired course when using a conventional VOR indicator. To avoid reverse sensing, your heading must generally agree with the course you select.

An HSI cannot reverse sense when tuned to a VOR station, even if you set it opposite your intended course or heading.

2-32   CA.VI.B.K1

To track outbound on the 180 radial of a VOR station, the recommended procedure is to set the OBS to

A – 360° and make heading corrections toward the CDI needle.

B – 180° and make heading corrections away from the CDI needle.

C – 180° and make heading corrections toward the CDI needle.

2-32. Answer C. GFDIC 2D, PHB
When using a conventional VOR indicator and tracking a radial, the course selector—omnibearing selector (OBS)—should indicate the approximate heading (allowing for wind correction) of the airplane. When tracking outbound on the 180° radial, you should have a FROM indication with 180° selected, which will result in proper sensing of the CDI.

SECTION D ■ Instrument Navigation

2-33   CA.VI.B.K1

To track inbound on the 215° radial of a VOR station, the recommended procedure is to set the OBS to

A – 215° and make heading corrections toward the CDI needle.

B – 215° and make heading corrections away from the CDI needle.

C – 035° and make heading corrections toward the CDI needle.

2-33. Answer C. GFDIC 2D, PHB

When using a conventional VOR indicator and tracking a radial, the course selector—omnibearing selector (OBS)—should indicate the approximate heading (allowing for wind correction) of the airplane. When tracking inbound on the 215° radial, you should have a TO indication with 035° selected, which will result in proper sensing of the CDI.

2-34   CA.VI.B.K1

(Refer to Figure 17.) Which illustration indicates that the airplane will intercept the 060° radial at a 60° angle inbound, if the present heading is maintained?

A – 6

B – 4

C – 5

2-34. Answer A. GFDIC 2D, PHB

To intercept the 060° radial inbound at a 60° angle, the HSI course arrow must be pointing at 240° with a TO indication, and the aircraft's heading needs to be either 300° or 180° (240° + 60° = 300°) or (240° – 60° = 180°).

2-35   CA.VI.B.K1

(Refer to Figure 17.) Which statement is true regarding illustration 2, if the present heading is maintained? The airplane will

A – cross the 180 radial at a 45° angle outbound.

B – intercept the 225 radial at a 45° angle.

C – intercept the 360 radial at a 45° angle inbound.

2-35. Answer C. GFDIC 2D, PHB

To intercept the 360° radial inbound at a 45° angle, the HSI course arrow must be pointing at 180° with a TO indication. The CDI is deflected to the right and the aircraft's heading is 225°, which provides a 45° intercept angle (225° – 45° = 180°).

2-36   CA.VI.B.K1

(Refer to Figure 17.) Which illustration indicates that the airplane will intercept the 060 radial at a 75° angle outbound, if the present heading is maintained?

A – 4

B – 5

C – 6

2-36. Answer B. GFDIC 2D, PHB

To intercept the 060° radial inbound at a 75° angle, the HSI course arrow must be pointing at 060° with a FROM indication or 240° with a TO indication (illustration 5). The heading of 345° provides a 75° intercept angle for flying the 060° radial outbound (060° + 360° – 345° = 75°).

2-37   CA.VI.B.K1

(Refer to Figure 17.) Which illustration indicates that the airplane should be turned 150° left to intercept the 360 radial at a 60° angle inbound?

A – 1

B – 2

C – 3

2-37. Answer A. GFDIC 2D, PHB

To intercept the 360° radial inbound, the HSI course arrow must be pointing at 180° with a TO indication. If the aircraft represented by illustration 1 turns 150° to the left, it will be on a heading of 240°, which provides a 60° intercept angle for the 180° course inbound on the 360° radial (240° − 60° = 180°).

2-38   CA.VI.B.K1

(Refer to Figure 17.) Which is true regarding illustration 4 if the present heading is maintained? The airplane will

A – cross the 060 radial at a 15° angle.

B – intercept the 240 radial at a 30° angle.

C – cross the 180 radial at a 75° angle.

2-38. Answer C. GFDIC 2D, PHB

The course arrow is on 240° with a TO indication (060° radial). On a heading of 255°, the aircraft is on a 15° intercept angle for the 060° radial so if the aircraft does not turn to intercept the radial when the CDI centers, the aircraft will cross the 060° radial at a 15° angle.

2-39   CA.VI.B.K1

When checking the course sensitivity of a VOR receiver, how many degrees should the OBS be rotated to move the CDI from the center to the last dot on either side?

A – 5° to 10°.

B – 10° to 12°.

C – 18° to 20°.

2-39. Answer B. GFDIC 2D, PHB

Course sensitivity may be checked by noting the number of degrees of change in the course selected as you rotate the course selector to move the CDI from the center to the last dot on either side. This should be between 10° and 12°.

2-40   CA.VI.B.K1

An aircraft 60 miles from a VOR station has a CDI indication of one-fifth deflection. This represents a course centerline deviation of approximately

A – 6 miles.

B – 2 miles.

C – 1 mile.

2-40. Answer B. GFDIC 2D, PHB

For VOR navigation, each dot on the course deviation scale of an HSI or a conventional VOR navigation indicator is 2°, or 200 feet per nautical mile. Typically, an indicator displays 5 dots to the right and left of center—each dot equals about one-fifth deflection. To determine the aircraft's lateral distance from a radial, multiply your distance from the VOR by 200 feet per dot of deflection and divide by 6,076 (feet per NM). The answer is 2 miles (60 x 200 = 12,000 ÷ 6,076 = 1.97).

2-41   CA.VI.B.K1

When must an operational check on the aircraft VOR equipment be accomplished to operate under IFR?

Within the preceding

A – 30 days or 30 hours of flight time.

B – 10 days or 10 hours of flight time.

C – 30 days.

2-41. Answer C. GFDIC 2D, FAR 91.171

To use a VOR for flight under IFR, the VOR system must have been tested for accuracy within the preceding 30 days. You can perform a VOR check, including using a VOT, ground and airborne checkpoints, or dual system check. When conducting a VOR check, you must record the date and place where the check was done, as well as the bearing error indicated. In addition, you must sign the record indicating that you have completed the check.

2-42   CA.I.B.K1b, CA.VI.B.K1

Which data must be recorded in the aircraft logbook or other record by a pilot making a VOR operational check for IFR operations?

A – VOR name or identification, place of operational check, amount of bearing error, and date of check.

B – Date of check, place of operational check, bearing error, and signature.

C – VOR name or identification, amount of bearing error, date of check, and signature.

2-42. Answer B. GFDIC 2D, FAR 91.171

To use a VOR for flight under IFR, the VOR system must have been tested for accuracy within the preceding 30 days. You can perform a VOR check, including using a VOT, ground and airborne checkpoints, or dual system check. When conducting a VOR check, you must record the date and place where the check was done, as well as the bearing error indicated. In addition, you must sign the record indicating that you have completed the check.

2-43   CA.VI.B.K1

What is the maximum bearing error (+ or -) allowed for an operational VOR equipment check when using an FAA-approved ground test signal?

A – 4 degrees

B – 6 degrees

C – 8 degrees

2-43. Answer A. GFDIC 2D, FAR 91.171

To use a VOR for flight under IFR, the VOR system must have been tested for accuracy within the preceding 30 days. When using a VOR test facility (VOT) the CDI must center on 180° TO or 360° FROM within ±4°.

2-44   CA.I.B.K1b

How should you make a VOR receiver check when the aircraft is located on the designated checkpoint on the airport surface?

A – Set the OBS on 180° plus or minus 4°; the CDI should center with a FROM indication.

B – Set the OBS on the designated radial. The CDI must center within plus or minus 4° of that radial with a FROM indication.

C – With the aircraft headed directly toward the VOR and the OBS set to 000°, the CDI should center within plus or minus 4° of that radial with a TO indication.

2-44. Answer B. GFDIC 2D, AIM, FAR 91.171

You can perform a VOR check, including using a VOT, ground and airborne checkpoints, or dual system check. VOT and checkpoint information is listed in the Associated Data section of the Chart Supplement. To use a ground checkpoint, taxi your aircraft to a designated point on the airport. After centering the CDI with a FROM indication, compare your VOR course selection to the published radial for that checkpoint. The maximum permissible error is ±4°.

For example, if the radial published in the Associated Data section is 250°, the course shown in the course selector—omnibearing selector (OBS)—when you center the CDI must be within 246° to 254°.

2-45   CA.I.B.K1b

When using a VOT to perform a VOR receiver check, the CDI should be centered and the OBS should indicate that the aircraft is on the

A – 090 radial.

B – 180 radial.

C – 360 radial.

2-45. Answer C. GFDIC 2D, AIM, FAR 91.171

VOR test facilities (VOTs) transmit only one radial—360°. Tune your VOR receiver and listen for a series of dots or a continuous tone that identifies the facility as a VOT. Determine that the needle centers, ±4° (ground or airborne) when the course selector is set to 180° with a TO indication, or 360° with a FROM indication.

2-46   CA.I.B.K1b

When the CDI needle is centered during an airborne VOR check, the omnibearing selector should read

A – within 4° of the selected radial.

B – within 6° of the selected radial.

C – 0° TO, only if you are due south of the VOR.

2-46. Answer B. GFDIC 2D, AIM, FAR 91.171

You can perform a VOR check, including using a VOT, ground and airborne checkpoints, or a dual system check. VOT and checkpoint information is listed in the Associated Data section of the Chart Supplement. Airborne checkpoints usually are located over easily identifiable terrain or prominent features on the ground. After centering the CDI with a FROM indication, compare your VOR course selection to the published radial for that checkpoint. The maximum permissible error is ±6°.

For example, if the radial published in the Associated Data section is 250°, the course shown in the course selector—omnibearing selector (OBS)—when you center the CDI must be within 244° to 256°.

2-47   CA.VI.B.K2

To comply with RNP standards, you must operate within what distance of the centerline of a route, path, or procedure?

A – 2 NM for approach operations; 1 NM for terminal operations; 0.3 NM for enroute operations.

B – 2 NM for enroute operations; 1 NM for terminal operations; 0.3 NM for approach operations.

C – 3 NM for enroute operations; 2 NM for terminal operations; 1 NM for approach operations.

2-47. Answer B. GFDIC 2D, AIM

Required navigation performance (RNP) is a set of standards that apply to both airspace and navigation equipment. To comply with RNP standards, your navigation equipment must be able to keep the airplane within:

- 2 NM for enroute operations.

- 1 NM for terminal operations.

- 0.3 NM for approach operations (the final approach course).

SECTION D ■ Instrument Navigation

2-48   CA.VI.B.K2

What is the wide area augmentation system (WAAS)?

A – WAAS enhances the accuracy of GPS by using a series of ground stations to generate a corrective message that is transmitted to the airplane by a geostationary satellite.

B – WAAS is a navigation computer in the airplane used in addition to GPS to calculate aircraft position with enhanced accuracy.

C – WAAS enhances the accuracy of GPS by using receivers to send corrective signals over a localized area, generally 20 to 30 miles.

2-48. Answer A. GFDIC 2D, AIM

The accuracy of GPS is enhanced with the use of the wide area augmentation system (WAAS), a series of ground stations that generate a corrective message that is transmitted to the airplane by a geostationary satellite. This corrective message improves navigational accuracy by accounting for positional drift of the satellites and signal delays caused by the ionosphere and other atmospheric factors.

2-49   CA.II.B.K3, CA.VI.B.K2

Prior to using GPS for IFR operations, what actions must you take?

A – For WAAS-certified GPS equipment, you must verify that RAIM will be available for the intended route and duration of the flight and ensure that your GPS navigational database is current.

B – For non-WAAS GPS equipment, you must verify that RAIM will be available for the intended route and duration of the flight and ensure that your GPS navigational database is current.

C – For all GPS equipment, you must verify that WAAS will be available for the intended route and duration of the flight and ensure that your GPS navigational database is current.

2-49. Answer A. GFDIC 2D, AIM

Prior to a flight under IFR with non-WAAS GPS equipment, you must confirm RAIM availability for the intended route and duration of the flight by checking NOTAMs, contacting Flight Service, accessing the FAA RAIM prediction website, or by using your GPS receiver's RAIM prediction function. If RAIM capability is lost during flight, you must begin to actively monitor an alternate means of navigation.

If you confirm WAAS coverage along the entire route of flight, you do not need to perform the RAIM prediction check prior to departure.

2-50   CA.VI.B.K2

A full-scale deviation of the CDI on an HSI used for GPS navigation equals what cross-track error in terminal sensitivity?

A – 2.0 nautical miles

B – 0.3 nautical miles

C – 1.0 nautical mile

2-50. Answer C. GFDIC 2D, AIM

For GPS units, the CDI has three different sensitivities, one each for enroute, terminal, and approach phase of flight with the following cross-track errors for a full-scale deviation:

- Enroute—2 NM (WAAS-certified GPS systems); 5 NM (non-WAAS systems).

- Terminal (within 30 NM of the departure or destination airport)—1 NM cross-track error.

- Approach (inside final approach)—0.3 NM.

2-51   CA.VI.B.K2

When using GPS equipment for navigation, what is auto-sequencing?

A – After passing a waypoint, the GPS display shows a FROM indication until 1/2 way to the next waypoint.

B – The GPS receiver senses when your aircraft passes a waypoint and automatically cycles to the next waypoint.

C – The GPS receiver automatically cycles to the next waypoint in your flight plan when you select Direct-To.

2-51. Answer B. GFDIC 2D, AIM

GPS equipment provides auto-sequencing of waypoints—when you program a departure, arrival, approach, or other route, the receiver senses when the airplane passes a waypoint and automatically cycles to the next waypoint. Some GPS equipment displays a message advising you to set the next course on the VOR indicator or HSI. Integrated systems, such as the G1000, automatically set the course on the HSI.

2-52   CA.VI.B.K2

What is a consideration when using a hand-held GPS for VFR navigation?

A – Position accuracy may degrade without notification.

B – RAIM capability will be maintained for the entire flight.

C – Waypoints will still be accurate even if the database is not current.

2-52. Answer A. GFDIC 2D, AIM

VFR GPS panel mount receivers and hand-held units have no RAIM alerting capability so you will not be alerted to the loss of the required number of satellites in view, or the detection of a position error. Systematically cross-check your GPS position with other navigation sources to verify your position.

To ensure the accuracy of waypoints and other data in the GPS system, you must verify that the navigation database and other databases are current prior to flight.

SECTION D ■ Instrument Navigation

CHAPTER 3

The Flight Environment

SECTION A

Airports, Airspace, and Flight Information

THE AIRPORT ENVIRONMENT

RUNWAY AND TAXIWAY MARKINGS

- Touchdown zone markers consist of groups of one, two, and three rectangular bars symmetrically arranged in pairs on either side of the runway centerline. These markings begin 500 feet from the landing threshold and provide distance information in 500-foot increments.

- The solid bold stripes of the aiming point markings (also referred to as the fixed distance markers) begin 1,000 feet from the landing threshold.

- A displaced threshold is marked by a solid white line extending across the runway perpendicular to the centerline. This line marks the point beyond which all normal takeoff and landing operations are permitted. Taxi, takeoff, and rollout areas are marked by white arrows leading to a displaced threshold.

- A 3-foot wide demarcation bar delineates a runway with a displaced threshold from a blast pad, stopway, or taxiway that precedes the runway. A demarcation is yellow because it is not located on the runway.

RUNWAY HOLDING POSITION MARKINGS

- Runway holding position markings, or hold lines, are used to keep aircraft clear of runways. At some airports, holding position signs might be used instead of, or in conjunction with, the hold lines painted on the runways and taxiways.

- Hold lines consist of two solid lines and two dashed lines usually placed between 125 and 250 feet from the runway centerline. Your aircraft is clear of the runway when it is on the side of the solid lines.

- Runway hold position markings on a runway identify the location of an intersecting runway and where you are expected to stop if you do not have clearance to proceed onto the intersecting runway.

- At some airports, holding position signs might be used instead of, or in conjunction with, the hold lines painted on the taxiways.

- At an uncontrolled airport, stop and check for traffic and cross the hold line only after ensuring that no one is on an approach to land. At a towered airport, the controller may ask you to hold short of the runway for landing traffic. In this case, stop before the hold line and proceed only after you are cleared to do so by the controller and you have checked for traffic.

- ILS critical areas are established near each localizer and glide slope antenna. When instructed by ATC to hold short of the ILS critical area, you must stop so that no part of the aircraft extends beyond the ILS holding position marking.

  - An ILS holding position marking on the pavement consists of two yellow solid lines spaced two feet apart connected by pairs of solid lines spaced ten feet apart.

  - A sign with an inscription in white on a red background is located adjacent to the ILS hold position markings.

  - The ILS critical area boundary sign has a yellow background with a black graphic depicting the ILS pavement holding position marking.

AIRPORT SIGNS

There are six basic types of airport signs:

- **Direction Signs** indicate directions of taxiways leading out of an intersection. They have black inscriptions on a yellow background and always contain arrows that show the approximate direction of turn.

- **Mandatory Instruction Signs** denote an entrance to a runway, a critical area, or an area prohibited to aircraft. These signs are red with white letters or numbers. Examples of mandatory instruction signs include:

    - Runway Holding Position Sign—located at the holding position on taxiways that intersect a runway or on runways that intersect other runways.

    - No Entry Sign—prohibits an aircraft from entering an area. Typically, this sign would be located on a taxiway intended to be used in only one direction or at the intersection of vehicle roadways with runways, taxiways, or aprons where the roadway may be mistaken as a taxiway or other aircraft movement surface.

- **Location Signs** identify either the taxiway or runway where your aircraft is located. These signs are black with yellow inscriptions and a yellow border. Location signs also identify the runway boundary or ILS critical area for aircraft exiting the runway. The runway boundary sign, which faces the runway and is visible to you when exiting the runway, is located adjacent to the holding position marking on the pavement, providing you with another visual cue to determine when you are clear of the runway.

- **Runway Distance Remaining Signs** provide distance remaining information to pilots during takeoff and landing operations. The signs are located along the sides of the runway, and the inscription consists of a white numeral on a black background. The signs indicate the distance remaining in thousands of feet. Runway distance remaining signs are recommended for runways used by turbojet aircraft.

- **Information Signs** advise you of such things as areas that cannot be seen from the control tower, applicable radio frequencies, and noise abatement procedures. These signs use yellow backgrounds with black inscriptions.

- **Destination Signs** indicate the general direction to a location on the airport, such as runways, aprons, terminals, military areas, civil aviation areas, cargo areas, international areas, and FBOs. They have black inscriptions on a yellow background and always have an arrow showing the direction of the taxiing route to that destination.

In addition to knowledge test questions about the purpose of runway and taxiway markings and airport signs, you might be required to identify specific signs and markings shown in illustrations. Refer to the FAA *Airport Sign and Marking — Quick Reference Guide* to review the various signs and markings.

SECTION A ■ **Airports, Airspace, and Flight Information**

AIRPORT SIGN AND MARKING – QUICK REFERENCE GUIDE

EXAMPLE	TYPE OF SIGN	PURPOSE	LOCATION/CONVENTION
4 - 22	Mandatory: Hold position for taxiway/ runway intersection.	Denotes entrance to runway from a taxiway.	Located L side of taxiway within 10 feet of hold position markings.
22 - 4	Mandatory: Holding position for runway/runway intersection.	Denotes intersecting runway.	Located L side of rwy prior to intersection, & R side if rwy more than 150' wide, used as taxiway, or has "land & hold short" ops.
4 - APCH	Mandatory: Holding position for runway approach area.	Denotes area to be protected for aircraft approaching or departing a runway.	Located on taxiways crossing thru runway approach areas where an aircraft would enter an RSA or apch/ departure airspace.
ILS	Mandatory: Holding position for ILS critical area/precision obstacle free zone.	Denotes entrance to area to be protected for an ILS signal or approach airspace.	Located on twys where the twys enter the NAVAID critical area or where aircraft on taxiway would violate ILS apch airspace (including POFZ).
⊖	Mandatory: No entry.	Denotes aircraft entry is prohibited.	Located on paved areas that aircraft should not enter.
B	Taxiway Location.	Identifies taxiway on which the aircraft is located.	Located along taxiway by itself, as part of an array of taxiway direction signs, or combined with a runway/ taxiway hold sign.
22	Runway Location.	Identifies the runway on which the aircraft is located.	Normally located where the proximity of two rwys to one another could cause confusion.
═ ═ ═	Runway Safety Area / OFZ and Runway Approach Area Boundary.	Identifies exit boundary for an RSA / OFZ or rwy approach.	Located on taxiways on back side of certain runway/ taxiway holding position signs or runway approach area signs.
▯▯▯▯	ILS Critical Area/POFZ Boundary.	Identifies ILS critical area exit boundary.	Located on taxiways on back side of ILS critical area signs.
J →	Direction: Taxiway.	Defines designation/direction of intersecting taxiway(s).	Located on L side, prior to intersection, with an array L to R in clockwise manner.
↖ L	Runway Exit.	Defines designation/direction of exit taxiways from the rwy.	Located on same side of runway as exit, prior to exit.
22 ↑	Outbound Destination.	Defines directions to take-off runway(s).	Located on taxi routes to runway(s). Never collocated or combined with other signs.
FBO ↘	Inbound Destination.	Defines directions to airport destinations for arriving aircraft.	Located on taxi routes to airport destinations. Never collocated or combined with other types of signs.
NOISE ABATEMENT PROCEDURES IN EFFECT 2300 - 0500	Information.	Provides procedural or other specialized information.	Located along taxi routes or aircraft parking/staging areas. May not be lighted.
▨▨▨	Taxiway Ending Marker.	Indicates taxiway does not continue beyond intersection.	Installed at taxiway end or far side of intersection, if visual cues are inadequate.
7	Distance Remaining.	Distance remaining info for take-off/landing.	Located along the sides of runways at 1000' increments.

EXAMPLE	TYPE OF MARKING	PURPOSE	LOCATION/CONVENTION
═ ═ ═	Holding Position.	Denotes entrance to runway from a taxiway.	Located across centerline within 10 feet of hold sign on taxiways and on certain runways.
▯▯▯	ILS Critical Area/POFZ Boundary.	Denotes entrance to area to be protected for an ILS signal or approach airspace.	Located on twys where the twys enter the NAVAID critical area or where aircraft on taxiway would violate ILS apch airspace (including POFZ).
┄┄┄	Taxiway/Taxiway Holding Position.	Denotes location on taxiway or apron where aircraft hold short of another taxiway.	Used at ATCT airports where needed to hold traffic at a twy/twy intersection. Installed provides wing clearance.
┄┄┄	Non-Movement Area Boundary.	Delineates movement area under control of ATCT, from non-movement area.	Located on boundary between movement and non-movement area. Located to ensure wing clearance for taxiing aircraft.
══════ Taxiway Edge.		Defines edge of usable, full strength taxiway.	Located along twy edge where contiguous shoulder or other paved surface NOT intended for use by aircraft.
┄┄┄┄ Dashed Taxiway Edge.		Defines taxiway edge where adjoining pavement is usable.	Located along twy edge where contiguous paved surface or apron is intended for use by aircraft.
[4-22] [4-22]	Surface Painted Holding Position.	Denotes entrance to runway from a taxiway.	Supplements elevated holding position signs. Required where hold line exceeds 200'. Also useful at complex intersections.
	Enhanced Taxiway Centerline.	Provides visual cue to help identify location of hold position.	Taxiway centerlines are enhanced 150' prior to a runway holding position marking.
↖ T	Surface Painted Taxiway Direction.	Defines designation/direction of intersecting taxiway(s).	Located L side for turns to left. R side for turns to right. Installed prior to intersection.
B	Surface Painted Taxiway Location.	Identifies taxiway on which the aircraft is located.	Located R side. Can be installed on L side if combined with surface painted hold sign.

Federal Aviation Administration

RUNWAY INCURSION AVOIDANCE

- The official definition of a runway incursion is "any occurrence at an airport involving an aircraft, vehicle, person, or object on the ground that creates a collision hazard or results in loss of separation with an aircraft taking off or intending to take off, landing, or intending to land."

- Runway incursions are primarily caused by errors associated with clearances, communication, airport surface movement, and positional awareness.

- Actions to help prevent a runway incursion include but are not limited to:

  - Review the airport diagram and complete as many checklist items as possible before taxi.

  - Read back (in full) all active runway crossing, hold short, or line up and wait clearances.

  - Do not become absorbed in other tasks, or conversation, while your airplane is moving.

  - If unsure of your position on the airport, stop and ask for assistance.

  - Monitor the radio to listen for other aircraft cleared onto your runway for takeoff or landing.

  - After landing, stay on the tower frequency until instructed to change frequencies.

  - To help others see your airplane during periods of reduced visibility or at night, use your exterior taxi/landing lights when practical.

LAND AND HOLD SHORT OPERATIONS

- During land and hold short operations (LAHSO), an aircraft is cleared to land and stop on the runway, holding short of an intersecting runway, intersecting taxiway, or some other designated point on the runway. LAHSO is an air traffic control tool that is used at selected airports to increase airport capacity and maintain system efficiency.

- To conduct LAHSO, you must have at least a private pilot certificate and you must take these actions:

  - During preflight planning, become familiar with all available information concerning LAHSO at the destination airport. The Airport/Facility Directory section of the Chart Supplement indicates the presence of LAHSO and includes the available landing distance (ALD) and runway slope, if it applies, for each LAHSO runway.

  - Determine which runway LAHSO combinations are acceptable for your airplane's landing performance and for your personal minimums.

  - During flight, have the published ALD and runway slope readily available and ensure that you can safely land and stop within the ALD with the existing conditions upon arrival.

- As pilot in command, you are responsible for the safety of the flight, and you have final authority to accept or decline any LAHSO clearance.

LIGHTING SYSTEMS

APPROACH LIGHT SYSTEM

- Normally, approach lights extend outward from the landing threshold to a distance of 2,400 to 3,000 feet from precision instrument runways and 1,400 to 1,500 feet from nonprecision instrument runways.

- High intensity white strobe lights on each side of the runway threshold called runway end identifier lights (REIL) help you see the runway threshold in reduced visibility or identify the threshold of a runway that is surrounded by a preponderance of other lighting or one that lacks contrast with surrounding terrain.

VISUAL GLIDE SLOPE INDICATORS

- After you have the runway environment in sight, visual glide slope indicators help you establish and maintain a safe descent path to the runway. Their purpose is to provide a clear visual means to determine if you are too high, too low, or on the correct glide path.

SECTION A ■ **Airports, Airspace, and Flight Information**

- Remaining on or above the proper glide path of a visual approach slope indicator (VASI) ensures safe obstruction clearance in the approach area—within ±10° of the extended runway centerline and out to 4 nautical miles from the threshold.

Two-Bar Visual Approach Slope Indicator (VASI)

- Provides one visual glide path, normally set to 3°. At some locations, the angle may be higher for obstacle clearance.
- Indicates an on-glide path indication when the far bars indicate red and the near bars show white.
- Consists of lights that are visible from 3 to 5 miles during the day and up to 20 miles at night.
- Glide path indications are:
    - On glide path—far bar is red, near bar is white; "red over white, you're all right."
    - Above glide path—both bars are white: you are too high.
    - Below glide path—both bars are red: you are too low.

Three-Bar Visual Approach Slope Indicator (VASI)

- Consists of three sets of light sources forming near, middle, and far bars.
- Provides two visual glide paths to the same runway:
    - The first glide path uses the near and middle bars and is the same as that provided by a standard two-bar VASI installation (normally 3°).
    - The second glide path uses the middle and far bars, is intended for use only by pilots of high-cockpit aircraft, and is about one-quarter of a degree (0.25°) steeper than the first. When on the upper glide path, the pilot sees red, white, and white. Pilots of high-cockpit aircraft use the middle and far bars to fly the upper glide path. In effect, these two bars constitute a 2-bar VASI for the upper glide path.
- Lower glide path indications are:
    - On glide path—2 far bars are red, near bar is white; "red over white, you're all right."
    - Above glide path—2 near bars are white: far bar is red or all 3 bars are white: you are too high.
    - Below glide path—all 3 bars are red: you are too low.
- Upper glide path indications are:
    - On glide path— 2 near bars are white, far bar is red; "red over white, you're all right."
    - Above glide path—all 3 bars are white: you are too high.
    - Below glide path— 2 far bars are red, near bar is white or all 3 bars are red: you are too low.

Precision Approach Path Indicator (PAPI)

- Is normally located on the left side of the runway and can be seen up to 5 miles during the day and 20 miles at night.
- Uses lights that are installed in a single row of two- or four-light units.
- Glide path indications for a four-light unit are:
    - All lights are white—high (over 3.5°).
    - Light on the far right is red and the other three are white—slightly high (3.2°).
    - Left two lights are white; right two lights are red—on glide path (3.0°).
    - Light on the far left is white and the other three are red—slightly low (2.8°).
    - All four lights are red—low (under 2.5°).

RUNWAY LIGHTING

- Runway edge lights are used to outline the runway during periods of darkness or restricted visibility. Runway edge lights include high intensity runway lights (HIRL), medium intensity runway lights (MIRL), and low intensity runway lights (LIRL).

- Runway edge lights are white, except on instrument runways where amber replaces white on the last 2,000 feet or half the runway length, whichever is less, to indicate a caution zone.

- Threshold lights, which form a line across the runway perpendicular to the centerline, mark the ends of the each runway.

- As you approach for landing, threshold lights appear green, indicating the beginning of the landing portion of the runway. As viewed during takeoff in the opposite direction, threshold lights appear red, marking the departure end of the runway.

- Displaced threshold lights are located on each side of the runway and appear green during approach to landing. If the displaced runway area is usable for taxi, takeoff, or rollout, the area short of the displaced threshold will have runway edge lights, which appear red while taking off toward the displaced threshold and white after the threshold.

- Runway centerline lights (RCLS) are flush-mounted in the runway to help you maintain the centerline during takeoff and landing.

- Land and hold short lights are a row of five flush-mounted flashing white lights installed at the hold short point, perpendicular to the centerline of the runway on which they are installed. These lights will normally be on when land and hold short operations are being conducted continuously.

- Runway status light (RWSL) system is a fully automated system that provides runway status information to pilots and surface vehicle operators to clearly indicate when it is unsafe to enter, cross, takeoff from, or land on a runway. Runway status lights are designed to reduce the number and severity of runway incursions.

AIRPORT BEACON AND OBSTRUCTION LIGHTS

- The airport beacon helps you to locate the airport at night and during conditions of reduced visibility.

- Operation of the beacon during daylight hours at an airport within controlled airspace (Class B, C, D, and E surface areas) often indicates that the ground visibility is less than 3 statute miles and/or the ceiling is less than 1,000 feet. However, because beacons are often turned on by photoelectric cells or time clocks, you must not rely on the airport beacon to indicate that the weather is below VFR minimums.

- Obstruction lights are installed on prominent structures such as towers, buildings, and sometimes power lines. Flashing red lights or high intensity strobe lights warn you of the obstructions.

AIRCRAFT LIGHTING

- The approved aircraft position lights for night operations are a green light on the right wingtip, a red light wingtip, and a white light on the tail.

- Flashing red and white anticollision lights are typically on the wingtips or tail.

AIRSPACE

ADS-B/TRANSPONDER REQUIREMENTS

- The FARs require that you have an operating transponder with Mode C capability and ADS-B Out equipment in Class A airspace, in Class B airspace, within 30 nautical miles of Class B primary airports, and in and above Class C airspace.

- You must have a transponder with Mode C capability and ADS-B Out equipment at or above 10,000 feet MSL (except at or below 2,500 feet AGL) even in uncontrolled airspace, over the 48 contiguous states.

- Even if you are not in airspace where transponders are required, if your aircraft is equipped with a transponder, the FARs require that it be turned on while operating in controlled airspace.

SECTION A ■ **Airports, Airspace, and Flight Information**

- If your transponder or ADS-B Out fails while you are operating in airspace that requires this equipment, ATC may authorize you to continue to your destination, including any intermediate stops, or to proceed to a place where repairs can be made.

CLASS G AIRSPACE (UNCONTROLLED)

- ATC does not exercise control of traffic and you are not required to communicate with controllers when operating in Class G airspace, unless a temporary control tower exists.

- Class G airspace typically starts at the surface and extends up to the base of the overlying controlled airspace (Class E), which is normally 700 or 1,200 feet AGL. In a few areas of the western U.S. and Alaska, Class G airspace can extend all the way up to 14,500 feet MSL, or to 1,500 feet AGL, whichever is higher.

CONTROLLED AIRSPACE

CLASS E AIRSPACE

- In Class E airspace, you cannot fly when the weather is below VFR minimums unless you are instrument rated, have filed an IFR flight plan, and have received a clearance from ATC.

- Federal airways, or Victor airways, are based on VOR or VORTAC navaids and are identified by a V and the airway number. Airways are normally 8 nautical miles wide, begin at 1,200 feet AGL, and extend up to, but not including, 18,000 feet MSL.

- To allow IFR traffic to remain in controlled airspace while transitioning from the enroute to the terminal environment, the base of Class E starts closer to the ground near many airports. At airports without control towers that have approved instrument approach procedures, Class E airspace begins either at 700 feet AGL or at the surface and these Class E areas might extend in the direction of the instrument approach.

- At airports where Class E begins at the surface, weather reporting services are provided by a weather observer or automatic weather observation equipment (ASOS/AWSS/AWOS).

CLASS D AIRSPACE

- An airport that has an operating control tower, but does not provide Class B or C airspace ATC services, is surrounded by Class D airspace.

- Class D airspace can be various sizes and shapes, depending on the instrument approach procedures established for that airport. Most Class D airspace is a circle with a radius of approximately 4 NM extending up to 2,500 feet AGL.

- On VFR charts, Class D boundaries are indicated by a blue dashed line and the upper limit altitude is shown in hundreds of feet MSL inside a blue dashed box.

- The control tower provides sequencing and traffic advisories to VFR aircraft operating into and out of the airport, and IFR traffic separation. You must establish two-way radio communication with the tower prior to entering Class D airspace and maintain radio contact during all operations to, from, or on that airport. A transponder is not required in Class D airspace.

- The airspace at an airport with a part-time control tower is designated as Class D only when the tower is in operation. At airports where the tower operates part time, the airspace changes to Class E, or a combination of Class E and Class G when the tower is closed.

CLASS C AIRSPACE

- Although some may be modified to fit unique aspects of a particular airport's location, Class C areas usually have similar dimensions from one location to another:
    - A 5 nautical mile radius core area extends from the surface to 4,000 feet above the elevation of the primary airport.
    - A 10 nautical mile radius shelf area usually extends from 1,200 feet to 4,000 feet above the airport elevation.
    - An outer area, where Class C services are available but not mandatory, normally extends out to 20 nautical miles from the primary airport.
- In addition to a two-way radio communication requirement, all aircraft operating in a Class C area and in all airspace above it must be equipped with a transponder with a Mode C capability and ADS-B Out equipment.
- When departing from a satellite airport without an operating control tower, you must establish and maintain two-way radio communications with the ATC facility having jurisdiction over the Class C airspace area as soon as practicable after departing.

CLASS B AIRSPACE

- You must be at least a private pilot, or a student pilot with the appropriate endorsement, and must receive an ATC clearance before you enter Class B airspace.
- Equipment requirements to fly in Class B airspace include:
    - Transponder with Mode C capability and ADS-B Out equipment within 30 nautical miles of the Class B area's primary airport from the surface to 10,000 feet MSL.
    - For all operations, two-way radio capable of communications with ATC on appropriate frequencies for that Class B airspace area.
    - For IFR operations, a VOR or TACAN receiver or a suitable RNAV system.

CLASS A AIRSPACE

- Class A airspace extends from 18,000 feet MSL up to and including FL600. Altitudes within Class A airspace are expressed to ATC by using the term flight level (FL). Class A covers the majority of the contiguous states and Alaska, as well as the area extending 12 nautical miles out from the U.S. coast.
- To operate within Class A airspace, you must:
    - Be instrument rated and current for instrument flight.
    - Operate under an IFR flight plan and in accordance with an ATC clearance at specified flight levels.
    - Set your altimeter to the standard setting of 29.92 inches Hg.
- Aircraft equipment requirements for Class A airspace are:
    - Instruments and equipment required by 91.205 for IFR operations.
    - ADS-B Out/Mode C transponder capability.
    - At or above 24,000 feet MSL (FL240), when VOR equipment is required for navigation, distance measuring equipment (DME) or a suitable RNAV system.
- If the DME or RNAV system fails in flight above FL240, you must immediately notify ATC. Then, you may continue to operate at or above FL240 and proceed to the next airport of intended landing where repairs can be made.

SECTION A ■ **Airports, Airspace, and Flight Information**

SPECIAL VFR

- You may only operate within the areas of Class B, C, D, or E airspace that extend to the surface around an airport, when the ground visibility is at least 3 statute miles and the cloud ceiling is at least 1,000 feet AGL. If ground visibility is not reported, you can use flight visibility.

- When the visibility is below 3 statute miles and/or the ceiling is below 1,000 feet AGL, you may obtain a special VFR clearance from the ATC facility having jurisdiction over the affected airspace.

- A special VFR clearance allows you to enter, leave, or operate within most Class D and Class E surface areas and in some Class B and Class C surface areas if the flight visibility is at least 1 statute mile and you can remain clear of clouds. At least 1 statute mile of ground visibility is required for takeoff and landing. However, if ground visibility is not reported, you must have at least 1 statute mile flight visibility.

- Special VFR is not permitted between sunset and sunrise unless you have a current instrument rating and the aircraft is equipped for instrument flight.

- The phrase NO SVFR included with the airport information on a VFR chart indicates that you cannot obtain a special VFR clearance to operate at the airport.

AIRSPEED LIMITATIONS

Maximum airspeeds designated by the FARs include:

- 250 KIAS—flights below 10,000 feet MSL.

- 200 KIAS—in Class C or D airspace, at or below 2,500 feet above the surface, and within 4 nautical miles of the primary airport.

- 200 KIAS—in airspace underlying a Class B area and in VFR corridors through Class B airspace.

AIRSPACE CLASS REVIEW

You can use the following table as a quick reference for the VFR weather minimums and operating requirements of each airspace class. When trying to remember the weather minimums, it is easier to remember the minimums that are the same (highlighted) and know the few exceptions.

	VFR Minimum Visibility	VFR Minimum Distance from Clouds	Minimum Pilot Qualifications	VFR Entry and Equipment Requirements	ATC Services
CLASS **A**	N/A	N/A	Instrument Rating	IFR Flight Plan IFR Clearance	All Aircraft Separation
CLASS **B**	3 SM	Clear of Clouds	Private Pilot Certificate Student Pilot Logbook Endorsement	ATC Clearance ADS-B/Mode C Transponder	All Aircraft Separation
CLASS **C**	3 SM	500 ft Below 1,000 ft Above 2,000 ft Horizontal	Student Pilot Certificate	Establish Radio Communication ADS-B/Mode C Transponder	IFR/IFR Separation IFR/VFR Separation VFR Traffic Advisories (workload permitting)
CLASS **D**	3 SM	500 ft Below 1,000 ft Above 2,000 ft Horizontal	Student Pilot Certificate	Establish Radio Communication	IFR/IFR Separation VFR Traffic Advisories (workload permitting)
CLASS **E**	Below 10,000 ft MSL: 3 SM At or Above 10,000 ft MSL: 5 SM	Below 10,000 ft MSL: 500 ft Below 1,000 ft Above 2,000 ft Horizontal At or Above 10,000 ft MSL: 1,000 ft Below 1,000 ft Above 1 SM Horizontal	Student Pilot Certificate	None	IFR/IFR Separation VFR Traffic Advisories on Request (workload permitting)
CLASS **G**	1,200 ft AGL and Below: Day 1 SM; Night 3 SM Below 10,000 ft MSL: Day 1 SM; Night 3 SM At or Above 10,000 MSL : 5 SM (above1,200 ft AGL)	1,200 ft AGL and Below: Day; Clear of Clouds Night; 500 ft Below, 1,000 ft Above, 2,000 ft Horizontal Below 10,000 ft MSL: 500 ft Below 1,000 ft Above 2,000 ft Horizontal (above 1,200 ft AGL) At or Above 10,000 ft MSL: 1,000 ft Below 1,000 ft Above 1 SM Horizontal (above 1,200 ft AGL)	Student Pilot Certificate	None	VFR Traffic Advisories on Request (workload permitting)

SECTION A ■ **Airports, Airspace, and Flight Information**

SPECIAL USE AIRSPACE

- Alert areas contain unusual types of aerial activities, such as parachute jumping and glider towing, or high concentrations of student pilot training. You do not need to obtain permission to enter an alert area. Pilots of participating aircraft and pilots transiting the area are equally responsible for collision avoidance, so you should be especially cautious when flying through alert areas.

- A military operations area (MOA) is a block of airspace in which military operations are conducted. VFR aircraft are not prevented from flying through active MOAs, but it is wise to avoid them when possible. If you do choose to fly in an MOA, you should exercise extreme caution when military activity is being conducted. Flight Service can advise you of the hours of operation of an MOA along your route, or you can check the special use airspace panel on the edge of your chart.

- Warning areas extend from three nautical miles outward from the coast of the United States and contain activity that may be hazardous to nonparticipating aircraft.

- Restricted areas often have invisible hazards to aircraft, such as artillery firing, aerial gunnery, or guided missiles. Permission to fly through restricted areas must be granted by the controlling agency.

- Prohibited areas are established for security or other reasons associated with the national welfare and contain airspace within which the flight of aircraft is prohibited.

OTHER AIRSPACE AREAS

- Other airspace areas include national security areas, local airport advisory areas, military training routes, parachute jump aircraft operations, and terminal radar service areas.

- Military training routes (MTRs) are established below 10,000 feet MSL for operations at speeds in excess of 250 knots. MTRs are classified as VR for VFR operations and IR for IFR operations.

- MTRs that are entirely at or below 1,500 feet AGL are identified by four-digit numbers, and those that have one or more segments above 1,500 feet AGL use three-digit numbers.

TEMPORARY FLIGHT RESTRICTIONS

- Types of TFRs include those that address disaster and hazards, space flight operations, VIP movement, emergency air traffic rules, air shows and sporting events on a case-by-case basis, and major sporting events.

- A Special Security Instructions standing NOTAM applies to any MLB, NFL, or NCAA division one football game, or any major motor speedway event.

- TFRs are issued in NOTAMs that specify the dimensions, restrictions, and effective times.

WASHINGTON DC SPECIAL FLIGHT RULES AREA

- The Washington DC Special Flight Rules Area (SFRA) includes all airspace within a 30 nautical mile radius of the Washington DC VOR (DCA) from the surface up to but not including FL180.

- Flight under VFR and general aviation aircraft operations are prohibited in the flight restricted zone (FRZ) of the SFRA—a ring of airspace within 13 to 15 nautical miles of the Washington DC VOR.

- If you are planning to fly under VFR within 60 nautical miles of the Washington DC VOR, you must complete the FAA Special Awareness Training course at faasafety.gov.

FLIGHT INFORMATION

CHART SUPPLEMENTS

- Chart Supplements include data that cannot be readily depicted in graphic form on charts. This data applies to public and joint-use airports, seaplane bases, and heliports, as well as navaids and airspace.

- Each Chart Supplement contains five primary sections:
    - The Airport/Facility Directory Legend—helps you interpret the information in an airport listing.
    - The Airport/Facility Directory (A/FD)—listings include airport identification and location information, runway data, airport services, weather data sources, communication and navaid frequencies, and airspace information.
    - Notices—include Aeronautical Chart Bulletins, Special Notices, and Regulatory Notices.

- Associated Data—contains information to help you prepare for flights under IFR, such as a list of VOR receiver checkpoints and VOR test facilities, preferred IFR routes, and tower enroute control (TEC) routes.
  - Airport Diagrams—diagrams of most towered airports and other selected nontowered airports and runway incursion hot spot information.
- You might be required to locate information in the Airport/Facility Directory (A/FD) section of a Chart Supplement. The A/FD Legend is provided in the Airman Knowledge Testing Supplement for the Commercial Certificate in Appendix A of this test guide. Examples of information that you might be required to locate include:
  - Runway data, such as the types of runway lighting available and land and hold short operations (LAHSO) information, which includes available landing distances (ALD) to the hold-short point.
  - Communications data, such as applicable frequencies for the airport, including ATIS, UNICOM, Flight Service, tower, ground control, approach, and departure.

NOTICES TO AIRMEN

- Notices to Airmen (NOTAMs) provide time-critical flight planning information regarding a facility, service, procedure, or hazard that is temporary or not known far enough in advance to be included in the most recent aeronautical charts or Chart Supplements.
- Two primary NOTAM types are:
  - NOTAM(D) (distant NOTAM)—disseminated for all navigational facilities that are part of the U.S. airspace system, and all public use airports, seaplane bases, and heliports listed in the Chart Supplements.
  - FDC NOTAMs—issued by the National Flight Data Center and contain regulatory information. For example, FDC NOTAMs may advise of changes in flight data which affect instrument approach procedures (IAP), aeronautical charts, and flight restrictions prior to normal publication.

FEDERAL AVIATION REGULATIONS

- The Federal Aviation Regulations (FARs) are under subject title 14, Aeronautics and Space of the Code of Federal Regulations (CFR). The Federal Register contains Notices of Proposed Rulemaking (NPRM), which inform pilots of pending regulation changes.
- NTSB 830 contains rules pertaining to the notification and reporting of aircraft accidents and incidents. For example, if an aircraft is involved in an accident that results in substantial damage to the aircraft, the nearest NTSB field office must be notified immediately. In addition, NTSB 830 also explains the requirements for the preservation of aircraft wreckage, mail, cargo, and records involving all civil aircraft in the United Sates.

NOTE: An asterisk appearing after an ACS code (i.e. CA.IV.A.K2) indicates that the question subject appears more than one time in the ACS. The code shown corresponds to the first instance of the subject in the ACS.*

3-1   CA.II.D.K3

The "yellow demarcation bar" marking indicates

A – a runway with a displaced threshold that precedes the runway.

B – a hold line from a taxiway to a runway.

C – the beginning of available runway for landing on the approach side.

3-1. Answer A. GFDIC 3A, AIM

A 3-foot wide demarcation bar delineates a runway with a displaced threshold from a blast pad, stopway, or taxiway that precedes the runway. A demarcation is yellow because it is not located on the runway.

3-2   CA.II.D.K3, CA.II.D.K6c

The runway holding position sign is located on

A – runways that intersect other runways.

B – taxiways protected from an aircraft approaching a runway.

C – runways that intersect other taxiways.

3-2. Answer A. GFDIC 3A, AIM

Runway holding position markings, or hold lines, are used to keep aircraft clear of runways. At some airports, holding position signs might be used instead of, or in conjunction with, the hold lines painted on the runways and taxiways. A runway holding position sign and runway holding position markings on a runway identify the location of an intersecting runway and where you are expected to stop if you do not have clearance to proceed onto the intersecting runway.

3-3   CA.II.D.K3, CA.II.D.K6c

Runway holding position markings on taxiways

A – identify where aircraft are prohibited to taxi when not cleared to proceed by ground control.

B – identify where aircraft are supposed to stop when not cleared to proceed onto the runway.

C – allow an aircraft permission onto the runway.

3-3. Answer B. GFDIC 3A, AIM

These signs are located at the holding position on taxiways that intersect a runway or on runways that intersect other runways. The inscription on the sign contains the designation of the intersecting runway. These signs are used on runways only when those runways are used for land and hold short operations (LAHSO) or for taxiing.

3-4   CA.II.D.K3

(Refer to Figure 51, item E.) This sign is a visual clue that

A – confirms the aircraft's location to be on Taxiway B.

B – warns the pilot of approaching Taxiway B.

C – indicates "B" holding area is ahead.

3-4. Answer A. GFDIC 3A, AIM

Location signs identify either the taxiway or runway where your aircraft is located. These signs are black with yellow inscriptions and a yellow border. In this case, the yellow letter B designates Taxiway Bravo.

3-5   CA.II.D.K3

(Refer to Figure 56, Item 1.) This sign confirms your position on

A – Runway 22.

B – routing to Runway 22.

C – Taxiway 22.

3-5. Answer B. GFDIC 3A, AIM

Destination signs indicate the general direction to a location on the airport, such as runways, aprons, terminals, military areas, civil aviation areas, cargo areas, international areas, and FBOs. They have black inscriptions on a yellow background and always have an arrow showing the direction of the taxiing route to that destination.

3-6   CA.II.D.K3

(Refer to Figure 56, Item 2.) This taxiway sign would be expected

A – at the intersection of Runway 04/22 departure end and the taxiway.

B – near the intersection of Runways 04 and 22.

C – at a taxiway intersecting Runway 04/22.

3-6. Answer A. GFDIC 3A, AIM
Mandatory instruction signs denote an entrance to a runway, a critical area, or an area prohibited to aircraft. These signs are red with white letters or numbers. An example of a mandatory instruction signs is a runway holding position sign, such as shown in Figure 56. If the runway holding position sign appears at the departure end of the runway, only the takeoff runway (in this case, Runway 4) will appear on the sign (4). At locations where a taxiway intersects a runway other than at the departure end, both runway numbers appear on the sign (4-22).

3-7   CA.II.D.K2, 3

(Refer to Figure 57.) You are directed to taxi to Runway 10. You see this sign at a taxiway intersection while taxiing. Which way should you proceed?

A – Left.

B – Right.

C – Straight ahead.

3-7. Answer C. GFDIC 3A, AIM
Destination signs indicate the general direction to a location on the airport, such as runways, aprons, terminals, military areas, civil aviation areas, cargo areas, international areas, and FBOs. They have black inscriptions on a yellow background and always have an arrow showing the direction of the taxiing route to that destination. The direction sign shown in Figure 57 indicates that Runway 10-21 is straight ahead, Runway 4 is to the left, and Runway 22 is to the right.

3-8   CA.II.D.K3

(Refer to Figure 60, item 1.) This sign is an indication

A – of an area where aircraft are prohibited.

B – that the taxiway does not continue.

C – of the general taxiing direction to a taxiway.

3-8. Answer B. GFDIC 3A, FAA Airport Sign and Marking—Quick Reference Guide
Item 1 in Figure 60 is a taxiway ending marker, which indicates that the taxiway does not continue beyond the location. If visual cues are inadequate, these signs are installed at the taxiway end or the far side of an intersection.

3-9   CA.II.D.K2, 3

(Refer to Figure 61.) Ground control has instructed you to taxi Alpha to Foxtrot to the active runway. According to the sign in the figure, which direction would you turn at this intersection to comply with ATC?

A – No turn is required.

B – The turn will be made to the right.

C – The turn will be made to the left.

3-9. Answer C. GFDIC 3A, AIM
Location signs identify either the taxiway or runway where your aircraft is located. These signs are black with yellow inscriptions and a yellow border. Direction signs indicate directions of taxiways leading out of an intersection. They have black inscriptions on a yellow background and always contain arrows that show the approximate direction of turn.

The location sign in Figure 61 indicates that you are on Taxiway Alpha and the direction sign indicates that you must turn slightly to the left to enter Taxiway Foxtrot.

SECTION A ■ **Airports, Airspace, and Flight Information**

3-10   CA.II.D.K2, 3

(Refer to Figure 64.) If cleared for an intersection takeoff on Runway 8, you see this sign at the intersection hold short position. Which way should you turn when taxiing onto the runway?

A – Left.

B – Right.

C – Need more information.

3-10. Answer A. GFDIC 3A, AIM

Mandatory instruction signs denote an entrance to a runway, a critical area, or an area prohibited to aircraft. These signs are red with white letters or numbers. An example of a mandatory instruction sign is a runway holding position sign, such as shown in Figure 64. At locations where a taxiway intersects a runway other than at the departure end, both runway numbers appear on the sign (26-8).

Runway holding signs are oriented in the same direction as the actual runway. When viewing this sign, the departure end of Runway 26 is to the left and the departure end of Runway 8 is to the right, which means the takeoff direction for Runway 8 is to the left. Turn left to use the remaining length of Runway 8.

3-11   CA.II.D.K2,3, 6c,

(Refer to Figure 64.) You see this sign when holding short of the runway. You receive clearance to back taxi on the runway for a full-length Runway 8 departure. Which way should you turn when first taxiing on to the runway for takeoff?

A – Left.

B – Right.

C – Need more information.

3-11. Answer B. GFDIC 3A, AIM

Mandatory instruction signs denote an entrance to a runway, a critical area, or an area prohibited to aircraft. These signs are red with white letters or numbers. An example of a mandatory instruction signs is a runway holding position sign, such as shown in Figure 64. At locations where a taxiway intersects a runway other than at the departure end, both runway numbers appear on the sign (26-8).

Runway holding signs are oriented in the same direction as the actual runway. When viewing this sign, the departure end of Runway 26 is to the left and the departure end of Runway 8 is to the right, which means you must turn right to back taxi to the Runway 8 threshold.

3-12   CA.II.D.K6b

When should pilots state their position on the airport when calling the tower for takeoff?

A – When visibility is less than 1 mile.

B – When parallel runways are in use.

C – When departing from a runway intersection.

3-12. Answer C. GFDIC 3A, AIM

When communicating with ground control or the tower, state your position on the airport surface. One of the position reports that you are required to make is when you are ready for takeoff from a runway intersection.

3-13   CA.II.D.K6d, e

Which is true regarding runway incursions?

A – To help prevent a runway incursion during periods of reduced visibility or at night use your exterior taxi/landing lights when practical.

B – A runway incursion is defined as any occurrence at an airport involving an aircraft, vehicle, person, or object on the ground that results in a collision.

C – Runway incursions are primarily caused by controller errors.

3-13. Answer A. GFDIC 3A, AFH

The official definition of a runway incursion is "any occurrence at an airport involving an aircraft, vehicle, person, or object on the ground that creates a collision hazard or results in loss of separation with an aircraft taking off or intending to take off, landing, or intending to land."

Runway incursions are primarily caused by errors associated with clearances, communication, airport surface movement, and positional awareness.

In addition to other actions you can take to prevent runway incursion, to help others see your airplane during periods of reduced visibility or at night, use your exterior taxi/landing lights when practical.

3-14   CA.III.A.K2

Which is a proper communication procedure to help prevent a runway incursion?

A – To prevent frequency congestion and to properly monitor the radio for other aircraft, do not read ATC clearances back in full during ground operations.

B – After landing at a controlled airport, immediately switch to the ground control frequency after you are clear of the runway.

C – Read back (in full) all active runway crossing, hold short, or line up and wait clearances.

3-14. Answer C. GFDIC 3A, AFH

Actions to help prevent a runway incursion include but are not limited to:

- Review the airport diagram and complete as many checklist items as possible before taxi.

- Read back (in full) all active runway crossing, hold short, or line up and wait clearances.

- Do not become absorbed in other tasks, or conversation, while your airplane is moving.

- If unsure of your position on the airport, stop and ask for assistance.

- Monitor the radio to listen for other aircraft cleared onto your runway for takeoff or landing.

- After landing, stay on the tower frequency until instructed to change frequencies.

- To help others see your airplane during periods of reduced visibility or at night, use your exterior taxi/landing lights when practical.

3-15   CA.IV.B.R3b*

A land and hold short (LAHSO) clearance

A – precludes a "Go Around" by ATC.

B – does not preclude a rejected landing.

C – requires a runway exit at the first taxiway.

3-15. Answer B. GFDIC 3A, AIM

After accepting a LAHSO clearance, you must adhere to that clearance unless you obtain an amended clearance or an emergency occurs. A LAHSO clearance does not preclude ATC from telling you to go around; that is an amended clearance. It also does not preclude you from a rejected landing, but because of the obvious hazard of going around when ATC expects you to hold short of another runway or taxiway, it is essential that you tell them immediately and take precautions to avoid collisions with conflicting traffic.

SECTION A ■ Airports, Airspace, and Flight Information

3-16   CA.IV.B.R3b*

Who has the final authority to accept or decline any land and hold short (LAHSO) clearance?

A – Pilot-in-command.

B – ATC tower controller.

C – ATC approach controller.

3-16. Answer A. GFDIC 3A, AIM

The pilot-in-command (PIC) of an aircraft has the final authority to accept or decline any LAHSO clearance. If the PIC elects to decline the clearance, ATC must be notified as soon as possible.

3-17   CA.IV.B.R3b*

When should you decline a land and hold short (LAHSO) clearance?

A – When it will compromise safety.

B – If runway surface is contaminated.

C – Only when the tower controller concurs.

3-17. Answer A. GFDIC 3A, AIM

The pilot-in-command (PIC) of an aircraft has the final authority to accept or decline a LAHSO clearance. If you determine that the LAHSO can compromise safety in any way, you should advise ATC that you are "unable" to accept the clearance.

3-18   CA.IV.B.R3b*

What is the minimum visibility and ceiling required for a pilot to receive a land and hold short clearance?

A – 3 statute miles and 1,500 feet.

B – 3 nautical miles and 1,000 feet.

C – 3 statute miles and 1,000 feet.

3-18. Answer C. GFDIC 3A, AIM

Pilots should only receive a LAHSO clearance when there is a minimum ceiling of 1,000 feet and 3 statute miles visibility. The intent of having "basic" VFR weather conditions is to allow pilots to maintain visual contact with other aircraft and ground vehicle operations.

3-19   CA.IV.B.R3b*

Once a pilot-in-command accepts a land and hold short (LAHSO) clearance, the clearance must be adhered to, just as any other ATC clearance, unless

A – an amended clearance is obtained or an emergency occurs.

B – the wind changes or available landing distance decreases.

C – Available landing distance decreases or density altitude increases.

3-19. Answer A. GFDIC 3A, AIM

Once you accept a LAHSO clearance, you must adhere to it, just as you would any other ATC clearance, unless you obtain an amended clearance or an emergency occurs. A LAHSO clearance does not preclude a rejected landing.

3-20   CA.IV.B.R3b*

What should you expect when you are told that LAHSO operations are in effect at your destination airport?

A – All aircraft must operate on an IFR clearance due to high traffic volume.

B – ATC may offer a clearance to land and hold short of a specified point on the runway.

C – Delays due to low IFR conditions and high traffic volume.

3-20. Answer B. GFDIC 3A, AIM

During land and hold short operations (LAHSO), an aircraft is cleared to land and stop on the runway, holding short of an intersecting runway, intersecting taxiway, or some other designated point on the runway. LAHSO is an air traffic control tool that is used at selected airports to increase airport capacity and maintain system efficiency.

3-21   CA.III.B.K1, S1

Light beacons producing red flashes indicate

A – an end of runway warning at the departure end.

B – a pilot should remain clear of an airport traffic pattern and continue circling.

C – obstructions or areas considered hazardous to aerial navigation.

3-21. Answer C. GFDIC 3A, AIM

Obstruction lights are installed on prominent structures such as towers, buildings, and sometimes power lines. Flashing red lights or high intensity strobe lights warn you of the obstructions.

End of runway warning lights at some airports are steady red, while a flashing red light from a control tower indicates that an airport is unsafe-do not land.

3-22   CA.II.D.K3

The middle and far bars of a 3-bar VASI will

A – both appear white to the pilot when on the upper glide path.

B – constitute a 2-bar VASI for using the lower glide path.

C – constitute a 2-bar VASI for using the upper glide path.

3-22. Answer C. GFDIC 3A, AIM

Pilots of high-cockpit aircraft use the middle and far bars of a 3-bar VASI to fly the upper glide path. In effect, these two bars constitute a 2-bar VASI for the upper glide path.

3-23   CA.II.D.K3

The operation of an airport rotating beacon during daylight hours may indicate that

A – the in-flight visibility is less than 3 miles and the ceiling is less than 1,500 feet within Class E airspace.

B – the ground visibility is less than 3 miles and/or the ceiling is less than 1,000 feet in Class B, C, or D airspace.

C – an IFR clearance is required to operate within the airport traffic area.

3-23. Answer B. GFDIC 3A, AIM

Operation of the beacon during daylight hours at an airport within controlled airspace (Class B, C, D, and E surface areas) often indicates that the ground visibility is less than 3 statute miles and/or the ceiling is less than 1,000 feet. However, because beacons are often turned on by photoelectric cells or time clocks, you must not rely on the airport beacon to indicate that the weather is below VFR minimums.

SECTION A ■ **Airports, Airspace, and Flight Information**

3-24   CA.II.D.K3

Which type of runway lighting consists of a pair of synchronized flashing lights, one on each side of the runway threshold?

A – MALSR.

B – HIRL.

C – REIL.

3-24. Answer C. GFDIC 3A, AIM

High intensity white strobe lights on each side of the runway threshold called runway end identifier lights (REIL) help you see the runway threshold in reduced visibility or identify the threshold of a runway that is surrounded by a preponderance of other lighting or one that lacks contrast with surrounding terrain.

3-25   CA.III.A.K9

What is a fully automated system that provides information to pilots and surface vehicle operators to clearly indicate when it is unsafe to enter, cross, takeoff from, or land on a runway?

A – Runway status light system.

B – Runway edge lights.

C – Threshold lights.

3-25. Answer A. GFDIC 3A, AIM

The runway status light system (RWSL) is a fully automated system that provides runway status information to pilots and surface vehicle operators to clearly indicate when it is unsafe to enter, cross, takeoff from, or land on a runway. Runway status lights are designed to reduce the number and severity of runway incursions.

Runway edge lights are used to outline the runway during periods of darkness or restricted visibility. Threshold lights, which form a line across the runway perpendicular to the centerline, mark the ends of the each runway.

3-26   CA.II.D.K5

During a night operation, the pilot of aircraft #1 sees only the green light of aircraft #2. If the aircraft are converging, which pilot has the right-of-way? The pilot of aircraft

A – #2; aircraft #2 is to the left of aircraft #1.

B – #2; aircraft #2 is to the right of aircraft #1.

C – #1; aircraft #1 is to the right of aircraft #2.

3-26. Answer C. GFDIC 3A, FAR 91.113

The approved aircraft position lights for night operations are a green light on the right wingtip, a red light wingtip, and a white light on the tail. If aircraft #1 sees only the green light of aircraft #2, the pilot would be looking at aircraft #2's right wingtip. Aircraft #1 has the right-of-way because it is to the right of aircraft #2.

3-27   CA.III.B.K1

When approaching to land at an airport without an operating control tower, in Class G airspace, you should

A – fly a left-hand traffic pattern at 800 feet AGL.

B – enter and fly a traffic pattern at 800 feet AGL.

C – make all turns to the left, unless otherwise indicated.

3-27. Answer C. GFDIC 3A, FAR 91.126

You must make all turns to the left unless the airport displays approved light signals or visual markings indicating that turns should be made to the right, in which case right turns are mandatory.

3-28   CA.I.E.K1, CA.III.A.K4

In the 48 contiguous states, excluding the airspace at or below 2,500 feet AGL, an operating transponder with Mode C capability and ADS-B Out equipment is required in all controlled airspace at and above

A – 12,500 feet MSL.

B – 10,000 feet MSL.

C – Flight level (FL) 180.

3-28. Answer B. GFDIC 3A, FAR 91.215, 91.225
The FARs require that you have an operating transponder with Mode C capability and ADS-B Out equipment at or above 10,000 feet MSL (except at or below 2,500 feet AGL) even in uncontrolled airspace, over the 48 contiguous states.

3-29   CA.I.E.K1

ADS-B Out equipment is required in all airspace

A – at and above 10,000 feet MSL, excluding at and below 2,500 feet AGL.

B – at and above 2,500 feet above the surface.

C – below 10,000 feet MSL, excluding at and below 2,500 feet AGL.

3-29. Answer A. GFDIC 3A, FAR 91.215, 91.225
The FARs require that you have an operating transponder with Mode C capability and ADS-B Out equipment at or above 10,000 feet MSL (except at or below 2,500 feet AGL) even in uncontrolled airspace, over the 48 contiguous states.

3-30   CA.I.E.K1, CA.III.A.K4

An operating transponder with Mode C capability and ADS-B Out equipment is required

A – below 10,000 feet MSL, excluding at and below 2,500 feet AGL.

B – in Class A airspace, in Class B airspace, within 30 nautical miles of Class B primary airports, and in and above Class C airspace.

C – in Class A airspace and within 30 nautical miles of Class B and Class C primary airports.

3-30. Answer B. GFDIC 3A, FAR 91.215, 91.225
The FARs require that you have an operating transponder with Mode C capability and ADS-B Out equipment in Class A airspace, in Class B airspace, within 30 nautical miles of Class B primary airports, and in and above Class C airspace.

You also must have a transponder with Mode C capability and ADS-B Out equipment at or above 10,000 feet MSL (except at or below 2,500 feet AGL) over the 48 contiguous states.

3-31   CA.I.E.K1

Unless otherwise authorized by ATC, which airspace requires the appropriate ADS-B Out equipment installed?

A – Within Class E airspace below the upper shelf of Class C Airspace.

B – Above the ceiling and within the lateral boundaries of Class D airspace up to 10,000 feet MSL.

C – Within Class G airspace 25 nautical miles from a Class B airport.

3-31. Answer C. GFDIC 3A, FAR 91.215, 91.225
The FARs require that you have an operating transponder with Mode C capability and ADS-B Out equipment in Class A airspace, in Class B airspace, within 30 nautical miles of Class B primary airports, and in and above Class C airspace.

You also must have a transponder with Mode C capability and ADS-B Out equipment at or above 10,000 feet MSL (except at or below 2,500 feet AGL) over the 48 contiguous states.

SECTION A ■ **Airports, Airspace, and Flight Information**

3-32   CA.I.E.K1, CA.III.A.K2, 4, 7

If the aircraft's transponder or ADS-B out equipment fails during flight within Class B airspace,

A – you should immediately request clearance to depart the Class B airspace.

B – ATC may authorize deviation from the transponder requirement to allow you to continue to the airport of ultimate destination.

C – you must immediately descend to 1,200 feet AGL and proceed to your destination.

3-32. Answer B. GFDIC 3A, FAR 91.215, 91.225

If your transponder or ADS-B Out fails while you are operating in airspace that requires this equipment, ATC may authorize you to continue to your destination, including any intermediate stops, or to proceed to a place where repairs can be made.

3-33   CA.I.E.K1

Your VFR flight will be conducted above 10,000 MSL in Class E airspace. What is the minimum flight visibility?

A – 3 NM.

B – 5 SM.

C – 1 SM.

3-33. Answer B. GFDIC 3A, FAR 91.155

When flying in Class E airspace above 10,000 feet MSL, visibility must be at least 5 statute miles and the aircraft must maintain at least 1,000 feet below, 1,000 feet above, and 1 statute mile horizontal cloud separation.

3-34   CA.I.E.K1, CA.I.E.S1

The minimum flight visibility for VFR flight in Class E airspace increases to 5 statute miles beginning at an altitude of

A – 14,500 feet MSL.

B – 10,000 feet MSL if above 1,200 feet AGL.

C – 10,000 feet MSL regardless of height above ground.

3-34. Answer C. GFDIC 3A, FAR 91.155

When flying in Class E airspace above 10,000 feet MSL, visibility must be at least 5 statute miles and the aircraft must maintain at least 1,000 feet below, 1,000 feet above, and 1 statute mile horizontal cloud separation. In Class G airspace, these minimums apply only if you are at or above 10,000 feet MSL and above 1,200 feet AGL.

3-35   CA.I.E.K1, CA.I.E.S1

What is the minimum flight visibility and proximity to cloud requirements for VFR flight, at 6,500 feet MSL, in Class C, D, and E airspace?

A – 1 mile visibility; clear of clouds.

B – 3 miles visibility; 1,000 feet above and 500 feet below.

C – 5 miles visibility; 1,000 feet above and 1,000 feet below.

3-35. Answer B. GFDIC 3A, FAR 91.155

When flying in Class C, Class D, or Class E airspace below 10,000 feet MSL, visibility must be at least 3 statute miles and the aircraft must maintain at least 1,000 feet above, 500 feet below, and 2,000 feet horizontal cloud separation.

3-36   CA.I.E.K1

When operating an aircraft in the vicinity of an airport with an operating control tower, in Class E airspace, you must establish communication prior to

A – 8 NM, and up to and including 3,000 feet AGL.

B – 5 NM, and up to and including 3,000 feet AGL.

C – 4 NM, and up to and including 2,500 feet AGL.

3-36. Answer C. GFDIC 3A, FAR 91.127
Sometimes, control towers are established in Class E airspace. These control towers might exist on a temporary basis to manage traffic for a special event at the airport. You must establish communication prior to 4 nautical miles from the airport, up to and including 2,500 feet AGL.

3-37   CA.I.E.K1

Excluding Hawaii, the vertical limits of the Federal Low Altitude airways extend from

A – 700 feet AGL up to, but not including, 14,500 feet MSL.

B – 1,200 feet AGL up to, but not including, 18,000 feet MSL.

C – 1,200 feet AGL up to, but not including, 14,500 feet MSL.

3-37. Answer B. GFDIC 3A, AIM
Federal airways, or Victor airways, are based on VOR or VORTAC navaids and are identified by a V and the airway number. Airways are normally 8 nautical miles wide, begin at 1,200 feet AGL, and extend up to, but not including, 18,000 feet MSL.

3-38   CA.I.E.K1, 2

When a dashed blue circle surrounds an airport on a sectional aeronautical chart, it will depict the boundary of

A – Special VFR airspace.

B – Class B airspace

C – Class D airspace.

3-38. Answer C. GFDIC 3A, AIM
Class D airspace can be various sizes and shapes, depending on the instrument approach procedures established for that airport. Most Class D airspace is a circle with a radius of approximately 4 NM extending up to 2,500 feet AGL.

On VFR charts, Class D boundaries are indicated by a blue dashed line and the upper limit altitude is shown in hundreds of feet MSL inside a blue dashed box.

3-39   CA.I.E.K1, CA.II.D.K6b

When approaching to land at an airport with an ATC facility, in Class D airspace, you must establish communications prior to

A – 10 NM, up to and including 3,000 feet AGL.

B – 30 SM, and be transponder equipped.

C – 4 NM, up to and including 2,500 feet AGL.

3-39. Answer C. GFDIC 3A, FAR 91.129
Although Class D airspace can be various sizes and shapes, depending on the instrument approach procedures established for that airport, most Class D airspace is a circle with a radius of approximately 4 NM extending up to 2,500 feet AGL.

You must establish two-way radio communication with the tower prior to entering Class D airspace and maintain radio contact during all operations to, from, or on that airport. A transponder is not required in Class D airspace.

SECTION A ■ Airports, Airspace, and Flight Information

3-40   CA.I.E.K1

What designated airspace associated with an airport becomes inactive when the control tower at that airport is not in operation?

A – Class D, which then becomes Class C.

B – Class D, which then becomes Class E.

C – Class B.

3-40. Answer B. GFDIC 3A, AIM

The airspace at an airport with a part-time control tower is designated as Class D only when the tower is in operation. At airports where the tower operates part time, the airspace changes to Class E, or a combination of Class E and Class G when the tower is closed.

3-41   CA.I.E.K1

The radius of the uncharted outer area of Class C airspace is normally

A – 20 NM.

B – 30 NM.

C – 40 NM.

3-41. Answer A. GFDIC 3A, AIM

Class C areas usually have similar dimensions from one location to another:

- A 5 nautical mile radius core area extends from the surface to 4,000 feet above the elevation of the primary airport.

- A 10 nautical mile radius shelf area usually extends from 1,200 feet to 4,000 feet above the airport elevation.

- An outer area, where Class C services are available but not mandatory, normally extends out to 20 nautical miles from the primary airport.

3-42   CA.I.E.K1, CA.III.A.K2, 4, 7

Which is true regarding flight operations from a satellite airport, without an operating control tower, within the Class C airspace area?

A – You must receive a takeoff clearance from the ATC facility having jurisdiction over the Class C airspace area.

B – Your aircraft must be equipped with a transponder with Mode C capability and ADS-B Out equipment.

C – Prior to takeoff, you must establish communication with the ATC facility having jurisdiction over the Class C airspace area.

3-42. Answer B. GFDIC 3A, FAR 91.130

In addition to a two-way radio communication requirement, all aircraft operating in a Class C area and in all airspace above it must be equipped with a transponder with a Mode C transponder and ADS-B Out equipment.

When departing from a satellite airport without an operating control tower, you must establish and maintain two-way radio communications with the ATC facility having jurisdiction over the Class C airspace area as soon as practicable after departing.

3-43   CA.I.E.K1, CA.III.A.K2, 7

You would like to enter Class B airspace and contact the approach controller. The controller responds to your initial radio call with "N125HF standby." May you enter the Class B airspace?

A – You must remain outside Class B airspace until the controller gives you a specific clearance.

B – You may continue into the Class B airspace and wait for further instructions.

C – You may continue into the Class B airspace without a specific clearance, if the aircraft is ADS-B equipped.

3-43. Answer A. GFDIC 3A, FAR 91.131

You must be at least a private pilot, or a student pilot with the appropriate endorsement, and must receive an ATC clearance before you enter Class B airspace.

3-44   CA.I.E.K1, CA.III.A.K4

Equipment requirements for operating within Class B airspace include

A – a transponder with Mode C capability and ADS-B Out equipment.

B – an RNAV system and a transponder with Mode C capability.

C – a two-way radio and ADS-B In equipment.

3-44. Answer A. GFDIC 3A, FAR 91.215

Equipment requirements to fly in Class B airspace include:

- Transponder with Mode C capability and ADS-B Out equipment within 30 nautical miles of the Class B area's primary airport from the surface to 10,000 feet MSL.

- For all operations, two-way radio capable of communications with ATC on appropriate frequencies for that Class B airspace area.

- For IFR operation, a VOR or TACAN receiver or a suitable RNAV system.

3-45   CA.I.E.K1, CA.III.A.K2, 7

Which is true regarding flight operations in Class B airspace?

A – You must receive an ATC clearance before operating an aircraft in that area.

B – Solo student pilot operations are not authorized.

C – Flight under VFR is not authorized unless you are instrument rated.

3-45. Answer A. GFDIC 3A, FAR 91.131

You must be at least a private pilot, or a student pilot with the appropriate endorsement, and must receive an ATC clearance before you enter Class B airspace.

SECTION A ■ **Airports, Airspace, and Flight Information**

3-46   CA.I.E.K1

Which is true regarding pilot certification requirements for operations in Class B airspace?

A – You must hold at least a private pilot certificate with an instrument rating.

B – You must hold at least a private pilot certificate.

C – Solo student pilot operations are not authorized.

3-46. Answer B. GFDIC 3A, FAR 91.131

You must be at least a private pilot, or a student pilot with the appropriate endorsement, and must receive an ATC clearance before you enter Class B airspace.

3-47   CA.I.E.K1, CA.III.A.K4

Which is equipment required to operate in Class A airspace?

A – DME or a suitable RNAV system.

B – ADS-B In equipment.

C – ADS-B Out/Transponder with Mode C capability.

3-47. Answer C. GFDIC 3A, FAR 91.135

Aircraft equipment requirements for Class A airspace are:

- Instruments and equipment required by 91.205 for IFR operations.
- ADS-B Out/Mode C transponder capability.
- At or above 24,000 feet MSL (FL240), when VOR equipment is required for navigation, distance measuring equipment (DME) or a suitable RNAV system.

3-48   CA.I.E.K1

To operate in Class A airspace, you must

A – use the altimeter setting provided by ATC.

B – be instrument rated and current for instrument flight.

C – file and activate a VFR flight plan.

3-48. Answer B. GFDIC 3A, FAR 91.135

To operate within Class A airspace:

- You must be instrument rated and current for instrument flight.
- You must operate under an IFR flight plan and in accordance with an ATC clearance at specified flight levels.
- You are required to set your altimeter to the standard setting of 29.92 inches Hg.

3-49   CA.I.E.K1

At some airports located in Class D airspace where ground visibility is not reported, takeoffs and landings under special VFR are

A – not authorized.

B – authorized by ATC if the flight visibility is at least 1 SM.

C – authorized only if the ground visibility is observed to be at least 3 SM.

3-49. Answer B. GFDIC 3A, FAR 91.157

A special VFR clearance allows you to enter, leave, or operate within most Class D and Class E surface areas and in some Class B and Class C surface areas if the flight visibility is at least 1 statute mile and you can remain clear of clouds. At least 1 statute mile of ground visibility is required for takeoff and landing. However, if ground visibility is not reported, you must have at least 1 statute mile flight visibility.

3-50   CA.I.E.K1

When operating an airplane for the purpose of takeoff or landing within Class D airspace under special VFR, what minimum distance from clouds and what visibility are required?

A – Remain clear of clouds, and the ground visibility must be at least 1 SM.

B – 500 feet beneath clouds, and the ground visibility must be at least 1 SM.

C – Remain clear of clouds, and the flight visibility must be at least 1 NM.

3-50. Answer A. GFDIC 3A, FAR 91.157
A special VFR clearance allows you to enter, leave, or operate within most Class D and Class E surface areas and in some Class B and Class C surface areas if the flight visibility is at least 1 statute mile and you can remain clear of clouds. At least 1 statute mile of ground visibility is required for takeoff and landing. However, if ground visibility is not reported, you must have at least 1 statute mile flight visibility.

3-51   CA.I.E.K1

To operate an airplane under special VFR within Class D airspace at night, which is required?

A – The Class D airspace must be specifically designated as a night SVFR area.

B – You must hold an instrument rating, but the airplane need not be equipped for instrument flight, as long as the weather will remain at or above SVFR minimums.

C – You must hold an instrument rating, and the airplane must be equipped for instrument flight.

3-51. Answer C. GFDIC 3A, FAR 91.157
Special VFR is not permitted between sunset and sunrise unless you have a current instrument rating and the aircraft is equipped for instrument flight.

3-52   CA.I.E.K1

What is the maximum indicated airspeed authorized in the airspace underlying Class B airspace?

A – 156 knots.

B – 200 knots.

C – 230 knots.

3-52. Answer B. GFDIC 3A, FAR 91.117
Maximum airspeeds designated by the FARs include:

- 250 KIAS—flights below 10,000 feet MSL.

- 200 KIAS—in Class C or D airspace, at or below 2,500 feet above the surface, and within 4 nautical miles of the primary airport.

- 200 KIAS—in airspace underlying a Class B area and in VFR corridors through Class B airspace.

3-53   CA.I.E.K1

Unless otherwise authorized or required by ATC, the maximum indicated airspeed permitted when at or below 2,500 feet AGL within 4 NM of the primary airport within Class C or D airspace is

A – 200 knots.

B – 180 knots.

C – 230 knots.

3-53. Answer A. GFDIC 3A, FAR 91.117
Maximum airspeeds designated by the FARs include:

- 250 KIAS—flights below 10,000 feet MSL.

- 200 KIAS—in Class C or D airspace, at or below 2,500 feet above the surface, and within 4 nautical miles of the primary airport.

- 200 KIAS—in airspace underlying a Class B area and in VFR corridors through Class B airspace.

SECTION A ■ **Airports, Airspace, and Flight Information**

3-54   CA.I.E.K3

What must you do or be aware of when transitioning through an alert area?

A – You must contact the controlling agency to ensure aircraft separation.

B – Non-participating aircraft may transit the area as long as they operate in accordance with their waiver.

C – Be aware that the area may contain unusual aeronautical activity or high volume of pilot training.

3-54. Answer C. GFDIC 3A, AIM

Alert areas contain unusual types of aerial activities, such as parachute jumping and glider towing, or high concentrations of student pilot training. You do not need to obtain permission to enter an alert area. Pilots of participating aircraft and pilots transiting the area are equally responsible for collision avoidance, so you should be especially cautious when flying through alert areas.

3-55   CA.I.E.K3

What is an activity that can cause an alert area to be established?

A – Military training.

B – Aerial gunnery.

C – Glider towing.

3-55. Answer C. GFDIC 3A, AIM

Examples of special use airspace include:

- Alert areas, which contain unusual types of aerial activities, such as parachute jumping and glider towing, or high concentrations of student pilot training.

- Military operations areas (MOA) in which military operations are conducted.

- Restricted areas, which often have invisible hazards to aircraft, such as artillery firing, aerial gunnery, or guided missiles.

3-56   CA.I.E.K3

You must obtain permission to fly under VFR through which special use airspace area?

A – Military operations area (MOA).

B – Restricted area.

C – Warning area.

3-56. Answer B. GFDIC 3A, AIM

Examples of special use airspace include:

- Restricted areas, which often have invisible hazards to aircraft, such as artillery firing, aerial gunnery, or guided missiles. Permission to fly through restricted areas must be granted by the controlling agency.

- Military operations areas (MOAs) in which military operations are conducted. VFR aircraft are not prevented from flying through active MOAs, but it is wise to avoid them when possible.

- Warning areas, which extend from three nautical miles outward from the coast of the United States, are depicted on charts to warn of activities that may be hazardous to nonparticipating aircraft.

3-57   CA.I.E.K3

Which is a characteristic of a military training route (MTR)?

A – Established for operations at speeds in excess of 200 knots.

B – Identified by a four-digit number if the operations occur above 1,500 feet AGL.

C – Classified as VR or IR.

3-57. Answer C. GFDIC 3A, AIM

Military training routes (MTRs) are established below 10,000 feet MSL for operations at speeds in excess of 250 knots. MTRs are classified as VR for VFR operations and IR for IFR operations. MTRs that are entirely at or below 1,500 feet AGL are identified by four-digit numbers, and those that have one or more segments above 1,500 feet AGL use three-digit numbers.

3-58   CA.I.E.K3

What is true regarding temporary flight restrictions (TFRs)?

A – TFRs are issued to designate special use airspace as an interim step between publication cycles of aeronautical charts.

B – NOTAMs specify the dimensions, restrictions, and effective times of TFRs.

C – The standard dimension of a TFR is a 10 NM mile ring that extends to 18,000 feet MSL.

3-58. Answer B. GFDIC 3A, AIM

Types of TFRs include those that address disasters and hazards, space flight operations, VIP movement, emergency air traffic rules, air shows and sporting events on a case-by-case basis, and major sporting events. TFRs are issued in NOTAMs that specify the dimensions, restrictions, and effective times.

3-59   CA.I.E.K3

What is a characteristic of the Washington DC Special Flight Rules Area (SFRA)?

A – Consists of the airspace within a 30 NM radius of the Washington DC VOR from the surface up to 10,000 feet MSL.

B – Includes a flight restricted zone (FRZ) within which all flight operations are prohibited.

C – Requires that you complete an FAA course prior to flying within 60 NM of the Washington DC VOR.

3-59. Answer C. GFDIC 3A, AIM

The Washington DC Special Flight Rules Area (SFRA) includes all airspace within a 30 nautical mile radius of the Washington DC VOR (DCA) from the surface up to but not including FL180. Flight under VFR and general aviation aircraft operations are prohibited in the flight restricted zone (FRZ) of the SFRA—a ring of airspace within 13 to 15 nautical miles of the Washington DC VOR.

If you are planning to fly under VFR within 60 nautical miles of the Washington DC VOR, you must complete the FAA Special Awareness Training course at faasafety.gov.

3-60   CA.II.D.K1, CA.II.D.K6a, e

You are preflight planning in the morning before an afternoon flight. Where would you find information regarding an "airport surface hot spot?"

A – Call Flight Service.

B – In the Chart Supplements U.S.

C – In the NOTAM's during your preflight briefing.

3-60. Answer B. GFDIC 3A, Chart Supplement

Chart Supplements include data that cannot be readily depicted in graphic form on charts. Each Chart Supplement contains five primary sections: Airport/Facility Directory Legend; Airport/Facility Directory; Notices; Associated Data; and Airport Diagrams. The Airport Diagrams section contains diagrams of most towered airports and other selected nontowered airports and runway incursion hot spot information.

SECTION A ■ **Airports, Airspace, and Flight Information**

3-61   CA.II.D.K1

What is the purpose of FDC NOTAMs?

A – To provide the latest information on the status of navigation facilities to all Flight Service facilities for scheduled broadcasts.

B – To issue notices for all airports and navigation facilities in the shortest possible time.

C – To advise of changes in flight data which affect instrument approach procedure (IAP), aeronautical charts, and flight restrictions prior to normal publication.

3-61. Answer C. GFDIC 3A, AIM

Notices to Airmen (NOTAMs) provide time-critical flight planning information regarding a facility, service, procedure, or hazard that is temporary or not known far enough in advance to be included in the most recent aeronautical charts or Chart Supplements.

FDC NOTAMs are issued by the National Flight Data Center and contain regulatory information. For example, FDC NOTAMs may advise of changes in flight data which affect instrument approach procedures (IAP), aeronautical charts, and flight restrictions prior to normal publication.

3-62   CA.III.A.K8

Which publication covers the procedures required for aircraft accident and incident reporting responsibilities for pilots?

A – FAR Part 61.

B – FAR Part 91.

C – NTSB Part 830.

3-62. Answer C. GFDIC 3A, NTSB 830

NTSB 830 contains rules pertaining to the notification and reporting of aircraft accidents and incidents. For example, if an aircraft is involved in an accident that results in substantial damage to the aircraft, the nearest NTSB field office must be notified immediately.

In addition, NTSB 830 also explains the requirements for the preservation of aircraft wreckage, mail, cargo, and records involving all civil aircraft in the United Sates.

3-63   CA.I.E.K1, 2

(Refer to Figure 52, area 1.) The floor of the Class E airspace above Georgetown Airport (Q61) is at

A – 3,823 feet MSL.

B – the surface.

C – 700 feet AGL.

3-63. Answer A. GFDIC 3A, Chart Legend

Class E airspace begins at 1,200 feet AGL on the hard side of the magenta band (where Georgetown Airport is located) and at 700 feet AGL on the soft side of the magenta band. The airport elevation is 2,623 feet MSL (2,623 + 1,200 = 3,823 feet MSL).

3-64   CA.I.E.K1, 2

(Refer to Figure 52, areas 2 and 3.) Which airports are located in Class E airspace?

A – McClellan and Rio Linda.

B – Sacramento Executive and McClellen.

C – Rio Linda and Van Dyke.

3-64. Answer A. GFDIC 3A, Chart Legend

Class E airspace begins at the surface within the dashed magenta line surrounding McClellen and Rio Linda Airports. The outer shelf area of the Class C surrounding Sacramento International Airport starts at 1,600 feet MSL so is above these two airports.

Sacramento Executive Airport is located in Class D airspace as indicated by the dashed blue circle. Van Dyke Airport is located on the soft side of the magenta band, which means that Class E airspace begins at 700 feet AGL.

3-65   CA.I.E.K1

(Refer to Figure 52, area 2.) When departing from Rio Linda (L36) Airport to the northwest at an altitude of 1,000 feet AGL, you

A – must make contact with McClellan (MCC) control tower as soon as practical after takeoff.

B – are not required to contact any ATC facilities if you do not enter the Class C Airspace.

C – must make contact with the Sacramento International (SMF) control tower immediately after takeoff.

3-65. Answer B. GFDIC 3A, Chart Legend, AIM

Rio Linda airport is located in Class E airspace below the floor of the 10 nautical mile radius shelf area of the Class C airspace designated for Sacramento International Airport. In this area, the ceiling of the Class C airspace is 4,100 feet MSL and the floor is 1,600 feet MSL as indicated by magenta numbers 41/16.

The elevation of Rio Linda is 46 feet MSL. At 1,000 feet AGL, your aircraft is at 1,046 feet MSL, which is below the floor of the Class C airspace. As long as you stay at this altitude and do not enter the 5 nautical mile radius area where the Class C airspace extends to the surface (41/SFC), you are not required to contact ATC. Nearby McClellan Airport (shown in magenta) does not have a control tower.

3-66   CA.I.E.K2, CA.VI.A.K3

(Refer to Figure 52, area 4) What is true regarding the obstructions south of Lincoln Regional Airport (LHM)?

A – The obstructions are lighted.

B – The height of the single obstruction is 406 feet MSL.

C – The height of the multiple obstructions is 472 feet AGL.

3-66. Answer B. GFDIC 3A, Chart Legend

The MSL height of the obstruction is listed first followed by the AGL height in parentheses. The height of the single obstruction is 406 feet MSL (296 feet AGL). The height of the multiple obstructions is 472 feet MSL (339 feet AGL). None of the obstructions are depicted with the symbol for lighting that appears in the chart legend.

3-67   CA.I.E.K2, CA.VI.A.K3

(Refer to Figure 52, area 4.) The terrain at the obstruction approximately 8 NM east southeast of the Lincoln Airport is approximately how much higher than the airport elevation?

A – 176 feet.

B – 827 feet.

C – 1,124 feet.

3-67. Answer B. GFDIC 3A, Chart Legend

The obstruction height is 1,245 feet MSL. Subtract the obstruction's AGL height (297 feet) from the MSL height to determine the MSL elevation of the terrain (1245 - 297 = 948). The difference between this elevation and the airport elevation is 827 feet (948 - 121 = 827).

3-68   CA.I.E.K1, 2

(Refer to Figure 52, area 5.) The floor of the Class E airspace over University Airport (EDU) is

A – the surface.

B – 700 feet AGL.

C – 1,200 feet AGL.

3-68. Answer B. GFDIC 3A, AIM

Class E airspace begins at 1,200 feet AGL on the hard side of the magenta band and at 700 feet AGL on the soft side of the magenta band (where University Airport is located).

SECTION A ■ Airports, Airspace, and Flight Information

3-69   CA.I.E.K1, 2

(Refer to Figure 52, area 6.) What is true about the airspace surrounding the airports in the area?

A – The ceiling of the Class D airspace surrounding Sacramento Mather Airport is 2,600 feet AGL.

B – Class E airspace over Rancho Murieta Airport begins at the surface.

C – When Sacramento Mather Tower is not operating, the airspace surrounding the airport is Class G with Class E beginning at 700 feet AGL.

3-69. Answer C. GFDIC 3A, Chart Legend
Sacramento Mather Airport is in Class D airspace as indicated by the dashed blue circle. The ceiling of the class D is 2,600 feet MSL as shown in the blue dashed square.

The star next to the control tower frequency indicates the tower operates part-time. The airspace at an airport with a part-time control tower is designated as Class D only when the tower is in operation—the airspace changes to Class E (beginning at 700 ft. AGL), or a combination of Class E and Class G, when the tower is closed.

3-70   CA.I.E.K1, 2

(Refer to Figure 52, area 7.) The floor of Class E airspace over the town of Woodland is

A – 700 feet AGL over part of the town and no floor over the remainder.

B – 1,200 feet AGL over part of the town and no floor over the remainder.

C – both 700 feet and 1,200 feet AGL.

3-70. Answer C. GFDIC 3A, Chart Legend, AIM
Class E airspace begins at 1,200 feet AGL on the hard side of the magenta band and at 700 feet AGL on the soft side of the magenta band. The town of Woodland is located in an area where the Class E floor transitions from 700 feet AGL to 1,200 feet AGL.

3-71   CA.I.E.K1, 2

(Refer to Figure 52, area 8). The traffic pattern altitude at the Auburn (AUN) Airport is 1,000 feet AGL. May you practice landings under VFR when the AWOS is reporting a ground visibility of 2 miles?

A – Yes, you will be operating in a combination of Class E and G airspace.

B – No, the reported ground visibility must be at least 3 miles.

C – No, the Class E airspace extends to the airport surface.

3-71. Answer A. GFDIC 3A, Chart Legend, 91.155
Class E airspace begins at 700 feet AGL on the soft side of the magenta band where Auburn Airport is located. At 1,000 feet AGL, you will be in Class E airspace where you must maintain the minimum visibility and cloud clearance requirements below 10,000 feet MSL, which are 3 statute miles flight visibility and 500 feet below, 1,000 feet above, and 2,000 horizontal from clouds.

Below 700 feet, you are operating in Class G airspace, where you must maintain 1 statute mile visibility and remain clear of clouds. The ground visibility is reported as 2 statute miles. You meet the basic VFR minimums specified by FAR 91.155. If you can maintain 1 statute mile visibility below 700 feet AGL (in Class G) and 3 statute miles visibility above 700 feet AGL (Class E) and meet the cloud clearance requirements.

3-72   CA.I.E.K1, 2
(Refer to Figure 52, area 8.) The floor of the Class E airspace over the town of Auburn is

A – 1,200 feet MSL.

B – 1,200 feet AGL.

C – 700 feet AGL.

3-72. Answer C. GFDIC 3A, Chart Legend
Class E airspace begins at 1,200 feet AGL on the hard side of the magenta band and at 700 feet AGL on the soft side of the magenta band. The town of Auburn is located on the soft side of the magenta band.

3-73   CA.I.D.K1, CA.I.E.K3
(Refer to Figure 52 area 9.) The alert area depicted within the magenta hash marks is an area in which

A – there is a high volume of pilot training activities or an unusual type of aerial activity.

B – the flight of aircraft is prohibited.

C – the flight of aircraft, while not prohibited, is subject to restriction.

3-73. Answer A. GFDIC 3A, AIM
Alert areas contain unusual types of aerial activities, such as parachute jumping and glider towing, or high concentrations of student pilot training. However, unlike prohibited or restricted areas, there are no restrictions to flight in alert areas.

3-74   CA.I.E.K3
(Refer to Figure 53.) You are planning a VFR west bound flight departing the Fresno Chandler Executive Airport (FCH) Airport and you will be passing through the active Lemoore C and A MOAs. What action should you take?

A – Exercise extreme caution while in the boundaries of the MOA.

B – Avoid the MOA, VFR, and IFR flights are prohibited during daylight hours.

C – Contact the aircraft operating in the MOA on the Guard frequency of 121.5.

3-74. Answer A. GFDIC 3A, AIM
A military operations area (MOA) is a block of airspace in which military operations are conducted. VFR aircraft are not prevented from flying through active MOAs, but it is wise to avoid them when possible. If you do choose to fly in an MOA, you should exercise extreme caution when military activity is being conducted. Flight Service can advise you of the hours of operation of an MOA along your route, or you can check the special use airspace panel on the edge of your chart.

3-75   CA.I.D.K1
(Refer to Figure 53, area 1.) The gray diagonal line is most likely

A – an arrival route.

B – a military training route.

C – a state boundary line.

3-75. Answer B. GFDIC 3A, AIM
Military training routes (MTRs) are depicted on sectional charts as gray lines. MTRs are established below 10,000 feet MSL for operations at speeds in excess of 250 knots.

MTRs are classified as VR for VFR operations and IR for IFR operations. MTRs that are entirely at or below 1,500 feet AGL are identified by four-digit numbers, and those that have one or more segments above 1,500 feet AGL use three-digit numbers. The IR/VR and number designation is not shown for this route on this portion of the chart.

State boundaries are dashed black lines. Arrival routes are not depicted on sectional charts.

SECTION A ■ **Airports, Airspace, and Flight Information**

3-76   CA.I.E.K1, 2

GIVEN:

Location................Madera Airport (MAE)
Altitude.................1,000 ft AGL

Position................7 NM north of Madera (MAE)
Time.....................3 p.m. local

Flight visibility.......1 SM

(Refer to Figure 53 between area 1 and area 2.) You are VFR approaching Madera Airport for a landing from the north. You

A – are in violation of the FARs; you need 3 miles of visibility under VFR.

B – may descend to 800 feet AGL (Pattern Altitude) after entering Class E airspace and continue to the airport.

C – are required to descend to below 700 feet AGL to remain clear of Class E airspace and may continue for landing.

3-76. Answer C. GFDIC 3A, Chart Legend, FAR 91.155

Class E airspace begins at 1,200 feet AGL on the hard side of the magenta band and at 700 feet AGL on the soft side of the magenta band. If you are currently 7 nautical miles north of the airport at 1,000 feet AGL, you are in Class G airspace, and your minimum visibility requirement is 1 statute mile. To remain in Class G airspace, you must descend below 700 feet as you near the airport.

If you remain at 1,000 feet AGL as you near the airport so that your aircraft is located in the area within the soft side of the magenta band, you are in Class E airspace and must maintain a minimum visibility of 3 statute miles.

3-77   CA.I.E.K2

(Refer to Figure 53, area 2.) What is indicated by the star next to the "L" in the airport information box for the Madera (MAE) airport north of area 2?

A – Special VFR is prohibited.

B – There is a rotating beacon at the field.

C – Lighting limitations exist.

3-77. Answer C. GFDPP 3A, Chart Legend

The star next to the "L" in the airport information indicates the airport/runway lighting operates part-time or is pilot-controlled.

3-78   CA.I.D.K2

(Refer to Figure 53, area 2.) The 16 indicates

A – an antenna top at 1,600 feet AGL.

B – the maximum elevation figure for that quadrangle.

C – the minimum safe sector altitude for that quadrangle.

3-78. Answer B. GFDPP 3A, Chart Legend

Maximum elevation figures (MEFs) are based on the highest known feature within a quadrangle bounded by lines of latitude and longitude. MEFs are rounded to the next 100-foot level and 100 to 300 feet is added to this figure, depending on the nature of the terrain or obstacle.

3-79   CA.I.E.K1

(Refer to Figure 53, area 4.) You plan to depart on a day VFR flight from the Firebaugh (F34) Airport. What is the floor of controlled airspace above this airport?

A – 1,200 feet above the airport.

B – 700 feet above the airport.

C – 1,500 feet above the airport.

3-79. Answer B. GFDIC 3A, Chart Legend, AIM
Class E airspace begins at 1,200 feet AGL on the hard side of the magenta band and at 700 feet AGL on the soft side of the magenta band (where Firebaugh Airport is located).

3-80   CA.I.E.K1, 2

(Refer to Figure 54, area 1.) What minimum altitude is required to avoid the Livermore Airport (LVK) Class D airspace?

A – 2,503 feet MSL.

B – 2,901 feet MSL.

C – 3,297 feet MSL.

3-80. Answer B. GFDIC 3A, Chart Legend, AIM
On VFR charts, Class D boundaries are indicated by a blue dashed line and the upper limit altitude is shown in hundreds of feet MSL inside a blue dashed box. In this case, the ceiling of the Class D airspace at Livermore Airport is 2,900 feet [29].

3-81   CA.I.E.K1, 2

(Refer to Figure 54, area 2.) What is the ceiling of the Class D Airspace of the Byron Airport (C83)?

A – 2,900 feet MSL.

B – 1,200 feet AGL.

C – Class D Airspace does not exist at Byron Airport.

3-81. Answer C. GFDIC 3A, Chart Legend, AIM
The magenta airport symbol indicates that Byron is a nontowered airport, which means Class D airspace does not exist at the airport. Class E airspace begins at 1,200 feet AGL on the hard side of the magenta band and at 700 feet AGL on the soft side of the magenta band (where Byron Airport is located). Class G airspace exists at the surface of Byron Airport.

3-82   CA.I.E.K1, 2, CA.III.A.K1

(Refer to Figure 54, area 2.) After departing from Byron Airport (C83) with a northeast wind, you discover you are approaching Livermore Class D airspace and flight visibility is approximately 2 1/2 miles. You must

A – stay below 700 feet to remain in Class G and return to Byron Airport to land.

B – stay below 1,200 feet to remain in Class G.

C – contact Livermore Control Tower on 119.65 and advise of your intentions.

3-82. Answer A. GFDIC 3A, FAR 91.155
Class E airspace begins at 1,200 feet AGL on the hard side of the magenta band and at 700 feet AGL on the soft side of the magenta band (where Byron Airport is located). Livermore Airport is located in Class D airspace as indicated by the blue color and dashed blue circle surrounding the airport.

In Class E and Class D airspace, a minimum visibility of 3 statute miles is required for flight under VFR. If you were to obtain a special VFR clearance, you would be allowed to enter, leave, or operate within the Class D airspace with a minimum flight visibility of 1 statute mile. However, you must request a special VFR clearance from Livermore Control Tower on 118.1, not 119.65 (the ATIS frequency).

SECTION A ■ Airports, Airspace, and Flight Information

3-83 CA.I.E.K3

(Refer to Figure 54, Area 3.) What is the significance of R-2531? This is a restricted area

A – for IFR aircraft.

B – where aircraft may never operate.

C – where often invisible hazards exist.

3-83. Answer C. GFDIC 3A, Chart Legend, AIM
Restricted areas often have invisible hazards to aircraft, such as artillery firing, aerial gunnery, or guided missiles. Permission to fly through restricted areas must be granted by the controlling agency.

3-84 CA.I.E.K1, 2

(Refer to Figure 54, area 6.) The Class C airspace at Metropolitan Oakland International Airport (OAK) which extends from the surface upward has a ceiling of

A – both 2,100 feet and 3,000 feet MSL.

B – 10,000 feet MSL.

C – 2,100 feet AGL.

3-84. Answer A. GFDIC 3A, Chart Legend
The "T/SFC" indicates the ceiling of the Oakland Class C airspace is at the floor of the overlying San Francisco Class B airspace. Above the Class C core area, which extends from the surface, the Class B sectors have floors as 2,100 feet MSL (100/21) and 3,000 feet MSL (100/30) with a ceiling of 10,000 feet MSL.

3-85 CA.II.D.K1, 6a

(Refer to Figure 66.) Which are characteristics of Runway 17R?

A – 7199 feet in length; PAPI located on the left side; right traffic pattern.

B – 5002 feet in length; PAPI located on the left side; right traffic pattern.

C – 50002 feet in length, right traffic pattern, displaced threshold.

3-85. Answer B. GFDIC 3A, A/FD Legend
The Runway Data section indicates that Runway 17R–35L is a hard-surfaced runway that is 5002 feet in length and 75 feet wide (H5002X75). Runway 17R has REIL, a PAPI with 4 lights on the left side of the runway (P4L), and a right traffic pattern applies (Rgt tfc).

3-86 CA.II.D.K1, CA.III.A.K1

(Refer to Figure 67.) What are the hours of operation (local time) of the control tower for the Yakima Air Terminal when daylight savings time is in effect?

A – 1400 to 0000.

B – 0800 to 1800.

C – 1300 to 2300.

3-86. Answer B. GFDIC 3A, A/FD Legend
The Airport Remarks section of the A/FD excerpt for Lubbock Executive Airpark indicates that the airport is attended from 1400Z to 0000Z. The symbol following the hours indicates that effective times are one hour earlier during periods of daylight savings time (1300Z to 2300Z). To convert to local time, subtract 5 hours (during daylight savings time as shown in the first line after the airport name, identifier, and distance/direction from the city) to determine the answer of 0800 to 1800 local time.

SECTION A ■ Airports, Airspace, and Flight Information

3-87 CA.II.D.K1, CA.III.A.K1

(Refer to Figure 67.) On what frequency could you communicate with Fort Worth Flight Service while on the ground at Lubbock Preston Smith International Airport?

A – 122.95.

B – 122.55.

C – 125.8.

3-87. Answer B. GFDIC 3A, A/FD Legend

The Communications section of the A/FD excerpt for Lubbock Preston Smith International Airport lists a remote communications outlet (RCO) for Fort Worth Radio on the frequency of 122.55.

3-88 CA.II.D.K1, CA.III.A.K1

(Refer to Figure 68.) What are the hours of operation (local time) of the control tower for the Addison Tower when daylight savings time is in effect?

A – The tower operates full time.

B – 1200 to 0400.

C – 0600 to 2200.

3-88. Answer C. GFDIC 3A, A/FD Legend

The Airspace section of the A/FD excerpt for Addison Airport notes that Class D service is available from 1200Z to 0400Z. The symbol after the hours indicates that effective times are one hour earlier during periods of daylight savings time (1100Z to 0300Z). To convert to local time, subtract 5 hours (during daylight savings time as shown in the first line after the airport name, identifier, and distance/direction from the city) to determine the answer of 0600 to 2200 local time.

On the Commercial Pilot Airman Knowledge Test, you might be presented with questions regarding FARs, such as right-of-way rules, that apply to VFR operations in the flight environment. These FARs were introduced to you as a private pilot. Examples of these types of questions follow.

3-89 CA.VI.A.R1

When in the vicinity of a VOR which is being used for navigation on VFR flights, it is important to

A – make 90° left and right turns to scan for other traffic.

B – exercise sustained vigilance to avoid aircraft that may be converging on the VOR from other directions.

C – pass the VOR on the right side of the radial to allow room for aircraft flying in the opposite direction on the same radial.

3-89. Answer B. AIM

When flying under VFR and using VOR navigation, you should be especially vigilant for other aircraft as you near a VOR or airway intersection due to the convergence of traffic.

SECTION A ■ **Airports, Airspace, and Flight Information**

3-90   CA.III.B.K3

While in flight a helicopter and an airplane are converging at a 90° angle, and the helicopter is located to the right of the airplane. Which aircraft has the right-of-way, and why?

A – The helicopter, because it is to the right of the airplane.

B – The helicopter, because helicopters have the right-of-way over airplanes.

C – The airplane, because airplanes have the right-of-way over helicopters.

3-90. Answer A. FAR 91.113

Because helicopters and airplanes are considered to have the same maneuverability, neither one has the right of way over the other. When two aircraft with the same maneuverability are converging at approximately the same altitude (except head-on, or nearly so), the aircraft to the other's right has the right-of-way. In this case, the helicopter has the right of way because it is on the right. In terms of the right-of-way rules, airplane and rotorcraft are given the same status for giving way to less maneuverable categories of aircraft.

3-91   CA.III.B.K3

An airplane is converging with a helicopter. Which aircraft has the right-of-way?

A – The aircraft on the left.

B – The aircraft on the right.

C – The faster of the two aircraft.

3-91. Answer B. FAR 91.113

Because helicopters and airplanes are considered to have the same maneuverability, neither one has the right of way over the other. When two aircraft with the same maneuverability are converging at approximately the same altitude (except head-on, or nearly so), the aircraft to the other's right has the right-of-way. In this case, the helicopter has the right of way because it is on the right. In terms of the right-of-way rules, airplane and rotorcraft are given the same status for giving way to less maneuverable categories of aircraft.

3-92   CA.III.B.K3

Two aircraft of the same category are approaching an airport for the purpose of landing. The right-of-way belongs to the aircraft

A – at the higher altitude.

B – at the lower altitude, but the pilot shall not take advantage of this rule to cut in front of or to overtake the other aircraft.

C – that is more maneuverable, and that aircraft may, with caution, move in front of or overtake the other aircraft.

3-92. Answer B. FAR 91.113

When two or more aircraft are approaching an airport for the purpose of landing, the aircraft at the lower altitude has the right-of-way, but it shall not take advantage of this rule to cut in front of another aircraft on final approach, or to overtake that aircraft.

3-93   CA.III.B.K3

A pilot flying a single-engine airplane observes a multi-engine airplane approaching from the left. Which pilot should give way?

A – The pilot of the multiengine airplane should give way; the single-engine airplane is to its right.

B – The pilot of the single-engine airplane should give way; the other airplane is to the left.

C – Each pilot should alter course to the right.

3-93. Answer A. FAR 91.113

When two aircraft of the same category are converging, that is, on intersecting courses, the aircraft to the right has the right of way.

3-94   CA.III.B.K3

Airplane A is overtaking airplane B. Which airplane has the right-of-way?

A – Airplane A; the pilot should alter course to the right to pass.

B – Airplane B; the pilot should expect to be passed on the right.

C – Airplane B; the pilot should expect to be passed on the left.

3-94. Answer B. FAR 91.113

When one aircraft is overtaking another, regardless of the categories of each aircraft, the aircraft being overtaken has the right of way over the aircraft that is passing. The faster aircraft should pass on the right.

3-95   CA.III.B.K3

An airplane is overtaking a helicopter. Which aircraft has the right-of-way?

A – Airplane; the airplane pilot should alter course to the left to pass.

B – Helicopter; the pilot should expect to be passed on the right.

C – Helicopter; the pilot should expect to be passed on the left.

3-95. Answer B. FAR 91.113

When one aircraft is overtaking another, regardless of the categories of each aircraft, the aircraft being overtaken has the right of way over the aircraft that is passing. The faster aircraft should pass on the right.

3-96   CA.I.D.K2

What is the minimum altitude and flight visibility required for aerobatic flight?

A – 1,500 feet AGL and 3 miles.

B – 2,000 feet MSL and 2 miles.

C – 3,000 feet AGL and 1 mile.

3-96. Answer A. FAR 91.303

No person may operate an aircraft in aerobatic flight below an altitude of 1,500 feet above the surface, or when flight visibility is less than three statute miles.

3-97   CA.I.D.R3

A pilot in command (PIC) of a civil aircraft may not allow any object to be dropped from that aircraft in flight

A – unless the PIC has permission to drop any object over private property.

B – if it creates a hazard to persons and property.

C – unless reasonable precautions are taken to avoid injury to property.

3-97. Answer B. FAR 91.15

According to FAR 91.15, no pilot in command of a civil aircraft may allow any object to be dropped in flight that creates a hazard to persons or property. The regulation provides an exception, that an object may be dropped if reasonable precautions are taken to avoid injury or damage to persons or property.

SECTION A ■ Airports, Airspace, and Flight Information

3-98   CA.III.A.K6

Which is an action you should take if you are unable to contact ATC as you are nearing an airport with a control tower?

A – Immediately squawk 7600 on our transponder.

B – Troubleshoot the problem by taking actions such as trying a different frequency; checking the radio volume and squelch; or switching to an alternate transceiver.

C – Enter the traffic pattern and land as soon as possible.

3-98. Answer B. GFDPP 5B, PHB

If you are unable to contact ATC:

- Ensure that you are using the correct frequency. Try a different frequency for the ATC facility, if available.
- Check the volume and squelch on your transceiver.
- Check the switch position on your audio control panel.
- Ensure that the headset mic and speaker plugs (or the handheld mic plug, if applicable) are properly inserted into the jacks.
- Try the handheld mic if you are using headsets.
- If your aircraft is equipped with more than one radio, try the alternate transceiver.
- If it is within range, try requesting assistance from the last ATC facility with which you had contact.
- If after taking these steps, you still are unable to contact ATC, follow the lost communication procedures.

3-99   CA.III.A.K3, 5

After you have a loss of communications, the control tower uses a light signal to direct you to give way to other aircraft and continue circling, the light is

A – flashing red.

B – steady red.

C – alternating red and green.

3-99. Answer B. GFDPP 5B, FAR 91.125

While in flight, a steady red light means give way and continue circling.

SECTION B
ATC Services

Chapter 3, Section B, of the *Commercial Pilot FAA Airman Knowledge Test Guide* corresponds to the same chapter and section of the *GFD Instrument/Commercial* textbook: ATC Clearances. Although this section focuses primarily on ATC services in the instrument flight environment, this section does provide a review of some basic ATC services and aircraft equipment, such as transponders and the ADS-B system that you were introduced to as a private pilot.

ADS-B SYSTEM

- The automatic dependent surveillance-broadcast (ADS-B) system incorporates the following components.
    - GPS provides aircraft position information.
    - ADS-B Ground Stations receive signals from aircraft and broadcast their lateral position, altitude, and velocity to controllers once per second.
    - ADS-B In receives the lateral position, altitude, and velocity of transmitting aircraft and presents this data on the cockpit display of traffic information (CDTI).
    - ADS-B Out transmits line-of-sight signals to ATC ground receivers and to aircraft receivers.
- With an effective range of 100 nautical miles, the ADS-B system provides precise real-time data that immediately indicates to controllers when an aircraft deviates from its assigned flight path.
- The ADS-B system displays aircraft with transponders that are not ADS-B equipped using the traffic information service-broadcast (TIS-B).
- ATC and pilots can use ADS-B to monitor aircraft surface movement. You can use this feature to increase situational awareness while taxiing and reduce the risk of runway incursions.
- ADS-B can provide the flight information service-broadcast (FIS-B) to suitably-equipped aircraft. FIS-B delivers a broad range of textual and graphical weather products, as well as other flight information, such as the location of temporary flight restrictions (TFRs) and special use airspace (SUA) status.

TERMINAL FACILITIES

TERMINAL RADAR APPROACH CONTROL

- Approach and departure control services are operated by terminal radar approach control (TRACON) facilities.
- In addition to providing IFR separation, TRACON controllers provide vectors to airports, around terrain, and to avoid hazardous weather. Controllers in TRACONs determine the arrival sequence for the control tower's designated airspace.

CONTROL TOWER

- When a control tower is operational, you are required to obtain a clearance prior to operating in a movement area. Movement areas are defined as runways, taxiways, and other areas that are used for taxiing, takeoffs, and landings, exclusive of loading ramps and parking areas.
- When communicating with ground control or the tower, state your position on the airport surface. One of the position reports that you are required to make is when you are ready for takeoff from a runway intersection.

ATIS

- Automatic terminal information service (ATIS) is a continuous, recorded broadcast of noncontrol information that helps to improve controller effectiveness and to reduce frequency congestion.

- ATIS is updated whenever any official weather is received, regardless of content change. It is also updated whenever airport conditions change. When a new ATIS is broadcast, it is changed to the next letter of the phonetic alphabet, such as Information Bravo or Information Charlie and so on.

- If the cloud ceiling is above 5,000 feet AGL and the visibility is more than 5 statute miles, inclusion of the ceiling/sky condition, visibility, and obstructions to vision in an ATIS message is optional.

ATC SERVICES FOR VFR AIRCRAFT

- TRACONs provide ATC services for VFR aircraft in the terminal area of airports typically in Class B, Class C, or TRSA airspace.

- To receive TRACON services at busy airports and airports in Class B and Class C airspace, obtain a transponder code and a departure frequency from clearance delivery prior to taxi. Under VFR, you must utilize Class B and C services.

- The controller's first responsibility is to aircraft flying on IFR flight plans. Factors such as the volume of traffic or frequency congestion might prevent controllers from providing VFR services.

INTERPRETING TRAFFIC ADVISORIES

- When giving traffic advisories and safety alerts, ATC references traffic from your airplane as if it were a clock with 12 o'clock corresponding to the nose of the airplane if the nose is aligned with the ground track.

- Wind correction angles do not appear on the ATC display so you must determine where to look for the traffic based on the controller's advisory and any wind correction angle you are applying.

NOTE: *An asterisk appearing after an ACS code (i.e. CA.IV.A.K2*) indicates that the question subject appears more than one time in the ACS. The code shown corresponds to the first instance of the subject in the ACS.*

You may encounter questions on the Commercial Airman Knowledge Test that apply to ATC services that you learned during private pilot training. Examples of these types of questions are included in this section.

SECTION B ■ ATC Services

3-100   CA.VI.B.K4

The ADS-B system incorporates which components?

A – ADS-B In to transmit line-of-sight signals to ATC ground receivers and to aircraft receivers.

B – ADS-B Out to receive the lateral position, altitude, and velocity of transmitting aircraft.

C – ADS-B ground stations to receive signals from aircraft and broadcast their lateral position, altitude, and velocity to controllers once per second.

3-100. Answer C. GFDIC 3B, AIM

The automatic dependent surveillance-broadcast (ADS-B) system incorporates the following components.

- GPS provides aircraft position information.

- ADS-B ground stations receive signals from aircraft and broadcast their lateral position, altitude, and velocity to controllers once per second.

- ADS-B In receives the lateral position, altitude, and velocity of transmitting aircraft and presents this data on the cockpit display of traffic information (CDTI).

- ADS-B Out transmits line-of-sight signals to ATC ground receivers and to aircraft receivers.

3-101   CA.VI.B.K4

The automatic dependent surveillance-broadcast (ADS-B) system enables ATC

A – to monitor ADS-B traffic data on a CDTI and alert you to conflicts.

B – to monitor ADS-B traffic within a range of 200 nautical miles.

C – to observe the movement of aircraft on the airport surface.

3-101. Answer C. GFDIC 3B, AIM

With an effective range of 100 nautical miles, the ADS-B system provides precise real-time data that immediately indicates to controllers when an aircraft deviates from its assigned flight path. ATC and pilots can use ADS-B to monitor aircraft surface movement. ADS-B In receives the lateral position, altitude, and velocity of transmitting aircraft and presents this data on the cockpit display of traffic information (CDTI).

3-102   CA.VI.B.K4

What is function of ADS-B In?

A – To transmit line-of-sight signals to ATC ground receivers and to aircraft receivers.

B – To receive the lateral position, altitude, and velocity of transmitting aircraft to present on a CDTI.

C – To receive signals from aircraft and broadcast their lateral position, altitude, and velocity to ATC.

3-102. Answer B. GFDIC 3B, AIM

The automatic dependent surveillance-broadcast (ADS-B) system incorporates the following components.

- GPS provides aircraft position information.

- ADS-B ground stations receive signals from aircraft and broadcast their lateral position, altitude, and velocity to controllers once per second.

- ADS-B In receives the lateral position, altitude, and velocity of transmitting aircraft and presents this data on the cockpit display of traffic information (CDTI).

- ADS-B Out transmits line-of-sight signals to ATC ground receivers and to aircraft receivers.

3-103   CA.VI.B.K4

What is the function of the ADS-B feature TIS-B?

A – Enables you to see aircraft with transponders that are not equipped with ADS-B on a cockpit display.

B – Delivers a broad range of textual and graphical weather products, as well as other flight information, such as the location of TFRs and special use airspace status.

C – Enables ATC to see an aircraft ID on their display for aircraft that are equipped with ADS-B Out.

3-103. Answer A. GFDIC 3B, AIM

The ADS-B system displays aircraft with transponders that are not ADS-B equipped using the traffic information service-broadcast (TIS-B). In addition to traffic data, ADS-B can provide the flight information service-broadcast (FIS-B) to suitably-equipped aircraft. FIS-B delivers a broad range of textual and graphical weather products, as well as other flight information, such as the location of temporary flight restrictions (TFRs) and special use airspace (SUA) status.

SECTION B ■ ATC Services

3-104   CA.III.B.K4

Absence of the sky condition and visibility on an ATIS broadcast specifically implies that

A – the ceiling is more than 5,000 feet and visibility is 5 miles or more.

B – the sky condition is clear and visibility is unrestricted.

C – the ceiling is at least 3,000 feet and visibility is 5 miles or more.

3-104. Answer A. GFDIC 3B, AIM

If the cloud ceiling is above 5,000 feet AGL and the visibility is more than 5 statute miles, inclusion of the ceiling/sky condition, visibility, and obstructions to vision in an ATIS message is optional.

3-105   CA.III.A.K7, CA.VI.B.K3

During a flight, the controller advises "traffic 2 o'clock 5 miles southbound." You are holding 20° correction for a crosswind from the right. Where should you look for the traffic?

A – 40° to the right of the aircraft's nose.

B – 20° to the right of the aircraft's nose.

C – Straight ahead.

3-105. Answer A. GFDIC 3B, AIM

When giving traffic advisories and safety alerts, ATC references traffic from your airplane as if it were a clock with 12 o'clock corresponding to the nose of the airplane if the nose is aligned with the ground track. Wind correction angles do not appear on the ATC display so in this example, the aircraft's nose is pointed 20° right of its ground track to compensate for a strong crosswind. In a no-wind situation, the 2 o'clock position would be 60° to the right of the nose. However, because the nose is already pointed toward the 2 o'clock position by 20°, you would only have to look further right by 40° to see the controller's advisory.

SECTION C
ATC Clearances

Chapter 3, Section C, of the *Commercial Pilot FAA Airman Knowledge Test Guide* corresponds to the same chapter and section of the *GFD Instrument/Commercial* textbook: ATC Clearances. Because this section is specific to instrument training, no FAA commercial pilot knowledge test questions apply.

SECTION C ■ ATC Clearances

CHAPTERS 4 – 8

Part II of the *GFD Instrument/Commercial* textbook: Instrument Charts and Procedures is composed of Chapters 4 through 8. These chapters are specific to instrument training, so no FAA commercial pilot knowledge test questions apply.

CHAPTER 9

Meteorology

SECTION A

Weather Factors

THE ATMOSPHERE

- The most common way of classifying the atmosphere is according to its thermal characteristics. The lowest layer, the troposphere, is where most weather occurs.

- In the troposphere, temperatures decrease with altitude up to the tropopause, where an abrupt change in the temperature lapse rate occurs. The average height of the troposphere in the middle latitudes is 36,000 to 37,000 feet.

- The top of the troposphere is called the tropopause and serves as the boundary between the troposphere and the stratosphere. The temperature in the lower part of the stratosphere experiences relatively small changes in temperature with an increase in altitude.

- The abrupt change in temperature lapse rate at the tropopause acts as a lid that confines most water vapor, and the associated weather, to the troposphere.

ATMOSPHERIC CIRCULATION

- Solar radiation strikes the Earth at different angles at different locations, depending on the latitude, the time of day, and the time of year. Cloud cover can also block solar radiation. This uneven heating of the Earth's surface is the driving force behind all weather.

- The primary cause of changes in the Earth's weather is the variation of solar energy received by the Earth's regions. In general, the most direct rays of the sun strike the Earth at latitudes near the equator. At higher latitudes sunlight is less concentrated—the poles receive the least direct light and solar energy.

PRESSURE AND WIND PATTERNS

- The unequal heating of the surface modifies air density, causing differences in pressure.

- Meteorologists plot pressure readings from weather reporting stations on charts and connect points of equal pressure with lines called isobars. The resulting pattern reveals the pressure gradient, or change in pressure over distance. When isobars are spread widely apart, the gradient is considered to be weak, and closely spaced isobars indicate a strong gradient.

- Isobars help identify pressure systems, which are classified as highs, lows, ridges, troughs, and cols.

  ○ A low pressure area or trough is an area of rising air, which results in generally unfavorable weather conditions.

  ○ A high pressure area or ridge is characterized by descending air, which encourages dissipation of clouds and results in generally favorable weather conditions.

- Because of wind circulation patterns, you will most likely experience a crosswind from the left when flying from a high to a low in the northern hemisphere, with stronger winds as you approach the low.

- Wind is caused by airflow from cool, dense high pressure areas into warm, less dense, low pressure areas. The stronger the gradient force, the stronger the wind.

- The rotation of the Earth causes Coriolis force, which counterbalances the pressure gradient force and deflects airflow to the right as it flows out of a high pressure area in the northern hemisphere. This effect results in clockwise circulation leaving a high and counterclockwise (cyclonic) circulation entering a low with winds parallel to the isobars.

- The airflow near the surface is influenced by friction with the surface, which weakens the effects of Coriolis force. As a result, pressure gradient force causes surface winds to cross the isobars at an angle. For this reason, wind direction tends to shift when you descend to within 2,000 feet of the surface.

LOCAL CONVECTIVE CIRCULATION

- Because land surfaces warm or cool more rapidly than water surfaces, land usually is warmer than water during the day, which creates a sea breeze—a wind that blows from cool water to warmer land.

- At night, land cools faster than water, and a land breeze blows from the cooler land to the warmer water.

- During the warm part of the day, air rises over the relatively warm land mass and sinks over the cooler water. This circulation pattern results in an onshore flow. At night, when the land cools more than the water, the circulation pattern reverses.

MOISTURE, PRECIPITATION, AND STABILITY

- Water vapor is added to the atmosphere through evaporation and sublimation.

  - Evaporation—heat is added to liquid water, changing it to a gas.

  - Sublimation—ice changes directly to water vapor, bypassing the liquid state.

- Water vapor is removed from the atmosphere by condensation and deposition.

  - Condensation—when the air becomes saturated, water vapor in the air becomes liquid.

  - Deposition—water vapor freezes directly to ice.

DEWPOINT

- The amount of water vapor the air can hold decreases with the air's temperature. When the air cools to the dewpoint, it contains all the moisture it can hold at that temperature, and is said to be saturated.

- Relative humidity increases as the temperature/dewpoint spread decreases. When the air is saturated, the relative humidity is 100%, water vapor condenses, and clouds, fog, or dew forms.

- On cool, still nights, if surface features and objects cool to a temperature below the dewpoint of the surrounding air, moisture condenses out of the air in the form of dew. Frost forms when the temperature of the collecting surface is below the dewpoint and the dewpoint is below freezing.

PRECIPITATION

- With low relative humidity, rain might evaporate before it reaches the surface. When this occurs, it is called virga. Virga appears as streamers of precipitation trailing from clouds.

- Freezing rain occurs when a deep layer aloft with above-freezing temperatures exists above a layer of below-freezing air. If the below-freezing layer is shallow, rain does not have time to freeze as ice pellets and rain drops freeze on contact with the airplane, the ground, or other exposed objects.

- Ice pellets (sleet) occur when a shallow layer aloft with above-freezing temperatures exists above a deep layer of below-freezing air. As the precipitation enters air that is below freezing, rain drops or partially melted snow freezes into ice pellets.

- Precipitation that forms by sublimation falls as snow if the air temperature remains below freezing. If snow falls into a shallow warm layer, the snowflakes partially melt. Melting (wet) snow indicates that the temperature is above freezing at your altitude.

STABILITY

- Stability is the atmosphere's resistance to vertical motion. The stability of a parcel of air determines whether it rises or sinks in relation to the air around it.

  - Stable air resists vertical movement. Air that is both cool and dry is stable. Stable air is associated with stratus clouds, poor visibility, and lack of turbulence.

  - Unstable air has a tendency to rise. The greatest instability occurs when the air is both warm and moist. Unstable air is associated with cumulus clouds, good visibility outside the clouds, and generally more extreme weather such as icing, heavy rain, hail, and turbulence.

SECTION A ■ **Weather Factors**

- Lifting of an air mass can be caused by frontal activity or convective currents that are generated by uneven heating of the Earth's surface. Lifting also can occur orographically, as when air is forced up a mountain slope. The stability of the air before it is lifted determines the type of clouds that will form.

  ○ If stable, moist air is forced up a slope, stratus-type clouds with little vertical development typically form. The stable air resists further upward movement.

  ○ If unstable, moist air is lifted aloft, clouds with vertical development usually form, such as towering cumulus or cumulonimbus clouds.

- Air that is lifted expands due to lower atmospheric pressure. As the air expands, it cools through adiabatic cooling. Conversely, air compresses and its temperature increases as it sinks.

- The dry adiabatic lapse rate (DALR) is 3°C (5.4°F) per 1,000 feet that a parcel of unsaturated air is lifted.

- Because of the latent heat contained in water vapor, stability is strongly related to the moisture of the lifted air. A saturated parcel continues to cool as it rises, but at a slower rate than if it were dry.

- Air is unstable when its adiabatic lapse rate is less than the ambient air lapse rate. The standard temperature at sea level is 15°C and decreases at an average rate of 2°C (3.5°F) per 1,000 feet. When the lapse rate causes the ambient, or surrounding, air to be colder than a lifted parcel of air, the lifted air tends to continue to rise and be unstable.

- Temperature inversions usually are confined to fairly shallow layers and might occur near the surface or at higher altitudes. Inversions usually develop in stable air with little or no wind and turbulence.

- One of the most familiar types of a ground- or surface-based inversion is from radiation cooling just above the ground on clear, cool, and still nights.

- A low-level temperature inversion combined with high relative humidity usually results in smooth air with poor visibility in fog, haze, or low clouds.

- The condensation level is the level at which the temperature and dewpoint converge, and a cloud forms in rising air. With the dewpoint decreasing at 1°F per 1,000 feet, and a dry adiabatic lapse rate of 5.4°F per 1,000 feet, the temperature and dewpoint converge at about 4.4°F (2.5°C) per 1,000 feet.

- To estimate cloud bases, divide the surface temperature/dewpoint spread by the rate that the temperature approaches the dewpoint. For example, if the surface temperature is 25°C and the surface dewpoint is 0°C, divide the 25°C spread by 2.5°C to get the approximate height of the cloud base in thousands of feet. In this case, 10,000 feet AGL.

- If you know the stability of an air mass, you can predict its characteristics.

	Stable Air	Unstable Air
Clouds	Wide areas of layered or stratiform clouds or fog; gray at low altitude, thin white at high altitude	Cumuliform with extensive vertical development; bright white to black; billowy
Precipitation	Small droplets in fog and low-level clouds; large droplets in thick stratified clouds; widespread and lengthy periods of rain or snow	Large drops in heavy rain showers; showers usually brief; hail possible
Visibility	Restricted for long periods	Poor in showers or thundershowers, good otherwise
Turbulence	Usually light or nonexistent	Moderate to severe
Icing	Moderate in mid-altitudes; freezing rain, rime, or clear ice	Moderate to severe clear ice
Other	Frost, dew, temperature inversions	High or gusty surface winds, lightning, tornadoes

CLOUDS

- Clouds occur when water vapor condenses. Cloud names are based on the terms cumulus (heap), stratus (layer), nimbus (rain), and cirrus (ringlet).

- Clouds are divided into four basic groups, or families, depending on their characteristics and the altitudes where they occur:

  ○ Low clouds—extend from near the surface to about 6,500 feet AGL; consist almost entirely of water; sometimes contain supercooled water that can create an icing hazard; include stratus, stratocumulus, and nimbostratus.

  ○ Middle clouds—have bases that range from about 6,500 feet AGL to 20,000 feet AGL; are composed of water, ice crystals, or supercooled water; can contain moderate turbulence and potentially severe icing; include altostratus and altocumulus.

  ○ High clouds—have bases that begin above 20,000 feet AGL; are composed mainly of ice crystals; seldom pose a serious turbulence or icing hazard; include cirrus, cirrostratus, and cirrocumulus.

  ○ Clouds with vertical development—have tops that sometimes exceeding 60,000 feet MSL; include cumulus, towering cumulus, and cumulonimbus.

- Cumulus clouds form when moist, unstable air is lifted and condenses. These clouds usually have flat bottoms and dome-shaped tops. The lifting of moist, unstable air results in good visibility outside the cloud, showery precipitation, and turbulence.

- Fair weather cumulus are widely spaced clouds that form in otherwise clear skies. These clouds generally form in unstable air, but are capped at the top by stable air. At and below the cloud level, you can expect turbulence, but little icing or precipitation.

- Towering cumulus clouds indicate a fairly deep layer of unstable air. These clouds contain moderate to heavy convective turbulence with icing and often develop into cumulonimbus clouds (thunderstorms).

- Stratus clouds can form when air is cooled from below, or when stable air is lifted up sloping terrain. The lifting of moist, stable air results in continuous precipitation, little or no turbulence, and poor visibility. Icing is possible if temperatures are at or near freezing.

- Stratus clouds also might form along with fog when rain falls through cooler air and raises the humidity to the saturation point.

- The prefixes alto and cirro denote cumulus and stratus clouds from the middle and high families, respectively.

- The prefix nimbo and the suffix nimbus denote clouds that produce rain. For example:

  ○ Cumulonimbus clouds, or thunderstorms, are large, vertically developed clouds that form in moist, unstable air. These clouds contain large amounts of moisture, icing, and lightning. The presence of both updrafts and downdrafts within the cloud create a great amount of turbulence.

  ○ Nimbostratus clouds are stratus clouds that produce rain. These clouds can be several thousand feet thick and contain large quantities of moisture.

AIR MASSES

- An air mass is a large body of air with fairly uniform temperature and moisture content. An air mass usually forms where air remains stationary or nearly stationary for several days.

- As an air mass moves over a warmer surface, its lower layers are heated, and vertical movement of the air develops. Depending on temperature and moisture levels, this can result in extreme instability, characterized by cumuliform clouds, turbulence, and good visibility outside the clouds.

- When an air mass flows over a cooler surface, its lower layers are cooled and vertical movement is inhibited. As a result, the stability of the air is increased.

FRONTS

- When an air mass moves out of its source region, it comes in contact with other air masses that have different moisture and temperature characteristics. The boundary between air masses is called a front and often contains hazardous weather.

- The most reliable indications that you are crossing a front are a change in wind direction and, less frequently, wind speed. The new direction of the wind is difficult to predict, but the wind always shifts to the right in the northern hemisphere as the front passes.

- Fronts are categorized as follows:

  ○ Cold front—separates an advancing mass of cold, dense, and stable air from an area of warm, lighter, and unstable air. Some general weather characteristics that occur with a cold front are: cumulus clouds, turbulence, showery precipitation, and strong, gusty winds. After the front passes, expect good visibility and cooler temperatures.

SECTION A ■ **Weather Factors**

○ Warm front—warm air moves over the top of cooler air at the surface. If the air is warm, moist, and stable, some general weather characteristics that occur with a warm front are stratus clouds, steady precipitation, and poor visibility. If the air is warm, moist, and unstable, cumulus clouds and showery precipitation can develop.

○ Stationary front—when the opposing forces of two air masses are balanced, the front that separates them might remain stationary and influence local flying conditions for several days. The weather in a stationary front usually is a mixture of that found in both warm and cold fronts.

○ Occluded front—occurs when a fast-moving cold front catches up to a slow-moving warm front.

OCCLUDED FRONTS

• A cold front occlusion develops when the fast-moving cold front is colder than the air ahead of the slow-moving warm front. In this case, the cold air replaces the cool air at the surface and forces the warm front aloft.

• A warm front occlusion occurs when the fast-moving cold front is warmer than the air ahead of the slow-moving warm front. In this case, the cold front rides up over the warm front, forcing the cold front aloft.

THE FRONTAL CYCLONE

• The surface development of a frontal cyclone in the northern hemisphere follows a distinctive life cycle. The frontal wave forms during these first two stages:

○ Pre-development stage—characterized by a stationary or slow-moving cold front with winds blowing in opposite directions on each side of the front.

○ Incipient (wave cyclone) stage—counterclockwise circulation around the low generates a frontal wave.

HIGH ALTITUDE WEATHER

• A jet stream is a narrow band of high speed winds that reaches its greatest speed near the tropopause.

• Typical jet stream speeds range between 60 knots and about 240 knots. Jet streams normally are several thousand miles long, several hundred miles wide, and a few miles thick.

• The polar front jet stream occurs at about 30°N to 60°N latitude. Although it exists year round, the polar front jet stream tends to be higher, weaker, and farther north in the summer.

NOTE: *An asterisk appearing after an ACS code (i.e. CA.IV.A.K2*) indicates that the question subject appears more than one time in the ACS. The code shown corresponds to the first instance of the subject in the ACS.*

9-1   CA.I.C.K3a, c

Which feature is associated with the tropopause?

A – Constant height above the Earth.

B – Abrupt change in temperature lapse rate.

C – Absolute upper limit of cloud formation.

9-1. Answer B. GFDIC 9A, AW
The lowest layer of the atmosphere, the troposphere, is where most weather occurs. In the troposphere, temperatures decrease with altitude up to the tropopause, where an abrupt change in the temperature lapse rate occurs. The tropopause serves as the boundary between the troposphere and the stratosphere. The temperature in the lower part of the stratosphere experiences relatively small changes in temperature with an increase in altitude.

9-2   CA.I.C.K3a, c

Which is true regarding the development of convective circulation?

A – Cool air must sink to force the warm air upward.

B – Warm air is less dense and rises on its own accord.

C – Warmer air covers a larger surface area than the cool air; therefore, the warmer air is less dense and rises.

9-2. Answer A. GFDIC 9A, AW

During the warm part of the day, air rises over the relatively warm land mass and sinks over the cooler water. This circulation pattern results in an onshore flow. At night, when the land cools more than the water, the cooler air sinks, forcing the warm air upward, which causes the circulation pattern to reverse.

9-3   CA.I.C.K3a, c

Convective circulation patterns associated with sea breezes are caused by

A – water absorbing and radiating heat faster than the land.

B – land absorbing and radiating heat faster than the water.

C – cool and less dense air moving inland from over the water, causing it to rise.

9-3. Answer B. GFDIC 9A, AW

Because land surfaces warm or cool more rapidly than water surfaces, land usually is warmer than water during the day, which creates a sea breeze—a wind that blows from cool water to warmer land.

At night, land cools faster than water, and a land breeze blows from the cooler land to the warmer water.

9-4   CA.I.C.K3b

What causes wind?

A – The Earth's rotation.

B – Air mass modification.

C – Pressure differences.

9-4. Answer C. GFDIC 9A, AW

The uneven heating of the Earth's surface creates circulation patterns, resulting in pressure differences. Wind is caused by airflow from cool, dense high pressure areas into warm, less dense, low pressure areas. The stronger the gradient force, the stronger the wind.

9-5   CA.I.C.K3b

In the Northern Hemisphere, the wind is deflected to the

A – right by Coriolis force.

B – right by surface friction.

C – left by Coriolis force.

9-5. Answer A. GFDIC 9A, AW

Coriolis force counterbalances pressure gradient force and deflects airflow to the right as it flows out of a high pressure area in the northern hemisphere. This effect results in clockwise circulation leaving a high and counterclockwise (cyclonic) circulation entering a low with winds parallel to the isobars.

SECTION A ■ **Weather Factors**

9-6   CA.I.C.K3b

What prevents air from flowing directly from high-pressure areas to low-pressure areas?

A – Coriolis force.

B – Surface friction.

C – Pressure gradient force.

9-6. Answer A. GFDIC 9A, AW

Wind is caused by airflow from cool, dense high pressure areas into warm, less dense, low pressure areas. The stronger the gradient force, the stronger the wind. The rotation of the Earth causes Coriolis force, which counterbalances the pressure gradient force and deflects airflow to the right as it flows out of a high pressure area in the northern hemisphere. This effect results in clockwise circulation leaving a high and counterclockwise (cyclonic) circulation entering a low with winds parallel to the isobars.

9-7   CA.I.C.K3a

While flying cross-country, in the Northern Hemisphere, you experience a continuous left crosswind which is associated with a major wind system. This indicates that you

A – are flying toward an area of generally unfavorable weather conditions.

B – have flown from an area of unfavorable weather conditions.

C – cannot determine weather conditions without knowing pressure changes.

9-7. Answer A. GFDIC 9A, AW

Because of wind circulation patterns, you will most likely experience a crosswind from the left when flying from a high to a low in the northern hemisphere, with stronger winds as you approach the low. Isobars help identify pressure systems, which are classified as highs, lows, ridges, troughs, and cols.

- A low pressure area or trough is an area of rising air, which results in generally unfavorable weather conditions.

- A high pressure area or ridge is characterized by descending air, which encourages dissipation of clouds and results in generally favorable weather conditions.

9-8   CA.I.C.K3a, CA.I.D.K2

There is a high pressure system that is located south of your planned route in the Northern Hemisphere on a west to east cross-country flight. To take advantage of favorable winds, you would plan your route

A – on the north side of the high pressure area.

B – on the south side of the high pressure area.

C – through the middle of the high pressure area.

9-8. Answer A. GFDIC 9A, AW

The rotation of the Earth causes Coriolis force, which counterbalances the pressure gradient force and deflects airflow to the right as it flows out of a high pressure area in the northern hemisphere. This effect results in clockwise circulation leaving a high. In this case the winds to the north of the high pressure area would be blowing from west to east and would provide a favorable tailwind for a west to east cross-country flight.

9-9   CA.I.C.K3a

Which is true with respect to a high- or low-pressure system?

A – A high-pressure area or ridge is an area of rising air.

B – A low-pressure area or trough is an area of descending air.

C – A high-pressure area or ridge is an area of descending air.

9-9. Answer C. GFDIC 9A, AW

Isobars help identify pressure systems, which are classified as highs, lows, ridges, troughs, and cols.

- A low pressure area or trough is an area of rising air, which results in generally unfavorable weather conditions.

- A high pressure area or ridge is characterized by descending air, which encourages dissipation of clouds and results in generally favorable weather conditions.

9-10   CA.I.C.K3b

The wind system associated with a low-pressure area in the Northern Hemisphere is

A – an anticyclone and is caused by descending cold air.

B – a cyclone and is caused by Coriolis force.

C – an anticyclone and is caused by Coriolis force.

9-10. Answer B. GFDIC 9A, AW

Coriolis force counterbalances pressure gradient force and deflects airflow to the right as it flows out of a high pressure area in the northern hemisphere. This effect results in clockwise circulation leaving a high and counterclockwise (cyclonic) circulation entering a low with winds parallel to the isobars.

9-11   CA.I.C.K3b

Why does the wind have a tendency to flow parallel to the isobars above the friction level?

A – Coriolis force tends to counterbalance the horizontal pressure gradient.

B – Coriolis force acts perpendicular to a line connecting the highs and lows.

C – Friction of the air with the Earth deflects the air perpendicular to the pressure gradient.

9-11. Answer A. GFDIC 9A, AW

The rotation of the Earth causes Coriolis force, which force counterbalances pressure gradient force and deflects airflow to the right as it flows out of a high pressure area in the northern hemisphere. This effect results in clockwise circulation leaving a high and counterclockwise (cyclonic) circulation entering a low with winds parallel to the isobars.

The airflow near the surface is influenced by friction with the surface, which weakens the effects of Coriolis force. As a result, pressure gradient force causes surface winds to cross the isobars at an angle. For this reason, wind direction tends to shift when you descend to within 2,000 feet of the surface.

9-12   CA.I.C.K3a

Which is true regarding high- or low-pressure systems?

A – A high-pressure area or ridge is an area of rising air.

B – A low-pressure area or trough is an area of rising air.

C – Both high- and low-pressure areas are characterized by descending air.

9-12. Answer B. GFDIC 9A, AW

Isobars help identify pressure systems, which are classified as highs, lows, ridges, troughs, and cols.

- A low pressure area or trough is an area of rising air, which results in generally unfavorable weather conditions.

- A high pressure area or ridge is characterized by descending air, which encourages dissipation of clouds and results in generally favorable weather conditions.

9-13   CA.I.C.K3a, CA.I.C.K3b

When flying into a low-pressure area in the Northern Hemisphere, the wind direction and velocity will be from the

A – left and decreasing.

B – left and increasing.

C – right and decreasing.

9-13. Answer B. GFDIC 9A, AW

Wind is caused by airflow from cool, dense high pressure areas into warm, less dense, low pressure areas. The stronger the gradient force, the stronger the wind. The rotation of the Earth causes Coriolis force, which counterbalances the pressure gradient force and deflects airflow to the right as it flows out of a high pressure area in the northern hemisphere.

This effect results in clockwise circulation leaving a high (to the right) and counterclockwise (cyclonic, to the left) circulation entering a low with winds parallel to the isobars. You will most likely experience a crosswind from the left when flying from a high to a low in the northern hemisphere, with stronger winds as you approach the low.

SECTION A ■ **Weather Factors**

9-14   CA.I.C.K3a

The general circulation of air associated with a high-pressure area in the Northern Hemisphere is

A – outward, downward, and clockwise.

B – outward, upward, and clockwise.

C – inward, downward, and clockwise.

9-14. Answer A. GFDIC 9A, AW

Coriolis force, which counterbalances the pressure gradient force and deflects airflow to the right as it flows out of a high pressure area in the northern hemisphere. This effect results in clockwise circulation leaving a high (to the right) and counterclockwise (cyclonic, to the left) circulation entering a low with winds parallel to the isobars.

Isobars help identify pressure systems, which are classified as highs, lows, ridges, troughs, and cols.

- A low pressure area or trough is an area of rising air, which results in generally unfavorable weather conditions.

- A high pressure area or ridge is characterized by descending air, which encourages dissipation of clouds and results in generally favorable weather conditions.

9-15   CA.I.C.K3a, CA.I.C.K3c

Every physical process of weather is accompanied by or is the result of

A – a heat exchange.

B – the movement of air.

C – a pressure differential.

9-15. Answer A. GFDIC 9A, AW

Every physical process of weather is accompanied by, or is the result of, a heat exchange. For example, the uneven heating of the Earth's surface is the driving force behind all weather. Another example is the evaporation of water when heat is added to liquid water, changing it to a gas.

9-16   CA.I.C.K3d

Moisture is added to air by

A – sublimation and condensation.

B – evaporation and condensation.

C – evaporation and sublimation.

9-16. Answer C. GFDIC 9A, AW

Water vapor is added to the atmosphere through evaporation and sublimation.

- Evaporation—heat is added to liquid water, changing it to a gas.

- Sublimation—ice changes directly to water vapor, bypassing the liquid state.

Water vapor is removed from the atmosphere by condensation and deposition.

- Condensation—when the air becomes saturated, water vapor in the air becomes liquid.

- Deposition—water vapor freezes directly to ice. .

9-17   CA.I.C.K3c

Which is true regarding actual air temperature and dewpoint temperature spread? The temperature spread

A – decreases as the relative humidity decreases.

B – decreases as the relative humidity increases.

C – increases as the relative humidity increases.

9-17. Answer B. GFDIC 9A, AW

The amount of water vapor the air can hold decreases with the air's temperature. When the air cools to the dewpoint, it contains all the moisture it can hold at that temperature, and is said to be saturated. Relative humidity increases as the temperature/dewpoint spread decreases. When the air is saturated, the relative humidity is 100%, water vapor condenses, and clouds, fog, or dew forms.

9-18   CA.I.C.K3d

Virga is best described as

A – streamers of precipitation trailing beneath clouds, which evaporate before reaching the ground.

B – wall cloud torrents trailing beneath cumulonimbus clouds, which dissipate before reaching the ground.

C – turbulent areas beneath cumulonimbus clouds.

9-18. Answer A. GFDIC 9A
With low relative humidity, rain might evaporate before it reaches the surface. When this occurs, it is called virga. Virga appears as streamers of precipitation trailing from clouds.

9-19   CA.I.C.K3a

What are the characteristics of an unstable atmosphere?

A – A cool, dry air mass.

B – A warm, humid air mass.

C – Descending air in the northern hemisphere.

9-19. Answer B. GFDIC 9A, AW
Stability is the atmosphere's resistance to vertical motion. The stability of a parcel of air determines whether it rises or sinks in relation to the air around it.

- Stable air resists vertical movement. Air that is both cool and dry is stable.

- Unstable air has a tendency to rise. The greatest instability occurs when the air is both warm and moist.

9-20   CA.I.C.K3c

What is the standard temperature at 6,500 feet?

A – 15 °C.

B – 2 °C.

C – 38 °F.

9-20. Answer B. GFDIC 9A, AW.
The standard temperature at sea level is 15°C and decreases at an average rate of 2°C (3.5°F) per 1,000 feet. Therefore, at 6,500 feet, the standard temperature is:
15°C − (6,500 ft × 2°C / 1,000 ft) = 2°C.

9-21   CA.I.C.K3c

What is the standard temperature at 10,000 feet?

A – −5°C.

B – −15°C.

C – +5°C.

9-21. Answer A. GFDIC 9A, AW
The standard temperature at sea level is 15°C and decreases at an average rate of 2°C (3.5°F) per 1,000 feet. Therefore, at 10,000 feet, the standard temperature is:
15°C − (10,000 ft × 2°C / 1,000 ft) = −5°C.

9-22   CA.I.C.K3c

What is the standard temperature at 20,000 feet?

A – −15°C.

B – −20°C.

C – −25°C.

9-22. Answer C. GFDIC 9A, AW
The standard temperature at sea level is 15°C and decreases at an average rate of 2°C (3.5°F) per 1,000 feet. Therefore, at 20,000 feet, the standard temperature is:
15°C − (20,000 ft × 2°C / 1,000 ft) = −25°C.

SECTION A ■ **Weather Factors**

9-23   CA.I.C.K3c

Which conditions are favorable for the formation of a surface based temperature inversion?

A – Clear, cool nights with calm or light wind.

B – Area of unstable air rapidly transferring heat from the surface.

C – Broad areas of cumulus clouds with smooth, level bases at the same altitude.

9-23. Answer A. GFDIC 9A, AW

Temperature inversions usually are confined to fairly shallow layers and might occur near the surface or at higher altitudes. Inversions usually develop in stable air with little or no wind and turbulence. One of the most familiar types of a ground- or surface-based inversion is from radiation cooling just above the ground on clear, cool nights.

9-24   CA.I.C.K3a, d, f

When conditionally unstable air with high-moisture content and very warm surface temperature is forecast, one can expect what type of weather?

A – Strong updrafts and stratonimbus clouds.

B – Restricted visibility near the surface over a large area.

C – Strong updrafts and cumulonimbus clouds.

9-24. Answer C. GFDIC 9A, AW

Lifting of an air mass can be caused by frontal activity or convective currents that are generated by uneven heating of the Earth's surface. The stability of the air before it is lifted determines the type of clouds that will form. If unstable, moist air is lifted aloft, clouds with vertical development usually form, such as towering cumulus or cumulonimbus clouds.

9-25   CA.I.C.K3c, f

What is the approximate base of the cumulus clouds if the temperature at 2,000 feet MSL is 10°C and the dewpoint is 1°C?

A – 3,000 feet MSL.

B – 4,000 feet MSL.

C – 6,000 feet MSL.

9-25. Answer C. GFDIC 9A, AW

To estimate cloud bases, divide the surface temperature/dewpoint spread by the rate that the temperature approaches the dewpoint. For example, if the surface temperature is 10°C and the surface dewpoint is 1°C, divide the 9°C spread by 2.5°C to get the approximate height of the cloud base in thousands of feet (3,600 feet AGL). Adding this number to the surface elevation of 2,000 feet MSL indicates a cloud base of 5,600 feet MSL (approximately 6,000 feet MSL).

9-26   CA.I.C.K3a, f

If clouds form as a result of very stable, moist air being forced to ascend a mountain slope, the clouds will be

A – cirrus type with no vertical development or turbulence.

B – cumulus type with considerable vertical development and turbulence.

C – stratus type with little vertical development and little or no turbulence.

9-26. Answer C. GFDIC 9A, AW

Lifting of an air mass can be caused by frontal activity or convective currents that are generated by uneven heating of the Earth's surface. Lifting also can occur orographically, as when air is forced up a mountain slope. The stability of the air before it is lifted determines the type of clouds that will form.

- If stable, moist air is forced up a slope, stratus-type clouds with little vertical development typically form. The stable air resists further upward movement.

- If unstable, moist air is lifted aloft, clouds with vertical development usually form, such as towering cumulus or cumulonimbus clouds.

9-27   CA.I.C.K3a, f

What determines the structure or type of clouds which will form as a result of air being forced to ascend?

A – The method by which the air is lifted.

B – The stability of the air before lifting occurs.

C – The relative humidity of the air after lifting occurs.

9-27. Answer B. GFDIC 9A, AW

Lifting of an air mass can be caused by frontal activity or convective currents that are generated by uneven heating of the Earth's surface. Lifting also can occur orographically, as when air is forced up a mountain slope. The stability of the air before it is lifted determines the type of clouds that will form.

- If stable, moist air is forced up a slope, stratus-type clouds with little vertical development typically form. The stable air resists further upward movement.

- If unstable, moist air is lifted aloft, clouds with vertical development usually form, such as towering cumulus or cumulonimbus clouds

9-28   CA.I.C.K3a, d, f

What are the characteristics of stable air?

A – Good visibility; steady precipitation; stratus clouds.

B – Poor visibility; steady precipitation; stratus clouds.

C – Poor visibility; intermittent precipitation; cumulus clouds.

9-28. Answer B. GFDIC 9A, AW

Stable air has these characteristics:

- Clouds—wide areas of layered or stratiform clouds or fog; gray at low altitude, thin white at high altitude.

- Precipitation—small droplets in fog and low-level clouds; large droplets in thick stratified clouds; widespread and lengthy periods of rain or snow.

- Visibility—restricted for long periods.

- Turbulence—usually light or nonexistent.

- Icing—moderate in mid-altitudes; freezing rain, rime, or clear ice.

- Other—frost, dew, temperature inversions.

9-29   CA.I.C.K3a, d, f

What are the characteristics of unstable air?

A – Good visibility; showery precipitation; cumulus clouds.

B – Poor visibility; steady precipitation; stratus clouds.

C – Poor visibility; intermittent precipitation; cumulus clouds.

9-29. Answer A. GFDIC 9A, AW

Unstable air has these characteristics:

- Clouds—cumuliform with extensive vertical development; bright white to black; billowy

- Precipitation—large drops in heavy rain showers; showers usually brief; hail possible

- Visibility—poor in showers or thundershowers, good otherwise

- Turbulence—moderate to severe

- Icing—moderate to severe clear ice

- Other—high or gusty surface winds, lightning, tornadoes

SECTION A ■ **Weather Factors**

9-30 CA.I.C.K3a

Which would decrease the stability of an air mass?

A – Warming from below.

B – Cooling from below.

C – Decrease in water vapor.

9-30. Answer A. GFDIC 9A, AW

Stability is the atmosphere's resistance to vertical motion. The stability of a parcel of air determines whether it rises or sinks in relation to the air around it. Stable air resists vertical movement. Air that is both cool and dry is stable. Unstable air has a tendency to rise.

The greatest instability occurs when the air is both warm and moist. Lifting of an air mass can be caused by frontal activity or convective currents that are generated by uneven heating of the Earth's surface. Lifting also can occur orographically, as when air is forced up a mountain slope.

9-31 CA.I.C.K3a, c

From which measurement of the atmosphere can stability be determined?

A – Atmospheric pressure.

B – The ambient lapse rate.

C – The dry adiabatic lapse rate.

9-31. Answer B. GFDIC 9A, AW

Air is unstable when its adiabatic lapse rate is less than the ambient air lapse rate. The standard temperature at sea level is 15°C and decreases at an average rate of 2°C (3.5°F) per 1,000 feet. When the lapse rate causes the ambient, or surrounding, air to be colder than a lifted parcel of air, the lifted air tends to continue to rise and be unstable.

9-32 CA.I.C.K3a, f

What type weather can one expect from moist, unstable air, and very warm surface temperatures?

A – Fog and low stratus clouds.

B – Continuous heavy precipitation.

C – Strong updrafts and cumulonimbus clouds.

9-32. Answer C. GFDIC 9A, AW

Unstable air has a tendency to rise. The greatest instability occurs when the air is both warm and moist. If unstable, moist air is lifted aloft, clouds with vertical development usually form, such as towering cumulus or cumulonimbus clouds.

9-33 CA.I.C.K3a, e

Which would increase the stability of an air mass?

A – Warming from below.

B – Cooling from below.

C – Decrease in water vapor.

9-33. Answer B. GFDIC 9A, AW

Stable air resists vertical movement. Air that is both cool and dry is stable. Stable air is associated with stratus clouds, poor visibility, and lack of turbulence.

Unstable air has a tendency to rise. The greatest instability occurs when the air is both warm and moist.

SECTION A ■ Weather Factors

9-34   CA.I.C.K3a, d, f

Which combination of weather-producing variables would likely result in cumuliform-type clouds, good visibility, and showery rain?

A – Stable, moist air and orographic lifting.

B – Unstable, moist air and orographic lifting.

C – Unstable, moist air and no lifting mechanism.

9-34. Answer B. GFDIC 9A, AW

Lifting of an air mass can occur orographically, as when air is forced up a mountain slope. If unstable, moist air is lifted aloft, clouds with vertical development usually form.

Unstable air has these characteristics:

- Clouds—cumuliform with extensive vertical development; bright white to black; billowy.
- Precipitation—large drops in heavy rain showers; showers usually brief; hail possible.
- Visibility—poor in showers or thundershowers, good otherwise.
- Turbulence—moderate to severe.
- Icing—moderate to severe clear ice.
- Other—high or gusty surface winds, lightning, tornadoes.

9-35   CA.I.C.K3a, f

What is a characteristic of stable air?

A – Stratiform clouds.

B – Fair weather cumulus clouds.

C – Temperature decreases rapidly with altitude.

9-35. Answer A. GFDIC 9A, AW

Stable air has these characteristics:

- Clouds—wide areas of layered or stratiform clouds or fog; gray at low altitude, thin white at high altitude.
- Precipitation—small droplets in fog and low-level clouds; large droplets in thick stratified clouds; widespread and lengthy periods of rain or snow.
- Visibility—restricted for long periods.
- Turbulence—usually light or nonexistent.
- Icing—moderate in mid-altitudes; freezing rain, rime, or clear ice.
- Other—frost, dew, temperature inversions.

9-36   CA.I.C.K3a, d, e, f

A moist, unstable air mass is characterized by

A – poor visibility and smooth air.

B – cumuliform clouds and showery precipitation.

C – stratiform clouds and continuous precipitation.

9-36. Answer B. GFDIC 9A, AW

Unstable air has these characteristics:

- Clouds—cumuliform with extensive vertical development; bright white to black; billowy.
- Precipitation—large drops in heavy rain showers; showers usually brief; hail possible.
- Visibility—poor in showers or thundershowers, good otherwise.
- Turbulence—moderate to severe.
- Icing—moderate to severe clear ice.
- Other—high or gusty surface winds, lightning, tornadoes.

SECTION A ■ **Weather Factors**

9-37   CA.I.C.K3a, e, l

When an air mass is stable, which of these conditions are most likely to exist?

A – Numerous towering cumulus and cumulonimbus clouds.

B – Moderate to severe turbulence at the lower levels.

C – Smoke, dust, haze, etc., concentrated at the lower levels with resulting poor visibility.

9-37. Answer C. GFDIC 9A, AW

Stable air has these characteristics:

- Clouds—wide areas of layered or stratiform clouds or fog; gray at low altitude, thin white at high altitude.
- Precipitation—small droplets in fog and low-level clouds; large droplets in thick stratified clouds; widespread and lengthy periods of rain or snow.
- Visibility—restricted for long periods.
- Turbulence—usually light or nonexistent.
- Icing—moderate in mid-altitudes; freezing rain, rime, or clear ice.
- Other—frost, dew, temperature inversions.

9-38   CA.I.C.K3a, e

Which is a characteristic of stable air?

A – Cumuliform clouds.

B – Excellent visibility.

C – Restricted visibility.

9-38. Answer C. GFDIC 9A, AW

Stable air has these characteristics:

- Clouds—wide areas of layered or stratiform clouds or fog; gray at low altitude, thin white at high altitude.
- Precipitation—small droplets in fog and low-level clouds; large droplets in thick stratified clouds; widespread and lengthy periods of rain or snow.
- Visibility—restricted for long periods.
- Turbulence—usually light or nonexistent.
- Icing—moderate in mid-altitudes; freezing rain, rime, or clear ice.
- Other—frost, dew, temperature inversions.

9-39   CA.I.C.K3a, d, e

Which is a characteristic typical of a stable air mass?

A – Cumuliform clouds.

B – Showery precipitation.

C – Continuous precipitation.

9-39. Answer C. GFDIC 9A, AW

Stable air has these characteristics:

- Clouds—wide areas of layered or stratiform clouds or fog; gray at low altitude, thin white at high altitude.
- Precipitation—small droplets in fog and low-level clouds; large droplets in thick stratified clouds; widespread and lengthy periods of rain or snow.
- Visibility—restricted for long periods.
- Turbulence—usually light or nonexistent.
- Icing—moderate in mid-altitudes; freezing rain, rime, or clear ice.
- Other—frost, dew, temperature inversions.

9-40   CA.I.C.K3a, f

The conditions necessary for the formation of stratiform clouds are a lifting action and

A – unstable, dry air.

B – stable, moist air.

C – unstable, moist air.

9-40. Answer B. GFDIC 9A, AW

Stable air resists vertical movement. Air that is both cool and dry is stable. Stable air is associated with stratus clouds, poor visibility, and lack of turbulence.

Unstable air has a tendency to rise. The greatest instability occurs when the air is both warm and moist.

9-41   CA.I.C.K3f, g

Which cloud types would indicate convective turbulence?

A – Cirrus clouds.

B – Nimbostratus clouds.

C – Towering cumulus clouds.

9-41. Answer C. GFDIC 9A, AW

Towering cumulus clouds indicate a fairly deep layer of unstable air. These clouds contain moderate to heavy convective turbulence with icing and often develop into cumulonimbus clouds (thunderstorms).

9-42   CA.I.C.K3a, f

The formation of either predominantly stratiform or predominantly cumuliform clouds is dependent upon the

A – source of lift.

B – stability of the air being lifted.

C – temperature of the air being lifted.

9-42. Answer B. GFDIC 9A, AW

If unstable, moist air is lifted aloft, clouds with vertical development usually form, such as towering cumulus or cumulonimbus clouds. Stable air resists vertical movement. Stable air is associated with stratus clouds, poor visibility, and lack of turbulence.

9-43   CA.I.C.K3h

The conditions necessary for the formation of cumulonimbus clouds are a lifting action and

A – unstable, dry air.

B – stable, moist air.

C – unstable, moist air.

9-43. Answer C. GFDIC 9A, AW

Cumulonimbus clouds, or thunderstorms, are large, vertically developed clouds that form in moist, unstable air. These clouds contain large amounts of moisture, icing, and lightning. The presence of both updrafts and downdrafts within the cloud create a great amount of turbulence.

9-44   CA.I.C.K3e, f, g

Which are characteristics of a cold air mass moving over a warm surface?

A – Cumuliform clouds, turbulence, and poor visibility.

B – Cumuliform clouds, turbulence, and good visibility.

C – Stratiform clouds, smooth air, and poor visibility.

9-44. Answer B. GFDIC 9A, AW

As an air mass moves over a warmer surface, its lower layers are heated, and vertical movement of the air develops. Depending on temperature and moisture levels, this can result in extreme instability, characterized by cumuliform clouds, turbulence, and good visibility outside the clouds.

When an air mass flows over a cooler surface, its lower layers are cooled and vertical movement is inhibited. As a result, the stability of the air is increased.

SECTION A ■ **Weather Factors**

9-45   CA.I.C.K3e

You have delayed your flight to allow a fast moving cold front to clear your destination airport before your arrival. What type of flying conditions would you expect after the front has passed?

A – A fast moving squall line with high winds and thunderstorms.

B – Clear skies with gusty, turbulent winds and cooler temperatures.

C – Low clouds, reduced visibility and showery, misty conditions.

9-45. Answer B. GFDIC 9A, AW

A cold front separates an advancing mass of cold, dense, and stable air from an area of warm, lighter, and unstable air. Some general weather characteristics that occur with a cold front are: cumulus clouds, turbulence, showery precipitation, and strong, gusty winds. After the front passes, expect good visibility and cooler temperatures.

Low clouds and poor visibility are typically associated with a warm front. A squall line often forms 50 to 200 miles ahead of a fast moving cold front.

9-46   CA.I.C.K3e

Frontal waves normally form on

A – slow moving cold fronts or stationary fronts.

B – slow moving warm fronts and strong occluded fronts.

C – rapidly moving cold fronts or warm fronts.

9-46. Answer A. GFDIC 9A, AW

The surface development of a frontal cyclone in the northern hemisphere follows a distinctive life cycle. During the first two stages, the frontal wave forms:

- Pre-development stage—characterized by a stationary or slow-moving cold front with winds blowing in opposite directions on each side of the front.

- Incipient (wave cyclone) stage—counterclockwise circulation around the low generates a frontal wave.

9-47   CA.I.C.K3e

Which weather phenomenon is always associated with the passage of a frontal system?

A – A wind change.

B – An abrupt decrease in pressure.

C – Clouds, either ahead or behind the front.

9-47. Answer A. GFDIC 9A, AW

The most reliable indications that you are crossing a front are a change in wind direction and, less frequently, wind speed. The new direction of the wind is difficult to predict, but the wind always shifts to the right in the northern hemisphere as the front passes.

9-48   CA.I.C.K3e

Which is true regarding a cold front occlusion? The air ahead of the warm front

A – is colder than the air behind the overtaking cold front.

B – is warmer than the air behind the overtaking cold front.

C – has the same temperature as the air behind the overtaking cold front.

9-48. Answer B. GFDIC 9A, AW

A frontal occlusion occurs when a fast-moving cold front catches up to a slow-moving warm front. The difference in temperature within each frontal system is a major factor that influences the type of front that develops. A cold front occlusion develops when the air ahead of the warm front is warmer than the overtaking cold front.

9-49   CA.I.C.K3a, b

During the winter months in the middle latitudes, the jet stream shifts toward the

A – north and speed decreases.

B – south and speed increases.

C – north and speed increases.

9-49. Answer B. GFDIC 9A, AW

A jet stream is a narrow band of high speed winds that reaches its greatest speed near the tropopause. Typical jet stream speeds range between 60 knots and about 240 knots. Jet streams normally are several thousand miles long, several hundred miles wide, and a few miles thick.

The polar front jet stream occurs at about 30°N to 60°N latitude. Although it exists year round, the polar front jet stream tends to be higher, weaker, and farther north in the summer. In the winter months, the jet stream shifts south and becomes stronger.

9-50   CA.I.C.K3a, b

The strength and location of the jet stream is normally

A – weaker and farther north in the summer.

B – stronger and farther north in the winter.

C – stronger and farther north in the summer.

9-50. Answer A. GFDIC 9A, AW

A jet stream is a narrow band of high speed winds that reaches its greatest speed near the tropopause. Typical jet stream speeds range between 60 knots and about 240 knots. Jet streams normally are several thousand miles long, several hundred miles wide, and a few miles thick.

The polar front jet stream occurs at about 30°N to 60°N latitude. Although it exists year round, the polar front jet stream tends to be higher, weaker, and farther north in the summer.

SECTION B
Weather Hazards and Ice Control Systems

THUNDERSTORMS

- Thunderstorm formation requires an unstable lapse rate, a lifting force, and a relatively high moisture level.

- Thunderstorms progress through three distinct stages—cumulus, mature, and dissipating.

    - Cumulus stage—characterized by continuous updrafts. A lifting action initiates the vertical movement of air. As the air rises and cools to its dewpoint, water vapor condenses into small water droplets or ice crystals. Heat released by the condensing vapor provides energy for the continued vertical growth of the cloud.

    - Mature stage—signaled by the beginning of precipitation at the surface. Downward rushing air spreads outward at the surface, producing a sharp drop in temperature, a rise in pressure, strong gusty surface winds, and turbulent conditions.

    - Dissipating stage—indicated by downdrafts becoming the dominant air movement within the cell. During this stage, the upper level winds often blow the top of the cloud downwind, creating the familiar anvil shape.

- Within the thunderstorm cloud, the strongest turbulence occurs in the shear between the updrafts and downdrafts. Near the surface, an area of low-level turbulence develops as the downdrafts spread out across the surface. The difference in speed and direction between the surrounding air and the cooler downdraft air creates a shear zone. The gusty winds and turbulence of this shear zone are not confined to the thunderstorm itself, but can extend outward for many miles from the center of the storm.

- Other weather phenomena might prevent you from seeing the characteristic shape of a thunderstorm. For example, a cumulonimbus cloud might be embedded, or contained within, other cloud layers making the thunderstorm impossible to see.

- As the thunderstorm advances, a roll cloud—a rolling, turbulent, circular-shaped cloud—might form at the lower leading edge of the cloud.

- A squall line is a narrow band of active thunderstorms that normally contains very severe weather, including heavy hail and destructive winds. Although it often forms 50 to 200 miles ahead of a fast-moving cold front, the existence of a front is not necessary for a squall line to form.

- Thunderstorms typically contain many severe weather hazards, such as lightning, hail, turbulence, gusty surface winds, and even tornadoes.

- Thunderstorm hazards are not confined to the cloud itself. For example, you can encounter turbulence in VFR conditions as far as 20 miles from the storm. Avoid thunderstorms by at least 20 miles.

- The cumulonimbus cloud is the visible part of a widespread system of turbulence and other weather hazards. Indications of severe turbulence within the storm system include the cumulonimbus cloud itself, very frequent lightning, and roll clouds.

- Lightning is a hazard that is always associated with thunderstorms and is found throughout the cloud. Although it rarely causes personal injury or substantial damage to the aircraft structure in flight, it can cause temporary loss of vision, puncture the aircraft skin, or damage electronic navigation and communication equipment.

- You can encounter hail in flight, even when no hail is reaching the surface. Hail can fall from the anvil-shaped top of the storm, and wind can carry it for a considerable distance ahead of the visible cloud.

- If the aircraft you are flying is equipped with a weather avoidance system, such as weather radar, you can use it to avoid thunderstorms. With radar, you should avoid intense thunderstorm echoes by at least 20 miles. Do not fly between intense radar echoes unless they are at least 40 miles apart.

- Airborne weather radar is designed as an aid for avoiding severe weather, not for penetrating it. Weather radar detects precipitation based on echo returns of significant raindrops; it does not detect minute droplets or other phenomenon such as hail, turbulence, and updrafts/downdrafts. Therefore, you should not rely on airborne radar to avoid instrument weather associated with clouds and fog or certain other severe weather conditions.

HYDROPLANING

- Hydroplaning is caused by a thin layer of standing water that separates the tires from the runway. Hydroplaning causes a substantial reduction in friction between the airplane tires and the runway surface and results in poor or nil braking action at high speeds.

- Hydroplaning is most likely at high speeds on wet, slushy, or snow-covered runways that have smooth textures.

TURBULENCE

- If you enter turbulence unexpectedly, or if you expect to encounter it during flight, or if you unintentionally enter a thunderstorm, slow the airplane to maneuvering speed (V_A) or less, or the recommended rough air penetration speed. Then, attempt to maintain a level flight attitude and accept variations in airspeed and altitude.

- If you encounter turbulent or gusty conditions during an approach to a landing, consider flying a power-on approach and landing at an airspeed slightly above the normal approach speed. This techninque helps to stabilize the airplane, giving you more control.

- Convective turbulence, which is also referred to as thermal turbulence, is typically a daytime phenomena that occurs over land in fair weather when winds are light. Turbulence is caused by vertical air currents, or thermals, that develop in air heated by contact with the warm surface below.

WAKE TURBULENCE

- Wake turbulence is created when an aircraft generates lift. The greatest vortex strength occurs when the generating aircraft is heavy, slow, in a clean configuration, and at a high angle of attack.

- Wingtip vortices from large commercial jets can induce uncontrollable roll rates in smaller airplanes. Vortices tend to sink below the flight path of the aircraft that generated them. You should avoid the area below and behind an aircraft generating wake turbulence, especially at low altitudes where even a momentary wake encounter could be hazardous.

- A light, quartering tailwind can move the upwind vortex of a landing airplane over the runway and forward into the touchdown zone.

- Vortices sinking close to the ground (within 100 to 200 feet), tend to move laterally over the ground at a speed of 2 or 3 knots. A crosswind decreases the lateral movement of the upwind vortex and increases the movement of the downwind vortex. Therefore, a crosswind could result in the upwind vortex remaining in the touchdown zone for a period of time and hasten the drift of the downwind vortex toward another runway.

- Follow these guidelines to avoid wake turbulence during takeoff and landing:

  - To avoid turbulence when landing behind a large airplane, stay above the large airplane's glide path and land beyond its touchdown point.

  - If a large airplane has just taken off as you approach to land, touch down well before the large airplane's liftoff point.

  - When departing after a large airplane has landed, lift off beyond its touchdown location.

  - When taking off behind a large airplane, lift off before the large airplane's rotation point and climb out above or upwind of its flight path.

- In a slow hover-taxi or stationary hover near the surface, helicopter main rotor(s) generate downwash that produces high velocity outwash vortices to a distance approximately three times the diameter of the rotor.

SECTION B ■ **Weather Hazards and Ice Control Systems**

- In forward flight, departing or landing helicopters produce a pair of strong, highspeed trailing vortices similar to the wingtip vortices of large fixed wing airplanes. Use caution when operating behind or crossing behind landing or departing helicopters.

CLEAR AIR TURBULENCE

- Clear air turbulence (CAT) usually is encountered above 15,000 feet, however, it can take place at any altitude and is often present with no visual warning.
- CAT can be caused by the interaction of layers of air with differing wind speeds. For example, weather products that predict clear air turbulence derive vertical wind shear values from forecast winds aloft. A vertical wind shear value of 6 knots per 1,000 feet is typically considered the threshold for moderate or greater turbulence.
- CAT often develops in or near the jet stream, which is a narrow band of high altitude winds near the tropopause.
- As a rule of thumb, CAT can be expected when a curving jet is found north of a deep low pressure system and can be particularly violent on the low pressure side of the jet stream when the wind speed at the core is 110 knots or greater.
- CAT is usually greater in an upper trough on the polar side of a jet stream.
- All pilots encountering CAT conditions are urgently requested to report the time, location and intensity of the CAT to the FAA facility with which they are maintaining radio contact.

MOUNTAIN WAVE TURBULENCE

- When stable air crosses a mountain barrier, it tends to flow in layers. When winds of at least 20 knots flow perpendicular to a mountain range, mountain waves can form, which can create very strong turbulence, particularly along the lee slopes downwind from the mountains.
- Below the crest of each mountain wave is an area of rotary circulation, or a rotor, which forms below the mountain peaks. Both the rotor and the waves can create violent turbulence. If sufficient moisture is present, a rotor cloud (sometimes called a roll cloud) might form in the rotors.
- If sufficient moisture is present, wave crests might be marked by lens-shaped (lenticular) altocumulus or cirrocumulus clouds. Winds within these clouds might be 50 knots or greater, but the clouds often appear stationary because they form in updrafts and dissipate in downdrafts. Because of this, they are sometimes called standing lenticular clouds.

REPORTING TURBULENCE

- Turbulence is considered to be occasional when it occurs less than one-third of a given time span, intermediate when it occurs one-third to two-thirds of the time, and continuous when it occurs more than two-thirds of the time.
- You can classify the intensity of turbulence using the following guidelines:
    ◦ Light—slight erratic changes in altitude or attitude; slight strain against seat belts. Light chop is slight, rapid bumpiness without appreciable changes in altitude or attitude.
    ◦ Moderate—changes in altitude or attitude, but the aircraft remains in positive control at all times; usually causes variations in indicated airspeed; occupants feel definite strains against seat belts. Moderate chop is rapid bumps or jolts without appreciable changes in altitude or attitude.
    ◦ Severe—large abrupt changes in altitude or attitude; usually causes large variations in indicated airspeed; aircraft might be momentarily out of control; occupants forced violently against seat belts.
    ◦ Extreme—aircraft practically impossible to control; might cause structural damage.

WIND SHEAR

- Wind shear is a sudden, drastic change in wind speed and/or direction. Wind shear can exist at any altitude and can occur in a vertical or horizontal direction.

- Wind shear is often associated with a strong low-level temperature inversion with strong winds above the inversion, a jet stream, a thunderstorm, or a frontal zone.

- Wind shear can materialize during a low-level temperature inversion when cold, still surface air is covered by warmer air that contains winds of 25 knots or more at 2,000 to 4,000 feet above the surface.

- With frontal activity, the most critical period for wind shear is either just before or just after frontal passage. The onset of low-level wind shear (LLWS) precedes a warm frontal passage and follows a cold frontal passage. Typical periods for critical LLWS with frontal passages are up to six hours before a warm front and one to three hours after a cold front.

- On an approach, monitor the power and vertical velocity required to maintain your glide path. You might have difficulty maintaining glide path using normal power settings and descent rates if you encounter wind shear. If you cannot regain a reasonable rate of descent and land without abnormal maneuvers, apply full power and go-around.

- The FAA recommends actions to take in order to maintain a stabilized final approach when encountering wind shear. For example, when flying a 3° glide slope/path to the runway, you encounter wind that shears from a:

    ○ Headwind to calm or tailwind. The indicated airspeed and lift decrease so the airplane tends to sink. Initially, you must add power and fly up to the glide slope/path. Then as your groundspeed increases, be prepared to reduce the power to increase your rate of descent and maintain the glide slope/path.

    ○ Tailwind to calm or headwind. The indicated airspeed and lift increase so the airplane tends to balloon. Initially, you must reduce power and fly down to the glide slope/path. Then as your groundspeed decreases, be prepared to add power to decrease your rate of descent and maintain the glide slope/path.

MICROBURST

- Microbursts are small-scale intense downdrafts that, on reaching the surface, spread outward in all directions from the downdraft center creating both vertical and horizontal wind shear that can be extremely hazardous to aircraft.

- A microburst downdraft is typically less than 1 mile in diameter as it descends from the cloud base to about 1,000 to 3,000 feet above the ground. In the transition zone near the ground, the downdraft changes to a horizontal outflow that can extend to approximately 2-1/2 miles in diameter. The downdrafts can be as strong as 6,000 ft/min.

- Horizontal winds near the surface can be as strong as 45 knots resulting in a 90 knot shear as the wind changes from a headwind to a tailwind across the microburst. These strong horizontal winds occur within a few hundred feet of the ground.

- A typical microburst intensifies for about 5 minutes after it first strikes the ground, with the maximum intensity winds lasting approximately 2 to 4 minutes. An individual microburst seldom lasts longer than 15 minutes from the time it strikes the ground until dissipation.

- If an aircraft inadvertently encounters a microburst at low altitude, at first a headwind increases performance followed by a decreasing headwind and a strong downdraft. Performance continues to deteriorate as the wind shears to a tailwind. The severe downdraft can result in an uncontrollable descent and impact with the ground.

WIND SHEAR WARNING SYSTEMS

- To help detect hazardous wind shear, low-level wind shear alert systems (LLWAS) have been installed at many airports. The LLWAS uses a system of anemometers placed at strategic locations around the airport to detect differences in the wind readings.

- Consult the Airport/Facility Directory listings in the Chart Supplement to determine if an airport has a LLWAS.

RESTRICTIONS TO VISIBILITY

- Restrictions to visibility can include fog, haze, smoke, smog, and dust.

- When operating VFR at night, one of the first indications of flying into areas of restricted visibility is the gradual disappearance of lights on the ground.

- Fog requires both sufficient moisture and condensation nuclei on which the water vapor can condense. Fog is more prevalent in industrial areas due to an abundance of condensation nuclei.

- Advection fog is caused when a low layer of warm, moist air moves over a cooler surface, which could be either land or water. This fog is most common under cloudy skies along coastlines, where sea breezes transport air from the warm water to cooler land.

- Advection fog is usually more persistent and extensive than radiation fog and can form rapidly during day or night.

- Upslope fog forms when moist, stable air is forced up a sloping land mass.

- Advection fog and upslope fog are both dependent upon wind for their formation. However, surface winds stronger than 15 knots tend to dissipate or lift advection fog into low stratus clouds.

- Radiation fog, also known as ground fog, forms over fairly level land areas on clear, calm, humid nights. As the surface cools by radiation, the adjacent air is also cooled to its dewpoint. Radiation fog usually occurs in stable air associated with a high pressure system.

- Haze is caused by a concentration of very fine dry particles that can restrict your visibility.

- Restrictions to visibility, such as haze, can create the illusion of being at a greater distance from a runway than you actually are, which can cause you to fly a lower approach.

- Precipitation-induced fog can form when warm rain or drizzle falls through a layer of cooler air near the surface and evaporation from the falling precipitation saturates the cool air. This type of fog is most commonly associated with warm fronts.

- Steam fog forms when very cold air moves over a warmer water surface.

COLD WEATHER OPERATIONS

Prior to a flight in cold weather

- Remove any frost, snow, or ice on the airplane.

- Inspect all control surfaces and their associated hinges, control rods, and cables for snow or ice that could interfere with their operation.

- Check the crankcase breather lines, because vapor from the engine can condense and freeze, preventing the release of air from the crankcase.

- Preheat the engine if temperatures are so low that you will experience difficulty starting the engine.

- Preheat the cabin to prevent instruments from being adversely affected by cold temperatures.

- Follow the manufacturer's recommended procedures for priming before you try to start the engine.

ICING

- The three types of structural ice are rime, clear, and mixed. The accumulation of ice on an aircraft increases drag and weight and decreases lift and thrust.

- Clear ice can develop in areas of large water droplets that are found in cumulus clouds or in freezing rain beneath a warm front inversion. Freezing rain means there is warmer air at higher altitudes. When the droplets flow over the aircraft structure and slowly freeze, they can glaze the aircraft's surfaces.

- Clear ice is the most serious of the various forms of ice because it has the fastest rate of accumulation, adheres tenaciously to the aircraft, and is more difficult to remove than rime ice.

- Just prior to the passage of a warm front when warm air extends up over the cold air preceding the front, you might encounter ice pellets formed by raindrops that have frozen while falling through colder air.

- Ice pellets normally do not adhere to an aircraft; but they always indicate there is freezing rain at a higher altitude. The altitude of the freezing rain decreases as you fly under the frontal zone

- Wind tunnel and flight tests indicate that ice, frost, or snow formations on the leading edge and upper surface of a wing, having a thickness similar to medium or coarse sandpaper, can reduce wing lift by as much as 30% and increase drag by 40%. These changes in lift and drag will significantly increase stall speed, reduce controllability, and alter aircraft flight characteristics.

- You can estimate the freezing level by using temperature lapse rates. For example, the standard, or average, temperature lapse rate is approximately 2°C per 1,000 feet. If the temperature at 1,350 feet MSL is 8°C, divide 8°C by 2°C to determine how much higher the freezing level is (8 ÷ 2 = 4). This means the freezing level is 4,000 feet above 1,350 feet MSL, or 5,350 feet MSL.

- You are least likely to encounter icing in high clouds, because these clouds consist of ice crystals and this already-frozen moisture will not adhere to your airframe.

- In weather forecasts or pilot reports, aircraft structural icing is normally classified as:

    - Trace—perceptible, but accumulation is nearly balanced by its rate of sublimation. Deicing equipment is unnecessary, unless icing is encountered for an extended period of time.

    - Light—can be a problem during prolonged exposure (over one hour) if you do not have adequate deicing/anti-icing equipment.

    - Moderate—even short encounters become potentially hazardous unless you use deicing/anti-icing equipment.

    - Severe—the rate of accumulation is greater than the reduction or control capabilities of the deicing/anti-icing equipment.

- In icing conditions, if workload permits, it is generally recommended that you periodically disengage the autopilot and manually fly the airplane to identify handling changes caused by airframe icing. The autopilot can mask the aerodynamic effects of icing and could cause control problems or a stall.

- If the autopilot limitations are exceeded in icing conditions, the autopilot can disconnect abruptly and you might be suddenly confronted by an unexpected control deflection.

- Airplanes are more vulnerable to ice accumulation during the initial climbout in icing conditions because lower speeds require a higher angle of attack. This high angle of attack exposes the underside of the airplane and its wings to the icing conditions and allows ice to accumulate further aft than it would in cruise flight. Climbing in icing conditions with the autopilot engaged in vertical speed (VS) mode is especially hazardous because the autopilot compensates for the loss of climb performance by increasing the pitch until the airplane stalls.

- Frost poses a serious hazard by interfering with smooth airflow over the wings and potentially causing early airflow separation, resulting in a loss of lift. Frost also increases drag and, when combined with the loss of lift, can prevent the aircraft from becoming airborne or can cause the wing to stall shortly after takeoff at an angle of attack that is lower than normal.

ICE CONTROL SYSTEMS

- Aircraft ice control systems consist of a combination of anti-icing and deicing equipment. Anti-icing equipment prevents the formation of ice, while deicing equipment removes the ice after it has formed.

- You must consult the FAA-approved aircraft flight manual (AFM) or pilot's operating handbook (POH) to determine if your aircraft is certified to operate in icing conditions.

- Examples of anti-icing and deicing equipment include:

    - Deicing boots that are pneumatically inflated to break the ice, allowing it to be carried away by the airstream.

    - Fluid anti-ice systems that use a pump to force a mixture of ethylene glycol, isopropyl alcohol, and water through the holes on a leading edge panel. This fluid runs back over the surface, forming a thin liquid film that prevents structural ice from forming.

    - Windshield ice control, such as a defrosters, anti-ice systems that use a flow of alcohol to coat a section of the windshield, and electrically heated wires.

    - Thermal anti-ice systems that heat the surfaces on airplanes to prevent ice formation.

SECTION B ■ Weather Hazards and Ice Control Systems

○ Propeller anti-ice systems that use alcohol discharged from nozzles that are pointed toward each blade root. Centrifugal force causes the alcohol to flow down the leading edge of the blade to prevent ice formation.

NOTE: *An asterisk appearing after an ACS code (i.e. CA.IV.A.K2*) indicates that the question subject appears more than one time in the ACS. The code shown corresponds to the first instance of the subject in the ACS.*

9-51   CA.I.C.K3h

Select the true statement pertaining to the life cycle of a thunderstorm.

A – Updrafts continue to develop throughout the dissipating stage of a thunderstorm.

B – The beginning of rain at the Earth's surface indicates the mature stage of the thunderstorm.

C – The beginning of rain at the Earth's surface indicates the dissipating stage of the thunderstorm.

9-51. Answer B. GFDIC 9B, AW

Thunderstorms progress through three distinct stages:

- Cumulus stage—characterized by continuous updrafts.
- Mature stage—signaled by the beginning of precipitation at the surface.
- Dissipating stage—indicated by downdrafts becoming the dominant air movement within the cell.

9-52   CA.I.C.K3h

Which weather phenomenon signals the beginning of the mature stage of a thunderstorm?

A – The start of rain.

B – The appearance of an anvil top.

C – Growth rate of cloud is maximum.

9-52. Answer A. GFDIC 9B, AW

Thunderstorms progress through three distinct stages:

- Cumulus stage—characterized by continuous updrafts.
- Mature stage—signaled by the beginning of precipitation at the surface.
- Dissipating stage—indicated by downdrafts becoming the dominant air movement within the cell.

9-53   CA.I.C.K3h

What feature is normally associated with the cumulus stage of a thunderstorm?

A – Roll cloud.

B – Continuous updraft.

C – Beginning of rain at the surface.

9-53. Answer B. GFDIC 9B, AW

Thunderstorms progress through three distinct stages:

- Cumulus stage—characterized by continuous updrafts.
- Mature stage—signaled by the beginning of precipitation at the surface.
- Dissipating stage—indicated by downdrafts becoming the dominant air movement within the cell.

9-54   CA.I.C.K3h

During the life cycle of a thunderstorm, which stage is characterized predominately by downdrafts?

A – Mature.

B – Developing.

C – Dissipating.

9-54. Answer C. GFDIC 9B, AW

Thunderstorms progress through three distinct stages:

- Cumulus stage—characterized by continuous updrafts.
- Mature stage—signaled by the beginning of precipitation at the surface.
- Dissipating stage—indicated by downdrafts becoming the dominant air movement within the cell.

9-55   CA.I.C.K3h

You are avoiding a thunderstorm that is in your flight path. You are over 20 miles from the cell however, you are under the anvil of the cell. Is this a hazard?

A – No, you are at a safe distance from the cell.

B – Yes, hail can be discharged from the anvil.

C – Yes, this is still in the area of dissipation.

9-55. Answer B. GFDIC 9B, AW

You can encounter hail in flight, even when no hail is reaching the surface. Hail can fall from the anvil-shaped top of the storm, and wind can carry it for a considerable distance ahead of the visible cloud.

9-56   CA.I.C.K3h

What visible signs indicate extreme turbulence in thunderstorms?

A – Base of the clouds near the surface, heavy rain, and hail.

B – Low ceiling and visibility, hail, and precipitation static.

C – Cumulonimbus clouds, very frequent lightning, and roll clouds.

9-56. Answer C. GFDIC 9B, AW

Thunderstorms typically contain many severe weather hazards, such as lightning, hail, turbulence, gusty surface winds, and even tornadoes. These hazards are not confined to the cloud itself. For example, you can encounter turbulence in VFR conditions as far as 20 miles from the storm.

The cumulonimbus cloud is the visible part of a widespread system of turbulence and other weather hazards. Indications of severe turbulence within the storm system include the cumulonimbus cloud itself, very frequent lightning, and roll clouds.

9-57   CA.I.C.K3h

The greatest threats to an aircraft operating in the vicinity of thunderstorms are:

A – thunder and heavy rain.

B – hail and turbulence.

C – precipitation static and low visibility.

9-57. Answer B. GFDIC 9B, AW

Thunderstorms typically contain many severe weather hazards, such as lightning, hail, turbulence, gusty surface winds and even tornadoes. Early in the mature stage of the thunderstorm, updrafts continue to increase up to speeds of 6,000 ft/min. The adjacent updrafts and downdrafts cause severe turbulence. You can encounter hail in flight, even when no hail is reaching the surface. Hail can cause extensive damage to your aircraft in a very short period of time.

SECTION B ■ Weather Hazards and Ice Control Systems

9-58   CA.I.C.K3d, h

Which statement is true concerning the hazards of hail?

A – Hail damage in horizontal flight is minimal due to the vertical movement of hail in the clouds.

B – Rain at the surface is a reliable indication of no hail aloft.

C – Hailstones may be encountered in clear air several miles from a thunderstorm.

9-58. Answer C. GFDIC 9B, AW

You can encounter hail in flight, even when no hail is reaching the surface. In addition, large hailstones have been encountered in clear air several miles from a thunderstorm. Hail can cause extensive damage to your aircraft in a very short period of time.

9-59   CA.I.C.K3d, h

Hail is most likely to be associated with

A – cumulus clouds.

B – cumulonimbus clouds.

C – stratocumulus clouds.

9-59. Answer B. GFDIC 9B, AW

Hail is commonly associated with cumulonimbus clouds (thunderstorms). You can encounter hail in flight, even when no hail is reaching the surface. In addition, large hailstones have been encountered in clear air several miles from a thunderstorm. Hail can cause extensive damage to your aircraft in a very short period of time.

9-60   CA.I.C.K3h

The most severe weather conditions, such as destructive winds, heavy hail, and tornadoes, are generally associated with

A – slow-moving warm fronts which slope above the tropopause.

B – squall lines.

C – fast-moving occluded fronts.

9-60. Answer B. GFDIC 9B, AW

A squall line is a narrow band of active thunderstorms which normally contains some of the most severe weather conditions.

9-61   CA.I.C.K3g, h

Of the following, which is accurate regarding turbulence associated with thunderstorms?

A – Outside the cloud, shear turbulence can be encountered 50 miles laterally from a severe storm.

B – Shear turbulence is encountered only inside cumulonimbus clouds or within a 5-mile radius of them.

C – Outside the cloud, shear turbulence can be encountered 20 miles laterally from a severe storm.

9-61. Answer C. GFDIC 9B, AW

Within the thunderstorm cloud, the strongest turbulence occurs in the shear between the updrafts and downdrafts. Near the surface, an area of low-level turbulence develops as the downdrafts spread out across the surface.

The difference in speed and direction between the surrounding air and the cooler downdraft air creates a shear zone. The gusty winds and turbulence of this shear zone are not confined to the thunderstorm itself, but can extend outward for many miles from the center of the storm. For example, you can encounter turbulence in VFR conditions as far as 20 miles from the storm. Avoid thunderstorms by at least 20 miles.

9-62   CA.I.C.K3h

Which statement is true regarding squall lines?

A – They are always associated with cold fronts.

B – They are slow in forming, but rapid in movement.

C – They are nonfrontal and often contain severe, steady-state thunderstorms.

9-62. Answer C. GFDIC 9B, AW

A squall line is a narrow band of active thunderstorms that normally contains very severe weather, including heavy hail and destructive winds. Although it often forms 50 to 200 miles ahead of a fast-moving cold front, the existence of a front is not necessary for a squall line to form.

9-63   CA.I.C.K3h, CA.I.C.K4

Thunderstorms identified as severe or giving an intense radar echo should be avoided by what distance?

A – 5 miles.

B – At least 25 miles.

C – At least 20 miles.

9-63. Answer C. GFDIC 9B, AIM

Thunderstorms typically contain many severe weather hazards, such as lightning, hail, turbulence, gusty surface winds, and even tornadoes. Thunderstorm hazards are not confined to the cloud itself. For example, you can encounter turbulence in VFR conditions as far as 20 miles from the storm. Avoid thunderstorms by at least 20 miles.

If the aircraft you are flying is equipped with a weather avoidance system, such as weather radar, you can use it to avoid thunderstorms. With radar, you should avoid intense thunderstorm echoes by at least 20 miles.

9-64   CA.I.C.K3h, CA.I.C.K4

Which is true regarding the use of airborne weather-avoidance radar for the recognition of certain weather conditions?

A – The radar scope provides no assurance of avoiding instrument weather conditions.

B – The avoidance of hail is assured when flying between and just clear of the most intense echoes.

C – The clear area between intense echoes indicates that visual sighting of storms can be maintained when flying between the echoes.

9-64. Answer A. GFDIC 9B, AW

Airborne weather radar is designed as an aid for avoiding severe weather, not for penetrating it. Weather radar detects precipitation based on echo returns of significant raindrops; it does not detect minute droplets or other phenomenon such as hail, turbulence, and updrafts/downdrafts. Therefore, you should not rely on airborne radar to avoid instrument weather associated with clouds and fog or certain other severe weather conditions.

9-65   CA.I.C.K3h, CA.I.C.K4

If airborne radar is indicating an extremely intense thunderstorm echo, you should avoid this thunderstorm by a distance of at least

A – 20 miles.

B – 10 miles.

C – 5 miles.

9-65. Answer A. GFDIC 9B, AW

If the aircraft you are flying is equipped with a weather avoidance system, such as weather radar, you can use it to avoid thunderstorms. With radar, you should avoid intense thunderstorm echoes by at least 20 miles. Do not fly between intense radar echoes unless they are at least 40 miles apart.

SECTION B ■ **Weather Hazards and Ice Control Systems**

9-66   CA.I.C.K3h, CA.I.C.K4

What minimum distance should exist between intense radar echoes before any attempt is made to fly between these thunderstorms?

A – 20 miles.

B – 30 miles.

C – 40 miles.

9-66. Answer C. GFDIC 9B, AW

If the aircraft you are flying is equipped with a weather avoidance system, such as weather radar, you can use it to avoid thunderstorms. With radar, you should avoid intense thunderstorm echoes by at least 20 miles. Do not fly between intense radar echoes unless they are at least 40 miles apart.

9-67   CA.I.C.K3g

If severe turbulence is encountered during flight, you should reduce the airspeed to

A – minimum control speed.

B – design-maneuvering speed.

C – maximum structural cruising speed.

9-67. Answer B. GFDIC 9B, PHB

If you enter turbulence unexpectedly, or if you expect to encounter it during flight, or if you unintentionally enter a thunderstorm, slow the airplane to maneuvering speed (V_A) or less, or the recommended rough air penetration speed. Then, attempt to maintain a level flight attitude and accept variations in airspeed and altitude.

9-68   CA.I.C.K3g

You are entering an area where significant clear air turbulence has been reported. Which action is appropriate upon encountering the first ripple?

A – Maintain altitude and airspeed.

B – Adjust airspeed to that recommended for rough air.

C – Enter a shallow climb or descent at maneuvering speed.

9-68. Answer B. GFDIC 9B, PHB

If you enter turbulence unexpectedly, or if you expect to encounter it during flight, or if you unintentionally enter a thunderstorm, slow the airplane to maneuvering speed (V_A) or less, or the recommended rough air penetration speed. Then, attempt to maintain a level flight attitude and accept variations in airspeed and altitude.

9-69   CA.I.C.K3g

Which is the best technique for minimizing the wing-load factor when flying in severe turbulence?

A – Change power settings, as necessary, to maintain constant airspeed.

B – Control airspeed with power, maintain wings level, and accept variations of altitude.

C – Set power and trim to obtain an airspeed at or below maneuvering speed, maintain wings level, and accept variations of airspeed and altitude.

9-69. Answer C. GFDIC 9B, PHB

If you enter turbulence unexpectedly, or if you expect to encounter it during flight, or if you unintentionally enter a thunderstorm, slow the airplane to maneuvering speed (V_A) or less, or the recommended rough air penetration speed. Then, attempt to maintain a level flight attitude and accept variations in airspeed and altitude.

9-70   CA.I.C.K3g, CA.IV.B.K3

When turbulence is encountered during the approach to a landing, what action is recommended and for what primary reason?

A – Increase the airspeed slightly above normal approach speed to attain more positive control.

B – Decrease the airspeed slightly below normal approach speed to avoid overstressing the airplane.

C – Increase the airspeed slightly above normal approach speed to penetrate the turbulence as quickly as possible.

9-70. Answer A. GFDIC 9B, AFH

If you encounter turbulent or gusty conditions during an approach to a landing, consider flying a power-on approach and landing at an airspeed slightly above the normal approach speed. This techninque helps to stabilize the airplane, giving you more control.

9-71   CA.I.C.K3b, CA.IV.B.K3

Which type of approach and landing is recommended during gusty wind conditions?

A – A power-on approach and power-on landing.

B – A power-off approach and power-on landing.

C – A power-on approach and power-off landing.

9-71. Answer A. GFDIC 9B, AFH

If you encounter turbulent or gusty conditions during an approach to a landing, consider flying a power-on approach and landing at an airspeed slightly above the normal approach speed. This tecinique helps to stabilize the airplane, giving you more control.

9-72   CA.I.C.K3g

Convective currents are most active on warm summer afternoons when winds are

A – light.

B – moderate.

C – strong.

9-72. Answer A. GFDIC 9B, AW

Convective turbulence, which is also referred to as thermal turbulence, is typically a daytime phenomena that occurs over land in fair weather when winds are light. Turbulence is caused by vertical air currents, or thermals, that develop in air heated by contact with the warm surface below.

9-73   CA.I.C.K3g, CA.II.F.R3*

Choose the correct statement regarding wake turbulence.

A – Vortex generation begins with the initiation of the takeoff roll.

B – The primary hazard is loss of control because of induced roll.

C – The greatest vortex strength is produced when the generating airplane is heavy, clean, and fast.

9-73. Answer B. GFDIC 9B, AIM

Wake turbulence is created when an aircraft generates lift. The greatest vortex strength occurs when the generating aircraft is heavy, slow, in a clean configuration, and at a high angle of attack.

Wingtip vortices from large commercial jets can induce uncontrollable roll rates in smaller airplanes Vortices tend to sink below the flight path of the aircraft that generated them.

SECTION B ■ Weather Hazards and Ice Control Systems

9-74   CA.I.C.K3g, CA.II.F.R3*

Which procedure should you follow to avoid wake turbulence if a large jet crosses your course from left to right approximately 1 mile ahead and at your altitude?

A – Make sure you are slightly above the path of the jet.

B – Slow your airspeed to V_A and maintain altitude and course.

C – Make sure you are slightly below the path of the jet and perpendicular to the course.

9-74. Answer A. GFDIC 9B, AIM
Wingtip vortices from large commercial jets can induce uncontrollable roll rates in smaller airplanes Vortices tend to sink below the flight path of the aircraft that generated them. You should avoid the area below and behind an aircraft generating wake turbulence. Because vortices sink, if a heavy aircraft crosses your course near your altitude, try to stay slightly above its path.

9-75   CA.I.C.K3g, CA.II.F.R3*

To avoid possible wake turbulence from a large jet airplane that has just landed prior to your takeoff, at which point on the runway should you plan to become airborne?

A – Past the point where the jet touched down.

B – At the point where the jet touched down, or just prior to this point.

C – Approximately 500 feet prior to the point where the jet touched down.

9-75. Answer A. GFDIC 9B, AIM
When taking off behind a large airplane that has just landed, you should plan on becoming airborne beyond the point where the large airplane touched down. Beyond this point, the jet's wake turbulence will be greatly diminished.

9-76   CA.I.C.K3g, CA.II.F.R3*

During a takeoff made behind a departing large jet airplane, you can minimize the hazard of wingtip vortices by

A – being airborne prior to reaching the jet's flight path until able to turn clear of its wake.

B – maintaining extra speed on takeoff and climbout.

C – extending the takeoff roll and not rotating until well beyond the jet's rotation point.

9-76. Answer A. GFDIC 9B, AIM
To avoid wake turbulence when taking off behind a large airplane, lift off before the large airplane's rotation point and climb out above or upwind of its flight path.

9-77   CA.I.C.K3g, CA.IV.B.R2d*

When landing behind a large airplane, which procedure should be followed for vortex avoidance?

A – Stay above its final approach flight path all the way to touchdown.

B – Stay below and to one side of its final approach flight path.

C – Stay well below its final approach flight path and land at least 2,000 feet behind.

9-77. Answer A. GFDIC 9B, AIM
To avoid wake turbulence when landing behind a large airplane, stay above the large airplane's glide path and land beyond its touchdown point.

9-78   CA.IV.A.R2d*

Your flight takes you in the path of a large aircraft. In order to avoid the vortices you should fly

A – at the same altitude as the large aircraft.

B – below the altitude of the large aircraft.

C – above the flight path of the large aircraft.

9-78. Answer C. GFDIC 9B, AIM

Wingtip vortices from large commercial jets can induce uncontrollable roll rates in smaller airplanes Vortices tend to sink below the flight path of the aircraft that generated them. You should avoid the area below and behind an aircraft generating wake turbulence.

9-79   CA.I.C.K3g, CA.II.F.R3*

With respect to vortex circulation, which is true?

A – Helicopters generate downwash turbulence, not vortex circulation.

B – The vortex strength is greatest when the generating aircraft is flying fast.

C – Vortex circulation generated by helicopters in forward flight trail behind in a manner similar to wingtip vortices generated by airplanes.

9-79. Answer C. GFDIC 9B, AIM

In forward flight, departing or landing helicopters produce a pair of strong, highspeed trailing vortices similar to the wingtip vortices of large fixed wing airplanes. Use caution when operating behind or crossing behind landing or departing helicopters.

9-80   CA.I.C.K3g, CA.II.F.R3*

Which is true with respect to vortex circulation in the wake turbulence generated by an aircraft?

A – Helicopters generate downwash turbulence only, not vortex circulation.

B – The vortex strength is greatest when the generating aircraft is heavy, clean, and slow.

C – When vortex circulation sinks into ground effect, it tends to dissipate rapidly and offer little danger.

9-80. Answer B. GFDIC 9B, AIM

Whenever an airplane generates lift, air spills over the wingtips causing wingtip vortices. The greatest vortex strength occurs when the generating aircraft is heavy, clean and slow.

In a slow hover-taxi or stationary hover near the surface, helicopter main rotor(s) generate downwash that produces high velocity outwash vortices to a distance approximately three times the diameter of the rotor.

9-81   CA.I.C.K3b, g

The minimum vertical wind shear value critical for probable moderate or greater turbulence is

A – 4 knots per 1,000 feet.

B – 6 knots per 1,000 feet.

C – 8 knots per 1,000 feet.

9-81. Answer B. GFDIC 9B, AWS

Weather products that predict clear air turbulence derive vertical wind shear values from forecast winds aloft. A vertical wind shear value of 6 knots per 1,000 feet is typically considered the threshold for moderate or greater turbulence.

SECTION B ■ **Weather Hazards and Ice Control Systems**

9-82   CA.I.C.K3g

A common location of clear air turbulence is

A – in an upper trough on the polar side of a jet stream.

B – near a ridge aloft on the equatorial side of a high-pressure flow.

C – south of an east/west oriented high-pressure ridge in its dissipating stage.

9-82. Answer A. GFDIC 9B, AC 00-30
Clear air turbulence (CAT) usually is encountered above 15,000 feet, however, it can take place at any altitude and is often present with no visual warning. CAT often develops in or near the jet stream, which is a narrow band of high altitude winds near the tropopause.

As a rule of thumb, CAT can be expected when a curving jet is found north of a deep low pressure system. CAT is usually greater in an upper trough on the polar side of a jet stream.

9-83   CA.I.C.K3b, g

A strong wind shear can be expected

A – in the jet stream front above a core having a speed of 60 to 90 knots.

B – if the 5°C isotherms are spaced between 7° to 10° of latitude.

C – on the low-pressure side of a jet stream core where the speed at the core is stronger than 110 knots.

9-83. Answer C. GFDIC 9B, AC 0030
As a rule of thumb, clear air turbulence, including wind shear can be expected when a curving jet is found north of a deep low pressure system and can be particularly violent on the low pressure side of the jet stream when the wind speed at the core is 110 knots or greater.

9-84   CA.I.C.K3b, g

Which type of jetstream can be expected to cause the greater turbulence?

A – A straight jetstream associated with a low-pressure trough.

B – A curving jetstream associated with a deep low-pressure trough.

C – A jetstream occurring during the summer at the lower latitudes.

9-84. Answer B. GFDIC 9B, AC 00-30
Clear air turbulence (CAT) usually is encountered above 15,000 feet, however, it can take place at any altitude and is often present with no visual warning. CAT often develops in or near the jet stream, which is a narrow band of high altitude winds near the tropopause.

As a rule of thumb, CAT can be expected when a curving jet is found north of a deep low pressure system. CAT is usually greater in an upper trough on the polar side of a jet strea

9-85   CA.I.C.K3f, g

The jet stream and associated clear air turbulence can sometimes be visually identified in flight by

A – dust or haze at flight level.

B – long streaks of cirrus clouds.

C – a constant outside air temperature.

9-85. Answer B. GFDIC 9B, AC 00-30
Clear air turbulence (CAT) often develops in or near the jet stream, which is a narrow band of high altitude winds near the tropopause. Jet streams can sometimes be identified by long streams of cirrus cloud formations or high, windswept-looking cirrus clouds.

As a rule of thumb, CAT can be expected when a curving jet is found north of a deep low pressure system. CAT is usually greater in an upper trough on the polar side of a jet stream.

9-86   CA.I.C.K3g

Turbulence that is encountered above 15,000 feet AGL not associated with cumuliform cloudiness, including thunderstorms, should be reported as

A – severe turbulence.

B – clear air turbulence.

C – convective turbulence.

9-86. Answer B. GFDIC 9B, AIM
Clear air turbulence (CAT) usually is encountered above 15,000 feet, however, it can take place at any altitude and is often present with no visual warning. All pilots encountering CAT conditions are urgently requested to report the time, location and intensity of the CAT to the FAA facility with which they are maintaining radio contact.

9-87   CA.I.C.K3b, g

The conditions most favorable to wave formation over mountainous areas are a layer of

A – stable air at mountaintop altitude and a wind of at least 20 knots blowing across the ridge.

B – unstable air at mountaintop altitude and a wind of at least 20 knots blowing across the ridge.

C – moist, unstable air at mountaintop altitude and a wind of less than 5 knots blowing across the ridge.

9-87. Answer A. GFDIC 9B, AW
When stable air crosses a mountain barrier, it tends to flow in layers. When winds of at least 20 knots flow perpendicular to a mountain range, mountain waves can form, which can create very strong turbulence, particularly along the lee slopes downwind from the mountains.

9-88   CA.I.C.K3b, f, g

 dangerous features of mountain waves is the turbulent areas in and

A – below rotor clouds.

B – above rotor clouds.

C – below lenticular clouds.

9-88. Answer A. GFDIC 9B, AW
When winds of at least 20 knots flow perpendicular to a mountain range, mountain waves can form, which can create very strong turbulence. Below the crest of each wave is an area of rotary circulation, or a rotor, which forms below the mountain peaks. Both the rotor and the waves can create violent turbulence. If sufficient moisture is present, a rotor cloud (sometimes called a roll cloud) might form in the rotors.

9-89   CA.I.C.K3b, g

When flying low over hilly terrain, ridges, or mountain ranges, the greatest potential danger from turbulent air currents will usually be encountered on the

A – leeward side when flying with a tailwind.

B – leeward side when flying into the wind.

C – windward side when flying into the wind.

9-89. Answer B. GFDIC 9B, AW
When winds of at least 20 knots flow perpendicular to a mountain range, mountain waves can form, which can create very strong turbulence, particularly along the lee slopes downwind from the mountains.

SECTION B ■ **Weather Hazards and Ice Control Systems**

9-90   CA.I.C.K3b, f, g

The presence of standing lenticular altocumulus clouds is a good indication of

A – lenticular ice formation in calm air.

B – very strong turbulence.

C – heavy icing conditions.

9-90. Answer B. GFDIC 9B, AW

When winds of at least 20 knots flow perpendicular to a mountain range, mountain waves can form, which can create very strong turbulence, particularly along the lee slopes downwind from the mountains. If sufficient moisture is present, characteristic clouds warn you of mountain waves. Wave crests might be marked by lens-shaped (lenticular) altocumulus or cirrocumulus clouds.

9-91   CA.I.C.K3g

You should report turbulence that momentarily causes slight, erratic changes in altitude and/or attitude as

A – light chop.

B – light turbulence.

C – moderate turbulence.

9-91. Answer B. GFDIC 9B, AIM

You can classify the intensity of turbulence using the following guidelines:

NOTE: the definition that applies to the correct answer is shown in bold.

- **Light—slight erratic changes in altitude or attitude; slight strain against seat belts.** Light chop is slight, rapid bumpiness without appreciable changes in altitude or attitude.

- Moderate—changes in altitude or attitude, but the aircraft remains in positive control at all times; usually causes variations in indicated airspeed; occupants feel definite strains against seat belts. Moderate chop is rapid bumps or jolts without appreciable changes in altitude or attitude.

- Severe—large abrupt changes in altitude or attitude; usually causes large variations in indicated airspeed; aircraft might be momentarily out of control; occupants forced violently against seat belts.

- Extreme—aircraft practically impossible to control; might cause structural damage.

9-92   CA.I.C.K3g

You should report turbulence that causes changes in altitude and/or attitude, but aircraft control remains positive, as

A – light.

B – severe.

C – moderate.

9-92. Answer C. GFDIC 9B, AIM

You can classify the intensity of turbulence using the following guidelines:

NOTE: the definition that applies to the correct answer is shown in bold.

- Light—slight erratic changes in altitude or attitude; slight strain against seat belts. Light chop is slight, rapid bumpiness without appreciable changes in altitude or attitude.

- **Moderate—changes in altitude or attitude, but the aircraft remains in positive control at all times;** usually causes variations in indicated airspeed; occupants feel definite strains against seat belts. Moderate chop is rapid bumps or jolts without appreciable changes in altitude or attitude.

- Severe—large abrupt changes in altitude or attitude; usually causes large variations in indicated airspeed; aircraft might be momentarily out of control; occupants forced violently against seat belts.

- Extreme—aircraft practically impossible to control; might cause structural damage.

9-93   CA.I.C.K3b

What is an important characteristic of wind shear?

A – It is present at only lower levels and exists in a horizontal direction.

B – It is present at any level and exists in only a vertical direction.

C – It can be present at any level and can exist in both a horizontal and vertical direction.

9-93. Answer C. GFDIC 9B, AW

Wind shear is a sudden, drastic change in wind speed and/or direction. Wind shear can exist at any altitude and can occur in a vertical or horizontal direction.

9-94   CA.I.C.K3b, c, h

Hazardous wind shear is commonly encountered

A – near warm or stationary frontal activity.

B – when the wind velocity is stronger than 35 knots.

C – in areas of temperature inversion and near thunderstorms.

9-94. Answer C. GFDIC 9B, AW

Wind shear is often associated with a strong low-level temperature inversion with strong winds above the inversion, a jet stream, a thunderstorm, or a frontal zone. Typical periods for critical low-level wind shear with frontal passages are up to six hours before a warm front and one to three hours after a cold front.

SECTION B ■ **Weather Hazards and Ice Control Systems**

9-95   CA.I.C.K3b, c

Low-level wind shear may occur when

A – surface winds are light and variable.

B – there is a low-level temperature inversion with strong winds above the inversion.

C – surface winds are above 15 knots and there is no change in wind direction and windspeed with height.

9-95. Answer B. GFDIC 9B, AW

Wind shear is a sudden, drastic change in wind speed and/or direction. Wind shear can materialize during a low-level temperature inversion when cold, still surface air is covered by warmer air that contains winds of 25 knots or more at 2,000 to 4,000 feet above the surface.

9-96   CA.I.C.K3b, c

If a temperature inversion is encountered immediately after takeoff or during an approach to a landing, a potential hazard exists due to

A – wind shear.

B – strong surface winds.

C – strong convective currents.

9-96. Answer A. GFDIC 9B, AW

Wind shear is a sudden, drastic change in wind speed and/or direction. Wind shear can materialize during a low-level temperature inversion when cold, still surface air is covered by warmer air that contains winds of 25 knots or more at 2,000 to 4,000 feet above the surface.

9-97   CA.I.C.K3b, CA.IV.B.K3

GIVEN:

Winds at 3,000 feet AGL...30 kts
Surface winds...calm

While on approach for landing, under clear skies with convective turbulence a few hours after sunrise, one should

A – increase approach airspeed slightly above normal to avoid stalling.

B – keep the approach airspeed at or slightly below normal to compensate for floating.

C – not alter the approach airspeed, these conditions are nearly ideal.

9-97. Answer A. GFDIC 9B, AW

The conditions indicated can create a wind shear hazard. When approaching to land in these conditions, flying at an approach speed slightly faster than normal can decrease the risk of stalling. If the wind shears from a strong headwind to no wind during descent, you could stall dangerously close to the ground.

9-98   CA.I.C.K3b, CA.IV.B.K3

During an approach, the most important and most easily recognized means of being alerted to possible wind shear is monitoring the

A – amount of trim required to relieve control pressures.

B – heading changes necessary to remain on the runway centerline.

C – power and vertical velocity required to remain on the proper glidepath.

9-98. Answer C. GFDIC 9B, AC 00-54

On an approach, monitor the power and vertical velocity required to maintain your glide path. You might have difficulty maintaining glide path using normal power settings and descent rates if you encounter wind shear. If you cannot regain a reasonable rate of descent and land without abnormal maneuvers, apply full power and go-around.

9-99   CA.I.C.K3b

During departure, under conditions of suspected low-level wind shear, a sudden decrease in headwind will cause

A – a loss in airspeed equal to the decrease in wind velocity.

B – a gain in airspeed equal to the decrease in wind velocity.

C – no change in airspeed, but groundspeed will decrease.

9-99. Answer A. GFDIC 9B, AC 00-54

Anytime you experience a sudden decrease in headwind, you will experience a performance decrease. This will equate to a loss of airspeed equal to the decrease in wind velocity and a corresponding loss of lift.

9-100   CA.I.C.K3b

The low level wind shear alert system (LLWAS) provides wind data and software process to detect the presence of a

A – rotating column of air extending from a cumulonimbus cloud.

B – change in wind direction and/or speed within a very short distance above the airport.

C – downward motion of the air associated with continuous winds blowing with an easterly component due to the rotation of the Earth.

9-100. Answer B. GFDIC 9B, AIM

Wind shear is a sudden, drastic change in wind speed and/or direction. Wind shear can exist at any altitude and can occur in a vertical or horizontal direction.

To help detect hazardous wind shear, low-level wind shear alert systems (LLWAS) have been installed at many airports. The LLWAS uses a system of anemometers placed at strategic locations around the airport to detect differences in the wind readings. Consult the Airport/Facility Directory listings in the Chart Supplement to determine if an airport has a LLWAS.

9-101   CA.I.C.K3l

When operating VFR at night, what is the first indication of flying into restricted visibility conditions?

A – Ground lights begin to take on an appearance of being surrounded by a halo or glow.

B – A gradual disappearance of lights on the ground.

C – Cockpit lights begin to take on an appearance of a halo or glow around them.

9-101. Answer B. GFDIC 9B, AFH

When operating VFR at night, one of the first indications of flying into areas of restricted visibility is the gradual disappearance of lights on the ground.

9-102   CA.I.C.K3j

A situation most conducive to the formation of advection fog is

A – a light breeze moving colder air over a water surface.

B – an air mass moving inland from the coastline during the winter.

C – a warm, moist air mass settling over a cool surface under no-wind conditions.

9-102. Answer B. GFDIC 9B, AW

Advection fog is caused when a low layer of warm, moist air moves over a cooler surface, which could be either land or water. This fog is most common under cloudy skies along coastlines, where sea breezes transport air from the warm water to cooler land.

SECTION B ■ **Weather Hazards and Ice Control Systems**

9-103   CA.I.C.K3j

Advection fog has drifted over a coastal airport during the day. What may tend to dissipate or lift this fog into low stratus clouds?

A – Nighttime cooling.

B – Surface radiation.

C – Surface winds of 15 knots or stronger.

9-103. Answer C. GFDIC 9B, AW

Advection fog is caused when a low layer of warm, moist air moves over a cooler surface, which could be either land or water. This fog is most common under cloudy skies along coastlines, where sea breezes transport air from the warm water to cooler land. However, surface winds stronger than 15 knots tend to dissipate or lift advection fog into low stratus clouds.

9-104   CA.I.C.K3j

In what ways do advection fog, radiation fog, and steam fog differ in their formation or location?

A – Radiation fog is restricted to land areas; advection fog is most common along coastal areas; steam fog forms over a water surface.

B – Advection fog deepens as windspeed increases up to 20 knots; steam fog requires calm or very light wind; radiation fog forms when the ground or water cools the air by radiation.

C – Steam fog forms from moist air moving over a colder surface; advection fog requires cold air over a warmer surface; radiation fog is produced by radiational cooling of the ground.

9-104. Answer A. GFDIC 9B, AW

Fog types differ in their formation or location:

- Radiation fog, also known as ground fog, forms over fairly level land areas on clear, calm, humid nights.

- Advection fog is caused when a low layer of warm, moist air moves over a cooler surface, which could be either land or water. This fog is most common under cloudy skies along coastlines, where sea breezes transport air from the warm water to cooler land.

- Steam fog forms when very cold air moves over a warmer water surface.

9-105   CA.I.C.K3j

With respect to advection fog, which statement is true?

A – It is slow to develop, and dissipates quite rapidly.

B – It forms almost exclusively at night or near daybreak.

C – It can appear suddenly during day or night, and it is more persistent than radiation fog.

9-105. Answer C. GFDIC 9B, AW

Advection fog is caused when a low layer of warm, moist air moves over a cooler surface, which could be either land or water. This fog is most common under cloudy skies along coastlines, where sea breezes transport air from the warm water to cooler land. Advection fog is usually more persistent and extensive than radiation fog and can form rapidly during day or night.

9-106   CA.I.C.K3e, j

Which in-flight hazard is most commonly associated with warm fronts?

A – Advection fog.

B – Radiation fog.

C – Precipitation-induced fog.

9-106. Answer C. GFDIC 9B, AW

Precipitation-induced fog can form when warm rain or drizzle falls through a layer of cooler air near the surface and evaporation from the falling precipitation saturates the cool air. This type of fog is most commonly associated with warm fronts.

9-107 CA.I.C.K3j

Fog produced by frontal activity is a result of saturation due to

A – nocturnal cooling.

B – adiabatic cooling.

C – evaporation of precipitation.

9-107. Answer C. GFDIC 9B, AW

Precipitation-induced fog can form when warm rain or drizzle falls through a layer of cooler air near the surface and evaporation from the falling precipitation saturates the cool air. This type of fog is most commonly associated with warm fronts.

9-108 CA.II.A.K3, K4

During preflight in cold weather, crankcase breather lines should receive special attention because they are susceptible to being clogged by

A – congealed oil from the crankcase.

B – moisture from the outside air which has frozen.

C – ice from crankcase vapors that have condensed and subsequently frozen.

9-108. Answer C. GFDIC 9B

To ensure proper engine operation, prior to a flight in cold weather:

- Check the crankcase breather lines, because vapor from the engine can condense and freeze, preventing the release of air from the crankcase.
- Preheat the engine if temperatures are so low that you will experience difficulty starting the engine.
- Follow the manufacturer's recommended procedures for priming before you try to start the engine.

9-109 CA.II.A.K3, K4

Which is true regarding preheating an aircraft during cold weather operations?

A – The cabin area as well as the engine should be preheated.

B – The cabin area should not be preheated with portable heaters.

C – Hot air should be blown directly at the engine through the air intakes.

9-109. Answer A. GFDIC 9B

To ensure proper engine and instrument operation, prior to a flight in cold weather

- Preheat the engine if temperatures are so low that you will experience difficulty starting the engine.
- Preheat the cabin to prevent instruments from being adversely affected by cold temperatures.

9-110 CA.I.C.K3d, e, i

Ice pellets encountered during flight normally are evidence that

A – a warm front has passed.

B – a warm front is about to pass.

C – there are thunderstorms in the area.

9-110. Answer B. GFDIC 9B, AW

Just prior to the passage of a warm front when warm air extends up over the cold air preceding the front, you might encounter ice pellets formed by raindrops that have frozen while falling through colder air.

Ice pellets normally do not adhere to an aircraft; but they always indicate there is freezing rain at a higher altitude. The altitude of the freezing rain decreases as you fly under the frontal zone.

SECTION B ■ Weather Hazards and Ice Control Systems

9-111   CA.I.C.K3d, e, i

What is indicated if ice pellets are encountered at 8,000 feet?

A – Freezing rain at higher altitude.

B – You are approaching an area of thunderstorms.

C – You will encounter hail if you continue your flight.

9-111. Answer A. GFDIC 9B, AW

Just prior to the passage of a warm front when warm air extends up over the cold air preceding the front, you might encounter ice pellets formed by raindrops that have frozen while falling through colder air.

Ice pellets normally do not adhere to an aircraft; but they always indicate there is freezing rain at a higher altitude. The altitude of the freezing rain decreases as you fly under the frontal zone.

9-112   CA.I.C.K3d, e, i

Ice pellets encountered during flight are normally evidence that

A – a cold front has passed.

B – there are thunderstorms in the area.

C – freezing rain exists at higher altitudes.

9-112. Answer C. GFDIC 9B, AW

Just prior to the passage of a warm front when warm air extends up over the cold air preceding the front, you might encounter ice pellets formed by raindrops that have frozen while falling through colder air.

Ice pellets normally do not adhere to an aircraft; but they always indicate there is freezing rain at a higher altitude. The altitude of the freezing rain decreases as you fly under the frontal zone

9-113   CA.I.C.K3d, i

Which situation would most likely result in freezing precipitation? Rain falling from air which has a temperature of

A – 32°F or less into air having a temperature of more than 32°F.

B – 0°C or less into air having a temperature of 0°C or more.

C – more than 32°F into air having a temperature of 32°F or less.

9-113. Answer C. GFDIC 9B, AW

Freezing rain means there is warmer air at higher altitudes. In order for precipitation to begin falling as a liquid and then freeze, rain typically must begin falling in air that is above freezing temperature (32°F/0°C) and continue falling through air that is below freezing temperature.

9-114   CA.I.C.K3k

Frost covering the upper surface of an airplane wing usually will cause

A – the airplane to stall at an angle of attack that is higher than normal.

B – the airplane to stall at an angle of attack that is lower than normal.

C – drag factors so large that sufficient speed cannot be obtained for takeoff.

9-114. Answer B. GFDIC 9B, PHB

Frost poses a serious hazard by interfering with smooth airflow over the wings and potentially causing early airflow separation, resulting in a loss of lift. Frost also increases drag and, when combined with the loss of lift, can prevent the aircraft from becoming airborne or can cause the wing to stall shortly after takeoff at an angle that is lower than normal.

9-115   CA.I.G.K1j

What is true regarding ice control systems?

A – Any aircraft equipped with anti-icing and deicing equipment may operate in icing conditions.

B – You must consult the FAA-approved aircraft flight manual or pilot's operating handbook to determine if your aircraft is certified to operate in icing conditions.

C – Anti-icing equipment is designed to remove ice after it had formed.

9-115. Answer B. GFDIC 9B, AC 91-13C

Aircraft ice control systems consist of a combination of anti-icing and deicing equipment. Anti-icing equipment prevents the formation of ice, while deicing equipment removes the ice after it has formed. You must consult the FAA-approved aircraft flight manual (AFM) or pilot's operating handbook (POH) to determine if your aircraft is certified to operate in icing conditions.

9-116   CA.I.G.K1j

Examples of de-icing and anti-icing systems include

A – anti-icing boots, that are pneumatically inflated to prevent the formation of ice on the wing.

B – thermal deicing systems that break ice from aircraft surfaces.

C – propeller anti-ice systems that use alcohol discharged from spinner nozzles to prevent ice formation.

9-116. Answer C. GFDIC 9B, AC 91-13C

Anti-icing equipment prevents the formation of ice, while deicing equipment removes the ice after it has formed. These systems include:

- Deicing boots that are pneumatically inflated to break the ice, allowing it to be carried away by the airstream.

- Thermal anti-ice systems that heat the surfaces on airplanes to prevent ice formation.

- Propeller anti-ice systems that use alcohol discharged from nozzles that are pointed toward each blade root. Centrifugal force causes the alcohol to flow down the leading edge of the blade to prevent ice formation.

SECTION B ■ **Weather Hazards and Ice Control Systems**

SECTION C
Aviation Weather Reports and Forecasts

OBSERVATIONS

AVIATION ROUTINE WEATHER REPORT

- An aviation routine weather report (METAR) is an observation of surface weather taken every hour that is reported in a standard format.

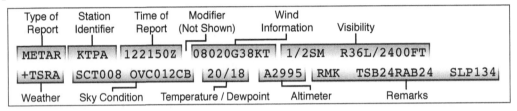

- A non-routine aviation weather report (SPECI) is issued when a significant change in one or more of the elements of a METAR has occurred.

- Prevailing visibility is the greatest distance an observer can see and identify objects through at least half of the horizon.

- Sometimes runway visual range (RVR) is reported following prevailing visibility. RVR is based on what a pilot in a moving aircraft should see when looking down the runway. RVR is a horizontal distance measured by a transmissometer located near the touchdown point of the runway.

- RVR is designated with an R, followed by the runway number, a slant (/), and the visual range in feet (FT). For example. R36L/2400FT means Runway 36 Left visual range is 2,400 feet.

- Weather or obstructions to vision that are present at the time of the observation are reported immediately after the visibility in the following order: intensity or proximity, descriptor, precipitation, obstruction to visibility, and any other weather phenomena.

WEATHER DESCRIPTOR CODES	
TS – Thunderstorm	DR –Low Drifting
SH –Shower(s)	MI – Shallow
FZ – Freezing	BC – Patches
BL – Blowing	PR – Partial

WEATHER PHENOMENA CODES	

Precipitation

RA — Rain	GR — Hail (> 1/4")
DZ — Drizzle	GS — Small Hail/Snow Pellets
SN — Snow	SG — Snow Grains
IC — Ice Crystals	PL — Ice Pellets
UP — Unknown Precipitation	

Obstructions to Visibility

FG — Fog	PY — Spray
BR — Mist	SA — Sand
FU — Smoke	DU — Dust
HZ — Haze	VA — Volcanic Ash

Other Weather Phenomena

SQ — Squall	SS — Sandstorm
DS — Duststorm	PO — Dust/Sand Whirls
FC — Funnel Cloud	
+FC — Tornado or Waterspout	

- Intensity or proximity of precipitation is shown just before the precipitation codes. The indicated intensity applies only to the first type of precipitation reported. Intensity levels are shown as light (–), moderate (no sign), or heavy (+).

- A ceiling is the above ground level (AGL) height of the lowest layer of clouds that is reported as broken (BKN) or overcast (OVC), or the vertical visibility into an obscuration, such as fog or haze. For example, VV008 indicates that the sky is obscured with a vertical visibility of 800 feet.

- If the top of a layer is known, you can easily determine its thickness. Add the airport elevation (MSL) to the height of the cloud base (AGL) found in a METAR observation. Then subtract this number from the height of the cloud tops.

- The beginning of the remarks section is indicated by the code RMK. The remarks section reports weather conditions, which are not covered in the previous sections of the METAR, that are considered significant to aircraft operations.

PILOT WEATHER REPORTS

- Pilot weather reports (PIREPs) are often your best source to confirm information such as the bases and tops of cloud layers, in-flight visibility, icing conditions, wind shear, and turbulence.

- In addition to a 3-letter identifier for the weather reporting location that is nearest to the reported phenomenon, PIREPS can contain up to 12 elements.

PIREP FORM		
3-Letter Station Identifier — — —	**Pilot Weather Report** 1. UA Routine Report	UUA Urgent Report
2. /OV	Location: In relation to a NAVAID	
3. /TM	Time: Coordinated Universal Time	
4. /FL	Altitude/Flight Level: Essential for turbulence and icing reports	
5. /TP	Aircraft Type: Essential for turbulence and icing reports	
Items 1 through 5 are mandatory for all PIREPs.		
6. /SK	Sky Cover: Cloud height and coverage (scattered, broken, or overcast)	
7. /WX	Flight Visibility and Weather: Flight visibility, precipitation, restrictions to visibility, etc.	
8. /TA	Temperature (Celsius): Essential for icing reports	
9. /WV	Wind: Direction in degrees and speed in knots	
10. /TB	Turbulence: Turbulence intensity, whether the turbulence occurred in or near clouds, and duration of turbulence	
11. /IC	Icing: Intensity and Type	
12. /RM	Remarks: For reporting elements not included or to clarify previously reported items	

SECTION C ■ **Aviation Weather Reports and Forecasts**

FORECASTS

TERMINAL AERODROME FORECAST

- The primary source for the forecast weather at a specific airport is the terminal aerodrome forecast (TAF). TAFs normally are valid for a 24-hour period and scheduled four times a day at 0000Z, 0600Z, 1200Z, and 1800Z for the area within a 5 statute mile radius from the center of an airport's runway complex.

- Each TAF contains these elements: type, ICAO station identifier, issuance date and time, valid period, and the forecast.

- The prevailing wind direction is forecast for any speed greater than or equal to 7 knots. When the prevailing wind direction is variable (variations in wind direction of 30 degrees or more), the wind direction is encoded as VRB. Two conditions where this can occur are very light winds (1 to 6 knots inclusive) and convective activity.

- A calm wind is forecast as 00000KT.

- When the expected prevailing visibility is 6 statute miles (SM) or less it is included in the forecast, followed by the letters, SM. Visibilities greater than (plus) 6 statute miles are indicated in the forecast by the letter P (P6SM).

- The letters SKC are used in a TAF to indicate "sky clear."

- The letters WS indicate that low-level wind shear that is not associated with convective activity might be present during the valid time of the forecast. For example, WS005/27050KT indicates that the wind at 500 feet AGL is 270° at 50 knots.

WIND AND TEMPERATURE ALOFT FORECAST

- The wind and temperature aloft forecast (FB) provides a forecast for wind direction in relation to true north, wind speed in knots, and temperature in degrees Celsius for selected stations and altitudes.

- An FB does not forecast winds within 1,500 feet of the station elevation, or temperatures for the 3,000-foot level or for any level within 2,500 feet of the station elevation.

- Wind direction and speed information on an FB are shown by a four-digit code. The first two digits are the wind direction in tens of degrees. Wind speed is shown by the second two digits. The last two digits indicate the temperature in degrees Celsius. All temperatures above 24,000 feet are negative and the minus sign is omitted.

- A code of 9900 on an (FB indicates light and variable winds (less than 5 knots).

- If the wind speed for a specific station is between 100 and 199 knots, subtract 50 from the wind direction code and add 100 to the speed. You can recognize this when you see a coded direction that exceeds "36" or 360.°

- When the wind speed at a specific station is forecast to be 200 knots or greater, 50 is added to the wind direction and the wind speed is coded as 99.

AIRMETS AND SIGMETS

- AIRMETs, SIGMETs, and convective SIGMETs are textual forecasts that advise enroute aircraft of the development of potentially hazardous weather.

- You can obtain these advisories from FIS-B during flight and, in some cases, ATC will broadcast the alert. In addition, you use these advisories during your preflight weather briefing to learn of the latest adverse conditions affecting your proposed flight.

- SIGMET and AIRMET conditions are considered widespread because they are for weather that affects an area of at least 3,000 square miles at any one time.

- AIRMETs (WAs) are issued every six hours, with amendments issued as necessary, for weather phenomena that are of operational interest to all aircraft, but hazardous mainly to light aircraft. AIRMETs are issued for:

  - IFR conditions (ceilings less than 1,000 feet or visibility less than 3 miles) and/or extensive mountain obscuration;

  - Moderate turbulence;

  - Sustained surface winds of 30 knots or greater;

  - Nonconvective low-level wind shear.

- SIGMETs (WSs) are unscheduled forecasts that are valid for four hours. However, if the SIGMET relates to hurricanes, it is valid for six hours. SIGMETs are issued for hazardous weather (other than convective activity) that is considered significant to all aircraft, including:

  - Severe icing;

  - Severe and extreme turbulence;

  - Clear air turbulence (CAT);

  - Dust storms and sandstorms lowering visibility to less than 3 miles;

  - Volcanic ash.

- Convective SIGMETs (WSTs) are issued for hazardous weather related to thunderstorms that is significant to the safety of all aircraft. Convective SIGMETS always imply severe or greater turbulence, severe icing, and low-level wind shear, so these items are not specified in the advisory.

- A WST consists of either an observation and a forecast or simply a forecast for any of the following phenomena:

  - Tornadoes.

  - Lines of thunderstorms, thunderstorms over a wide area, and embedded thunderstorms.

  - Hail ¾ inch in diameter or more.

  - Wind gusts to 50 knots or greater.

SEVERE WEATHER REPORTS AND FORECASTS

- The convective outlook (AC) is a national forecast of thunderstorm activity for the following 24-hour period that describes areas in which there is a slight, moderate, or high risk of severe thunderstorms, as well as areas of general thunderstorm activity. The convective outlook issuance schedule may cover 8 days of forecasts.

- Severe weather watch bulletins (WWs) are issued only when required to define an area of possible severe thunderstorms or tornadoes.

NOTE: An asterisk appearing after an ACS code (i.e. CA.IV.A.K2) indicates that the question subject appears more than one time in the ACS. The code shown corresponds to the first instance of the subject in the ACS.*

SECTION C ■ **Aviation Weather Reports and Forecasts**

9-117   CA.I.C.K2, CA.II.A.K4

What is the thickness of the cloud layer given a field elevation of 1,500 feet MSL with tops of the overcast at 7,000 feet MSL?

METAR KHOB 151250Z 17006KT 4SM OVC010 13/11 A2998

A – 4,500 feet.

B – 6,500 feet.

C – 5,500 feet.

9-117. Answer A. GFDIC 9C, AIM

A ceiling is the above ground level (AGL) height of the lowest layer of clouds that is reported as broken (BKN) or overcast (OVC), or the vertical visibility into an obscuration. If the top of a layer is known, you can easily determine its thickness. Add the airport elevation (MSL) to the height of the cloud base (AGL) found in a METAR observation. Then subtract this number from the height of the cloud tops.

1,000 feet AGL (OVC010) + 1,500 feet MSL (field elevation) = 2,500 feet MSL

7,000 feet MSL (top of the overcast) – 2,500 feet MSL = 4,500 feet

9-118   CA.I.C.K2, CA.II.A.K4

The remarks section of the aviation routine weather report (METAR) contains the following coded information. What does it mean?

RMK FZDZB42 WSHFT 30 FROPA

A – Freezing drizzle below 4,200 feet and wind shear.

B – Wind shift at 30 minutes past the hour due to frontal passage.

C – Freezing drizzle with cloud bases below 4,200 feet.

9-118. Answer B. GFDIC 9C, AIM

The beginning of the remarks section is indicated by the code RMK. The remarks section reports weather conditions, which are not covered in the previous sections of the METAR, that are considered significant to aircraft operations

In this example, freezing drizzle (FZDZ) began at 42 minutes past the hour (B42), and a wind shift occurred at thirty minutes past the hour (30). The contraction for frontal passage (FROPA) may be added when there is reasonable certainty that the wind shift was the result of frontal passage.

9-119   CA.I.C.K2, CA.II.A.K4

What is meant by the Special METAR weather observation for KBOI?

SPECI KBOI 091854Z 32005KT 1 1/2SM RA BR OVC007 17/16 A2990 RMK RAB12

A – Rain and fog are creating an overcast at 700 feet AGL; rain began at 1912Z.

B – The temperature-dew point spread is 1°C; rain began at 1812Z.

C – Rain and overcast at 1200 feet AGL.

9-119. Answer B. GFDIC 9C, AIM

Interpret the Special METAR as follows:

NOTE: the portions of the METAR that apply to the correct answer are shown in bold.

- 091854Z—issued on the 9th of the month at 1854 UTC (Zulu).
- 32005KT—wind from 320° at 5 knots.
- 1 1/2SM—prevailing visibility 1 1/2 statute miles.
- **RA BR—rain, mist.**
- OVC007—overcast ceiling at 700 feet AGL.
- **17/16—temperature 17, dewpoint 16.**
- A2990—altimeter setting 29.90.
- RMK RAB12—remarks: rain began at 12 minutes past the hour.

9-120   CA.I.C.K2, CA.II.A.K4

The station originating the following METAR observation has a field elevation of 5,000 feet MSL. If the sky cover is one continuous layer, what is the thickness of the cloud layer? (Top of overcast reported at 8,000 feet MSL).

METAR KHOB 151250Z 17006KT 4SM OVC005 13/11 A2998

A – 2,500 feet.

B – 3,500 feet.

C – 4,000 feet.

9-120. Answer A. GFDIC 9C, AIM

A ceiling is the above ground level (AGL) height of the lowest layer of clouds that is reported as broken (BKN) or overcast (OVC), or the vertical visibility into an obscuration. If the top of a layer is known, you can easily determine its thickness. Add the airport elevation (MSL) to the height of the cloud base (AGL) found in a METAR observation. Then subtract this number from the height of the cloud tops.

500 feet AGL (OVC010) + 5,000 feet MSL (field elevation) = 5,500 feet MSL

8,000 feet MSL (top of the overcast) – 5,500 feet MSL = 2,500 feet

9-121   CA.I.C.K2, CA.II.A.K4

Refer to the excerpt from the following METAR report:

KTUS 08004KT 4SM HZ 26/04 A2995 RMK RAE36

At approximately what altitude AGL should bases of convective-type cumuliform clouds be expected?

A – 4,400 feet.

B – 8,800 feet.

C – 17,600 feet.

9-121. Answer B. GFDIC 9C, AW

Temperature and dewpoint converge at 2.5°C per 1,000 feet of altitude. The temperature/dewpoint spread at the surface, according to the METAR, is 26°C – 4°C = 22°C. The bases of cumulus clouds are at the altitude where the spread is zero: 22°C ÷ (2.5°C/1,000 feet) = 8,800 feet AGL.

9-122   CA.I.C.K2, CA.II.A.K4

What significant cloud coverage is reported by this pilot report?

KMOB UA/OV 15NW MOB 1340Z/SK 025 OVC 045/075 OVC 080/090 OVC

A – Three (3) separate overcast layers exist with bases at 2,500, 7,500 and 9,000 feet.

B – The top of the lower overcast is 2,500 feet; base and top of second overcast layer are 4,500 and 9,000 feet, respectively.

C – The base of the second overcast layer is 2,500 feet; top of second overcast layer is 7,500 feet; base of third layer is 9,000 feet.

9-122. Answer A. GFDIC 9C, AIM

Interpret the PIREP as follows:

NOTE: the portions of the PIREP that apply to the correct answer are shown in bold.

- UA—pilot report
- OV 15 NM MOB 1340Z—15 nautical miles northwest of MOB at 1340 UTC (Zulu).
- SK 025 OVC 045—overcast layer with a **base at 2,500 feet MSL** and tops at 4,500 feet MSL.
- 075 OVC 080—overcast layer with a **base at 7,500 feet MSL** and tops at 8,000 feet MSL.
- 090 OVC—overcast layer with a **base at 9,000 feet MSL** with no tops reported.

SECTION C ■ **Aviation Weather Reports and Forecasts**

9-123   CA.I.C.K2, CA.II.A.K4

Interpret this PIREP.

MRB UA/OV MRB/TM1430/FL060/TPC182/SK BKN BL/WX RA/TB MDT.

A – Ceiling 6,000 feet intermittently below moderate thundershowers; turbulence increasing westward.

B – FL600, intermittently below clouds; moderate rain, turbulence increasing with the wind.

C – At 6,000 feet; between layers; moderate rain; moderate turbulence.

9-123. Answer C. GFDIC 9C, AIM

Interpret the PIREP as follows:

- Type of Report: routine PIREP (UA)
- Location (OV): over Martinsburg (MRB)
- Time (TM): 1430Z
- Altitude/Flight Level (FL): 6,000 feet MSL (060)
- Aircraft Type (TP): Cessna 182 (C182)
- Sky Cover (SK): broken (BKN), between layers (BL)
- Flight Visibility and Weather (WX): moderate rain (RA)

NOTE: Qualifiers for precipitation intensity are "-" for light:, no sign for moderate; "+" for heavy

- Turbulence (TB): moderate (MDT)

9-124   CA.I.C.K2

Terminal aerodrome forecasts (TAF) are issued how many times a day and cover what period of time?

A – Four times daily and are usually valid for a 24 hour period.

B – Six times daily and are usually valid for a 24 hour period including a 4-hour categorical outlook.

C – Four times daily and are valid for 12 hours including a 6-hour categorical outlook.

9-124. Answer A. GFDIC 9C, AWS

The primary source for the forecast weather at a specific airport is the terminal aerodrome forecast (TAF). TAFs normally are valid for a 24-hour period and scheduled four times a day at 0000Z, 0600Z, 1200Z, and 1800Z for the area within a 5 statute mile radius from the center of an airport's runway complex.

9-125   CA.I.C.K2, CA.II.A.K4

Which statement pertaining to the following terminal aerodrome forecast (TAF) is true?

TAF KMEM 091730Z 2218/2318 15005KT 5SM HZ BKN060 FM2300 VRB04KT P6SM SKC

A – Wind in the outlook period implies surface winds are forecast to be greater than 5 KTS

B – Wind direction is from 160° at 4 KTS and reported visibility is 6 statute miles.

C – SKC in the valid period indicates no significant weather and sky clear.

9-125. Answer C. GFDIC 9C, AIM

Interpret the TAF as follows:

NOTE: the portions of the TAF that apply to the correct answer are shown in bold.

- 091730Z—issued on the 9th of the month at 1730 UTC (Zulu).
- 0918/1018—valid from the 9th of the month at 1800 UTC (Zulu) to the 10th at 1800 UTC (Zulu) the 22
- 15005KT—wind from 150° at 5 knots.
- 5SM—prevailing visibility 5 statute miles.
- HZ—haze.
- BKN060—broken ceiling at 6,000 feet AGL.
- FM2300—from 2300 UTC (Zulu) temperature.
- VRB04KT—wind variable at 4 knots.
- P6SM—visibility greater than 6 statute miles.
- **SKC—sky clear.**

9-126   CA.I.C.K2

What is the meaning of the terms PROB40 2102 +TSRA as used in a terminal aerodrome forecasts (TAF)?

A – Probability of heavy thunderstorms with rain showers below 4000 feet at time 2102.

B – Between 2100Z and 0200Z there is a forty percent (40%) probability of thunderstorms with heavy rain.

C – Beginning at 2102Z forty percent (40%) probability of heavy thunderstorms and rain showers.

9-126. Answer B. GFDIC 9C, AIM

The probability group (PROB40) in a TAF is used to indicate there is between a 30% and 49% probability of thunderstorms or precipitation events and associated conditions occurring in the forecast period. This is followed by beginning and ending time and then by the conditions that are expected. In this example, there is approximately a 40 percent probability of a thunderstorm and heavy rain between 2100Z and 0200Z. There is no mention of showers (SH).

9-127   CA.I.C.K2, CA.II.A.K4

In the following TAF for HOU, what is the ceiling and visibility forecast on the 7th day of the month at 0600Z?

KHOU 061734Z 0618/0718 16014G22KT P6SM VCSH BKN018 BKN035

FM070100 17010KT P6SM BKN015 OVC025

FM070500 17008KT 4SM BR SCT008 OVC012

FM071000 18005KT 3SM BR OVC007

FM071500 23008KT 5SM BR VCSH SCT008 OVC015

A – Visibility 6 miles with a broken ceiling at 15,000 feet MSL.

B – 4 nautical miles of visibility and an overcast ceiling at 700 feet MSL.

C – 4 statute miles visibility and an overcast ceiling at 1,200 feet AGL.

9-127. Answer C. GFDIC 9C, AIM

In a terminal aerodrome forecast (TAF), FM is used to indicate that a change in the existing weather is expected, with the hour of the expected change following "FM." In this example, the weather is expected to change at 0100Z, 0500Z, 1000Z and 1500Z on the 7th. The forecast from 0500Z to 1000Z would include the time of 0600Z. Interpret the TAF for this time period as follows:

NOTE: the portions of the TAF that apply to the correct answer are shown in bold.

- FM07050—from 0500 UTC (Zulu).
- 17008KT—wind from 170° at 8 knots.
- **4SM—4 statute miles visibility.**
- BR—mist
- SCT008—scattered clouds at 800 feet AGL.
- OVC012—overcast ceiling at 1,200 feet AGL.

9-128   CA.I.C.K2

What does the contraction VRB in the terminal aerodrome forecast (TAF) mean?

A – Wind speed is variable throughout the period.

B – Cloud base is variable.

C – Wind direction is variable.

9-128. Answer C. GFDIC 9C, AWS

The prevailing wind direction is forecast for any speed greater than or equal to 7 knots. When the prevailing wind direction is variable (variations in wind direction of 30 degrees or more), the wind direction is encoded as VRB. Two conditions where this can occur are very light winds (1 to 6 knots inclusive) and convective activity.

SECTION C ■ **Aviation Weather Reports and Forecasts**

9-129　CA.I.C.K2

The visibility entry in a terminal aerodrome forecast (TAF) of P6SM implies that the prevailing visibility is expected to be greater than

A – 6 nautical miles.

B – 6 statute miles.

C – 6 kilometers.

9-129. Answer B. GFDIC 9C, AWS

When the expected prevailing visibility is 6 statute miles (SM) or less it is included in the forecast, followed by the letters, SM. Visibilities greater than (plus) 6 statute miles are indicated in the forecast by the letter P (P6SM).

9-130　CA.I.C.K2

What values are used for wind and temperature aloft forecasts?

A – True direction and MPH.

B – True direction and knots.

C – Magnetic direction and knots.

9-130. Answer B. GFDIC 9C, AWS

The wind and temperature aloft forecast (FB) provides a forecast for wind direction in relation to true north, wind speed in knots, and temperature in degrees Celsius for selected stations and altitudes.

9-131　CA.I.C.K2, CA.II.A.K4

Decode the excerpt from the wind and temperature aloft forecast (FB) for OKC at 39,000 feet.

FT	3000	9000	12000	24000	39000
OKC	9900	2018+00	2130-06	2361-30	830558

A – Wind 130° at 50 knots, temperature -58°C.

B – Wind 330° at 105 knots, temperature -58°C.

C – Wind 330° at 205 knots, temperature -58°C.

9-131. Answer B. GFDIC 9C, AWS

If the wind speed for a specific station is between 100 and 199 knots, subtract 50 from the wind direction code and add 100 to the speed. You can recognize this when you see a coded direction that exceeds "36" or 360.°

In this example, "830558" indicates the wind at OKC is from 330° (83 – 50 = 33 or 330°) at 105 knots (05 + 100 = 105 knots). The last two digits of the sequence always represents the temperature. All temperatures above 24,000 feet are negative; therefore, the minus sign is omitted for temperatures above 24,000 feet.

9-132　CA.I.C.K2, K3i

What type of in-flight weather advisory provides an enroute pilot with information regarding the possibility of moderate icing, moderate turbulence, winds of 30 knots or more at the surface and extensive mountain obscuration?

A – Convective SIGMETs and SIGMETs.

B – Terminal aerodrome forecasts.

C – AIRMETs.

9-132. Answer C. GFDIC 9C, AWS

AIRMETs, SIGMETs, and convective SIGMETs are textual forecasts that advise enroute aircraft of the development of potentially hazardous weather. In addition, you use these advisories during your preflight weather briefing to learn of the latest adverse conditions affecting your proposed flight.

AIRMETs (WAs) are issued every six hours, with amendments issued as necessary, for weather phenomena that are of operational interest to all aircraft, but hazardous mainly to light aircraft. AIRMETs are issued for:

- IFR conditions (ceilings less than 1,000 feet or visibility less than 3 miles) and/or extensive mountain obscuration:
- Moderate turbulence:
- Sustained surface winds of 30 knots or greater;
- Nonconvective low-level wind shear.

9-133   CA.I.C.K2, K3l

What in-flight weather advisory contains a forecast for volcanic ash?

A – SIGMET.

B – AIRMET.

C – METAR.

9-133. Answer A. GFDIC 9C, AIM

SIGMETs (WSs) are unscheduled forecasts that are valid for four hours. However, if the SIGMET relates to hurricanes, it is valid for six hours. SIGMETs are issued for hazardous weather (other than convective activity) that is considered significant to all aircraft, including:

- Severe icing;
- Severe and extreme turbulence;
- Clear air turbulence (CAT);
- Dust storms and sandstorms lowering visibility to less than 3 miles;
- Volcanic ash.

9-134   CA.I.C.K2, K3g, i, l

SIGMETs are issued as a warning of weather conditions which are hazardous

A – to all aircraft.

B – particularly to heavy aircraft.

C – particularly to light airplanes.

9-134. Answer A. GFDIC 9C, AIM

SIGMETs (WSs) are unscheduled forecasts that are valid for four hours. However, if the SIGMET relates to hurricanes, it is valid for six hours. SIGMETs are issued for hazardous weather (other than convective activity) that is considered significant to all aircraft, including:

- Severe icing;
- Severe and extreme turbulence;
- Clear air turbulence (CAT);
- Dust storms and sandstorms lowering visibility to less than 3 miles;
- Volcanic ash.

9-135   CA.I.C.K2

Which correctly describes the purpose of Convective SIGMETs (WST)?

A – They consist of an hourly observation of tornadoes, significant thunderstorm activity, and large hailstone activity.

B – They contain both an observation and a forecast of all thunderstorm and hailstone activity. The forecast is valid for 1 hour only.

C – They consist of either an observation and a forecast or just a forecast for tornadoes, significant thunderstorm activity, or hail greater than or equal to 3/4 inch in diameter.

9-135. Answer C. GFDIC 9E, AIM

Convective SIGMETs (WSTs) are issued for hazardous weather related to thunderstorms that is significant to the safety of all aircraft.

A WST consists of either an observation and a forecast or simply a forecast for any of the following phenomena:

- Tornadoes.
- Lines of thunderstorms, thunderstorms over a wide area, and embedded thunderstorms.
- Hail ¾ inch in diameter or more.
- Wind gusts to 50 knots or greater.

SECTION C ■ Aviation Weather Reports and Forecasts

SECTION D
Graphic Weather Products

OVERVIEW

- Graphic weather products use information gathered from ground observations, weather radar, satellites, and other sources to give you a pictorial view of large scale weather patterns and trends.

- You can obtain graphic weather products online from the National Weather Service (NWS) Aviation Weather Center (AWC) at aviationweather.gov, from Flight Service at 1800wxbrief.com, and other vendors.

- When interpreting graphic weather products, refer to the legend provided by the source for the particular product. However, some standard symbology applies to a variety of analysis and forecast charts to display weather phenomena, precipitation, turbulence, and winds.

Symbol	Meaning	Symbol	Meaning	Symbol	Meaning
=	Mist	∿●	Freezing Drizzle	Ψ	Moderate Icing
≡	Fog	∿●	Freezing Rain	Ψ	Severe Icing
∞	Haze	◬	Ice Pellets	⌃	Moderate Turbulence
∾	Smoke	✳	Snow	⌃	Severe Turbulence
❟	Drizzle	▽̇	Rain Shower	૬	Tropical Storm
●	Rain	▽̣	Snow Shower	૬	Hurricane (Typhoon)
		⏃	Thunderstorms		

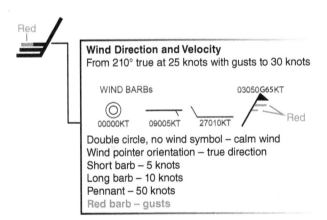

Wind Direction and Velocity
From 210° true at 25 knots with gusts to 30 knots

WIND BARBs   03050G65KT

00000KT   09005KT   27010KT

Double circle, no wind symbol – calm wind
Wind pointer orientation – true direction
Short barb – 5 knots
Long barb – 10 knots
Pennant – 50 knots
Red barb – gusts

ANALYSIS

SURFACE ANALYSIS CHART

- The surface analysis chart is an analyzed depiction of surface weather observations. By reviewing this chart, you obtain a picture of atmospheric pressure patterns at the Earth's surface.

- Standard chart symbols depict areas of equal pressure, the positions of highs, lows, ridges, and troughs, the location and type of fronts, and various boundaries, such as drylines, which separate moist and dry air masses.

- Isobars—lines of equal pressure—are depicted as solid lines spaced at intervals of 4 millibars (mb), each labeled with the pressure. For example: 1008 is 1,008 mb.

- Isobars that are close together indicate a higher pressure gradient because the pressure changes over a shorter distance, resulting in stronger winds.

FORECASTS

AVIATION FORECASTS

- Aviation forecasts are presented for the entire continental U.S. and divided into specific regions. These forecasts are updated every 3 hours and provide forecast snapshots for 3, 6, 9, 12, 15, and 18 hours in the future. These forecasts include the aviation surface forecast and the aviation cloud forecast.

- The aviation surface forecast provides visibility, weather phenomena, and winds (including wind gusts) with depictions of the boundaries of AIRMETs for IFR conditions and sustained surface winds of 30 knots or more. Use this information to interpret the aviation surface forecast:

    ○ The legend in the lower left corner of the weather graphic displays the colors used for areas of LIFR, IFR, MVFR, and VFR weather conditions.

    ○ Standard symbols represent precipitation. The number of symbols indicates the intensities of drizzle, rain, and snow: two—light, three—moderate, and four—heavy. A mixture of two precipitation types is shown as two symbols separated by a slash.

    ○ Wind is plotted in increments of 5 knots. The wind direction is depicted by a stem (line) pointed in the direction from which the wind is blowing. Add the values of the pennants (50 knots), barbs (10 knots) and half-barbs (5 knots) to determine wind speed. Gusts are shown by red barbs.

- The aviation cloud forecast provides cloud coverage, bases, layers, and tops and includes depictions of the boundaries of AIRMETs for mountain obscuration and icing. Use this information to interpret the aviation cloud forecast:

    ○ The legend in the lower left corner of the weather graphic displays the colors used for cloud coverage—few, scattered, broken, and overcast.

    ○ Text next to station symbols provides cloud bases, layers, and tops in feet MSL.

U.S. LOW-LEVEL SIGNIFICANT WEATHER (SIGWX) CHART

- Significant weather prognostic (prog) charts are available from the AWC for low-level, midlevel, and high-level forecasts for varying time periods depending on the chart.

- The U.S. low-level significant weather (SigWx) chart is designed to help you plan flights to avoid areas of low visibilities and ceilings, as well as areas where turbulence and icing might exist. Forecast freezing levels are also depicted on the SigWx panels.

- The forecast covers altitudes from FL240 and below. Two charts (12 and 24 hours) are issued and the weather conditions depicted are forecast to exist during the valid time of the chart.

- Bold, dashed brown lines enclose areas of moderate or greater turbulence. Standard symbols for moderate and severe turbulence are shown.

- Below the turbulence symbol, the vertical extent of the turbulence layers is specified by top and base heights separated by a slash. For example, 180/100 indicates that turbulence can be expected from the top at FL180 to the base at 10,000 feet MSL. If the base height is omitted, the turbulence is forecast to reach the surface.

- Forecast freezing level height contours for the highest freezing level are typically drawn at 4,000-foot intervals with dashed lines and labeled in hundreds of feet MSL. A zigzag line labeled SFC normally shows where the freezing level is at the surface.

SECTION D ■ Graphic Weather Products

U.S. HIGH-LEVEL SIGNIFICANT WEATHER (SIGWX) CHART

- High-level significant weather (SigWx) charts cover altitudes from FL250 to FL630. These charts present forecasts for thunderstorms, tropical cyclones, squall lines, moderate or greater turbulence, widespread dust storms and sandstorms, tropopause heights, the location of the jet streams, and volcanic activity.

- The abbreviation CB refers to the expected occurrence of widespread cumulonimbus clouds. Red scalloped lines enclose these areas. The coverage and height of the cloud bases and tops is typically indicated in a box with an arrow pointing to the specific area. Bases that extend below FL250 (the lowest altitude limit of the chart) are encoded as XXX.

- Enclosed areas of cumulonimbus clouds also imply the presence of moderate or greater turbulence and icing conditions.

- Areas of moderate or greater turbulence are enclosed by bold, dashed yellow lines. Standard symbols for moderate and severe turbulence are shown. The vertical extent of the turbulence layers is specified by top and base heights separated by a horizontal line. Bases that extend below FL250 (the lowest altitude limit of the chart) are encoded as XXX.

- A jet stream axis with a wind speed of more than 80 knots is identified by a bold (green) line. An arrowhead is used to indicate wind direction. A standard wind symbol (light green) identifies wind velocity—a pennant represents 50 knots and a barb represents 10 knots. The flight level is placed adjacent to each wind symbol to identify the altitude of the jet stream core or axis.

- Three-digit numbers in boxes represent the forecast height of the tropopause in hundreds of feet MSL, or flight levels. Centers of high (H) and low (L) tropopause heights are enclosed by polygons.

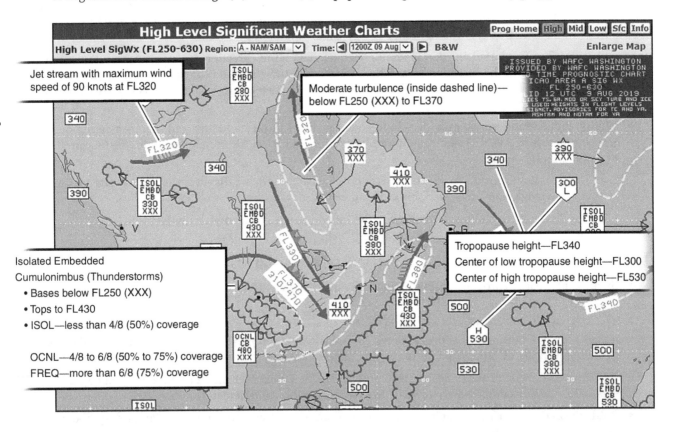

NOTE: *An asterisk appearing after an ACS code (i.e. CA.IV.A.K2*) indicates that the question subject appears more than one time in the ACS. The code shown corresponds to the first instance of the subject in the ACS.*

9-136   CA.I.C.K2

Which chart provides a ready means of locating observed frontal positions and pressure centers?

A – Surface analysis chart.

B – Constant pressure analysis chart.

C – Weather depiction chart.

9-136. Answer A. GFDIC 9D, AWS

The surface analysis chart is an analyzed depiction of surface weather observations. By reviewing this chart, you obtain a picture of atmospheric pressure patterns at the Earth's surface. Standard chart symbols depict areas of equal pressure, the positions of highs, lows, ridges, and troughs, the location and type of fronts, and various boundaries, such as drylines, which separate moist and dry air masses.

9-137   CA.I.C.K2

On a surface analysis chart, the solid lines that depict sea level pressure patterns are called

A – isobars.

B – isogons.

C – millibars.

9-137. Answer A. GFDIC 9D, AWS

On surface analysis charts, isobars—lines of equal pressure—are depicted as solid lines spaced at intervals of 4 millibars (mb), each labeled with the pressure. For example: 1008 is 1,008 mb. Isobars that are close together indicate a higher pressure gradient because the pressure changes over a shorter distance, resulting in stronger winds.

9-138   CA.I.C.K2

With regard to wind flow patterns shown on surface analysis charts; when the isobars are

A – close together, the pressure gradient force is slight and wind velocities are weaker.

B – not close together, the pressure gradient force is greater and wind velocities are stronger.

C – close together, the pressure gradient force is greater and wind velocities are stronger.

9-138. Answer C. GFDIC 9D, AWS

On surface analysis charts, isobars—lines of equal pressure—are depicted as solid lines spaced at intervals of 4 millibars (mb), each labeled with the pressure. For example: 1008 is 1,008 mb. Isobars that are close together indicate a higher pressure gradient because the pressure changes over a shorter distance, resulting in stronger winds.

9-139   CA.I.C.K2

On a surface analysis chart, close spacing of the isobars indicates

A – weak pressure gradient.

B – strong pressure gradient.

C – strong temperature gradient.

9-139. Answer B. GFDIC 9D, AWS

On surface analysis charts, isobars—lines of equal pressure—are depicted as solid lines spaced at intervals of 4 millibars (mb), each labeled with the pressure. For example: 1008 is 1,008 mb. Isobars that are close together indicate a higher pressure gradient because the pressure changes over a shorter distance, resulting in stronger winds.

9-140   CA.I.C.K2

On surface analysis charts, widely spaced isobars indicate a

A – weak pressure gradient.

B – strong pressure gradient.

C – relatively turbulent wind.

9-140. Answer A. GFDIC 9D, AWS

On surface analysis charts, isobars—lines of equal pressure—are depicted as solid lines spaced at intervals of 4 millibars (mb), each labeled with the pressure. For example: 1008 is 1,008 mb. Isobars that are close together indicate a higher pressure gradient because the pressure changes over a shorter distance, resulting in stronger winds.

SECTION D ■ **Graphic Weather Products**

9-141   CA.I.C.K2

Which weather chart depicts conditions forecast to exist at a specific time in the future?

A – Freezing level chart.

B – Surface analysis chart.

C – U.S. low-level significant weather (SigWx) chart.

9-141. Answer C. GFDIC 9D, AWS

The U.S. low-level significant weather (SigWx) chart is designed to help you plan flights to avoid areas of low visibilities and ceilings, as well as areas where turbulence and icing might exist. Forecast freezing levels are also depicted on the SigWx panels.

The forecast covers altitudes from FL240 and below. Two charts (12 and 24 hours) are issued and the weather conditions depicted are forecast to exist during the valid time of the chart.

9-142   CA.I.C.K2

What is the upper limit of the low level significant weather prognostic chart?

A – 30,000 feet.

B – 24,000 feet.

C – 18,000 feet.

9-142. Answer B. GFDIC 9D, AWS

The U.S. low-level significant weather (SigWx) chart is designed to help you plan flights to avoid areas of low visibilities and ceilings, as well as areas where turbulence and icing might exist. Forecast freezing levels are also depicted on the SigWx panels.

The forecast covers altitudes from FL240 and below. Two charts (12 and 24 hours) are issued and the weather conditions depicted are forecast to exist during the valid time of the chart.

9-143   CA.I.C.K2, K3g, i

What weather phenomenon is implied within an area enclosed by small scalloped lines on a U.S. high-level significant weather prognostic chart?

A – Cirriform clouds, light to moderate turbulence, and icing.

B – Cumulonimbus clouds, icing, and moderate or greater turbulence.

C – Cumuliform or standing lenticular clouds, moderate to severe turbulence, and icing.

9-143. Answer B. GFDIC 9D, AWS

High-level significant weather (SigWx) charts cover altitudes from FL250 to FL630. These charts present forecasts for thunderstorms, tropical cyclones, squall lines, moderate or greater turbulence, widespread dust storms and sandstorms, tropopause heights, the location of the jet streams, and volcanic activity.

The abbreviation CB refers to the expected occurrence of widespread cumulonimbus clouds. Red scalloped lines enclose these areas. Enclosed areas of cumulonimbus clouds also imply the presence of moderate or greater turbulence and icing conditions.

9-144   CA.I.C.K2

The U.S. high-level significant weather prognostic chart forecasts significant weather for what airspace?

A – FL180 to FL450.

B – FL250 to FL450.

C – FL250 to FL630.

9-144. Answer C. GFDIC 9D, AWS

High-level significant weather (SigWx) charts cover altitudes from FL250 to FL630. These charts present forecasts for thunderstorms, tropical cyclones, squall lines, moderate or greater turbulence, widespread dust storms and sandstorms, tropopause heights, the location of the jet streams, and volcanic activity.

SECTION E
Sources of Weather Information

PREFLIGHT WEATHER SOURCES

FLIGHT SERVICE AND NWS

- You can call Flight Service for a phone briefing for your specific flight at 1-800-WX-BRIEF or obtain an online weather briefing and other weather information at 1800wxbrief.com. Types of briefings include:
    - Standard briefing when you are planning a flight and have not obtained preliminary weather or a previous briefing.
    - Abbreviated briefing when you need only one or two specific items or would like to update weather information from a previous briefing or other weather sources.
    - Outlook briefing when your proposed departure time is six or more hours in the future to obtain forecast information that helps you make an initial judgment about the feasibility of your flight.
- When you need to update a previous briefing during flight, contact Flight Service for current weather information along your route, including PIREPs.
- You can obtain preliminary and supplemental weather information directly from the National Weather Service (NWS) online at the Aviation Weather Center (AWC) site.

IN-FLIGHT WEATHER SOURCES

CENTER WEATHER ADVISORIES

- A center weather advisory (CWA) is an unscheduled weather advisory issued by an ARTCC to alert pilots of existing or anticipated adverse weather conditions within the next two hours.
- A CWA can be initiated when an AIRMET or SIGMET has not been issued but, based on current PIREPs, conditions meet those criteria.
- A CWA can be issued to supplement an existing in-flight advisory as well as any conditions that currently or will soon adversely affect the safe flow of traffic within the ARTCC area of responsibility.
- ARTCCs broadcast CWAs and other hazardous weather information once on all frequencies, except emergency (121.5), when any part of the area described is within the area described is within when any part of the area described is within 150 miles of the airspace under the ARTCC jurisdiction. In terminal areas, local control and approach control might limit these broadcasts to weather occurring within 50 miles of the airspace under their jurisdiction.

AUTOMATED WEATHER REPORTING SYSTEMS

- Automated weather observation systems include:
    - Automated weather observing system (AWOS)—broadcasts specific information depending on the type of system. AWOS-3 can report the altimeter setting, wind speed, direction and gusts, temperature, dew point, visibility, and cloud and ceiling data.
    - Automated surface observing system (ASOS)—in addition to broadcasting the same elements as AWOS, measures and reports variable cloud height, variable visibility, and rapid pressure changes, as well as precipitation type, intensity, accumulation, and beginning and ending times. In addition, ASOS is capable of measuring wind shifts and peak winds and some ASOS stations can determine the difference between liquid precipitation and frozen or freezing precipitation.

○ Automated weather sensor system (AWSS)—has the same capabilities as ASOS, but is operated by the FAA rather than the NWS.

- ASOS/AWSS/AWOS information is broadcast over discrete VHF frequencies or the voice portions of local navaids. You can normally receive these weather report transmissions within 25 miles of the site and up to 10,000 feet AGL.

DATA LINK WEATHER AND AIRBORNE WEATHER RADAR

- Data link weather services are often included with GPS and electronic flight bag (EFB) flight deck or tablet display systems. The weather information displayed using a data link is near realtime but should not be thought of as instantaneous, up-to-date information.

- The NEXRAD radar image that you view on your cockpit display can be up to 5 minutes old. Even small-time differences between the age indicator and actual conditions can be critical to flight safety. At no time should you use the images as storm penetrating radar to navigate through a line of thunderstorms.

- Airborne weather radar is prone to many of the same limitations as ground-based systems—it cannot detect water vapor, lightning, or wind shear.

NOTE: An asterisk appearing after an ACS code (i.e. CA.IV.A.K2*) indicates that the question subject appears more than one time in the ACS. The code shown corresponds to the first instance of the subject in the ACS.

9-145   CA.I.C.K1
The most current enroute and destination flight information for planning an instrument flight should be obtained from

A – the ATIS broadcast.

B – Flight Service.

C – Notices to Airmen.

9-145. Answer B. GFDIC 9E, AIM
Flight Service is your primary FAA source of preflight weather information. Call for a phone briefing for your specific flight at 1-800-WX-BRIEF or obtain an online weather briefing and other weather information at 1800wxbrief.com.

9-146   CA.I.C.K1
Obtain an outlook briefing when

A – your proposed departure time is six or more hours in the future.

B – you need only one or two specific items to update weather information from other weather sources.

C – your proposed departure time is within the next 2 hours.

9-146. Answer A. GFDIC 9E, AWS
Types of Flight Service briefings include:

- Standard briefing when you are planning a flight and have not obtained preliminary weather or a previous briefing.

- Abbreviated briefing when you need only one or two specific items or would like to update weather information from a previous briefing or other weather sources.

- Outlook briefing when your proposed departure time is six or more hours in the future to obtain forecast information that helps you make an initial judgment about the feasibility of your flight.

9-147 CA.I.C.K1

A center weather advisory is

A – a scheduled weather advisory issued by Flight Service to alert you to current AIRMETs and SIGMETs.

B – an unscheduled weather advisory issued by an ARTCC to alert you to existing or anticipated adverse weather conditions within the next two hours.

C – an unscheduled weather advisory issued by an ARTCC to alert you to adverse weather conditions occurring within 50 miles of the ARTCC facility.

9-147. Answer B. GFDIC 9E, AWS

A center weather advisory (CWA) is an unscheduled weather advisory issued by an ARTCC to alert pilots of existing or anticipated adverse weather conditions within the next two hours. A CWA can be initiated when a SIGMET has not been issued but, based on current PIREPs, conditions meet those criteria.

ARTCCs broadcast CWAs and other hazardous weather information when any part of the area described is within 150 miles of the airspace under the ARTCC jurisdiction. In terminal areas, local control and approach control might limit these broadcasts to weather occurring within 50 miles of the airspace under their jurisdiction.

9-148 CA.I.C.K1

Weather advisory broadcasts, including center weather advisories and SIGMETS, are provided by

A – ARTCCs on all frequencies, except emergency, when any part of the area described is within 150 miles of the airspace under their jurisdiction.

B – Flight service on 122.2 MHz and adjacent VORs, when any part of the area described is within 200 miles of the airspace under their jurisdiction.

C – ARTCCs on all frequencies, except emergency, only when any part of the area described is within 50 miles of the airspace under their jurisdiction.

9-148. Answer A. GFDIC 9E, AIM

ARTCCs broadcast CWAs and other hazardous weather information once on all frequencies, except emergency, when any part of the area described is within the area described is within when any part of the area described is within 150 miles of the airspace under the ARTCC jurisdiction. In terminal areas, local control and approach control might limit these broadcasts to weather occurring within 50 miles of the airspace under their jurisdiction.

9-149 CA.I.C.K1

Which information is broadcast by an ASOS?

A – AIRMETs and SIGMETs that affect an area within 50 miles of the transmission site.

B – variable cloud height, variable visibility, precipitation type, intensity, and beginning and ending times.

C – visibility, cloud and ceiling data, and instrument approach in use.

9-149. Answer B. GFDIC 9E, AWS

An automated surface observing system (ASOS) broadcasts the same elements as an AWOS, such as the altimeter setting, wind speed, direction and gusts, temperature, dew point, visibility, and cloud and ceiling data. In addition, ASOS measures and reports variable cloud height, variable visibility, and rapid pressure changes, as well as precipitation type, intensity, accumulation, and beginning and ending times.

SECTION E ■ Sources of Weather Information

9-150   CA.I.C.K1

Which is true regarding flight deck weather information?

A – Data link weather is instantaneous up-to-date weather information

B – Airborne weather radar can detect water vapor, lightning, or wind shear.

C – NEXRAD radar images on a flight deck display are should not be used to navigate through a line of thunderstorms.

9-150. Answer C. GFDIC 9E, AWS

Data link weather services are often included with GPS and electronic flight bag (EFB) flight deck or tablet display systems. The weather information displayed using a data link is near real-time but should not be thought of as instantaneous, up-to-date information.

The NEXRAD radar image that you view on your cockpit display can be up to 5 minutes old. Even small-time differences between the age indicator and actual conditions can be critical to flight safety. At no time should you use the images as storm penetrating radar to navigate through a line of thunderstorms.

Airborne weather radar is prone to many of the same limitations as ground-based systems—it cannot detect water vapor, lightning, or wind shear.

9-151   CA.I.C.K2

An in-flight aviation weather advisory, such as a CWA or a SIGMET broadcast by ATC include what type of information?

A – Forecasts for potentially hazardous flying conditions for enroute aircraft.

B – State and geographic areas with reported ceilings and visibilities below VFR minimums.

C – IFR conditions, turbulence, and icing within a valid period for the listed states.

9-151. Answer A. GFDIC 9E, AIM

In-Flight Aviation Weather Advisories are forecasts to advise enroute aircraft of potentially hazardous weather. Included are convective SIGMETs, SIGMETs, and AIRMETs, using VORs, airports, or other well known geographic areas to describe the location of hazardous weather along a route.

CHAPTER 10

Chapter 10 of the *GFD Instrument/Commercial* textbook: IFR Flight Considerations is specific to instrument training, so no FAA commercial pilot knowledge test questions apply.

CHAPTER 11

Advanced Systems

SECTION A
High Performance Powerplants

CARBURETORS

- Ice can form inside a carburetor due to the temperature drop caused by venturi effect and fuel vaporization. If you miss the indications of carburetor ice, the engine loses power and might even stop running.

- Using carburetor heat can help prevent icing, but because the warm air is less dense than cold air, the engine produces less power when carburetor heat is on. When the same amount of fuel is mixed with less dense air (more fuel than air by weight), the fuel/air mixture is enriched.

FUEL INJECTION SYSTEM DESIGN AND OPERATION

- Fuel injection systems can increase engine efficiency by providing the same amount of fuel to every cylinder, which allows for more precise mixture control. This improves engine performance and reduces fuel waste. It also promotes safety by reducing the risk of induction system icing.

- Most operating difficulties of fuel-injected engines occur when pilots do not follow the manufacturer's recommended procedures.

- Proper use of the electric/auxiliary fuel pump minimizes vapor lock problems.

MIXTURE CONTROL

- Set the mixture control to achieve a fuel/air ratio that provides the most power for any given throttle setting.

- To maintain the correct fuel/air ratio, you must lean the mixture as you gain altitude. During a descent from high altitude, enrich the mixture.

- As altitude increases, the density of air decreases while the density of the fuel remains the same, creating a progressively richer mixture, which can reduce power output and cause engine roughness. The roughness normally is due to spark plug fouling from excessive carbon buildup on the plugs.

FUEL PUMPS

- Fuel injection systems depend on fuel pumps to force fuel into the cylinders under pressure.

- An engine-driven fuel pump operates whenever the engine is turning.

- An electric fuel pump, (sometimes referred to as the auxiliary fuel pump) provides fuel under pressure to the fuel/ air control unit for engine starting and/or emergency use.

OPERATING PROCEDURES

- Priming the engine with the auxiliary fuel pump sprays fuel directly into the intake ports of each cylinder.

- Priming provides a combustible mixture for starting and purges any vapors, or air pockets, from the injection system. If not eliminated, fuel vapors can prevent the injection system from functioning properly.

- A fuel-injected engine can be difficult to restart a few minutes after shutdown—the residual heat in the engine can boil the fuel in the injection system's lines and components, and the resulting bubbles can cause vapor lock, which interferes with fuel metering and pumping.

- The objective of the flooded engine starting procedure is to purge the excess fuel from the cylinders until you obtain a combustible fuel/air ratio. This procedure typically involves opening the throttle fully to provide maximum airflow through the cylinders and setting the mixture control to the idle-cutoff position before cranking the engine.

- If the ignition switch is off, the magneto will continue to fire if the ground wire between the magneto and the ignition switch becomes disconnected. The magneto might send a current to the spark plugs and the engine could start if any rotation of the crankshaft/propeller occurs and a small amount of fuel is in the cylinders.

- To check the ignition system for a broken ground wire, idle the engine before shutting it down and momentarily turn the ignition switch to OFF, then, turn the switch back to both. If the engine continues to run without hesitation the ground wire is broken. This check should be accomplished in accordance with the manufacturer's recommendations in the aircraft flight manual (AFM) or the pilot's operating handbook (POH).

ENGINE MONITORING

- Oil provides two important functions in an engine, lubrication and cooling by reducing friction and removing some of the heat from the cylinders. The oil pressure gauge provides a direct indication of the oil system operation.

- High oil temperature indications can be caused by several factors, including a low oil quantity, a plugged oil line, or a defective temperature gauge.

- The exhaust gas temperature gauge (EGT) measures the temperature of the exhaust gases leaving the combustion chamber. Generally, the exhaust temperature increases as you lean the mixture until the optimum fuel/air ratio is achieved.

- A cylinder head temperature gauges (CHT) gauge uses one or more thermocouple probes to sense the temperature of the metal of the combustion chamber.

ABNORMAL COMBUSTION

- Detonation is the uncontrolled, explosive combustion of fuel, which can produce damaging pressures and temperatures inside the engine's cylinders.

- Detonation usually causes high CHT and is most likely to occur when operating at high power settings.

- Common causes include using a lower fuel grade than specified by the manufacturer, operating with high manifold pressures combined with low RPM, or using too lean a mixture at high power settings.

- Preignition occurs when the fuel/air mixture ignites prior to the firing of the spark plug. Premature ignition is usually caused by a residual hot spot in the combustion chamber, often created by a small carbon deposit on a spark plug, a cracked spark plug insulator, or other damage in the cylinder that causes some part to stay hot enough to ignite the fuel/air charge.

INDUCTION ICING

- Fuel injection systems are less likely than carbureted systems to develop internal icing, so there is no need for an induction air heater like those used for carburetor heat. However, impact ice can block the induction air filter or intake air scoop of either system. As ice blocks the intake, the engine's performance decreases due to the reduced airflow.

- Most airplanes have an alternate air source that draws warmer, unfiltered air from inside the cowling to supply the engine intake. Depending on the aircraft design, the alternate air source might be automatic or manual.

- You can check the operation of a manual alternate air system during your preflight runup by observing an RPM drop when you switch to the alternate air source.

TURBOCHARGING SYSTEMS

- A turbocharger system produces increased intake air density. This allows the engine to develop more power and also provides a much higher service ceiling.

SECTION A ■ **High Performance Powerplants**

- When operating an aircraft with a turbocharger system, make slow throttle adjustments and monitor MAP and RPM carefully to prevent overboosting the engine. When flying an airplane with an automatic waste gate system, be sure the engine's oil temperature is within normal limits before applying full throttle.

CONSTANT-SPEED PROPELLERS

PROPELLER PRINCIPLES

- Propeller efficiency is the ratio of thrust horsepower to brake horsepower.

- A fixed-pitch propeller is most efficient only at one particular RPM and airspeed.

- Propeller efficiency is the ratio of thrust horsepower (THP) to brake horsepower (BHP). The main advantage of a constant-speed propeller is that it converts a high percentage of brake horsepower into thrust horsepower over a wide range of RPM and airspeed combinations by allowing the selection of the most efficient engine RPM for the given conditions.

- Because the tips of propeller blades move so much faster through the air than the blade roots, the airfoil shape and its blade angle vary along the length of the blade. Variations in the geometric pitch (twisting) of the blades enables the propeller to operate with a relatively constant angle of attack along its length when in cruising flight.

CONSTANT-SPEED PROPELLER OPERATION

- After you have set the RPM, a device called a governor automatically adjusts the blade angle to maintain that RPM, even if you make a change in airspeed or flight attitude.

- In general, use the propeller control to:

  ◦ Increase the blade angle to decrease RPM—high pitch/large angle of attack = low RPM.

  ◦ Decrease the blade angle to increase RPM—low pitch/small angle of attack = high RPM.

POWER CONTROLS

- An airplane with a constant-speed propeller has separate controls for engine power and propeller RPM. Use the throttle control to set engine power, which is indicated on the manifold pressure gauge. Use the propeller control to adjust engine RPM, which is the same as the propeller RPM and is indicated on the tachometer.

- To avoid engine stress and possible damage, ensure that the manifold pressure is within allowable limits before you reduce the RPM with the propeller control. Conversely, when you increase power, be sure that the engine's RPM is high enough to handle the increased manifold pressure before you advance the throttle.

- In general, when reducing power, pull back the throttle before the propeller control; when increasing power, push the propeller control forward before increasing the throttle.

- When you move the throttle too quickly, counterweights that are mounted on the engine crankshaft to damp out torsional vibration can shift out of place and begin hammering on their mountings. This detuning of the counterweights can damage the magnetos, oil pump, and other engine parts and in extreme cases, can cause the crankshaft to break.

FADEC

- Full authority digital engine control (FADEC) is a computer that continuously monitors engine speed, temperature, and pressure through a series of sensors to calculate and deliver the correct amount of fuel for each injector.

- FADEC systems do not have magnetos or mixture controls, and automatically handle engine priming.

- FADEC-equipped aircraft have a single power lever for the engine—just set the lever to the desired power, and the computer adjusts the engine and propeller.

NOTE: *An asterisk appearing after an ACS code (i.e. CA.IV.A.K2*) indicates that the question subject appears more than one time in the ACS. The code shown corresponds to the first instance of the subject in the ACS.*

11-1   CA.I.G.K1c, e

Applying carburetor heat will

A – not affect the mixture.

B – lean the fuel/air mixture.

C – enrich the fuel/air mixture.

11-1. Answer C. GFDIC 11A, PHB

When you apply carburetor heat, warm, less dense air is introduced into the carburetor. When the same amount of fuel is mixed with less dense air (more fuel than air by weight), the fuel/air mixture is enriched.

11-2   CA.I.G.K1c

Leaving the carburetor heat on during takeoff

A – leans the mixture for more power on takeoff.

B – will decrease the takeoff distance.

C – will increase the ground roll.

11-2. Answer C. GFDIC 11A, PHB

Using carburetor heat can help prevent icing, but because the warm air is less dense than cold air, the engine produces less power when carburetor heat is on. This decrease in engine performance will increase the ground roll.

11-3   CA.I.G.K1c, e

Fuel/air ratio is the ratio between the

A – volume of fuel and volume of air entering the cylinder.

B – weight of fuel and weight of air entering the cylinder.

C – weight of fuel and weight of air entering the carburetor.

11-3. Answer B. GFDIC 11A, PHB

Set the mixture control to achieve a fuel/air ratio that provides the most power for any given throttle setting. To maintain the correct fuel/air ratio, you must lean the mixture as you gain altitude. As altitude increases, the density (and weight) of air decreases while the density (and weight) of the fuel remains the same.

11-4   CA.I.G.K1c, e

You control the air/fuel ratio with the

A – throttle.

B – mixture control.

C – manifold pressure.

11-4. Answer B. GFDIC 11A, AFH

Set the mixture control to achieve a fuel/air ratio that provides the most power for any given throttle setting. To maintain the correct fuel/air ratio, you must lean the mixture as you gain altitude. During a descent from high altitude, enrich the mixture.

SECTION A ■ **High Performance Powerplants**

11-5   CA.I.G.K1c, e

The best power mixture is that fuel/air ratio at which

A – cylinder head temperatures are the coolest.

B – the most power can be obtained for any given throttle setting.

C – a given power can be obtained with the highest manifold pressure or throttle setting.

11-5. Answer B. GFDPP 11A, PHB
Set the mixture control to achieve a fuel/air ratio that provides the most power for any given throttle setting. To maintain the correct fuel/air ratio, you must lean the mixture as you gain altitude. During a descent from high altitude, enrich the mixture.

11-6   CA.I.G.K1c, e

The mixture control can be adjusted, which

A – prevents the fuel/air combination from becoming too rich at higher altitudes.

B – regulates the amount of air flow through the carburetor's venturi.

C – prevents the fuel/air combination from becoming lean as the airplane climbs.

11-6. Answer A. GFDPP 11A, PHB
To maintain the correct fuel/air ratio, you must lean the mixture as you gain altitude. As altitude increases, the density of air decreases while the density of the fuel remains the same, creating a progressively richer mixture, which can reduce power output and cause engine roughness.

11-7   CA.I.G.K1c, e

Unless adjusted, the fuel/air mixture becomes richer with an increase in altitude because the amount of fuel

A – decreases while the volume of air decreases.

B – remains constant while the volume of air decreases.

C – remains constant while the density of air decreases.

11-7. Answer C. GFDIC 11A, PHB
To maintain the correct fuel/air ratio, you must lean the mixture as you gain altitude. As altitude increases, the density of air decreases while the density of the fuel remains the same, creating a progressively richer mixture, which can reduce power output and cause engine roughness.

11-8   CA.I.G.K1c, e

The basic purpose of adjusting the fuel/air mixture control at altitude is to

A – decrease the fuel flow to compensate for decreased air density.

B – decrease the amount of fuel in the mixture to compensate for increased air density.

C – increase the amount of fuel in the mixture to compensate for the decrease in pressure and density of the air.

11-8. Answer A. GFDIC 11A, PHB
To maintain the correct fuel/air ratio, you must lean the mixture as you gain altitude. As altitude increases, the density of air decreases while the density of the fuel remains the same, creating a progressively richer mixture, which can reduce power output and cause engine roughness.

11-9   CA.I.G.K1c, K2

At high altitudes, an excessively rich mixture will cause the

A – engine to overheat.

B – fouling of spark plugs.

C – engine to operate smoother even though fuel consumption is increased.

11-9. Answer B. GFDIC 11A, PHB

To maintain the correct fuel/air ratio, you must lean the mixture as you gain altitude. As altitude increases, the density of air decreases while the density of the fuel remains the same, creating a progressively richer mixture, which can reduce power output and cause engine roughness. The roughness normally is due to spark plug fouling from excessive carbon buildup on the plugs.

11-10   CA.I.G.K1c, K2

Fouling of spark plugs is more apt to occur if the aircraft

A – gains altitude with no mixture adjustment.

B – descends from altitude with no mixture adjustment.

C – throttle is advanced very abruptly.

11-10. Answer A. GFDIC 11A, PHB

To maintain the correct fuel/air ratio, you must lean the mixture as you gain altitude. As altitude increases, the density of air decreases while the density of the fuel remains the same, creating a progressively richer mixture, which can reduce power output and cause engine roughness. The roughness normally is due to spark plug fouling from excessive carbon buildup on the plugs.

11-11   CA.II.C.K1, 2, 3

Which is true regarding starting a fuel-injected engine?

A – Vapor lock typically occurs in cold weather conditions if the engine has not been started for a significant period of time.

B – Using the electric/auxiliary fuel pump to prime the engine can help purge vapors from the injection system.

C – A typical procedure for starting a flooded engine involves initially setting the throttle to idle and setting the mixture control to the idle-cutoff position.

11-11. Answer B. GFDIC 11A, PHB

Priming the engine provides a combustible mixture for starting and purges any vapors, or air pockets, from the injection system. A fuel-injected engine can be difficult to restart a few minutes after shutdown—the residual heat in the engine can boil the fuel in the injection system's lines and components, and the resulting bubbles can cause vapor lock, which interferes with fuel metering and pumping.

The objective of the flooded engine starting procedure is to purge the excess fuel from the cylinders until you obtain a combustible fuel/air ratio. This procedure typically involves opening the throttle fully to provide maximum airflow through the cylinders and setting the mixture control to the idle-cutoff position before cranking the engine.

11-12   CA.I.G.K1c, K2

The most probable reason an engine continues to run after the ignition switch has been turned off is

A – carbon deposits glowing on the spark plugs.

B – a magneto ground wire is in contact with the engine casing.

C – a broken magneto ground wire.

11-12. Answer C. GFDIC 11A, PHB

If the ignition switch is off, the magneto will continue to fire if the ground wire between the magneto and the ignition switch becomes disconnected.

SECTION A ■ **High Performance Powerplants**

11-13   CA.I.G.K1c, K2

If the ground wire between the magneto and the ignition switch becomes disconnected, the engine

A – will not operate on one magneto.

B – cannot be started with the switch in the BOTH position.

C – could accidently start if the propeller is moved with fuel in the cylinder.

11-13. Answer C. GFDIC 11A, PHB

If the ignition switch is off, the magneto will continue to fire if the ground wire between the magneto and the ignition switch becomes disconnected. The magneto might send a current to the spark plugs and the engine could start if any rotation of the crankshaft/propeller occurs and a small amount of fuel is in the cylinders.

11-14   CA.I.G.K1c, K2

Before shutdown, while at idle, the ignition key is momentarily turned OFF. The engine continues to run with no interruption; this

A – is normal because the engine is usually stopped by moving the mixture to idle cut-off.

B – should not normally happen. Indicates a magneto not grounding in OFF position.

C – is an undesirable practice, but indicates that nothing is wrong.

11-14. Answer B. GFDIC 11A, PHB

If the ignition switch is off, the magneto will continue to fire if the ground wire between the magneto and the ignition switch becomes disconnected. The magneto might send a current to the spark plugs and the engine could start if any rotation of the crankshaft/propeller occurs and a small amount of fuel is in the cylinders.

11-15   CA.I.G.K1c, K2

A way to detect a broken magneto primary grounding lead is to

A – idle the engine and momentarily turn the ignition off.

B – add full power, while holding the brakes, and momentarily turn off the ignition.

C – run on one magneto, lean the mixture, and look for a rise in manifold pressure.

11-15. Answer A. GFDIC 11A, PHB

If the ignition switch is off, the magneto will continue to fire if the ground wire between the magneto and the ignition switch becomes disconnected. The magneto might send a current to the spark plugs and the engine could start if any rotation of the crankshaft/propeller occurs and a small amount of fuel is in the cylinders.

To check the ignition system for a broken ground wire, idle the engine before shutting it down and momentarily turn the ignition switch to OFF, then, turn the switch back to both. If the engine continues to run without hesitation, the ground wire is broken. This check should be accomplished in accordance with the manufacturer's recommendations in the aircraft flight manual (AFM) or the pilot's operating handbook (POH).

11-16   CA.I.G.K1e

For internal cooling, reciprocating aircraft engines are especially dependent on

A – a properly functioning cowl flap augmenter.

B – the circulation of lubricating oil.

C – the proper freon/compressor output ratio.

11-16. Answer B. GFDIC 11A, PHB

Oil provides two important functions in an engine, lubrication and cooling by reducing friction and removing some of the heat from the cylinders.

11-17   CA.I.G.K1e, K2, CA.IX.C.K1a, c

An abnormally high engine oil temperature indication may be caused by

A – a defective bearing.

B – the oil level being too low.

C – operating with an excessively rich mixture.

11-17. Answer B. GFDIC 11A, PHB

High oil temperature indications can be caused by several factors, including a low oil quantity, a plugged oil line, or a defective temperature gauge.

11-18   CA.I.G.K1c, K2, CA.IX.C.K1a

Detonation may occur at high-power settings when

A – the fuel mixture ignites instantaneously instead of burning progressively and evenly.

B – an excessively rich fuel mixture causes an explosive gain in power.

C – the fuel mixture is ignited too early by hot carbon deposits in the cylinder.

11-18. Answer A. GFDIC 11A, PHB

Detonation is the uncontrolled, explosive combustion of fuel, which can produce damaging pressures and temperatures inside the engine's cylinders. Detonation usually causes high CHT and is most likely to occur when operating at high power settings.

11-19   CA.I.G.K1c, K2, CA.IX.C.K1a

Detonation can be caused by

A – a "rich" mixture.

B – using a lower grade of fuel than recommended.

C – low engine temperatures.

11-19. Answer B. GFDIC 11A, PHB

Detonation is the uncontrolled, explosive combustion of fuel, which can produce damaging pressures and temperatures inside the engine's cylinders. Detonation usually causes high CHT and is most likely to occur when operating at high power settings. Common causes include using a lower fuel grade than specified by the manufacturer, operating with high manifold pressures combined with low RPM, or using too lean a mixture at high power settings

SECTION A ■ High Performance Powerplants

11-20 CA.I.G.K1c, K2, CA.IX.C.K1a

The uncontrolled firing of the fuel/air charge in advance of normal spark ignition is known as

A – instantaneous combustion.

B – detonation.

C – preignition.

11-20. Answer C. GFDIC 11A, PHB

Preignition occurs when the fuel/air mixture ignites prior to the firing of the spark plug. Premature ignition is usually caused by a residual hot spot in the combustion chamber, often created by a small carbon deposit on a spark plug, a cracked spark plug insulator, or other damage in the cylinder that causes some part to stay hot enough to ignite the fuel/air charge.

11-21 CA.I.G.K1c, K2, CA.IX.C.K1b

Which is true about induction icing in fuel-injected engines?

A – Fuel-injected engines are more susceptible to ice formation than carbureted engines.

B – An alternate air source provides warm unfiltered air from inside the cowling to supply the engine intake in the event of induction icing

C – An induction air heater, similar to carburetor heat prevents ice formation.

11-21. Answer B. GFDIC 11A, PHB

Fuel injection systems are less likely than carbureted systems to develop internal icing, so there is no need for an induction air heater like those used for carburetor heat. However, impact ice can block the induction air filter or intake air scoop of either system. As ice blocks the intake, the engine's performance decreases due to the reduced airflow.

Most airplanes have an alternate air source that draws warmer, unfiltered air from inside the cowling to supply the engine intake. Depending on the aircraft design, the alternate air source might be automatic or manual.

11-22 CA.II.F.K1

When switching to the engine alternate air source during a pre-takeoff check, you determine that it is operating properly when you observe

A – a decrease in RPM.

B – an increase in RPM.

C – no change in RPM.

11-22. Answer A. GFDIC 11A, AFH

Most airplanes have an alternate air source that draws warmer, unfiltered air from inside the cowling to supply the engine intake. Depending on the aircraft design, the alternate air source might be automatic or manual.

You can check the operation of a manual alternate air system during your preflight runup by observing an RPM drop when you switch to the alternate air source.

11-23 CA.I.G.K1c

Propeller efficiency is the

A – ratio of thrust horsepower to brake horsepower.

B – actual distance a propeller advances in one revolution.

C – ratio of geometric pitch to effective pitch.

11-23. Answer A. GFDIC 11A, PHB

Propeller efficiency is the ratio of thrust horsepower to brake horsepower. A fixed-pitch propeller is most efficient only at one particular RPM and airspeed. The main advantage of a constant-speed propeller is that it converts a high percentage of brake horsepower (BHP) into thrust horsepower (THP) over a wide range of RPM and airspeed combinations by allowing the selection of the most efficient engine RPM for the given conditions.

11-24   CA.I.G.K1c

A fixed-pitch propeller is designed for best efficiency only at a given combination of

A – altitude and RPM.

B – airspeed and RPM.

C – airspeed and altitude.

11-24. Answer B. GFDIC 11A, PHB

A fixed-pitch propeller is most efficient only at one particular RPM and airspeed. The main advantage of a constant-speed propeller is that it converts a high percentage of brake horsepower (BHP) into thrust horsepower (THP) over a wide range of RPM and airspeed combinations by allowing the selection of the most efficient engine RPM for the given conditions.

11-25   CA.I.G.K1c

The reason for variations in geometric pitch (twisting) along a propeller blade is that it

A – permits a relatively constant angle of incidence along its length when in cruising flight.

B – prevents the portion of the blade near the hub from stalling during cruising flight.

C – permits a relatively constant angle of attack along its length when in cruising flight.

11-25. Answer C. GFDIC 11A, PHB

Because the tips of propeller blades move so much faster through the air than the blade roots, the airfoil shape and its blade angle vary along the length of the blade. Variations in the geometric pitch (twisting) of the blades enables the propeller to operate with a relatively constant angle of attack along its length when in cruising flight.

11-26   CA.I.G.K1c

To establish a climb after takeoff in an aircraft equipped with a constant-speed propeller, the output of the engine is reduced to climb power by decreasing manifold pressure and

A – increasing RPM by decreasing propeller blade angle.

B – decreasing RPM by decreasing propeller blade angle.

C – decreasing RPM by increasing propeller blade angle.

11-26. Answer C. GFDIC 11A, AFH

After you have set the RPM, a device called a governor automatically adjusts the blade angle to maintain that RPM, even if you make a change in airspeed or flight attitude. In general, use the propeller control to:

- Increase the blade angle to decrease RPM—high pitch/large angle of attack = low RPM.

- Decrease the blade angle to increase RPM—low pitch/small angle of attack = high RPM.

11-27   CA.I.G.K1c

To develop maximum power and thrust during takeoff, a constant-speed propeller should be set to a blade angle that will produce a

A – large angle of attack and low RPM.

B – small angle of attack and high RPM.

C – large angle of attack and high RPM.

11-27. Answer B. GFDIC 11A, AFH

After you have set the RPM, a device called a governor automatically adjusts the blade angle to maintain that RPM, even if you make a change in airspeed or flight attitude. In general, use the propeller control to:

- Increase the blade angle to decrease RPM—high pitch/large angle of attack = low RPM.

- Decrease the blade angle to increase RPM—low pitch/small angle of attack = high RPM.

SECTION A ■ **High Performance Powerplants**

11-28   CA.I.G.K1c

Which statement best describes the operating principle of a constant-speed propeller?

A – As throttle setting is changed by the pilot, the prop governor causes pitch angle of the propeller blades to remain unchanged.

B – The propeller control regulates the engine RPM, and in turn, the propeller RPM.

C – A high blade angle, or increased pitch, reduces the propeller drag and allows more engine power for takeoffs.

11-28. Answer B. GFDIC 11A, PHB

An airplane with a constant-speed propeller has separate controls for engine power and propeller RPM. Use the throttle control to set engine power, which is indicated on the manifold pressure gauge. Use the propeller control to adjust engine RPM, which is the same as the propeller RPM and is indicated on the tachometer.

11-29   CA.I.G.K1c

In aircraft equipped with constant-speed propellers and normally-aspirated engines, which procedure should be used to avoid placing undue stress on the engine components? When power is being

A – decreased, reduce the RPM before reducing the manifold pressure.

B – increased, increase the RPM before increasing the manifold pressure.

C – increased or decreased, the RPM should be adjusted before the manifold pressure.

11-29. Answer B. GFDIC 11A, PHB

To avoid engine stress and possible damage, ensure that the manifold pressure is within allowable limits before you reduce the RPM with the propeller control. Conversely, when you increase power, be sure that the engine's RPM is high enough to handle the increased manifold pressure before you advance the throttle.

In general, when reducing power, pull back the throttle before the propeller control; when increasing power, push the propeller control forward before increasing the throttle.

11-30   CA.I.G.K1c, K2

A detuning of engine crankshaft counterweights is a source of overstress that can be caused by

A – rapid opening and closing of the throttle.

B – carburetor ice forming on the throttle valve.

C – operating with an excessively rich fuel/air mixture.

11-30. Answer A. GFDIC 11A

When you move the throttle too quickly, counterweights that are mounted on the engine crankshaft to damp out torsional vibration can shift out of place and begin hammering on their mountings. This detuning of the counterweights can damage the magnetos, oil pump, and other engine parts and in extreme cases, can cause the crankshaft to break.

SECTION B
Supplemental Oxygen and Pressurization

OXYGEN SYSTEMS

- Constant-flow, adjustable-flow and altitude-compensated oxygen systems are all continuous-flow designs, and are capable of providing adequate respiration up to 25,000 feet.

- Constant-flow systems are used on many reciprocating-engine airplanes to provide continuous oxygen delivery at a constant flow rate.

- Oxygen masks that are used with continuous-flow oxygen systems are usually oronasal rebreather designs that dilute oxygen with a portion of exhaled air, to provide increased oxygen supply duration.

- Diluter-demand and pressure-demand oxygen systems only allow oxygen to flow when you inhale, and are capable of providing diluted or 100% oxygen.

- For flights as high as 40,000 feet, diluter-demand or pressure-demand oxygen systems are used. For flights above 40,000 feet, a pressure-demand system must be used.

- The style of mask used with diluter-demand and pressure-demand oxygen systems is a quick-donning design, which:

  - Can be put on rapidly.
  - Provides a tighter seal around your nose and mouth than an oronasal rebreather mask.
  - Improves oxygen delivery when you are flying at high altitude.
  - Does not use a rebreather bag for oxygen dilution—uses a valve in the regulator unit that opens to allow cabin air into the mask to mix with oxygen when you are flying at an altitude that permits a diluted oxygen supply.

- A pulse-demand system is an electronic oxygen controller that detects when a user begins to inhale and provides a measured amount of oxygen during each breath. The oxygen savings from these systems can be as high as 85 percent.

- Aviator's breathing oxygen (ABO) must be 99.5% pure oxygen with no more than 0.005 milligrams of water per liter.

- A chemical oxygen generator provides an emergency oxygen supply, and is primarily used in pressurized airplanes in the event of a cabin decompression.

OXYGEN SERVICING

- Aviator's breathing oxygen is usually stored in a high-pressure cylinder that is typically serviced to between 1,800 to 1,850 psi with a maximum pressure of approximately 2,200 psi.

- Never leave a high-pressure cylinder exposed to heat or direct sunlight for an extended because oxygen expands when heated and the cylinder pressure could increase above maximum limits.

- To prevent moisture from entering an oxygen cylinder, do not allow tank pressure to deplete below 50 psi.

- To prevent a fire, never allow smoking or open flames near an oxygen system while it is in use. In addition, keep oxygen fittings free of grease, oil and hydraulic fluids.

CABIN PRESSURIZATION

- Pressurization systems increase the pressure inside an airplane to produce a lower cabin pressure altitude. In addition, some pressurization systems enable you to control the cabin "rate of climb" to maintain a comfortable environment.

- A basic pressurization system begins operating at a particular altitude, whereas a system with a cabin pressure control enables you to set the altitude where pressurization begins and, with most systems, control the cabin "rate of climb."

- When a pressurization system is operating at less-than-maximum differential pressure and is able to maintain the cabin pressure altitude at the preset level, it is considered to be operating in the isobaric range.

- When the maximum cabin differential pressure is reached, a cabin pressurization system operates in the differential range to avoid exceeding the maximum psid—the cabin altitude must increase if the airplane climbs higher.

- The pressurization instruments include the cabin rate-of-climb indicator and the cabin/differential pressure indicators.

- If a pressurized cabin decompresses, you must descend to an altitude where oxygen is not required. If the decompression is rapid or explosive, you should be checked by an aeromedical examiner for altitude-induced decompression sickness (DCS).

NOTE: *An asterisk appearing after an ACS code (i.e. CA.IV.A.K2*) indicates that the question subject appears more than one time in the ACS. The code shown corresponds to the first instance of the subject in the ACS.*

11-31   CA.I.G.K1l, CA.VIII.A.K3a

Which is a characteristic of the continuous-flow oxygen systems?

A – Provide adequate respiration up to 45,000 feet.

B – Use masks that dilute oxygen with exhaled air.

C – Include the diluter-demand system design.

11-31. Answer B. GFDIC 11B, PHB

Constant-flow, adjustable-flow and altitude-compensated oxygen systems are all continuous-flow designs, and are capable of providing adequate respiration up to 25,000 feet. Oxygen masks that are used with continuous-flow oxygen systems are usually oronasal rebreather designs that dilute oxygen with a portion of exhaled air to provide increased oxygen supply duration.

11-32   CA.I.G.K1l, CA.VIII.A.K3a

Which is a characteristic of demand-type oxygen systems?

A – Only provide 100% oxygen.

B – Provide continuous oxygen delivery at a constant flow rate.

C – Include pressure-demand systems used above 40,000 feet.

11-32. Answer C. GFDIC 11B, PHB

Diluter-demand and pressure-demand oxygen systems only allow oxygen to flow when you inhale, and are capable of providing diluted or 100% oxygen. For flights as high as 40,000 feet, diluter-demand or pressure-demand oxygen systems are used. For flights above 40,000 feet, a pressure-demand system must be used.

11-33 CA.I.G.K1l, CA.VIII.A.K3a

Which is a characteristic of the quick-donning mask design?

A – Typically used with continuous-flow oxygen systems.

B – Used with demand oxygen systems to improve oxygen delivery at high altitudes.

C – Uses a rebreather bag for oxygen dilution.

11-33. Answer B. GFDIC 11B, PHB

The style of mask used with diluter-demand and pressure-demand oxygen systems is a quick-donning design, which:

- Can be put on rapidly.
- Provides a tighter seal around your nose and mouth than an oronasal rebreather mask.
- Improves oxygen delivery when you are flying at high altitude.
- Does not use a rebreather bag for oxygen dilution—uses a valve in the regulator unit that opens to allow cabin air into the mask to mix with oxygen when you are flying at an altitude that permits a diluted oxygen supply.

11-34 CA.I.G.K1l, CA.VIII.A.K3a

Which is a characteristic of a pulse-demand oxygen system?

A – Detects when a user begins to inhale before providing oxygen.

B – Provides continuous oxygen delivery at a constant flow rate.

C – Uses an increased amount of oxygen compared to other systems.

11-34. Answer A. GFDIC 11B, PHB

A pulse-demand system is an electronic oxygen controller that detects when a user begins to inhale and provides a measured amount of oxygen during each breath. The oxygen savings from these systems can be as high as 85 percent.

11-35 CA.I.G.K1l, CA.VIII.A.K3b

Which is a characteristic of aviator's breathing oxygen?

A – Stored in high-pressure cylinders that should not be allowed to decrease below 50 psi.

B – Must have no more than 0.010 milligrams water per liter.

C – Must be 99.5% pure oxygen in cylinders serviced to 1,000 psi.

11-35. Answer A. GFDIC 11B, PHB

Aviator's breathing oxygen (ABO) must be 99.5% pure oxygen with no more than 0.005 milligrams of water per liter. ABO is usually stored in a high-pressure cylinder that is typically serviced to between 1,800 to 1,850 psi. To prevent moisture from entering an oxygen cylinder, do not allow tank pressure to deplete below 50 psi.

11-36 CA.I.G.K1l, CA.VIII.A.K3c

As a precaution when using or servicing supplemental oxygen, do not allow

A – tank pressure to deplete below 1,000 psi.

B – smoking or open flames near the system.

C – a cylinder to be exposed to heat, which can cause the pressure to decrease below minimum limits.

11-36. Answer B. GFDIC 11B, PHB

To prevent a fire, never allow smoking or open flames near an oxygen system while it is in use. In addition, keep oxygen fittings free of grease, oil and hydraulic fluids. Aviator's breathing oxygen is usually stored in a high-pressure cylinder that is typically serviced to between 1,800 to 1,850 psi with a maximum pressure of approximately 2,200 psi.

Never leave a high-pressure cylinder exposed to heat or direct sunlight for an extended amount of time because oxygen expands when heated and the cylinder pressure could increase above maximum limits. To prevent moisture from entering an oxygen cylinder, do not allow tank pressure to deplete below 50 psi.

SECTION B ■ Supplemental Oxygen and Pressurization

11-37   CA.I.G.K1i, CA.VIII.B.K1

Which is a correct definition of a term that applies to pressurization?

A – Cabin pressure altitude is the equivalent altitude inside a pressurized cabin.

B – Cabin differential pressure is the difference between the actual cabin air pressure and the pressure set by the cabin pressure control.

C – Equivalent pressure altitude is equal to the outside air pressure at a given altitude.

11-37. Answer A. GFDIC 11B, AFH

Pressurization is accomplished by pumping air into an aircraft that is adequately sealed to limit the rate at which air escapes from the cabin. The air pressure increases to produce a cabin environment equivalent to that at a lower altitude. Cabin pressure altitude is a term that describes the equivalent altitude inside the cabin. Cabin differential pressure is the difference between the cabin air pressure and the outside air pressure.

11-38   CA.I.G.K1i, CA.VIII.B.K1

What is the function of the outflow valve of a pressurization system?

To regulate the amount of air pressure in the cabin, an outflow

A – Vents the pressurized air overboard if the primary system valve fails.

B – Is operated manually by the pilot to adjust the amount of air vented out of the cabin.

C – Opens and closes to allow the pressurized air to vent out of the cabin at a controlled rate.

11-38. Answer C. GFDIC 11B, PHB

To regulate the amount of air pressure in the cabin, an outflow valve opens and closes to allow the pressurized air to vent out of the cabin at a controlled rate. The safety/dump valve vents the pressurized air overboard if the outflow valve fails.

11-39   CA.I.G.K1i, CA.VIII.B.K1, K2a, b

Which is true regarding a failure of the pressurization system?

A – Rapid decompression occurs if the cabin pressure changes in less than 0.5 seconds.

B – Your ability to detect gradual decompression can be impaired by hypoxia.

C – An annunciator light illuminates when the cabin pressure altitude decreases below 12,500 feet.

11-39. Answer B. GFDIC 11B, AFH

Depending on how quickly it occurs, decompression affects the airplane occupants in different ways:

- Explosive decompression—cabin pressure changes in less than 0.5 seconds.

- Rapid decompression—complete pressurization loss occurs in less than 10 seconds.

- Gradual decompression—you might not be aware of a subtle change in cabin pressure and as cabin altitude increases, your ability to detect decompression is impaired by hypoxia.

To alert the flight crew of loss of pressure, an annunciator light illuminates when the cabin pressure altitude exceeds a preset value—typically 10,000 feet or 12,500 feet.

SECTION C
Retractable Landing Gear

LANDING GEAR SYSTEMS

- Landing gear systems can be operated through a hydraulic system, an electrically driven motor, or a hybrid of the two methods.

- The electrical gear system consists of a reversible motor that drives a series of rods, levers, cables, and bellcranks that raise and lower the gear.

- The gear cycle refers to the process that the gear goes through during extension and retraction. The electric motor moves the gear up or down and it continues to operate until the up or down limit switch on the motor's gearbox is tripped.

- In a hydraulic gear system, hydraulic fluid flows under pressure through valves and downlocks to the gear actuating cylinders to raise and lower the gear.

- An electrohydraulic system utilizes an electric pump to pressurize a hydraulic system for gear extension and retraction.

GEAR SYSTEM SAFETY

- Gear position indicators enable you to determine the location of the gear in the gear cycle. Position lights are one common gear position indicator, and they consist of three green lights and one red light.

- As a reminder to pilots to lower the gear before landing, a gear warning horn sounds when the airplane is configured for landing with the gear in an unsafe position.

- Most retractable landing gear systems incorporate a safety switch, or squat switch, to ensure that the gear does not retract when the airplane is sitting on the ground.

- Maximum landing gear extension speed (V_{LE}) is the fastest speed at which you can fly with the landing gear extended, and maximum landing gear operating speed (V_{LO}) is the highest speed at which you can safely operate the landing gear.

OPERATING PROCEDURES

- Preflight the landing gear system before each flight, including a check for loose bolts, cracks and corrosion, and foreign objects in the wheel wells.

- The gear switch is often shaped differently from the flap switch to aid you in discriminating between the two.

- Besides the gear position indicators, a pitch change, a change in airspeed, and the sound of the gear mechanism enable you to determine if the gear is operating properly.

- One or more circuit breakers protect the landing gear system from electrical overloads.

- Recycling the landing gear after takeoff from a slushy runway can help prevent the build-up of ice on the landing gear.

- The position indicator lights are your primary means of determining gear position. If one or more fail to illuminate, check the bulbs and the circuit breakers before attempting to lower the gear manually.

- The four most common kinds of emergency gear extension systems are the hand crank, the hydraulic hand pump, the freefall, and the carbon dioxide (CO_2) pressurized systems. Check the AFM/POH to determine the proper method for operating the system on your airplane.

- If departing from a runway with wet snow or slush on the takeoff surface, do not retract the landing gear immediately so that any wet snow or slush can be air-dried or blown from the tires.

NOTE: An asterisk appearing after an ACS code (i.e. CA.IV.A.K2*) indicates that the question subject appears more than one time in the ACS. The code shown corresponds to the first instance of the subject in the ACS.

SECTION C ▪ Retractable Landing Gear

11-40   CA.I.G.K1d

14 CFR part 1 defines V_{LE} as

A – maximum landing gear extended speed.

B – maximum landing gear operating speed.

C – maximum leading edge flaps extended speed.

11-40. Answer A. GFDIC 11C, FAR 1.2

V_{LE} is the maximum allowable speed with the landing gear extended. V_{LO} is the maximum landing gear operating speed.

11-41   CA.I.G.K1d

When departing from a runway that is covered with snow or slush, what could you do to prevent damage to the landing gear due to the conditions?

A – Do not retract the landing gear immediately to allow the gear to air-dry.

B – Immediately retract the landing gear so it can be heated in the gear wells.

C – Fly at a speed above the green arc of the airspeed indicator to remove the snow and slush.

11-41. Answer A. GFDIC 11C, AC 91-13

If departing from an runway with wet snow or slush on the takeoff surface, do not retract the landing gear immediately so that any wet snow or slush can be air-dried or blown from the tires.

11-42   CA.I.G.K1d

If necessary to take off from a slushy runway, the freezing of landing gear mechanisms can be minimized by

A – recycling the gear.

B – delaying gear retraction.

C – increasing the airspeed to V_{LE} before retraction.

11-42. Answer B. GFDIC 11C, AC 91-13

If departing from an runway with wet snow or slush on the takeoff surface, do not retract the landing gear immediately so that any wet snow or slush can be air-dried or blown from the tires.

11-43   CA.I.G.K1d

Which is a characteristic of a retractable landing gear system?

A – A warning horn and annunciator light typically alert you to raise the gear immediately after takeoff.

B – In a hydraulic system, hydraulic fluid flows under pressure to and from gear actuating cylinders to raise and lower the gear.

C – When the airplane is configured for landing with the gear in an unsafe position, a safety switch triggers automatic gear extension.

11-43. Answer B. GFDIC 11C, PHB

Landing gear systems can be operated through a hydraulic system, an electrically driven motor, or a hybrid of the two methods. In a hydraulic gear system, hydraulic fluid flows under pressure through valves and downlocks to the gear actuating cylinders to raise and lower the gear.

As a reminder to pilots to lower the gear before landing, a gear warning horn sounds when the airplane is configured for landing with the gear in an unsafe position. Most retractable landing gear systems incorporate a safety switch, or squat switch, to ensure that the gear does not retract when the airplane is sitting on the ground.

11-44   PLT138   CA.I.G.K1d

Which of these are systems are used for emergency gear extension?

A – Hydraulic hand pump, freefall, and squat switch.

B – Hand crank, hydraulic hand pump, and electrohydraulic system.

C – Hand crank, hydraulic hand pump, and carbon dioxide (CO2) pressurized system.

11-44. Answer C. GFDIC 11C, AC 91-13C
The four most common kinds of emergency gear extension systems are the hand crank, the hydraulic hand pump, the freefall, and the carbon dioxide (CO2) pressurized systems. Check the AFM/POH to determine the proper method for operating the system on your airplane.

SECTION C ■ **Retractable Landing Gear**

CHAPTER 12

Aerodynamics and Performance Limitations

SECTION A
Advanced Aerodynamics

- The four fundamental flight maneuvers—straight-and-level flight, turns, climbs, and descents—are controlled by changing the balance between the four aerodynamic forces: lift, thrust, drag, and weight.

- The opposing aerodynamic forces are balanced in unaccelerated (steady-state) flight. Lift balances weight, and thrust balances drag—the airplane is in a state of dynamic equilibrium, and no acceleration occurs in any direction.

- A change in any one of the four forces results in an acceleration until equilibrium is reestablished. An imbalance in the forces, such as when you initiate a climb or descent, causes the airplane to change speed and direction until it reaches a new equilibrium. After you restore equilibrium in the climb or descent, the vector sums of the opposing forces are balanced.

LIFT

- The wing causes the air moving past it to curve downward, creating a strong downwash behind the wing. Lift is the reaction that results from the action of forcing air downward.

- The air pressure above a wing is reduced because the shape of the airfoil and the angle of attack cause air to flow faster over the upper surface of the wing.

- Air flowing along the lower surface of the wing slows down, causing its pressure to increase, and adding to lift.

- Relative wind is directly opposite the flight path of the airplane.

- The angle between the chord line of the wing and the relative wind is the angle of attack.

- Lift acts perpendicular to the relative wind, regardless of the wing's angle of attack.

- Drag acts opposite the flight path, in the same direction as the relative wind.

- The pressure distribution pattern of airflow around the wing changes as you vary the angle of attack. Regions of positive and negative pressure move along the upper and lower surface of the wing as the angle of attack is changed.

- The angle of incidence is the small angle formed by the chord line and the longitudinal axis of the airplane. The angle of incidence generally provides the proper angle of attack for level flight at cruising speed.

LIFT EQUATION

- For any wing, a definite mathematical relationship exists between lift, angle of attack, airspeed, altitude, and the size of the wing. These factors correspond to the terms coefficient of lift (CL), velocity, air density, and wing surface area and their relationship is expressed in the lift equation.

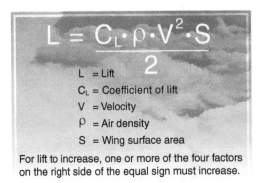

$$L = \frac{C_L \cdot \rho \cdot V^2 \cdot S}{2}$$

L = Lift
C_L = Coefficient of lift
V = Velocity
ρ = Air density
S = Wing surface area

For lift to increase, one or more of the four factors on the right side of the equal sign must increase.

- For any particular amount of lift, a specific combination of angle of attack and airspeed applies.
    - If you reduce the airspeed and maintain your altitude (air density) and airplane configuration (wing area), the lift equation shows that you must increase the coefficient of lift (angle of attack) to generate sufficient lift to maintain altitude.
    - If you increase airspeed, you must reduce the angle of attack to stay at the same altitude.
- Lift is proportional to the square of the velocity, or airspeed, so doubling your airspeed quadruples the amount of lift, if the other factors remain the same.

CONTROLLING LIFT

- When you change the angle of attack of the wing, you also change lift and drag forces.
- In general, increasing the angle of attack increases both lift and drag. If drag is increased without changing thrust, airspeed will decrease in level flight. You can directly affect lift, and indirectly change drag and airspeed by changing the angle of attack.

HIGH-LIFT DEVICES

TRAILING-EDGE FLAPS

- Trailing-edge flaps increase both lift and drag. Because flaps increase the coefficient of lift, they also decrease the stall speed. Raising the flaps increases the stall speed, so consider this increase before you raise the flaps at low airspeeds or high angles of attack.
- Extending flaps can increase the airplane's rate of descent without increasing airspeed. Consequently, you can extend flaps to perform a steeper landing approach at a slower airspeed.

LEADING-EDGE DEVICES

- Fixed slots direct airflow to the upper wing surface and delay airflow separation at higher angles of attack.
- Slats move forward and down to enable the air below the wing to flow over the wing's upper surface, delaying airflow separation.
- Leading-edge flaps (generally only found on jets) usually increase both wing camber and area to create adequate lift at relatively low takeoff and landing speeds.

DRAG

INDUCED DRAG

- The greater the angle of attack, the more drag is produced.
- At low speeds, a wing must fly at a higher angle of attack to generate enough lift to support the airplane, and more high pressure air from the lower surface flows around the wingtips, forming more powerful vortices, which are the primary cause of induced drag.
- Induced drag increases with a decrease in airspeed.

GROUND EFFECT

- When an airplane flies within a distance from the ground (or water) surface equal to its own wingspan or less, the amount of induced drag decreases. This reduction in induced drag is due to changes in the upwash pattern ahead of the wing, and the downwash and wingtip vortices behind the wing.
- With the reduction in induced drag, the amount of thrust necessary is also reduced, allowing the airplane to lift off at a lower-than-normal speed.

SECTION A ■ **Advanced Aerodynamics**

- If you try to climb out of ground effect at too low of an airspeed, the greater induced drag can result in marginal initial climb performance, the airplane settling back to the runway, or a stall. As an airplane climbs out of ground effect, more thrust is required.

PARASITE DRAG

- Parasite drag increases with an increase in speed. The rate of increase is proportional to the square of the airspeed, so doubling your speed quadruples parasite drag.

TOTAL DRAG

- On the total drag graph, the intersection of the induced drag and parasite drag lines corresponds with a point on the total drag line where drag is at a minimum. This point is where the aircraft is operating at the best ratio of lift to drag, or L/D_{MAX}.

HIGH-DRAG DEVICES

- Spoilers are deployed from the upper surfaces of wings to spoil the smooth airflow, reducing lift and increasing drag.

- Depending on the airplane, spoilers are used for roll control, enabling the airplane to descend without gaining speed, and help shorten ground roll after landing on some airplanes—one of the advantages being the virtual elimination of adverse yaw.

LOAD FACTOR

- The load factor is defined as the load the wings are supporting divided by the total weight of the airplane.

- A heavily loaded airplane has a higher stall speed than the same airplane with a light load—the heavily loaded airplane must use a higher angle of attack to generate the required lift at any given speed than when lightly loaded.

- To find the weight of an object that is subject to a positive G force, multiply the weight of the object times the number of Gs. For example, 90 pounds of baggage multiplied by 3.5 Gs equals 315 pounds.

- Airplane structures are designed to withstand greater loads than normal flight is likely to produce. Aircraft category load limits are:

   ○ Normal category—3.8 positive Gs and 1.52 negative Gs.

   ○ Utility category—4.4 positive G's and 1.76 negative Gs.

   ○ Acrobatic category—6 positive Gs and 3 negative Gs.

V-G DIAGRAM

- A V-g diagram applies to one airplane type and the information is valid only for a specific weight, configuration, and altitude.

- V-g diagrams show the maximum amount of positive or negative lift the airplane is capable of generating at a given speed, the safe load factor limits, and the load factor, or number of Gs, the airplane can sustain at various speeds.

- Flying within the boundaries depicted by the diagram minimizes the risk of stalls, spins, and structural damage.

- The horizontal positive and negative load factor limits represent the structural limitations of the airplane (for example, 3.8 Gs and 1.52 Gs for a normal category airplane).

- Maximum structural cruising speed, V_{NO}, is the top speed of the normal operating range and corresponds to the upper limit of the green arc on the airspeed indicator. Do not exceed this speed in rough air.

- Never-exceed speed (V_{NE}) corresponds to the red line on the airspeed indicator. Flying faster than V_{NE} could cause control surface flutter, airframe structural damage, or failure.

- The range from V_{NO} to V_{NE} is the caution range represented by the yellow arc on the airspeed indicator. Because turbulence and gusts are more likely to cause high load factors at higher speeds, use this speed range only in smooth air.

AIRCRAFT STABILITY

- Static stability is the airplane's initial tendency when disturbed from equilibrium in one of three ways:
    - Positive static stability—returns toward equilibrium.
    - Negative static stability—moves away from equilibrium.
    - Neutral static stability—remains in new position and does not return to or move away from equilibrium.
- Dynamic stability describes how the airplane responds over time to a displacement from equilibrium.
- Combining the characteristics of static and dynamic stability describes a variety of stability conditions:
    - Positive non-oscillatory dynamic stability—the airplane returns directly to equilibrium without oscillation.
    - Positive oscillatory dynamic stability—the airplane returns to equilibrium after a series of oscillations.
    - Positive static, neutral dynamic stability—oscillations neither decrease nor increase in amplitude.
    - Positive static and negative dynamic stability—over time, oscillations increase and becomes more divergent. The divergence will continue until the pilot intervenes or the airplane is destroyed.
- Longitudinal stability involves the pitching motion, or tendency, of the airplane to move about its lateral axis.

TURNS

- When you roll the airplane into a bank, some of the lift of the wings is directed to the side, and it is this horizontal component of lift that causes the airplane to turn.
- Diverting a portion of lift to turn the airplane reduces the vertical component of lift available to support the airplane's weight. Therefore, to maintain altitude in a turn, you must increase the angle of attack by adding elevator back pressure to increase the vertical component of lift.

LOAD FACTOR IN TURNS

- Load factor in turns increases at steeper bank angles, as does the stall speed.
- The constant load factor generated in a coordinated, level turn depends on the bank angle. Load factor remains constant if no change in bank angle occurs.
- Load factor in turns increases at steeper bank angles, as does the stall speed. In a coordinated, level turn at a given bank angle, all airplanes will experience the same load factor and the same percentage of increase in stall speed over their wings-level stall speed.

RATE AND RADIUS OF TURN

- Rate and radius of turn vary with both airspeed and bank angle but load factor remains constant if no change in bank angle occurs. For example:

    When the angle of bank is held constant, decreasing the airspeed:
    - increases the turn radius.
    - decreases the turn rate.
    - has no effect on the load factor.

SECTION A ■ **Advanced Aerodynamics**

When the angle of bank is held constant, decreasing the airspeed:

- decreases the turn radius.

- increases the turn rate.

- has no effect on the load factor.

When the airspeed is held constant, increasing the bank angle:

- decreases the turn radius.

- increases the turn rate.

- increases the load factor.

When the airspeed is held constant, decreasing the bank angle:

- increases the turn radius.

- decreases the turn rate.

- decreases the load factor.

STALL AND SPIN AWARENESS

CAUSES OF STALLS

- The stall always occurs at the same angle of attack for any particular airfoil, regardless of air density, weight, load factor, attitude, airspeed, or thrust/power. However, several of these factors affect the stall speed.

- If you increase the weight of the airplane or the load factor or decrease the power, you must increase the angle of attack at any given airspeed to generate a corresponding amount of lift so stall speed increases.

- As the CG is moved forward, the tail-down force necessary for level flight increases and stall speed increases. Because the wing must fly at a higher angle of attack to generate the greater tail-down forces, the wing is closer to its stalling angle of attack for any given airspeed.

- If the center of gravity is too far aft, the stall speed decreases, but the elevator/stabilator control might not have enough authority to reduce the angle of attack, making recovery impossible.

- Stall speed increases rapidly as G-loading increases during maneuvers such as steep turns. This increase in stall speed is because the load factor multiplies the effective weight of the airplane, which must be balanced by a similar increase in lift from the wings, necessitating a higher angle of attack.

SPINS

- Stalling with crossed controls is a major cause of spins, and usually happens when either too much or not enough rudder is used for existing yawing forces.

- If an airplane stalls with crossed controls, it is likely to enter a spin. The spin rotation is usually in the direction of the rudder being applied, regardless of which wing is raised.

- Because moving the CG aft decreases longitudinal stability and reduces pitch control forces in most airplanes, an aft CG tends to make the airplane easier to stall. After a spin is entered, an airplane with its CG farther aft tends to have a flatter spin attitude.

- A flat spin is characterized by a near level pitch and roll attitude with the spin axis near the CG of the airplane. The upward flow over the tail could render the elevators and rudder ineffective, making recovery impossible.

HIGH SPEED FLIGHT

- Critical Mach number is the speed of an aircraft in which airflow over any part of the aircraft or structure first reaches (but does not exceed) Mach 1.0.

- The drag incurred in the transonic region due to shock wave formation and airflow separation is known as wave drag.

- When speed exceeds the critical Mach number by about 10 percent, wave drag increases sharply. Associated with drag rise are Mach buffet, trim and stability changes, and a decrease in control force effectiveness.

NOTE: An asterisk appearing after an ACS code (i.e. CA.IV.A.K2*) indicates that the question subject appears more than one time in the ACS. The code shown corresponds to the first instance of the subject in the ACS.

12-1   CA.I.F.K3

Name the four fundamentals involved in maneuvering an aircraft.

A – Power, pitch, bank, and trim.

B – Thrust, lift, turns, and glides.

C – Straight-and-level flight, turns, climbs, and descents.

12-1. Answer C. GFDIC 12A, AFH

The four fundamental flight maneuvers—straight-and-level flight, turns, climbs, and descents—are controlled by changing the balance between the four aerodynamic forces.

12-2   CA.I.F.K3

Which statement is true regarding the opposing forces acting on an airplane in steady-state level flight?

A – These forces are equal.

B – Thrust is greater than drag and weight and lift are equal.

C – Thrust is greater than drag and lift is greater than weight.

12-2. Answer A. GFDIC 12A, PHB

Opposing aerodynamic forces are balanced in unaccelerated (steady-state) flight. Lift balances weight, and thrust balances drag—the airplane is in a state of dynamic equilibrium, and no acceleration occurs in any direction.

12-3   CA.I.F.K3

When transitioning from straight-and-level flight to a constant airspeed climb, the angle of attack and lift

A – are increased and remain at a higher lift-to-weight ratio to maintain the climb.

B – remain the same and maintain a steady state lift-to-weight ratio during the climb.

C – are momentarily increased and lift returns to a steady state during the climb.

12-3. Answer C. GFDIC 12A, PHB

A change in any one of the four forces—lift, weight, thrust, drag—results in an acceleration until equilibrium is reestablished. An imbalance in the forces, such as when you initiate a climb or descent, causes the airplane to change speed and direction until it reaches a new equilibrium. After you restore equilibrium in the climb or descent, the vector sums of the opposing forces are balanced.

SECTION A ■ **Advanced Aerodynamics**

12-4   CA.I.F.K3

Which is true regarding the forces acting on an aircraft in a steady-state descent? The sum of all

A – upward forces is less than the sum of all downward forces.

B – rearward forces is greater than the sum of all forward forces.

C – forward forces is equal to the sum of all rearward forces.

12-4. Answer C. GFDIC 12A, PHB

A change in any one of the four forces—lift, weight, thrust, drag—results in an acceleration until equilibrium is reestablished. An imbalance in the forces, such as when you initiate a climb or descent, causes the airplane to change speed and direction until it reaches a new equilibrium. After you restore equilibrium in the climb or descent, the vector sums of the opposing forces are balanced.

12-5   CA.I.F.K3

During the transition from straight-and-level flight to a climb, the angle of attack is increased and lift

A – is momentarily decreased.

B – remains the same.

C – is momentarily increased.

12-5. Answer C. GFDIC 12A, PHB

The opposing aerodynamic forces are balanced in unaccelerated (steady-state) straight-and-level flight. Lift balances weight, and thrust balances drag—the airplane is in a state of dynamic equilibrium, and no acceleration occurs in any direction.

A change in any one of the four forces results in an acceleration until equilibrium is reestablished. For example, increasing power and the angle of attack in straight-and-level flight momentarily increases lift. After you restore equilibrium in the climb, the vector sums of the opposing forces are balanced.

12-6   CA.I.F.K3, CA.VII.A.K1*

Lift on a wing is most properly defined as the

A – force acting perpendicular to the relative wind.

B – reduced pressure resulting from a laminar flow over the upper camber of an airfoil, which acts perpendicular to the mean camber.

C – differential pressure acting perpendicular to the chord of the wing.

12-6. Answer A. GFDIC 12A, PHB

Relative wind is directly opposite the flight path of the airplane. The angle between the chord line of the wing and the relative wind is the angle of attack. Lift generally acts perpendicular to the relative wind, regardless of the wing's angle of attack.

12-7   CA.I.F.K3

An aircraft airfoil is designed to produce lift resulting from a difference in the

A – negative air pressure below and a vacuum above the wing's surface.

B – vacuum below the wing's surface and greater air pressure above the wing's surface.

C – higher air pressure below the wing's surface and lower air pressure above the wing's surface.

12-7. Answer C. GFDIC 12A, PHB

The wing is designed to produce lift resulting from:

- The air moving past the wing curves downward, creating a strong downwash behind the wing. Lift is the reaction that results from the action of forcing air downward.

- The air pressure above a wing is reduced because the shape of the airfoil and the angle of attack cause air to flow faster over the upper surface of the wing.

- Air flowing along the lower surface of the wing slows down, causing its pressure to increase, and adding to lift.

12-8   CA.I.F.K3

The angle of attack of a wing directly controls the

A – angle of incidence of the wing.

B – amount of airflow above and below the wing.

C – distribution of pressure acting on the wing.

12-8. Answer C. GFDIC 12A, PHB

The pressure distribution pattern of airflow around the wing changes as you vary the angle of attack. Regions of positive and negative pressure move along the upper and lower surface of the wing as the angle of attack is changed.

The angle of incidence is the small angle formed by the chord line and the longitudinal axis of the airplane and is not controlled by the angle of attack.

12-9   CA.I.F.K3

On a wing, the force of lift acts perpendicular to and the force of drag acts parallel to the

A – chord line.

B – flight path.

C – longitudinal axis.

12-9. Answer B. GFDIC 12A, PHB

Relative wind is directly opposite the flight path of the airplane. The angle between the chord line of the wing and the relative wind is the angle of attack. Lift acts perpendicular to the relative wind, regardless of the wing's angle of attack. Drag acts opposite the flight path, in the same direction as the relative wind.

12-10   CA.I.F.K3

In theory, if the angle of attack and other factors remain constant and the airspeed is doubled, the lift produced at the higher speed will be

A – the same as at the lower speed.

B – two times greater than at the lower speed.

C – four times greater than at the lower speed.

12-10. Answer C. GFDIC 12A, PHB

For any wing a definite mathematical relationship exists between lift, angle of attack, airspeed, altitude, and the size of the wing. These factors correspond to the terms coefficient of lift (CL), velocity, air density, and wing surface area and their relationship is expressed in the lift equation. Lift is proportional to the square of the velocity, or airspeed, so doubling your airspeed quadruples the amount of lift, if the other factors remain the same.

12-11   CA.I.F.K3

Which is true regarding the force of lift in steady, unaccelerated flight?

A – There is a corresponding indicated airspeed required for every angle of attack to generate sufficient lift to maintain altitude.

B – An airfoil will always stall at the same indicated airspeed; therefore, an increase in weight will require an increase in speed to generate sufficient lift to maintain altitude.

C – At lower airspeeds the angle of attack must be less to generate sufficient lift to maintain altitude.

12-11. Answer A. GFDIC 12A, PHB

For any particular amount of lift, a specific combination of angle of attack and airspeed applies.

- If you reduce the airspeed and maintain your altitude (air density) and airplane configuration (wing area), the lift equation shows that you must increase the coefficient of lift (angle of attack) to generate sufficient lift to maintain altitude.

- If you increase airspeed, you must reduce the angle of attack to stay at the same altitude.

SECTION A ■ **Advanced Aerodynamics**

SECTION A ■ Advanced Aerodynamics

12-12   CA.I.F.K3

To hold an airplane in level flight at airspeeds from very slow to very fast, you must coordinate thrust and

A – angle of incidence.

B – gross weight.

C – angle of attack.

12-12. Answer C. GFDIC12A, PHB

For any particular amount of lift, a specific combination of angle of attack and airspeed applies.

- If you reduce the airspeed and maintain your altitude (air density) and airplane configuration (wing area), the lift equation shows that you must increase the coefficient of lift (angle of attack) to generate sufficient lift to maintain altitude.

- If you increase airspeed, you must reduce the angle of attack to stay at the same altitude.

12-13   CA.I.F.K3

What changes in airplane longitudinal control must be made to maintain altitude while the airspeed is being decreased?

A – Increase the angle of attack to produce more lift than drag.

B – Increase the angle of attack to compensate for the decreasing lift.

C – Decrease the angle of attack to compensate for the increasing drag.

12-13. Answer B. GFDIC 12A, PHB

For any particular amount of lift, a specific combination of angle of attack and airspeed applies.

- If you reduce the airspeed and maintain your altitude (air density) and airplane configuration (wing area), the lift equation shows that you must increase the coefficient of lift (angle of attack) to generate sufficient lift to maintain altitude.

- If you increase airspeed, you must reduce the angle of attack to stay at the same altitude.

12-14   CA.I.F.K3

To generate the same amount of lift as altitude is increased, an airplane must be flown at

A – the same true airspeed regardless of angle of attack.

B – a lower true airspeed and a greater angle of attack.

C – a higher true airspeed for any given angle of attack.

12-14. Answer C. GFDIC 12A, PHB

For any wing a definite mathematical relationship exists between lift, angle of attack, airspeed, altitude, and the size of the wing. These factors correspond to the terms coefficient of lift (CL), velocity, air density, and wing surface area and their relationship is expressed in the lift equation.

Because air density decreases with altitude, the airplane must fly at a higher true airspeed for any given angle of attack to generate the same lift as at a lower altitude.

12-15   CA.I.F.K3

By changing the angle of attack of a wing, you can control the airplane's

A – lift, airspeed, and drag.

B – lift, airspeed, and CG.

C – lift and airspeed, but not drag.

12-15. Answer A. GFDIC 12A, PHB

When you change the angle of attack of the wing, you also change lift and drag forces. In general, increasing the angle of attack increases both lift and drag. If drag is increased without changing thrust, airspeed will decrease in level flight. You can directly affect lift, and indirectly change drag and airspeed by changing the angle of attack.

12-16　CA.I.F.K2c, CA.I.F.K3, CA.VII.A.K1

Which is true regarding the use of flaps during level turns?

A – The lowering of flaps increases the stall speed.

B – The raising of flaps increases the stall speed.

C – Raising flaps will require added forward pressure on the yoke or stick.

12-16. Answer B. GFDIC 12A, PHB

Trailing-edge flaps increase both lift and drag. Because flaps increase the coefficient of lift, they also decrease the stall speed. Raising the flaps increases the stall speed so consider this increase before you raise the flaps at low airspeeds or high angles of attack.

12-17　CA.I.F.K2c, CA.I.F.K3

One of the main functions of flaps during the approach and landing is to

A – decrease the angle of descent without increasing the airspeed.

B – provide the same amount of lift at a slower airspeed.

C – decrease lift, thus enabling a steeper-than-normal approach to be made.

12-17. Answer B. GFDIC 12A, PHB

Trailing-edge flaps increase both lift and drag. Because flaps increase the coefficient of lift, they also decrease the stall speed. Raising the flaps increases the stall speed so consider this increase before you raise the flaps at low airspeeds or high angles of attack.

Extending flaps can increase the airplane's rate of descent without increasing airspeed. Consequently, you can extend flaps to perform a steeper landing approach at a slower airspeed.

12-18　CA.I.F.K2b, c, CA.I.F.K3

Both lift and drag would be increased when which of these devices are extended?

A – Flaps.

B – Spoilers.

C – Slats.

12-18. Answer A. GFDIC 12A, PHB

Flaps increase both lift and drag.

Spoilers are deployed from the upper surfaces of wings to spoil the smooth airflow, reducing lift and increasing drag.

Slats increase lift but generally do not increase drag—slats move forward and down to enable the air below the wing to flow over the wing's upper surface, delaying airflow separation.

12-19　CA.I.F.K3, CA.VII.A.K1*

Which statement is true relative to changing angle of attack?

A – An increase in angle of attack decreases pressure below the wing, and increases drag.

B – An increase in angle of attack increases drag.

C – A decrease in angle of attack increases pressure below the wing, and decreases drag.

12-19. Answer B. GFDIC 12A, PHB

The greater the angle of attack, the more drag is produced. At low speeds, a wing must fly at a higher angle of attack to generate enough lift to support the airplane, and more high pressure air from the lower surface flows around the wingtips, forming more powerful vortices, which are the primary cause of induced drag.

SECTION A ■ **Advanced Aerodynamics**

12-20 CA.I.F.K3

Which is true regarding aerodynamic drag?

A – Induced drag is created entirely by air resistance.

B – All aerodynamic drag is created entirely by the production of lift.

C – Induced drag is a by-product of lift and is greatly affected by changes in airspeed.

12-20. Answer C. GFDIC 12A, PHB

The greater the angle of attack, the more drag is produced. At low speeds, a wing must fly at a higher angle of attack to generate enough lift to support the airplane, and more high pressure air from the lower surface flows around the wingtips, forming more powerful vortices, which are the primary cause of induced drag.

Induced drag increases with a decrease in airspeed. Parasite drag increases with an increase in speed.

12-21 CA.I.F.K3, CA.IV.C.K4

An airplane leaving ground effect will

A – experience a reduction in ground friction and require a slight power reduction.

B – experience an increase in induced drag and require more thrust.

C – require a lower angle of attack to maintain the same lift coefficient.

12-21. Answer B. GFDIC 12A, PHB

When an airplane flies within a distance from the ground (or water) surface equal to its own wingspan or less, the amount of induced drag decreases. With the reduction in induced drag, the amount of thrust necessary is also reduced, allowing the airplane to lift off at a lower-than-normal speed.

If you try to climb out of ground effect at too low of an airspeed, the greater induced drag can result in marginal initial climb performance, the airplane settling back to the runway, or a stall. As an airplane climbs out of ground effect, more thrust is required.

12-22 CA.I.F.K3, CA.IV.C.K4

If the same angle of attack is maintained in ground effect as when out of ground effect, lift will

A – increase, and induced drag will decrease.

B – decrease, and parasite drag will increase.

C – increase, and induced drag will increase.

12-22. Answer A. GFDIC 12A, PHB

When an airplane flies within a distance from the ground (or water) surface equal to its own wingspan or less, the amount of induced drag decreases.

Ground effect can cause floating during the landing flare. Because the wing is able to create more lift at the same angle of attack in ground effect, you might need to slightly reduce the pitch angle to maintain a descent.

12-23 CA.IV.C.K4

To produce the same lift while in ground effect as when out of ground effect, the airplane requires

A – a lower angle of attack.

B – the same angle of attack.

C – a greater angle of attack.

12-23. Answer A. GFDIC 12A, PHB

When an airplane flies within a distance from the ground (or water) surface equal to its own wingspan or less, the amount of induced drag decreases. Therefore, in ground effect, a lower angle of attack is required to produce the same amount of lift as when out of ground effect.

12-24 CA.I.F.K3, CA.VII.A.K1*

As airspeed decreases in level flight below that speed for maximum lift/drag ratio, total drag of an airplane

A – decreases because of lower parasite drag.

B – increases because of increased induced drag.

C – increases because of increased parasite drag.

12-24. Answer B. GFDIC 12A, PHB

At low speeds, a wing must fly at a higher angle of attack to generate enough lift to support the airplane, and more high pressure air from the lower surface flows around the wingtips, forming more powerful vortices, which are the primary cause of induced drag.

12-25 CA.I.F.K3

In theory, if the airspeed of an airplane is doubled while in level flight, parasite drag will become

A – twice as great.

B – half as great.

C – four times greater.

12-25. Answer C. GFDIC 12A, PHB

Although induced drag diminishes with speed, parasite drag increases with an increase in speed. The rate of increase is proportional to the square of the airspeed, so doubling your speed quadruples parasite drag.

12-26 CA.I.F.K3

(Refer to Figure 1.) At the airspeed represented by point A, in steady flight, the airplane will

A – have its maximum L/D ratio.

B – have its minimum L/D ratio.

C – be developing its maximum coefficient of lift.

12-26. Answer A. GFDIC 12A, PHB

On the total drag graph, the intersection of the induced drag and parasite drag lines corresponds with a point on the total drag line where drag is at a minimum. This point is where the aircraft is operating at the best ratio of lift to drag, or L/D_{MAX}.

12-27 CA.I.F.K3

(Refer to Figure 1.) At an airspeed represented by point B, in steady flight, you can expect to obtain the airplane's maximum

A – endurance.

B – glide range.

C – coefficient of lift.

12-27. Answer B. GFDIC 12A, PHB

Point B corresponds to the airspeed where the airplane obtains the maximum ratio of lift to drag, L/D_{MAX}. This point provides both maximum range and the best power-off glide speed. Any increase or decrease from that specified for L/D_{MAX} will result in a reduced glide distance.

12-28 CA.IX.B.K2a

What performance is characteristic of flight at maximum lift/drag ratio in a propeller-driven airplane? Maximum

A – gain in altitude over a given distance.

B – range and maximum distance glide.

C – coefficient of lift and minimum coefficient of drag.

12-28. Answer B. GFDIC 12A, PHB

On the total drag graph, the intersection of the induced drag and parasite drag lines corresponds with a point on the total drag line where drag is at a minimum. Flying your aircraft at L/D_{MAX} provides both maximum range and the best power-off glide speed. Any decrease or increase in airspeed from that specified for L/D_{MAX} will result in reduced range or gliding distance.

SECTION A ■ **Advanced Aerodynamics**

12-29 CA.I.F.K3, CA.VII.A.K1, CA.VII.B.K1*
The ratio between the total airload imposed on the wing and the gross weight of an aircraft in flight is known as

A – load factor and directly affects stall speed.

B – aspect load and directly affects stall speed.

C – load factor and has no relation with stall speed.

12-30 CA.I.F.K3, CA.VII.A.K1
Load factor is the lift generated by the wings of an airplane at any given time

A – divided by the total weight of the airplane.

B – multiplied by the total weight of the airplane.

C – divided by the basic empty weight of the airplane.

12-31 CA.I.F.K3, CA.VII.A.K1
A load factor of 1.2 means the total load on an aircraft's structure is 1.2 times its

A – gross weight.

B – load limit.

C – gust factor.

12-32 CA.I.F.K3, CA.V.A.K2d
While executing a 60° level turn, your aircraft is at a load factor of 2.0. What does this mean?

A – The total load on the aircraft's structure is two times its weight.

B – The load factor is over the load limit.

C – The gust factor is two times the total load limit.

12-29. Answer A. GFDIC 12A, PHB
The load factor is defined as the load the wings are supporting divided by the total weight of the airplane. A heavily loaded airplane has a higher stall speed than the same airplane with a light load—the heavily loaded airplane must use a higher angle of attack to generate the required lift at any given speed than when lightly loaded. Load factor in turns increases at steeper bank angles, as does the stall speed.

12-30. Answer A. GFDIC 12A, PHB
The load factor is defined as the load the wings are supporting divided by the total weight of the airplane. A heavily loaded airplane has a higher stall speed than the same airplane with a light load—the heavily loaded airplane must use a higher angle of attack to generate the required lift at any given speed than when lightly loaded. Load factor in turns increases at steeper bank angles, as does the stall speed.

12-31. Answer A. GFDIC 12A, PHB
The load factor is defined as the load the wings are supporting divided by the total weight of the airplane. A heavily loaded airplane has a higher stall speed than the same airplane with a light load—the heavily loaded airplane must use a higher angle of attack to generate the required lift at any given speed than when lightly loaded. Load factor in turns increases at steeper bank angles, as does the stall speed.

12-32. Answer A. GFDIC 12A, PHB
The load factor is defined as the load the wings are supporting divided by the total weight of the airplane. Load factor in turns increases at steeper bank angles, as does the stall speed.

When an airplane is certified in the normal category, for example, each part of the structure is designed to withstand 3.8 positive Gs and 1.52 negative Gs.

12-33   CA.I.F.K3, CA.VII.A.K1*

Baggage weighing 90 pounds is placed in a normal category airplane's baggage compartment which is placarded at 100 pounds. If this airplane is subjected to a positive load factor of 3.5 Gs, the total load of the baggage would be

A – 315 pounds and would be excessive.

B – 315 pounds and would not be excessive.

C – 350 pounds and would not be excessive.

12-33. Answer B. GFDIC 12A, PHB

To find the weight of an object that is subject to a positive G force, multiply the weight of the object times the number of Gs. For example, 90 pounds of baggage multiplied by 3.5 Gs equals 315 pounds.

Airplane structures are designed to withstand greater loads than normal flight is likely to produce. When an airplane is certified in the normal category, for example, each part of the structure is designed to withstand 3.8 positive Gs and 1.52 negative Gs.

12-34   CA.I.F.K3, CA.VII.B.K1*

In a rapid recovery from a dive, the effects of load factor would cause the stall speed to

A – increase.

B – decrease.

C – not vary.

12-34. Answer A. GFDIC 12A, PHB

A rapid pull-up from a dive increases the load factor or "G" forces imposed on the airplane, and stall speed increases in proportion to the square root of the load factor.

12-35   CA.I.F.K3

Maximum structural cruising speed is the maximum speed at which an airplane can be operated during

A – abrupt maneuvers.

B – normal operations.

C – flight in smooth air.

12-35. Answer B. GFDIC 12A, PHB

Maximum structural cruising speed, V_{NO}, is the top speed of the normal operating range and corresponds to the upper limit of the green arc on the airspeed indicator. Do not exceed this speed in rough air.

The range from V_{NO} to V_{NE} is the caution range represented by the yellow arc on the airspeed indicator. Because turbulence and gusts are more likely to cause high load factors at higher speeds, use this speed range only in smooth air.

12-36   CA.I.F.K3

Why should flight speeds above V_{NE} be avoided?

A – Excessive induced drag will result in structural failure.

B – Design limit load factors may be exceeded, if gusts are encountered.

C – Control effectiveness is so impaired that the aircraft becomes uncontrollable.

12-36. Answer B. GFDIC 12A, PHB

Never-exceed speed (V_{NE}) corresponds to the red line on the airspeed indicator. Flying faster than V_{NE} could cause control surface flutter, airframe structural damage, or failure. The range from V_{NO} to V_{NE} is the caution range represented by the yellow arc on the airspeed indicator. Because turbulence and gusts are more likely to cause high load factors at higher speeds, use this speed range only in smooth air.

SECTION A ■ **Advanced Aerodynamics**

12-37   CA.I.F.R2

Structural damage or failure is more likely to occur in smooth air at speeds above

A – V_{NO}.

B – V_A.

C – V_{NE}.

12-37. Answer A. GFDIC 12A, PHB

Maximum structural cruising speed, VNO, is the top speed of the normal operating range and corresponds to the upper limit of the green arc on the airspeed indicator. Do not exceed this speed in rough air.

The range from VNO to VNE is the caution range represented by the yellow arc on the airspeed indicator. Because turbulence and gusts are more likely to cause high load factors at higher speeds, use this speed range only in smooth air.

12-38   CA.I.F.K3

(Refer to Figure 5.) The horizontal line from point C to point E represents the

A – ultimate load factor.

B – positive limit load factor.

C – airspeed range for normal operations.

12-38. Answer B. GFDIC 12A, PHB

V-g diagrams show the maximum amount of positive or negative lift the airplane is capable of generating at a given speed, the safe load factor limits, and the load factor, or number of Gs, the airplane can sustain at various speeds. Flying within the boundaries depicted by the diagram minimizes the risk of stalls, spins, and structural damage.

The horizontal line at 3.8 Gs (point C to point E), and at –1.52 Gs (point I to point G), indicate the positive and negative load factor limits, respectively, for a normal category airplane.

12-39   CA.I.F.K3

(Refer to Figure 5.) The vertical line from point E to point F is represented on the airspeed indicator by the

A – upper limit of the yellow arc.

B – upper limit of the green arc.

C – blue radial line.

12-39. Answer A. GFDIC 12A, PHB

V-g diagrams show the maximum amount of positive or negative lift the airplane is capable of generating at a given speed, the safe load factor limits, and the load factor, or number of Gs, the airplane can sustain at various speeds.

The vertical line from point E to point F represents never-exceed speed (V_{NE})—the upper limit of the yellow arc that corresponds to the red line on the airspeed indicator. Flying faster than V_{NE} could cause control surface flutter, airframe structural damage, or failure. The range from V_{NO} to V_{NE} is the caution range represented by the yellow arc on the airspeed indicator. Because turbulence and gusts are more likely to cause high load factors at higher speeds, use this speed range only in smooth air.

12-40   CA.I.F.K3

(Refer to Figure 5.) The vertical line from point D to point G is represented on the airspeed indicator by the maximum speed limit of the

A – green arc.

B – yellow arc.

C – white arc.

12-40. Answer A. GFDIC 12A, PHB

V-g diagrams show the maximum amount of positive or negative lift the airplane is capable of generating at a given speed, the safe load factor limits, and the load factor, or number of Gs, the airplane can sustain at various speeds.

The vertical line from point D to point G represents maximum structural cruising speed, V_{NO}, which is the top speed of the normal operating range and corresponds to the upper limit of the green arc on the airspeed indicator. Do not exceed this speed in rough air.

12-41   CA.I.F.K3

If the airplane attitude remains in a new position after the elevator control is pressed forward and released, the airplane displays

A – neutral longitudinal static stability.

B – positive longitudinal static stability.

C – neutral longitudinal dynamic stability.

12-41. Answer A. GFDIC 12A, PHB

Longitudinal stability involves the pitching motion, or tendency, of the airplane to move about its lateral axis. Static stability is the airplane's initial tendency when disturbed from equilibrium in one of three ways:

- Positive static stability—return toward equilibrium.
- Negative static stability—moves away from equilibrium.
- Neutral static stability—remains in new position and does not return to or move away from equilibrium.

If the airplane remains in the new pitch attitude after elevator control pressures are released following a pitch displacement, the airplane is exhibiting neutral longitudinal static stability.

12-42   CA.I.F.K3

If the airplane attitude initially tends to return to its original position after the elevator control is pressed forward and released, the airplane displays

A – positive dynamic stability.

B – positive static stability.

C – neutral dynamic stability.

12-42. Answer B. GFDIC 12A, PHB

Static stability is the airplane's initial tendency when disturbed from equilibrium in one of three ways:

- Positive static stability—return toward equilibrium.
- Negative static stability—moves away from equilibrium.
- Neutral static stability—remains in new position and does not return to or move away from equilibrium.

If the airplane returns to the original pitch attitude after elevator control pressures are released following a pitch displacement, the airplane is exhibiting positive static stability.

SECTION A ■ **Advanced Aerodynamics**

12-43   CA.I.F.K3

Longitudinal dynamic instability in an airplane can be identified by

A – bank oscillations becoming progressively steeper.

B – pitch oscillations becoming progressively steeper.

C – trilatitudinal roll oscillations becoming progressively steeper.

12-43. Answer B. GFDIC 12A, PHB

Longitudinal stability involves the pitching motion, or tendency, of the airplane to move about its lateral axis. Dynamic stability describes how the airplane responds over time to a displacement from equilibrium.

Combining the characteristics of static and dynamic stability describes a variety of stability conditions. Longitudinal instability in an airplane can be defined as positive static and negative dynamic stability—over time, oscillations increase and becomes more divergent. The divergence will continue until the pilot intervenes or the airplane is destroyed.

12-44   CA.I.F.K3, CA.I.G.K1a

Longitudinal stability involves the motion of the airplane controlled by its

A – rudder.

B – elevator.

C – ailerons.

12-44. Answer B. GFDIC 12A, PHB

Longitudinal stability involves the pitching motion, or tendency, of the airplane to move about its lateral axis. The elevator controls an airplane's pitching moment.

12-45   CA.I.F.K3

A propeller, rotating clockwise as seen from the rear, creates a spiraling slipstream. The spiraling slipstream, along with torque effect, tends to rotate the airplane to the

A – right around the vertical axis, and to the left around the longitudinal axis.

B – left around the vertical axis, and to the right around the longitudinal axis.

C – left around the vertical axis, and to the left around the longitudinal axis.

12-45. Answer B. GFDIC 12A, PHB

As the slipstream produced by a clockwise rotating propeller (as seen from the rear) wraps around the fuselage, some of it strikes the left side of the vertical fin. This tends to rotate the airplane to the left around the vertical axis. Because the vertical fin is above the longitudinal axis, the spiraling slipstream also tends to rotate the aircraft to the right around the longitudinal axis.

12-46   CA.I.F.K3

(Refer to Figure 3.) If an airplane glides at an angle of attack of 10°, how much altitude will it lose in 1 statute mile?

A – 240 feet.

B – 480 feet.

C – 960 feet.

12-46. Answer B. GFDIC 12A, PHB

To find the L/D ratio for a particular angle of attack (in this case, 10°):

1. Locate the angle of attack at the bottom of the graph.

2. Move up the vertical reference line until you intersect the L/D curve.

3. Move right horizontally until reaching the L/D scale and read the L/D ratio of approximately 11. An 11:1 ratio means that the airplane travels 11 feet horizontally in the glide for every foot of altitude lost.

4. To find the total altitude lost in 1 statute mile, divide 5,280 ft by the L/D ratio of 11. The answer is 480 ft (5,280 ÷ 11 = 480 ft).

For nautical miles, divide 6,076 by the L/D radio of 11 (6,076 ÷ 11 = 552).

12-47   CA.I.F.K3

(Refer to Figure 3.) How much altitude will this airplane lose in 3 statute miles of gliding at an angle of attack of 8°?

A – 440 feet.

B – 880 feet.

C – 1,320 feet.

12-47. Answer C. GFDIC 12A, PHB

To find the L/D ratio for a particular angle of attack (in this case 8°):

1. Locate the angle of attack at the bottom of the graph.

2. Move up the vertical reference line until you intersect the L/D curve.

3. Move right horizontally until reaching the L/D scale and read the L/D ratio of approximately 12. A 12:1 ratio means that the airplane travels 12 feet horizontally in the glide for every foot of altitude lost.

4. To find the total altitude lost in 1 statute mile, divide 5,280 ft by the L/D ratio of 12. The answer is 440 ft (5,280 ÷ 12 = 440). Therefore, the airplane will lose approximately 1,320 ft in 3 statue miles (440 × 3 = 1,320 ft).

For nautical miles, divide 6,076 by the L/D radio of 12 (6,076 ÷ 12 = 506) and multiply by 3 (506 × 3 = 1,518 ft).

SECTION A ■ **Advanced Aerodynamics**

12-48   CA.I.F.K3

(Refer to Figure 3.) The L/D ratio at a 2° angle of attack is approximately the same as the L/D ratio for a

A – 9.75° angle of attack.

B – 10.5° angle of attack.

C – 16.5° angle of attack.

12-48. Answer C. GFDIC 12A, PHB

To find the L/D$_{MAX}$ value for a particular angle of attack:

1. Locate the 2° angle of attack on the x-axis of the graph and then move vertically to the L/D curved line.

2. Move right until you intersect the L/D curved line.

3. Follow the vertical reference line down to the corresponding angle of attack (16.5°) on the x-axis of the graph.

12-49   CA.I.F.K3

As the angle of bank is increased, the vertical component of lift

A – decreases and the horizontal component of lift increases.

B – increases and the horizontal component of lift decreases.

C – decreases and the horizontal component of lift remains constant.

12-49. Answer A. GFDIC 12A, PHB

When you roll the airplane into a bank, some of the lift of the wings is directed to the side, and it is this horizontal component of lift that causes the airplane to turn.

Diverting a portion of lift to turn the airplane reduces the vertical component of lift available to support the airplane's weight. Therefore, to maintain altitude in a turn, you must increase the angle of attack by adding elevator back pressure to increase the vertical component of lift.

12-50   CA.I.F.K3, CA.I.G.K1a

Why is it necessary to increase back elevator pressure to maintain altitude during a turn? To compensate for the

A – loss of the vertical component of lift.

B – loss of the horizontal component of lift and the increase in centrifugal force.

C – rudder deflection and slight opposite aileron throughout the turn.

12-50. Answer A. GFDIC 12A, PHB

When you roll the airplane into a bank, some of the lift of the wings is directed to the side, and it is this horizontal component of lift that causes the airplane to turn.

Diverting a portion of lift to turn the airplane reduces the vertical component of lift available to support the airplane's weight. Therefore, to maintain altitude in a turn, you must increase the angle of attack by adding elevator back pressure to increase the vertical component of lift.

12-51   CA.I.F.K3

To maintain altitude during a turn, the angle of attack must be increased to compensate for the decrease in the

A – forces opposing the resultant component of drag.

B – vertical component of lift.

C – horizontal component of lift.

12-51. Answer B. GFDIC 12A, AFH

When you roll the airplane into a bank, some of the lift of the wings is directed to the side, and it is this horizontal component of lift that causes the airplane to turn.

Diverting a portion of lift to turn the airplane reduces the vertical component of lift available to support the airplane's weight. Therefore, to maintain altitude in a turn, you must increase the angle of attack by adding elevator back pressure to increase the vertical component of lift.

12-52 CA.I.F.K3

If airspeed is increased during a level turn, what action would be necessary to maintain altitude? The angle of attack

A – and angle of bank must be decreased.

B – must be increased or angle of bank decreased.

C – must be decreased or angle of bank increased.

12-52. Answer C. GFDIC 12A, AFH

When you roll the airplane into a bank, the horizontal component of lift causes the airplane to turn. Diverting a portion of lift to turn the airplane reduces the vertical component of lift available to support the airplane's weight. However, if you increase airspeed, the vertical component of lift increases.

To maintain the same vertical lift component and prevent a climb, you must compensate by either increasing the angle of bank (changing part of the vertical lift component to the horizontal lift component), and/or by decreasing the angle of attack.

12-53 CA.V.A.K2d, CA.VII.B.K1*, CA.VII.D.K1

For a given angle of bank, in any airplane, the load factor imposed in a coordinated turn

A – is constant and the stall speed increases.

B – varies with the rate of turn.

C – is constant and the stall speed decreases.

12-53. Answer A. GFDIC 12A, PHB

The constant load factor generated in a coordinated, level turn depends on the bank angle. Load factor remains constant if no change in bank angle occurs. Load factor in turns increases at steeper bank angles, as does the stall speed. In a coordinated, level turn at a given bank angle, all airplanes will experience the same load factor and the same percentage of increase in stall speed over their wings-level stall speed.

12-54 CA.I.F.K3, CA.V.A.K2d

Airplane wing loading during a level coordinated turn in smooth air depends upon the

A – rate of turn.

B – angle of bank.

C – true airspeed.

12-54. Answer B. GFDIC 12A, PHB

The constant load factor generated in a coordinated, level turn depends on the bank angle. Load factor remains constant if no change in bank angle occurs. Load factor in turns increases at steeper bank angles, as does the stall speed. In a coordinated, level turn at a given bank angle, all airplanes will experience the same load factor and the same percentage of increase in stall speed over their wings-level stall speed.

12-55 CA.VII.D.K1

(Refer to Figure 4.) What increase in load factor would take place if the angle of bank were increased from 60° to 80°?

A – 3 Gs.

B – 3.5 Gs.

C – 4 Gs.

12-55. Answer C. GFDIC 12A, PHB

To find the increase in load factor from a 60° bank to a 80° bank:

1. Locate the 60° angle of attack on the x-axis of the graph and then move vertically to the load factor curved line.

2. Move right to read the load factor of 2 Gs on the y-axis.

3. Locate the 80° angle of attack on the x-axis of the graph and then move vertically to the load factor curved line.

4. Move right to read the load factor of 6 Gs on the y-axis.

5. Subtract the load factor at 60° bank from the load factor at 80° bank to find the increase (6 − 2 = 4 Gs).

SECTION A ■ **Advanced Aerodynamics**

12-56   CA.VII.B.K1*, CA.VII.D.K1

(Refer to Figure 4.) What is the stall speed of an airplane under a load factor of 2 Gs if the unaccelerated stall speed is 60 knots?

A – 66 knots.

B – 74 knots.

C – 84 knots.

12-56. Answer C. GFDIC 12A, PHB

To find the increase in stall speed at a 2-G load factor:

1. Locate the the load factor of 2 Gs on the y-axis on the right side of the graph.

2. Move left to the load factor curved line. 2 Gs intersects this line at a 60° bank angle.

3. Move vertically to intersect the stall speed increase line.

4. Move horizontally from the intersection point on the stall speed increase line to the y-axis on the left side to read the percent increase in stall speed of 40%.

5. Multiply the stall speed by a 140% (60 × 1.4 = 84 knots).

12-57   CA.V.A.K2e

Which is correct with respect to rate and radius of turn for an airplane flown in a coordinated turn at a constant altitude?

A – For a specific angle of bank and airspeed, the rate and radius of turn will not vary.

B – To maintain a steady rate of turn, the angle of bank must be increased as the airspeed is decreased.

C – The faster the true airspeed, the faster the rate and larger the radius of turn regardless of the angle of bank.

12-57. Answer A. GFDIC 12A, PHB

Airspeed and bank angle are the two variables in determining rate and radius of turn. If these variables remain constant, rate and radius of turn will remain constant. The rate of turn varies directly with bank angle and is inversely proportional to airspeed.

12-58   CA.V.A.K2e

To increase the rate of turn and at the same time decrease the radius, you should

A – increase the bank and decrease airspeed.

B – increase the bank and increase airspeed.

C – maintain the bank and decrease airspeed.

12-58. Answer A. GFDIC 12A, PHB

Rate and radius of turn vary with both airspeed and bank angle. For example:

When the angle of bank is held constant, decreasing the airspeed:

- decreases the turn radius.

- increases the turn rate.

When the airspeed is held constant, increasing the bank angle:

- decreases the turn radius.

- increases the turn rate.

12-59   CA.V.A.K2e

To maintain a standard-rate turn as the airspeed decreases, the bank angle of the airplane will need to

A – decrease.

B – increase.

C – remain constant.

12-59. Answer A. GFDIC 12A, PHB

Rate and radius of turn vary with both airspeed and bank angle. For example:

When the angle of bank is held constant, decreasing the airspeed:

- decreases the turn radius.
- increases the turn rate.

When the airspeed is held constant, increasing the bank angle:

- decreases the turn radius.
- increases the turn rate.

Because the turn rate increases when the airspeed decreases, you must also decrease the bank angle to maintain the same rate of turn at a slower airspeed.

12-60   CA.V.A.K2d, e

If the airspeed is decreased from 98 knots to 85 knots during a coordinated level 45° banked turn, the load factor will

A – remain the same, but the radius of turn will decrease.

B – decrease, and the rate of turn will decrease.

C – remain the same, but the radius of turn will increase.

12-60. Answer A. GFDIC 12A, PHB

Rate and radius of turn vary with both airspeed and bank angle but load factor remains constant if no change in bank angle occurs. For example:

When the angle of bank is held constant, decreasing the airspeed:

- decreases the turn radius.
- increases the turn rate.
- has no effect on the load factor.

12-61   CA.V.A.K2d, e

If the airspeed is increased from 89 knots to 98 knots during a coordinated level 45° banked turn, the load factor will

A – decrease, and the radius of turn will decrease.

B – remain the same, but the radius of turn will increase.

C – increase, but the rate of turn will decrease.

12-61. Answer B. GFDIC 12A, PHB

Rate and radius of turn vary with both airspeed and bank angle but load factor remains constant if no change in bank angle occurs. For example:

When the angle of bank is held constant, increasing the airspeed:

- decreases the turn radius.
- increases the turn rate.
- has no effect on the load factor.

12-62   CA.V.A.K2d, e

While maintaining a constant angle of bank and altitude in a coordinated turn, an increase in airspeed will

A – decrease the rate of turn resulting in a decreased load factor.

B – decrease the rate of turn resulting in no change in load factor.

C – increase the rate of turn resulting in no change in load factor.

12-62. Answer B. GFDIC 12A, PHB

Rate and radius of turn vary with both airspeed and bank angle but load factor remains constant if no change in bank angle occurs. For example:

When the angle of bank is held constant, increasing the airspeed:

- decreases the turn radius.
- increases the turn rate.
- has no effect on the load factor.

SECTION A ■ **Advanced Aerodynamics**

12-63   CA.I.F.K3, CA.V.A.K2d

While holding the angle of bank constant in a level turn, if the rate of turn is varied, the load factor would

A – remain constant regardless of air density and the resultant lift vector.

B – vary depending upon speed and air density provided the resultant lift vector varies proportionately.

C – vary depending upon the resultant lift vector.

12-63. Answer A. GFDIC 12A, PHB

Rate and radius of turn vary with both airspeed and bank angle but load factor remains constant if no change in bank angle occurs. For example:

When the angle of bank is held constant, increasing the airspeed:

- increases the turn radius.
- decreases the turn rate.
- has no effect on the load factor.

When the angle of bank is held constant, decreasing the airspeed:

- decreases the turn radius.
- increases the turn rate.
- has no effect on the load factor.

12-64   CA.V.A.K2d, e

If the airspeed is increased from 90 knots to 135 knots during a level 60° banked turn, the load factor will

A – increase as well as the stall speed.

B – decrease and the stall speed will increase.

C – remain the same but the radius of turn will increase.

12-64. Answer C. GFDIC 12A, PHB

Rate and radius of turn vary with both airspeed and bank angle but load factor remains constant if no change in bank angle occurs. For example:

When the angle of bank is held constant, increasing the airspeed:

- increases the turn radius.
- decreases the turn rate.
- has no effect on the load factor.

When the angle of bank is held constant, decreasing the airspeed:

- decreases the turn radius.
- increases the turn rate.
- has no effect on the load factor.

12-65   CA.VII.B.K1*, CA.VII.D.K1

An airplane will stall at the same

A – angle of attack regardless of the attitude with relation to the horizon.

B – airspeed regardless of the attitude with relation to the horizon.

C – angle of attack and attitude with relation to the horizon.

12-65. Answer A. GFDIC 12A, AFH

The stall always occurs at the same angle of attack for any particular airfoil, regardless of weight, load factor, attitude, airspeed, or thrust/power. However, several factors of these affect the stall speed.

12-66   CA.VII.B.K1*, CA.VII.D.K1

The angle of attack at which a wing stalls remains constant regardless of

A – weight, dynamic pressure, bank angle, or pitch attitude.

B – dynamic pressure, but varies with weight, bank angle, and pitch attitude.

C – weight and pitch attitude, but varies with dynamic pressure and bank angle.

12-66. Answer A. GFDIC 12A, PHB

The stall always occurs at the same angle of attack for any particular airfoil, regardless of air density, weight, load factor, attitude, airspeed, or thrust/power. However, several of these factors affect the stall speed. For example, if you increase weight or the load factor by increasing the bank angle, or decrease the power, you must increase the angle of attack at any given airspeed to generate a corresponding amount of lift so stall speed increases.

Dynamic pressure is expressed in the lift equation as air density multiplied by velocity squared divided by 2.

12-67   CA.VII.B.K1*, CA.VII.D.K1

Stall speed is affected by

A – weight, load factor, and power.

B – load factor, angle of attack, and power.

C – angle of attack, weight, and air density.

12-67. Answer A. GFDIC 12A, AFH

The stall always occurs at the same angle of attack for any particular airfoil, regardless of air density, weight, load factor, attitude, airspeed, or thrust/power. However, several factors affect the stall speed. For example, if you increase the weight of the airplane or the load factor or decrease the power, you must increase the angle of attack at any given airspeed to generate a corresponding amount of lift so stall speed increases.

12-68   CA.VII.B.K4*

Recovery from a stall in any airplane becomes more difficult when its

A – center of gravity moves aft.

B – center of gravity moves forward.

C – elevator trim is adjusted nose down.

12-68. Answer A. GFDIC 12A, PHB

If the center of gravity is too far aft, the stall speed decreases, but the elevator/stabilator control might not have enough authority to reduce the angle of attack, making recovery impossible.

As the CG is moved forward, the tail-down force necessary for level flight increases and stall speed increases. Because the wing must fly at a higher angle of attack to generate the greater tail-down forces, the wing is closer to its stalling angle of attack for any given airspeed.

12-69   CA.VII.B.K1*

The stalling speed of an airplane is most affected by

A – changes in air density.

B – variations in flight altitude.

C – variations in airplane loading.

12-69. Answer C. GFDIC 12A, AFH

Stall speed increases rapidly as G-loading increases during maneuvers such as steep turns. This increase in stall speed is because the load factor multiplies the effective weight of the airplane, which must be balanced by a similar increase in lift from the wings, necessitating a higher angle of attack. In addition, the weight of the airplane and location of the CG affects stall speed.

Although changes in air density due to temperature and altitude affect stall speed, the effect of these variations is not as significant as airplane loading.

SECTION A ■ **Advanced Aerodynamics**

12-70   CA.I.G.K1a, CA.VII.B.K3, CA.VII.E.K1, 2

A left side slip is used to counteract a crosswind drift during the final approach for landing. An over-the-top spin would most likely occur if the controls were used in which of the following ways? Holding the stick

A – too far back and applying full right rudder.

B – in the neutral position and applying full right rudder.

C – too far to the left and applying full left rudder.

12-70. Answer A. GFDIC 12A, PHB

Stalling with crossed controls is a major cause of spins, and usually happens when either too much or not enough rudder is used for existing yawing forces. In this case, applying too much right rudder while applying left aileron and applying excessive elevator back pressure could result in a stall/spin situation.

If an airplane stalls with crossed controls, it is likely to enter a spin. The spin rotation is usually in the direction of the rudder being applied, regardless of which wing is raised.

12-71   CA.VII.E.K1, 2, 3

In small airplanes, normal recovery from spins may become difficult if the

A – CG is too far rearward, and rotation is around the longitudinal axis.

B – CG is too far rearward, and rotation is around the CG.

C – spin is entered before the stall is fully developed.

12-71. Answer B. GFDIC 12A, PHB

Because moving the CG aft decreases longitudinal stability and reduces pitch control forces in most airplanes, an aft CG tends to make the airplane easier to stall. After a spin is entered, an airplane with its CG farther aft tends to have a flatter spin attitude. A flat spin is characterized by a near level pitch and roll attitude with the spin axis near the CG of the airplane. The upward flow over the tail could render the elevators and rudder ineffective, making recovery impossible.

12-72   CA.I.F.K3, CA.I.G.K1a

What could be one result of exceeding critical Mach number?

A – Propeller stall.

B – Reduction in drag.

C – Aircraft control difficulties.

12-72. Answer C. GFDIC 12A, PHB

Critical Mach number is the speed of an aircraft in which airflow over any part of the aircraft or structure first reaches (but does not exceed) Mach 1.0. The drag incurred in the transonic region due to shock wave formation and airflow separation is known as wave drag.

When speed exceeds the critical Mach number by about 10 percent, wave drag increases sharply. Associated with drag rise are Mach buffet, trim and stability changes, and a decrease in control force effectiveness.

SECTION B
PREDICTING PERFORMANCE

FACTORS AFFECTING PERFORMANCE

- Factors affecting aircraft performance include:
    - Atmospheric conditions—temperature, wind, humidity
    - Pilot technique
    - Airplane configuration
    - Airport environment/runway conditions
    - Weight and balance (loading/center of gravity)
- Although standard atmospheric conditions are the foundation for estimating airplane performance, airplanes are rarely flown in conditions that match the standard atmosphere. Calculating aircraft performance takes differences between standard and existing conditions into account.

DENSITY ALTITUDE

- The density of the air directly influences the performance of your airplane by altering the lift of the airframe, as well as the ability of the engine to produce power.
- Both reciprocating and turbine engines produce less thrust as air density decreases and/or temperature increases, because these factors reduce the mass of the air passing through the engine.
- In propeller-driven airplanes, propeller efficiency is reduced when there are fewer air molecules to act upon.
- Jet thrust is the reaction force resulting from accelerating mass backward, so a reduction in the mass going into the engine reduces thrust if other factors remain the same.
- Density altitude is pressure altitude corrected for nonstandard temperature, and is equal to pressure altitude only when standard atmospheric conditions exist at that level.
- For a given pressure altitude, density altitude increases when temperature increases.
- Most performance charts do not require you to compute density altitude. Instead, the computation is built into the performance chart itself. All you have to do is enter the correct pressure altitude and the temperature on the chart.
- Some pilot's operating handbooks/aircraft flight manuals (POHs/AFMs) contain a density altitude chart. However, you can find density altitude using an electronic or a mechanical flight computer by taking these steps:
1. Enter pressure altitude.
2. Enter the outside air temperature (OAT).
3. Compute density altitude.

SURFACE WINDS

- Take these steps to determine the crosswind component using a wind component chart.
1. Determine the angle between the wind and the runway (for example, runway direction 080° − wind direction 010° = angle 70°)
2. Locate the intersection of the angle and wind velocity.
3. Move vertically to the x-axis to read the approximate wind component perpendicular to the runway (crosswind component).
    - Angle 70° / 18 knots: 17-knot crosswind component

4. Move horizontally to the y-axis to read the approximate wind component parallel to the runway (headwind).

- Angle 70° / 18 knots: 6-knot headwind component

RUNWAY CONDITIONS

- The gradient, or slope, of the runway is expressed as a percentage. For example, a gradient of 2 percent means the runway height changes 2 feet for each 100 feet of runway length. Positive gradients are uphill, and negative gradients are downhill.

- A positive gradient (uphill)

  - increases takeoff distance.

  - decreases landing distance.

- A negative gradient (downhill)

  - decreases takeoff distance.

  - increases landing distance.

- Wet or icy runways decrease braking effectiveness and increase landing distances. Braking effectiveness is reported as good, fair, poor, or nil, or some combination of these terms.

- Hydroplaning is when the tires are separated from the runway surface by a thin layer of water. Hydroplaning not only increases stopping distances, it can also lead to complete loss of airplane control.

PILOT'S OPERATING HANDBOOK

- Operating limitations are contained in the approved flight manual (AFM), approved manual materials, markings and placards, or any combination of these. For most modern airplanes, the pilot's operating handbook (POH) is the approved flight manual.

- Performance charts contained in the POH are typically presented in a logical order, beginning with general information and flight planning calculations and progressing through takeoff, climb, cruise, descent, and landing.

PERFORMANCE CHARTS

The Commercial Pilot Airmen Knowledge Test presents a variety of different performance charts in both table and graph formats. Sample test questions contained in this section present step-by-step explanations for determining performance using charts contained in the FAA figures of the Computer Testing Supplement for Commercial Pilot. Consider the following when using the performance charts:

- Read the given conditions in the question and associated conditions on the chart carefully. You must consider an assortment of criteria when using performance charts, such as optional flap settings, power settings, or correction factors for different runway conditions.

- Apply any corrections to your solution that are indicated in notes on the performance chart.

- Interpolate to determine performance values that are not specifically listed on the chart. Interpolation is the estimation of an unknown value between two known values. For example, if the performance table only provides information for 2,000 and 4,000 feet, and you need to find a value for an altitude of 3,000 feet, you can find the midpoint between the values provided to estimate the value for 3,000 feet.

TAKEOFF CHARTS

- Takeoff charts usually incorporate compensation for pressure altitude, outside air temperature, airplane weight, and headwind or tailwind component.

- Manuals include separate charts for normal and obstacle takeoff distances, two- or three-bladed propellers, various flap settings, or specific pilot techniques, such as short field or maximum effort.

CLIMB PERFORMANCE CHARTS

- Two different types of climb performance charts enable you to determine:
  - The maximum rate of climb for various combinations of air temperature, pressure altitude, airplane weight, and airspeed.
  - The time, fuel, and distance required to climb from one altitude to another based on temperature, airplane weight, and the altitudes concerned.
- Using the time, fuel, and distance to climb chart is a two-step process. First, find the values for your cruising altitude, then find and subtract the values for your takeoff altitude.

CRUISE PERFORMANCE CHARTS

- Cruise performance charts include variables such as manifold pressure, propeller RPM, fuel flow settings, and pressure altitude.
- Range is the distance the airplane can travel on a given amount of fuel.
- Endurance is the amount of time an airplane can remain airborne on a given amount of fuel.

DESCENT CHARTS

- Use descent charts to predict the time, fuel, and distance to descend from your cruising altitude to your destination.

LANDING DISTANCE CHARTS

- Landing distance charts usually incorporate compensation for pressure altitude, outside air temperature, airplane weight, and headwind or tailwind component.
- Charts typically provide the ground roll and the landing distance from a height of 50 feet.

STALL SPEEDS

- Stall speed varies with factors such as weight, CG location, configuration, and bank angle.
- Because of the change in stall speed, airplanes are usually flown at a higher approach speed when they are heavily loaded.

NOTE: An asterisk appearing after an ACS code (i.e. CA.IV.A.K2*) indicates that the question subject appears more than one time in the ACS. The code shown corresponds to the first instance of the subject in the ACS.

SECTION B ■ **Predicting Performance**

12-73   CA.I.F.K2a, b

Which is true regarding factors that affect aircraft performance?

A – Performance is always determined using standard atmospheric conditions.

B – Pilot technique does not affect aircraft performance.

C – Atmospheric conditions, airplane configuration, and weight and balance affect aircraft performance.

12-73. Answer C. GFDIC 12B, PHB

Factors affecting aircraft performance include:

- Atmospheric conditions—temperature, wind, humidity
- Pilot technique
- Airplane configuration
- Airport environment/runway conditions
- Weight and balance (loading/center of gravity)

Although standard atmospheric conditions are the foundation for estimating airplane performance, airplanes are rarely flown in conditions that match the standard atmosphere. Calculating aircraft performance takes differences between standard and existing conditions into account.

12-74   CA.I.C.K3c, CA.I.F.K1, 2a

As air temperature increases, density altitude will

A – decrease.

B – increase.

C – remain the same.

12-74. Answer B. GFDIC 12B, PHB

Density altitude is pressure altitude corrected for nonstandard temperature, and is equal to pressure altitude only when standard atmospheric conditions exist at that level. For a given pressure altitude, density altitude increases when temperature increases.

12-75   CA.I.F.K2a

Density altitude is the vertical distance above mean sea level in the standard atmosphere at which

A – pressure altitude is corrected for standard temperature.

B – a given atmospheric density is to be found.

C – temperature, pressure, altitude, and humidity are considered.

12-75. Answer B. GFDIC 12B, PHB

Density altitude is pressure altitude corrected for nonstandard temperature, and is equal to pressure altitude only when standard atmospheric conditions exist at that level. For a given pressure altitude, density altitude increases when temperature increases.

12-76   CA.I.F.K2a

What effect, if any, would a change in ambient temperature or air density have on gas turbine engine performance?

A – As air density decreases, thrust increases.

B – As temperature increases, thrust increases.

C – As temperature increases, thrust decreases.

12-76. Answer C. GFDIC 12B, AFH

Both reciprocating and turbine engines produce less thrust as air density decreases and/or temperature increases, because these factors reduce the mass of the air passing through the engine.

In propeller-driven airplanes, propeller efficiency is reduced when there are fewer air molecules to act upon. Jet thrust is the reaction force resulting from accelerating mass backward, so a reduction in the mass going into the engine reduces thrust if other factors remain the same.

12-77   CA.I.F.K1, CA.IV.A.K1*

The performance tables of an aircraft for takeoff and climb are based on

A – pressure/density altitude.

B – cabin altitude.

C – true altitude.

12-77. Answer A. GFDIC 12B, PHB
Most performance charts do not require you to compute density altitude. Instead, the computation is built into the performance chart itself. All you have to do is enter the correct pressure altitude and the temperature on the chart. This means the charts reflect density altitude.

12-78   CA.I.F.K1, CA.I.F.K2a
GIVEN:

Pressure altitude...12,000 ft

Outside air temperature...+50°F

From the conditions given, the approximate density altitude is

A – 11,900 feet.

B – 14,130 feet.

C – 18,150 feet.

12-78. Answer B. GFDIC 12B, PHB
Some POHs/AFMs contain a density altitude chart. However, you can find density altitude using an electronic or a mechanical flight computer by taking these steps:

1. Enter pressure altitude—12,000 feet.

2. Enter the outside air temperature—50°F/10°C.

3. Compute density altitude—14,134 feet.

12-79   CA.I.F.K1, CA.I.F.K2a
GIVEN:

Pressure altitude...5,000 ft

Outside air temperature...+30°C

From the conditions given, the approximate density altitude is

A – 7,200 feet.

B – 7,800 feet.

C – 9,000 feet.

12-79. Answer B. GFDIC 12B, PHB
Some POHs/AFMs contain a density altitude chart. However, you can find density altitude using an electronic or a mechanical flight computer by taking these steps:

1. Enter pressure altitude—5,000 feet.

2. Enter the outside air temperature—30°C/86°F.

3. Compute density altitude—7,801 feet.

12-80   CA.I.F.K1, CA.I.F.K2a
GIVEN:

Pressure altitude...6,000 ft

Outside air temperature...+30°F

From the conditions given, the approximate density altitude is

A – 9,000 feet.

B – 5,500 feet.

C – 5,000 feet.

12-80. Answer B. GFDIC 12B, PHB
This question requires you to compute density altitude. To do this use the following steps.

1. Enter pressure altitude—6,000 feet.

2. Enter the outside air temperature—30°F/-1.1°C.

3. Compute density altitude—5,496 feet.

SECTION B ■ **Predicting Performance**

12-81   CA.I.F.K1, CA.I.F.K2a

GIVEN:

Pressure altitude...7,000 ft

Outside air temperature...+15°C

From the conditions given, the approximate density altitude is

A – 5,000 feet.

B – 8,500 feet.

C – 9,500 feet.

12-81. Answer B. GFDIC 12B, PHB

This question requires you to compute density altitude. To do this use the following steps.

1. Enter pressure altitude—7,000 feet.

2. Enter the outside air temperature—15°C/59°F.

3. Compute density altitude—8,595 feet.

12-82   CA.I.F.K1, CA.I.F.K2a, d

(Refer to Figure 31.) If the tower-reported surface wind is 010° at 18 knots, what is the crosswind component for a Rwy 08 landing?

A – 7 knots.

B – 15 knots.

C – 17 knots.

12-82. Answer C. GFDIC 12B, PHB

Take these steps to determine the crosswind component:

1. Determine the angle between the wind and the runway: 080° – 010° = 70°:

2. Locate the intersection of the angle and wind velocity.

3. Move vertically to the x-axis to read the approximate wind component perpendicular to the runway (crosswind component).

Angle 70° / 18 knots: 17-knot crosswind component

12-83   CA.I.F.K1, CA.I.F.K2a, d

(Refer to Figure 31.) The surface wind is 180° at 25 knots. What is the crosswind component for a RWY 13 landing?

A – 19 knots.

B – 21 knots.

C – 23 knots.

12-83. Answer A. GFDIC 12B, PHB

Take these steps to determine the crosswind component:

1. Determine the angle between the wind and the runway: 180° – 130° = 50°:

2. Locate the intersection of the angle and wind velocity.

3. Move vertically to the x-axis to read the approximate wind component perpendicular to the runway (crosswind component).

Angle 50° / 25 knots: 19-knot crosswind component

12-84   CA.I.F.K1, CA.I.F.K2a, d, CA.IV.A.K1*
(Refer to Figure 31.) What is the headwind component for a Rwy 13 takeoff if the surface wind is 190° at 15 knots?

A – 7 knots.

B – 13 knots.

C – 15 knots.

12-84. Answer A. GFDIC 12B, PHB
Take these steps to determine the headwind component:

1. Determine the angle between the wind and the runway: 190° − 130° = 60°:

2. Locate the intersection of the angle and wind velocity.

3. Move horizontally to the y-axis to read the approximate wind component parallel to the runway (headwind component).

Angle 60° / 15 knots: 7-knot headwind component

12-85   CA.I.F.K1, CA.I.F.K2a, d
(Refer to Figure 31.) Rwy 30 is being used for landing. Which surface wind would exceed the airplane's crosswind capability of 0.2 V_{S0}, if V_{S0} is 60 knots?

A – 260° at 20 knots.

B – 275° at 25 knots.

C – 315° at 35 knots.

12-85. Answer A. GFDIC 12B, PHB
In this example, the aircraft's maximum crosswind component is 12 knots (.2 × 60 = 12). Take these steps to determine which of the indicated choices exceeds this value:

1. Determine the angle between the wind and the runway for each possible answer:

- 300° − 260° = 40°

- 300° − 275° = 25°

- 315° − 300° = 15°

2. Locate the intersection of the angle and wind velocity.

3. Move vertically to the x-axis to read the approximate wind component perpendicular to the runway (crosswind component).

- **Angle 40° / 20 knots: 13-knot crosswind component**

- Angle 25° / 25 knots: 10-knot crosswind component

- Angle 15° / 25 knots: 4-knot crosswind component

12-86   CA.I.F.K1, CA.I.F.K2d, CA.IV.A.K1*
What effect does an uphill runway slope have on takeoff performance?

A – Increases takeoff speed.

B – Increases takeoff distance.

C – Decreases takeoff distance.

12-86. Answer B. GFDIC 12B, PHB
The gradient, or slope, of the runway is expressed as a percentage. For example, a gradient of 2 percent means the runway height changes 2 feet for each 100 feet of runway length. Positive gradients are uphill, and negative gradients are downhill. A positive gradient increases takeoff distance.

SECTION B ■ **Predicting Performance**

12-87   CA.I.F.K1, CA.I.F.K2a, d, CA.IV.A.K1*

(Refer to Figure 32.)

GIVEN:

Temperature...50°F

Pressure altitude...2,000 feet

Weight ... 2,700 lb

Wind ... Calm

What is the total takeoff distance over a 50-foot obstacle?

A – 800 feet.

B – 650 feet.

C – 1050 feet.

12-87. Answer A. GFDIC 12B, PHB

To determine the total takeoff distance over a 50-foot obstacle:

1. Enter the graph at the outside air temperature of 50°F.

2. Go up to the diagonal line for the pressure altitude of 2,000 feet.

3. Move right horizontally to the reference line, then diagonally to intersect the vertical guideline for the total weight of 2,700 pounds.

4. Move right horizontally to the y-axis to read the takeoff distance over a 50-foot obstacles of approximately 800 feet.

12-88   CA.I.F.K1, CA.I.F.K2a, d, CA.IV.A.K1*

(Refer to Figure 32.)

GIVEN:

Temperature...100°F

Pressure altitude...4,000 ft

Weight...3,200 lb

Wind...Calm.

What is the ground roll required for takeoff over a 50-foot obstacle?

A – 1,180 feet.

B – 1,350 feet.

C – 1,850 feet.

12-88. Answer B. GFDIC 12B, PHB

To determine the total takeoff distance over a 50-foot obstacle:

1. Enter the graph at the outside air temperature of 100°F.

2. Go up to the diagonal line for the pressure altitude of 4,000 feet.

3. Move right horizontally to the reference line, then diagonally to intersect the vertical guideline for the total weight of 3,200 pounds.

4. Move right horizontally to the y-axis to read the takeoff distance over a 50-foot obstacles of approximately 1,350 feet.

12-89   CA.I.F.K1, CA.I.F.K2a, d, CA.IV.A.K1*
(Refer to Figure 32.)

GIVEN:

Temperature...30°F

Pressure altitude...6,000 ft

Weight...3,300 lb

Headwind...20 kts

What is the total takeoff distance over a 50-foot obstacle?

A – 1,100 feet.

B – 1,300 feet.

C – 1,500 feet.

12-89. Answer C. GFDIC 12B, PHB
To determine the total takeoff distance over a 50-foot obstacle:

1. Enter the graph at the outside air temperature of 30°F.

2. Go up to the diagonal line for the pressure altitude of 6,000 feet.

3. Move right horizontally to the reference line, then diagonally to intersect the vertical guideline for the total weight of 3,300 pounds.

4. Move right horizontally to the second reference line, then diagonally to parallel the headwind guidelines, to intersect the vertical guideline for the wind speed of 20 knots.

5. Move right horizontally to the y-axis to read the takeoff distance over a 50-foot obstacles of approximately 1,500 feet.

12-90   CA.I.F.K1, CA.I.F.K2a, d, CA.IV.A.K1*
(Refer to Figure 32.) What is the total takeoff distance required to clear a 50-foot obstacle with the following conditions.

Temperature...50 °F

Pressure altitude...4,000 ft

Weight...3,200 lb

Headwind...15 kts.

A – 1,200 feet.

B – 880 feet.

C – 700 feet.

12-90. Answer A. GFDIC 12B, PHB
To determine the total takeoff distance over a 50-foot obstacle:

1. Enter the graph at the outside air temperature of 50°F.

2. Go up to the diagonal line for the pressure altitude of 4,000 feet.

3. Move right horizontally to the reference line, then diagonally to intersect the vertical guideline for the total weight of 3,200 pounds.

4. Move right horizontally to the second reference line, then diagonally to parallel the headwind guidelines, to intersect the vertical guideline for the wind speed of 15 knots.

5. Move right horizontally to the y-axis to read the takeoff distance over a 50-foot obstacle of approximately 1,200 feet.

SECTION B ■ **Predicting Performance**

12-91   CA.I.F.K1, CA.I.F.K2a, d, CA.IV.A.K1*
(Refer to Figure 32.)

GIVEN:

Temperature...75°F

Pressure altitude...6,000 ft

Weight...2,900 lb

Headwind...20 kts

To safely take off over a 50-foot obstacle in 1,000 feet, what weight reduction is necessary?

A – 50 pounds.

B – 100 pounds.

C – 300 pounds.

12-91. Answer C. GFDIC 12B, PHB
To determine the total takeoff distance over a 50-foot obstacle:

1. Enter the graph at the outside air temperature of 75°F.

2. Go up to the diagonal line for the pressure altitude of 6,000 feet.

3. Move right horizontally to the reference line, then diagonally to intersect the vertical guideline for the total weight of 2,900 pounds.

4. Move right horizontally to the second reference line, then diagonally to parallel the headwind guidelines, to intersect the vertical guideline for the wind speed of 20 knots.

5. Move right horizontally to the y-axis to read the takeoff distance over a 50-foot obstacles of approximately 1,450 feet.

To determine the takeoff weight that would reduce the total takeoff distance to 1,000 feet:

1. Enter the chart at 1,000 feet on the right side on the y-axis and move left horizontally to intersect the vertical guideline for the wind speed of 20 knots.

2. Move left parallel to the diagonal reference lines to the vertical reference line. Move horizontally until intersect the original diagonal line that you used extending to the right of the first reference line.

3. Move vertically down to weight along the x-axis of 2,600 pounds.

4. Subtract 2,600 pounds from the original weight of 2,900 pounds for a required weight reduction of 300 pounds (2,900 - 2,600 = 300).

5. intersect the 2,600 pound line. This point corresponds with the original mark on reference line number 1 and requires a weight reduction of 300 pounds.

12-92 CA.I.F.K1

(Refer to Figure 8.) Approximately how much fuel would be consumed when climbing at 75 percent power for 7 minutes?

A – 1.82 gallons.

B – 1.97 gallons.

C – 2.13 gallons.

12-92. Answer C. GFDIC 12B, PHB

To determine the fuel consumption during the climb:

1. Follow the Takeoff and Climb diagonal line to where it intersects the vertical line of 75% maximum continuous power.

2. Move left horizontally to the fuel flow of 18.25 gallons per hour on the y-axis.

3. Use a flight computer or calculator to determine that the total fuel consumed during 7 minutes at a rate of 18.25 gallons per hour is approximately 2.13 gallons: $18.25 \div 60 \times 7 = 2.13$.

12-93 CA.I.F.K1

(Refer to Figure 8.) Determine the amount of fuel consumed during takeoff and climb at 70 percent power for 10 minutes.

A – 2.66 gallons.

B – 2.88 gallons.

C – 3.2 gallons.

12-93. Answer B. GFDIC 12B, PHB

To determine the fuel consumption during the climb:

1. Follow the Takeoff and Climb diagonal line to where it intersects the vertical line of 70% maximum continuous power (midway between 65% and 75%).

2. Move left horizontally to the fuel flow of 17.25 gallons per hour on the y-axis.

3. Use a flight computer or calculator to determine that the total fuel consumed during 10 minutes at a rate of 17.25 gallons per hour is approximately 2.88 gallons: $17.25 \div 60 \times 10 = 2.88$.

SECTION B ■ **Predicting Performance**

12-94   CA.I.F.K1

(Refer to Figure 9.)

GIVEN:

Aircraft weight...3,500 lb

Airport pressure altitude...4,000 ft

Temperature...21°C

Using a normal climb, approximately how much fuel would be used from engine start to 10,000 feet pressure altitude?

A – 23 pounds.

B – 31 pounds.

C – 35 pounds.

12-94. Answer C. GFDIC 12B, PHB

To determine the fuel to used to climb, subtract the fuel shown on the table at 4,000 feet from the fuel at 10,000 feet.

1. At the aircraft weight of 3,500 pounds, move right to the pressure altitude column.

2. Read the fuel used at 4,000 feet—11 pounds.

3. Read the fuel used at 10,000 feet—31 pounds.

4. Subtract the 2 values to determine the fuel used: 31 – 11 = 20 pounds of fuel.

5. Note 2—increase time, fuel, and distance by 10% for each 10°C above standard temperature (1% change for every 1°C).

   • Standard temperature at sea level is 15°C and the standard lapse rate is 2°C per 1,000-foot increase in altitude. Standard temperature for an airport at 4,000 feet is 7°C (15°C – 8°C = 7°C).

   • Subtract the standard temperature from the outside air temperature: 21°C – 7°C = 14°C.

   • Because a 14°C difference exists between the actual temperature and standard, increase the fuel used by 14%: 20 × 1.14 = 22.8 pounds.

6. Note 1—add 12 pounds for engine start, taxi and takeoff: 22.8 + 12 = 34.8 pounds.

12-95   CA.I.F.K1

(Refer to Figure 9.)

GIVEN:

Aircraft weight...3,800 lb

Airport pressure altitude...4,000 ft

Temperature...26°C

Using a normal climb, approximately how much fuel would be used from engine start to 12,000 feet pressure altitude?

A – 46 pounds.

B – 51 pounds.

C – 58 pounds.

12-95. Answer C. GFDIC 12B, PHB

To determine the fuel to used to climb, subtract the fuel shown on the table at 4,000 feet from the fuel at 12,000 feet.

1. At the aircraft weight of 3,800 pounds, move right to the pressure altitude column.

2. Read the fuel used at 4,000 feet—12 pounds.

3. Read the fuel used at 12,000 feet—51 pounds.

4. Subtract the 2 values to determine the fuel used: 51 – 12 = 39 pounds of fuel.

5. Note 2—increase time, fuel, and distance by 10% for each 10°C above standard temperature (1% change for every 1°C).

   • Standard temperature at sea level is 15°C and the standard lapse rate is 2°C per 1,000-foot increase in altitude. Standard temperature for an airport at 4,000 feet is 7°C (15°C – 8°C = 7°C).

   • Subtract the standard temperature from the outside air temperature: 26°C – 7°C = 19°C.

   • Because a 19°C difference exists between the actual temperature and standard, increase the fuel used by 19%: 39 × 1.19 = 46.4 pounds.

6. Note 1—add 12 pounds for engine start, taxi and takeoff: 46.4 + 12 = 58.4 pounds.

SECTION B ■ Predicting Performance

12-96　CA.I.F.K1

(Refer to Figure 10.)

GIVEN:

Aircraft weight...3,200 lb

Airport pressure altitude...2,000 ft

Temperature...27°C

Using a maximum rate of climb, approximately how much fuel would be used from engine start to 6,000 feet pressure altitude?

A – 10 pounds.

B – 14 pounds.

C – 24 pounds.

12-96. Answer C. GFDIC 12B, PHB

To determine the fuel to used to climb, subtract the fuel shown on the table at 2,000 feet from the fuel at 6,000 feet.

1. At the aircraft weight of 3,200 pounds, move right to the pressure altitude column.

2. Read the fuel used at 2,000 feet—4 pounds.

3. Read the fuel used at 6,000 feet—14 pounds.

4. Subtract the 2 values to determine the fuel used: 14 – 4 = 10 pounds of fuel.

5. Note 2—increase time, fuel, and distance by 10% for each 10°C above standard temperature (1% change for every 1°C).

   • Standard temperature at sea level is 15°C and the standard lapse rate is 2°C per 1,000-foot increase in altitude. Standard temperature for an airport at 2,000 feet is 11°C (15°C – 4°C = 11°C).

   • Subtract the standard temperature from the outside air temperature: 27°C – 11°C = 16°C.

   • Because a 16°C difference exists between the actual temperature and standard, increase the fuel used by 16%: 10 × 1.16 = 11.6 pounds.

6. Note 1—add 12 pounds for engine start, taxi and takeoff: 11.6 + 12 = 23.6 pounds.

12-97   CA.I.F.K1

(Refer to Figure 10.)

GIVEN:

Aircraft weight...3,800 lb

Airport pressure altitude...4,000 ft

Temperature...30°C

Using a maximum rate of climb, approximately how much fuel would be used from engine start to 10,000 feet pressure altitude?

A – 28 pounds.

B – 35 pounds.

C – 40 pounds.

12-97. Answer C. GFDIC 12B, PHB

To determine the fuel to used to climb, subtract the fuel shown on the table at 4,000 feet from the fuel at 10,000 feet.

1. At the aircraft weight of 3,800 pounds, move right to the pressure altitude column.

2. Read the fuel used at 4,000 feet—12 pounds.

3. Read the fuel used at 10,000 feet—35 pounds.

4. Subtract the 2 values to determine the fuel used: 35 – 12 = 23 pounds of fuel.

5. Note 2—increase time, fuel, and distance by 10% for each 10°C above standard temperature (1% change for every 1°C).

   • Standard temperature at sea level is 15°C and the standard lapse rate is 2°C per 1,000-foot increase in altitude. Standard temperature for an airport at 4,000 feet is 8°C (15°C – 8°C = 7°C).

   • Subtract the standard temperature from the outside air temperature: 30°C – 7°C = 23°C.

   • Because a 23°C difference exists between the actual temperature and standard, increase the fuel used by 23%: 23 × 1.23 = 28.29 pounds.

6. Note 1—add 12 pounds for engine start, taxi and takeoff: 28.29 + 12 = 40.29 pounds.

SECTION B ■ **Predicting Performance**

12-98   CA.I.D.K3a, c, CA.I.F.K1

(Refer to Figure 13.)

GIVEN:

Aircraft weight...3,400 lb

Airport pressure altitude...6,000 ft

Temperature at 6,000 ft...10°C

Using a maximum rate of climb under the given conditions, approximately how much fuel would be used from engine start to a pressure altitude of 16,000 feet?

A – 43 pounds.

B – 45 pounds.

C – 49 pounds.

12-98. Answer A. GFDIC 12B, PHB

To determine the fuel to used to climb, subtract the fuel shown on the table at 6,000 feet from the fuel at 16,000 feet.

1. At the aircraft weight of 3,400 pounds, move right to the pressure altitude column.

2. Interpolate between the 4,000 feet and 8,000-feet to determine 14 pounds of fuel.

3. Read the fuel used at 16,000 feet—39 pounds.

4. Subtract the 2 values to determine the fuel used: 39 – 14 = 25 pounds of fuel.

5. Note 2—increase time, fuel, and distance by 10% for each 10°C above standard temperature (1% change for every 1°C).

   - Standard temperature at sea level is 15°C and the standard lapse rate is 2°C per 1,000-foot increase in altitude. Standard temperature for an airport at 6,000 feet is 3°C (15°C – 12°C = 3°C).

   - Subtract the standard temperature from the outside air temperature: 10°C – 3°C = 7°C.

   - Because a 7°C difference exists between the actual temperature and standard, increase the fuel used by 7%: 25 × 1.07 = 26.75 pounds.

6. Note 1—add 16 pounds for engine start, taxi and takeoff: 26.75 + 16 = 42.75 pounds.

12-99 CA.I.D.K3a, CA.I.F.K1

(Refer to Figure 13.)

GIVEN:

Aircraft weight...4,000 lb

Airport pressure altitude...2,000 ft

Temperature at 2,000 ft...32°C

Using a maximum rate of climb under the given conditions, how much time would be required to climb to a pressure altitude of 8,000 feet?

A – 7 minutes.

B – 8.5 minutes.

C – 11.2 minutes.

12-99. Answer B. GFDIC 12B, PHB

To determine the time to climb, subtract the time shown on the table at 2,000 feet from time at 8,000 feet.

1. At the aircraft weight of 4,000 pounds, move right to the pressure altitude column.

2. Interpolate between the sea level time to climb and 4,000 feet to determine 2 minutes.

3. Read the time at 8,000 feet—9 minutes.

4. Subtract the 2 values to determine the time to climb: 9 – 2 = 7 minutes.

5. Note 2—increase time, fuel, and distance by 10% for each 10°C above standard temperature (1% change for every 1°C).

- Standard temperature at sea level is 15°C and the standard lapse rate is 2°C per 1,000-foot increase in altitude. Standard temperature for an airport at 2,000 feet is 11°C (15°C – 4°C = 11°C).

- Subtract the standard temperature from the outside air temperature: 32°C – 11°C = 21°C.

- Because a 21°C difference exists between the actual temperature and standard, increase the time to climb by 21%: 7 × 1.21 = 8.47 minutes.

SECTION B ■ **Predicting Performance**

12-100   CA.I.D.K3a, c, CA.I.F.K1

(Refer to Figure 14.)

GIVEN:

Aircraft weight...3,700 lb

Airport pressure altitude...4,000 ft

Temperature at 4,000 ft...21°C

Using a normal climb under the given conditions, approximately how much fuel would be used from engine start to a pressure altitude of 12,000 feet?

A – 30 pounds.

B – 37 pounds.

C – 45 pounds.

12-101   CA.I.D.K3a, CA.I.F.K1

(Refer to Figure 15.)

GIVEN:

Airport pressure altitude...4,000 ft

Airport temperature...12°C

Cruise pressure altitude...9,000 ft

Cruise temperature...–4°C

What will be the distance required to climb to cruise altitude under the given conditions?

A – 6 miles.

B – 8.5 miles.

C – 11 miles.

12-100. Answer C. GFDIC 12B, PHB

To determine the fuel to used to climb, subtract the fuel shown on the table at 4,000 feet from the fuel at 12,000 feet.

1. At the aircraft weight of 3,700 pounds, move right to read the fuel at the 4,000 feet—12 pounds.

2. Read the fuel used at 12,000 feet—37 pounds.

3. Subtract the 2 values to determine the fuel used: 37 – 12 = 25 pounds of fuel.

4. Note 2—increase time, fuel, and distance by 10% for each 7°C above standard temperature (1% change for every 1°C).

   - Standard temperature at sea level is 15°C and the standard lapse rate is 2°C per 1,000-foot increase in altitude. Standard temperature for an airport at 4,000 feet is 7°C (15°C – 8°C = 7°C).

   - Subtract the standard temperature from the outside air temperature: 21°C – 7°C = 14°C.

   - Because a 14°C difference exists between the actual temperature and standard, increase the fuel used by 14%: 25 × 1.14 = 28.5 pounds.

5. Note 1—add 16 pounds for engine start, taxi and takeoff: 28.5 + 16 = 44.5 pounds.

12-101. Answer B. GFDIC 12B, PHB

To determine the distance to climb, subtract the distance to climb from sea level to the airport elevation from the distance to climb from sea level to 9,000 feet.

1. Enter the graph at the outside air temperature for the cruise altitude of –4°C.

2. Go up to the diagonal line for the pressure altitude of 9,000 feet (midway between the 8,000 and 10,000 feet).

3. Move right horizontally to the distance line.

4. Move down to read the distance of 14 NM.

5. Repeat steps 1 through 4 for the temperature of 12°C and elevation of 4,000 feet to determine a distance of 5.5 NM.

6. Determine the distance to climb from the airport to 9,000 feet: 14 – 5.5 = 8.5 NM.

12-102 CA.I.D.K3a, c, CA.I.F.K1, CA.VI.A.K6
(Refer to Figure 8.)

GIVEN:

Fuel quantity...47 gal

Power-cruise (lean)...55 percent

Approximately how much flight time would be available with a night VFR fuel reserve remaining?

A – 3 hours 8 minutes.

B – 3 hours 22 minutes.

C – 3 hours 43 minutes.

12-102. Answer B. GFDIC 12B, PHB
To determine the available flight time with 47 gallons of fuel on board:

1. Follow the Cruise (Lean) diagonal line to where it intersects the vertical line of 55% maximum continuous power.

2. Move left horizontally to the fuel flow of 11.4 gallons per hour on the y-axis.

3. Use a flight computer or calculator to determine a total time by dividing the 47 gallons on board by the fuel flow rate: 47 ÷ 11.4 = 4.12 (4 hours and 7 minutes).

4. FAR 91.151 requires a fuel reserve of 45 minutes at normal cruise speed for night VFR flying. Subtract 45 minutes from your total time of 4:07 for approximately 3 hours and 22 minutes of flight time available.

12-103 CA.I.D.K3a, c, CA.I.F.K1, CA.VI.A.K6
(Refer to Figure 8.)

GIVEN:

Fuel quantity...65 gal

Best power-level flight...55 percent

Approximately how much flight time would be available with a day VFR fuel reserve remaining?

A – 4 hours 17 minutes.

B – 4 hours 30 minutes.

C – 5 hours 4 minutes.

12-103. Answer B. GFDIC 12B, PHB
To determine the available flight time with 65 gallons of fuel on board:

1. Follow the Cruise (Lean) diagonal line to where it intersects the vertical line of 55% maximum continuous power.

2. Move left horizontally to the fuel flow of 13 gallons per hour on the y-axis.

3. Use a flight computer or calculator to determine a total time by dividing the 65 gallons on board by the fuel flow rate: 65 ÷ 13 = 5 hours.

4. FAR 91.151 requires a fuel reserve of 30 minutes at normal cruise speed for day VFR flying. Subtract 30 minutes from your total time of 5:00 for approximately 4 hours and 30 minutes of flight time available.

SECTION B ■ **Predicting Performance**

12-104 CA.I.D.K3a, c, CA.I.F.K1, CA.VI.A.K6
(Refer to Figure 8.) With 38 gallons of fuel aboard at cruise power (55 percent), how much flight time is available with night VFR fuel reserve still remaining?

A – 2 hours 35 minutes.

B – 2 hours 49 minutes.

C – 3 hours 20 minutes.

12-104. Answer A. GFDIC 12B, PHB
To determine the available flight time with 38 gallons of fuel on board:

1. Follow the Cruise (Lean) diagonal line to where it intersects the vertical line of 55% maximum continuous power.

2. Move left horizontally to the fuel flow of 11.4 gallons per hour on the y-axis.

3. Use a flight computer or calculator to determine a total time by dividing the 38 gallons on board by the fuel flow rate: 38 ÷ 11.4 = 3.33 (3 hours and 20 minutes).

4. FAR 91.151 requires a fuel reserve of 45 minutes at normal cruise speed for night VFR flying. Subtract 45 minutes from your total time of 3:20 for approximately 2 hours and 35 minutes of flight time available.

12-105 CA.I.D.K3a, c, CA.I.F.K1
(Refer to Figure 11.) If the cruise altitude is 7,500 feet, using 64 percent power at 2500 RPM, what would be the range with 48 gallons of usable fuel?

A – 635 miles.

B – 645 miles.

C – 810 miles.

12-105. Answer C. GFDIC 12B, PHB
To determine the range with 48 gallons of usable fuel on board:

1. At the altitude of 7,500 feet, move right to the 2,500 row under RPM. (Note, this is also 64% BHP.)

2. Move right to the RANGE (MILES) column below the heading 48 GAL (NO RESERVE) to read 810 miles.

12-106 CA.I.D.K3a, c, CA.I.F.K1
(Refer to Figure 11.) What would be the endurance at an altitude of 7,500 feet, using 52 percent power with 48 gallons of usable fuel?

A – 6.1 hours.

B – 7.7 hours.

C – 8.0 hours.

12-106. Answer B. GFDIC 12B, PHB
To determine the endurance with 48 gallons of usable fuel on board:

1. At the altitude of 7,500 feet, move right to the 52% row under % BHP RPM. (Note, this is 2,300 RPM.)

2. Move right to the ENDURANCE (HOURS) column below the heading 48 GAL (NO RESERVE) to read 7.7 hours.

12-107 CA.I.D.K3a, c, CA.I.F.K1
(Refer to Figure 11.) What would be the approximate true airspeed and fuel consumption per hour at an altitude of 7,500 feet, using 52 percent power?

A – 103 MPH TAS, 6.3 GPH.

B – 105 MPH TAS, 6.2 GPH.

C – 105 MPH TAS, 6.6 GPH.

12-107. Answer B. GFDIC 12B, PHB
To determine the true airspeed and fuel consumption:

1. At the altitude of 7,500 feet, move right to the 52% row under % BHP RPM. (Note, this is 2,300 RPM.)

2. Move right to the TAS MPH to read 105 mph.

3. Move right to the GAL/HOUR column to read 6.2 gallons per hour.

12-108 CA.I.D.K3a, c, CA.I.F.K1

(Refer to Figure 12.)

GIVEN:

Pressure altitude...18,000 ft

Temperature...–21°C

Power...2400 RPM, 28 inches MP

Recommended lean mixture

Usable fuel...425 lb

What is the approximate flight time available under the given conditions? (Allow for VFR day fuel reserve.)

A – 3 hours 46 minutes.

B – 4 hours 1 minute.

C – 4 hours 31 minutes.

12-109 CA.I.D.K3a, c, CA.I.F.K1

(Refer to Figure 12.)

GIVEN:

Pressure altitude...18,000 ft

Temperature...–41°C

Power...2500 RPM, 26 inches MP

Recommended lean mixture

Usable fuel...318 lb

What is the approximate flight time available under the given conditions? (Allow for VFR night fuel reserve.)

A – 2 hours 27 minutes.

B – 3 hours 12 minutes.

C – 3 hours 42 minutes.

12-108. Answer B. GFDIC 12B, PHB

To determine the available flight time with 425 pounds of fuel on board:

1. At 2,400 RPM, move right to the 28 inches row under MP.

2. Move right to the PPH column under the heading STANDARD TEMPERATURE –21°C to read the fuel flow of 94 pounds per hour.

3. Use a flight computer or calculator to determine a total time by dividing the 425 pounds on board by the fuel flow rate: 425 ÷ 94 = 4.52 (4 hours and 31 minutes).

4. FAR 91.151 requires a fuel reserve of 30 minutes at normal cruise speed for day VFR flying. Subtract 30 minutes from your total time of 4:31 for an available flight time of 4 hours and 1 minute.

12-109. Answer A. GFDIC 12B, PHB

To determine the available flight time with 318 pounds of fuel on board:

1. At 2,500 RPM, move right to the 26 inches row under MP.

2. Move right to the PPH column under the heading 20°C BELOW STANDARD TEMPERATURE –41°C to read the fuel flow of 99 pounds per hour.

3. Use a flight computer or calculator to determine a total time by dividing the 318 pounds on board by the fuel flow rate: 318 ÷ 99 = 3.21 (3 hours and 12 minutes).

4. FAR 91.151 requires a fuel reserve of 45 minutes at normal cruise speed for night VFR flying. Subtract 45 minutes from your total time of 3:12 for an available flight time of 2 hours and 27 minutes.

SECTION B ■ **Predicting Performance**

12-110 CA.I.D.K3a, c, CA.I.F.K1

(Refer to Figure 12.)

GIVEN:

Pressure Altitude...18,000 ft

Temperature...−1°C

Power...2200 RPM, 20 inches MP

Best fuel economy

Usable fuel...344 lb

What is the approximate flight time available under the given conditions? (Allow for VFR day fuel reserve.)

A – 4 hours 50 minutes.

B – 5 hours 20 minutes.

C – 5 hours 59 minutes.

12-111 CA.I.D.K3a, c, CA.I.F.K1

(Refer to Figure 34.)

GIVEN:

Pressure altitude...6,000 ft

Temperature...+3°C

Power...2200 RPM, 22 inches MP

Usable fuel available...465 lb

What is the maximum available flight time under the conditions stated?

A – 6 hours 27 minutes.

B – 6 hours 39 minutes.

C – 6 hours 56 minutes.

12-110. Answer B. GFDIC 12B, PHB

To determine the available flight time with 344 pounds of fuel on board:

1. At 2,200 RPM, move right to the 20 inches row under MP.

2. Move right to the PPH column under the heading 20°C ABOVE STANDARD TEMPERATURE −1°C to read the fuel flow of 59 pounds per hour.

3. Use a flight computer or calculator to determine a total time by dividing the 344 pounds on board by the fuel flow rate: 344 ÷ 59 = 5.83 (5 hours and 50 minutes).

4. FAR 91.151 requires a fuel reserve of 30 minutes at normal cruise speed for day VFR flying. Subtract 30 minutes from your total time of 5:50 for an available flight time of 5 hours and 20 minutes.

12-111. Answer B. GFDIC 12B, PHB

To determine the maximum available flight time with 465 pounds of fuel on board:

1. At 2,200 RPM, move right to the 22 inches row under MP.

2. Move right to the PPH column under the heading STANDARD TEMPERATURE +3°C to read the fuel flow of 70 pounds per hour.

3. Use a flight computer or calculator to determine a total time by dividing the 465 pounds on board by the fuel flow rate: 465 ÷ 70 = 6.64 (6 hours and 39 minutes).

Note: When planning an actual flight, remember that FAR 91.151 requires a fuel reserve of 30 minutes at normal cruise speed for day VFR flying and 45 minutes for night VFR flying.

12-112 CA.I.D.K3a, c, CA.I.F.K1

(Refer to Figure 34.)

GIVEN:

Pressure altitude...6,000 ft

Temperature...−17°C

Power...2300 RPM, 23 inches MP

Usable fuel available...370 lb

What is the maximum available flight time under the conditions stated?

A – 4 hours 20 minutes.

B – 4 hours 30 minutes.

C – 4 hours 50 minutes.

12-113 CA.I.D.K3a, c, CA.I.F.K1

(Refer to Figure 34.)

GIVEN:

Pressure altitude...6,000 ft

Temperature...+13°C

Power...2500 RPM, 23 inches MP

Usable fuel available...460 lb

What is the maximum available flight time under the conditions stated?

A – 4 hours 58 minutes.

B – 5 hours 7 minutes.

C – 5 hours 12 minutes.

12-112. Answer B. GFDIC 12B, PHB

To determine the maximum available flight time with 370 pounds of fuel on board:

1. At 2,300 RPM, move right to the 23 inches row under MP.

2. Move right to the PPH column under the heading 20°C BELOW STANDARD TEMPERATURE −17°C to read the fuel flow of 82 pounds per hour.

3. Use a flight computer or calculator to determine a total time by dividing the 370 pounds on board by the fuel flow rate: 370 ÷ 82 = 4.51 (4 hours and 30 minutes).

Note: When planning an actual flight, remember that FAR 91.151 requires a fuel reserve of 30 minutes at normal cruise speed for day VFR flying and 45 minutes for night VFR flying.

12-113. Answer C. GFDIC 12B, PHB

To determine the maximum available flight time with 460 pounds of fuel on board:

1. At 2,500 RPM, move right to the 23 inches row under MP.

2. Move right to the PPH column under the heading STANDARD TEMPERATURE to read the fuel flow of 90 pounds per hour.

3. Move right to the PPH column under the heading 20°C ABOVE STANDARD TEMPERATURE +13°C to read the fuel flow of 87 pounds per hour.

4. Interpolate between the fuel flows of 90 and 87 to determine a fuel flow of 88.5 pounds per hour.

5. Use a flight computer or calculator to determine a total time by dividing the 460 pounds on board by the fuel flow rate: 460 ÷ 88.5 = 5.19 (5 hours and 12 minutes).

Note: When planning an actual flight, remember that FAR 91.151 requires a fuel reserve of 30 minutes at normal cruise speed for day VFR flying and 45 minutes for night VFR flying.

SECTION B ■ **Predicting Performance**

12-114 CA.I.D.K3c

If fuel consumption is 80 pounds per hour and groundspeed is 180 knots, how much fuel is required for an airplane to travel 477 NM?

A – 205 pounds.

B – 212 pounds.

C – 460 pounds.

12-114. Answer B. GFDIC 12B, PHB

Use your flight computer or calculate the fuel requirement mathematically.

1. Time enroute = 477 NM ÷ 180 NM/hr = 2.65 hr (2 hours and 39 minutes)

2. Fuel required = 2.65 hr × 80 lb/hr = 212 pounds

12-115 CA.I.D.K3c

If an airplane is consuming 95 pounds of fuel per hour at a cruising altitude of 6,500 feet and the groundspeed is 173 knots, how much fuel is required to travel 450 NM?

A – 247 pounds.

B – 265 pounds.

C – 284 pounds.

12-115. Answer A. GFDIC 12B, PHB

Use your flight computer or calculate the fuel requirement mathematically.

1. Time enroute = 450 NM ÷ 173 NM/hr = 2.6 hr (2 hours and 36 minutes)

2. Fuel required = 2.65 hr × 95 lb/hr = 247 pounds

12-116 CA.I.D.K3c

If an airplane is consuming 12.5 gallons of fuel per hour at a cruising altitude of 8,500 feet and the groundspeed is 145 knots, how much fuel is required to travel 435 NM?

A – 27 gallons.

B – 34 gallons.

C – 38 gallons.

12-116. Answer C. GFDIC 12B, PHB

Use your flight computer or calculate the fuel requirement mathematically.

1. Time enroute = 435 NM ÷ 145 NM/hr = 3 hours

2. Fuel required = 3 hr × 12.5 gallons = 37.5 gallons

12-117 CA.I.D.K3c

If an aircraft is consuming 9.5 gallons of fuel per hour at a cruising altitude of 6,000 feet and the groundspeed is 135 knots, how much fuel is required to travel 420 NM?

A – 27 gallons.

B – 30 gallons.

C – 35 gallons.

12-117. Answer B. GFDIC 12B, PHB

Use your flight computer or calculate the fuel requirement mathematically.

1. Time enroute = 420 NM ÷ 135 NM/hr = 3.11 hr (3 hours and 7 minutes)

2. Fuel required = 3.11 hr × 9.5 gal/hr = 29.6 gallons

12-118 CA.I.D.K3c

If an airplane is consuming 14.8 gallons of fuel per hour at a cruising altitude of 7,500 feet and the groundspeed is 167 knots, how much fuel is required to travel 560 NM?

A – 50 gallons.

B – 53 gallons.

C – 57 gallons.

12-118. Answer A. GFDIC 12B, PHB

Use your flight computer or calculate the fuel requirement mathematically.

Time enroute = 560 NM ÷ 167 NM/hr = 3.35 hr (3 hours and 21 minutes)

Fuel required = 3.35 hr × 14.8 gal/hr = 49.6 gallons

12-119 CA.I.F.K1, CA.I.F.K2a, d, CA.IV.B.K2*
(Refer to Figure 35.)

GIVEN:

Temperature...70°F

Pressure altitude...Sea level

Weight...3,400 lb

Headwind...16 kts

Determine the approximate ground roll.

A – 689 feet.

B – 716 feet.

C – 1,275 feet.

12-119. Answer A. GFDIC 12B, PHB

To determine the approximate ground roll:

1. Enter the graph at the outside air temperature of 70°F.

2. Go up to the diagonal line for the pressure altitude of sea level.

3. Move right horizontally to the reference line, then diagonally to intersect the vertical guideline for the total weight of 3,400 pounds.

4. Move right horizontally to the second reference line, then diagonally to parallel the headwind guidelines to intersect the vertical guideline for the wind speed of 16 knots.

5. Move right horizontally to the y-axis to read the total landing distance over a 50-foot obstacle of approximately 1,300 feet.

6. As indicated in the note under Associated Conditions, to determine the ground roll, multiply the total landing distance by .53: 1,300 × .53 = 689 feet.

SECTION B ■ **Predicting Performance**

12-120 CA.I.F.K1, CA.I.F.K2a, d, CA.IV.B.K2*

(Refer to Figure 35.)

GIVEN:

Temperature...85°F

Pressure altitude...6,000 ft

Weight...2,800 lb

Headwind...14 kts

Determine the approximate ground roll.

A – 742 feet.

B – 1,280 feet.

C – 1,480 feet.

12-120. Answer A. GFDIC 12B, PHB

To determine the approximate ground roll:

1. Enter the graph at the outside air temperature of 85°F.

2. Go up to the diagonal line for the pressure altitude of 6,000 feet.

3. Move right horizontally to the reference line, then diagonally to intersect the vertical guideline for the total weight of 2,800 pounds.

4. Move right horizontally to the second reference line, then diagonally to parallel the headwind guidelines to intersect the vertical guideline for the wind speed of 14 knots.

5. Move right horizontally to the y-axis to read the total landing distance over a 50-foot obstacle of approximately 1,400 feet.

6. As indicated in the note under Associated Conditions, to determine the ground roll, multiply the total landing distance by .53: 1,400 × .53 = 742 feet.

12-121 CA.I.F.K1, CA.I.F.K2a, d, CA.IV.B.K2*

(Refer to Figure 35.)

GIVEN:

Temperature...50°F

Pressure altitude...Sea level

Weight...3,000 lb

Headwind...10 kts

Determine the approximate ground roll.

A – 425 feet.

B – 636 feet.

C – 836 feet.

12-121. Answer B. GFDIC 12B, PHB

To determine the approximate ground roll:

1. Enter the graph at the outside air temperature of 50°F.

2. Go up to the diagonal line for the pressure altitude of 6,000 feet.

3. Move right horizontally to the reference line, then diagonally to intersect the vertical guideline for the total weight of 3,000 pounds.

4. Move right horizontally to the second reference line, then diagonally to parallel the headwind guidelines to intersect the vertical guideline for the wind speed of 10 knots.

5. Move right horizontally to the y-axis to read the total landing distance over a 50-foot obstacle of approximately 1,200 feet.

6. As indicated in the note under Associated Conditions, to determine the ground roll, multiply the total landing distance by .53: 1,200 × .53 = 636 feet.

12-122 CA.I.F.K1, CA.I.F.K2a, d, CA.IV.B.K2*
(Refer to Figure 35.)

GIVEN:

Temperature...80°F

Pressure altitude...4,000 ft

Weight...2,800 lb

Headwind...24 kts

What is the total landing distance over a 50-foot obstacle?

A – 1,125 feet.

B – 1,250 feet.

C – 1,325 feet.

12-122. Answer A. GFDIC 12B, PHB
To determine the total landing distance over a 50-foot obstacle:

1. Enter the graph at the outside air temperature of 80°F.

2. Go up to the diagonal line for the pressure altitude of 4,000 feet.

3. Move right horizontally to the reference line, then diagonally to intersect the vertical guideline for the total weight of 2,800 pounds.

4. Move right horizontally to the second reference line, then diagonally to parallel the headwind guidelines to intersect the vertical guideline for the wind speed of 24 knots.

5. Move right horizontally to the y-axis to read the total landing distance over a 50-foot obstacle of approximately 1,125 feet.

12-123 CA.VII.B.K1*
(Refer to Figure 2.) Select the correct statement regarding stall speeds.

A – Power-off stalls occur at higher airspeeds with the gear and flaps down.

B – In a 60° bank, the airplane stalls at a lower airspeed with the gear up.

C – Power-on stalls occur at lower airspeeds in shallower banks.

12-123. Answer C. GFDIC 12B, PHB
Manufacturers provide charts to help you estimate the stall speed for various conditions. According to the stall speed table, stall speeds are lower with power on and higher with power off. With power on, most airplanes stall at a lower airspeed because of the airflow over the wings induced by the propeller.

12-124 CA.I.F.K2c, CA.VII.B.K1*
(Refer to Figure 2.) Select the correct statement regarding stall speeds. The airplane will stall

A – 10 knots higher in a power-on 60° bank with gear and flaps up than with gear and flaps down.

B – 25 knots lower in a power-off, flaps-up, 60° bank, than in a power-off, flaps-down, wings-level configuration.

C – 10 knots higher in a 45° bank, power-on stall than in a wings-level stall with flaps up.

12-124. Answer A. GFDIC 12B, PHB
Manufacturers provide charts to help you estimate the stall speed for various conditions. According to the stall speed table, the difference between the power-on stall speed in a 60° bank with gear and flaps up (76 knots) and the power-on stall speed with gear and flaps down (66 knots) is 10 knots.

SECTION B ■ **Predicting Performance**

On the Commercial Pilot Airman Knowledge Test, you might be presented with basic VFR flight planning questions that provide conditions derived from performance charts and require the use of an electronic or mechanical flight computer. These flight planning concepts were introduced to you as a private pilot. Examples of these types of questions follow.

12-125 CA.VI.A.K1

What procedure could you use to navigate under VFR from one point to another when ground references are not visible?

A – Dead reckoning.

B – Pilotage.

C – VFR is not allowed in these circumstances.

12-125. Answer A. GFDPP 12B, PHB
Dead reckoning is navigating by time, speed, distance, and direction calculations. Navigating by reference to landmarks is called pilotage.

12-126 CA.I.C.K3

You are pilot-in-command of a VFR flight that you think will be within the fuel range of your aircraft. As part of your preflight planning you must

A – be familiar with all instrument approaches at the destination airport.

B – list an alternate airport on the flight plan, and confirm adequate takeoff and landing performance at the destination airport.

C – obtain weather reports, forecasts, and fuel requirements for the flight.

12-126. Answer C. GFDPP 12A, FAR 91.103
According to FAR 91.103, as pilot in command, you must become familiar with all available information concerning that flight. For a flight under IFR or not in the vicinity of an airport, this information must include weather reports and forecasts, fuel requirements, alternatives available if the planned flight cannot be completed, and any known traffic delays of which the pilot in command has been advised by ATC.

12-127 CA.VI.A.K4a, b, c

Which is an action you should take when planning your route for a VFR cross-country?

A – Use a preferred VFR route listed in the appropriate Chart Supplement.

B – Plan your route to avoid all special use airspace.

C – Select easily identifiable checkpoints and plot a course that you provides options if you have to divert.

12-127. Answer B. GFDPP 11A, PHB
When developing a route for a VFR cross-country flight, consider significant terrain and obstacles along the route and determine airspace requirements. Decide if you would like to circumnavigate any busy airspace and locate any special use airspace that might affect your route.

Modify your course to include appropriate navaids and plan a route that gives you options if you have to divert. Select easily identifiable checkpoints, such as prominent landmarks and navaids, to keep track of your position, monitor your progress, and provide references for contacting ATC.

SECTION B ■ **Predicting Performance**

12-128 CA.I.D.K2, CA.VI.A.K4b

VFR cruising altitudes are required to be maintained when flying

A – at 3,000 feet or more AGL, based on true course.

B – more than 3,000 feet AGL, based on magnetic course.

C – at 3,000 feet or more above MSL, based on magnetic heading.

12-128. Answer B. GFDPP 9A, FAR 91.159

When operating an aircraft under VFR in level cruising flight, VFR cruising altitudes begin at 3,000 feet AGL. In addition, the altitudes are based on magnetic course.

12-129 CA.I.D.K4

When filling out a flight plan form you should enter

A – your initial cruising altitude even if you plan to change altitude later in the flight.

B – the usable fuel on board in gallons and pounds.

C – all legs of the flight with stops expected to be more than one hour.

12-129. Answer B. GFDPP 9A, PHB

You can find specific guidelines for filling out a flight plan form at 1800wxbrief.com and in the AIM. For example, enter your initial cruising altitude, even if you plan to change altitude later in the flight. If you will be making a stop on your flight, the FAA recommends that you file a separate flight plan for each leg if the stop is expected to be more than one hour. Enter the usable fuel on board in hours and minutes.

12-130 CA.I.D.K3a, CA.VI.A.K5

True course measurements on a sectional aeronautical chart should be made at a meridian near the midpoint of the course because the

A – values of isogonic lines change from point to point.

B – angles formed by isogonic lines and lines of latitude vary from point to point.

C – angles formed by lines of longitude and the course line vary from point to point.

12-130. Answer C. GFDPP 9A, PHB

Because the longitude lines (meridians) converge toward the poles in the map projection used for sectional charts, the longitude lines toward the ends of the course would give slightly different true course readings. Measuring near the center of the course will put you on a nearly perfect great circle route between your departure and destination airports.

SECTION B ■ **Predicting Performance**

12-131 CA.I.D.K3a, c

An airplane departs an airport under the following conditions:

Airport elevation...1,000 ft

Cruise altitude...9,500 ft

Rate of climb...500 ft/m

Average true airspeed...135 kts

True course...215°

Average wind velocity...290° at 20 kts

Variation...3° W

Deviation...-2°

Average fuel consumption...13 gal/hr

Determine the approximate time, compass heading, distance, and fuel consumed during the climb.

A – 14 minutes, 234°, 26 NM, 3.9 gallons.

B – 17 minutes, 224°, 36 NM, 3.7 gallons.

C – 17 minutes, 242°, 31 NM, 3.5 gallons.

12-131. Answer B. GFDPP 12B, PHB

To determine the approximate time, compass heading, distance, and fuel consumed during the climb:

1. Determine the total height of the climb from the airport elevation of 1,000 feet to the cruise altitude of 9,500 feet: 9,500 feet – 1,000 feet = 8,500 feet.

2. Determine the time to climb by dividing the height of the climb by the rate of climb: 8,500 feet ÷ 500 feet/minute = 17 minutes.

3. Enter the following given information into your flight computer to calculate a true heading and groundspeed.

   • Wind: 290° at 20 knots

   • True course: 215°

   • True airspeed: 135 knots

   True heading = 223°
   Groundspeed = 128 knots

4. Determine the compass heading by adding the variation of 3°W to and subtracting the deviation of -2° from the true heading: 223° + 3° – 2° = 224°.

5. Enter into a flight computer the time of 17 minutes and the groundspeed of 128 knots to determine a distance of 36.4 nautical miles.

6. Enter into a flight computer the time of 17 minutes and a fuel flow of 13.0 gallons per hour to determine the fuel consumption of 3.7 gallons.

12-132 CA.I.D.K3a

An airplane departs an airport under the following conditions:

Airport elevation...1,500 ft

Cruise altitude...9,500 ft

Rate of climb...500 ft/m

Average true airspeed...160 kts

True course...145°

Average wind velocity...080° at 15 kts

Variation...5° E

Deviation...-3°

Average fuel consumption...4 gal/hr.

Determine the approximate time, compass heading, distance, and fuel consumed during the climb.

A – 14 minutes, 128°, 35 NM, 3.2 gallons.

B – 16 minutes, 132°, 41 NM, 3.7 gallons.

C – 16 minutes, 128°, 32 NM, 3.8 gallons.

12-132. Answer B. GFDPP 12B, PHB

To determine the approximate time, compass heading, distance, and fuel consumed during the climb:

1. Determine the total height of the climb from the airport elevation of 1,500 feet to the cruise altitude of 9,500 feet: 9,500 feet – 1,500 feet = 8,000 feet.

2. Determine the time to climb by dividing the height of the climb by the rate of climb: 8,000 feet ÷ 500 feet/minute = 16 minutes.

3. Enter the following given information into your flight computer to calculate a true heading and groundspeed.

- Wind: 080° at 15 knots

- True course: 145°

- True airspeed: 160 knots

True heading = 140°
Groundspeed = 153 knots

4. Determine the compass heading by subtracting the variation of 5°E and the deviation of -3° from the true heading: 140° – 5° – 3° = 132°.

5. Enter into a flight computer the time of 16 minutes and the groundspeed of 153 knots to determine a distance of 40.8 nautical miles.

6. Enter into a flight computer the time of 16 minutes and a fuel flow of 14.0 gallons per hour to determine the fuel consumption of 3.7 gallons.

SECTION B ▪ **Predicting Performance**

12-133 CA.I.D.K3a, b, c, CA.VI.A.K1, 5
GIVEN:

Wind...175° at 20 kts

Distance...135 NM

True course...075°

True airspeed...80 kts

Fuel consumption...105 lb/hr

Determine the time enroute and fuel consumption.

A – 1 hour 28 minutes and 73.2 pounds.

B – 1 hour 38 minutes and 158 pounds.

C – 1 hour 40 minutes and 175 pounds.

12-133. Answer C. GFDPP 12B, PHB
To determine the time enroute and fuel consumption:

1. Enter the following given information into your flight computer to calculate a true heading and groundspeed.

   • Wind: 175° at 20 knots

   • True course: 075°

   • True airspeed: 80 knots

   Groundspeed = 81 knots

2. To determine the estimated time enroute (ETE), divide the distance of 135 nautical miles by the groundspeed of 81 knots: 135 ÷ 81 = 1.66 (1 hour and 40 minutes).

3. To calculate your fuel consumption, multiply your ETE of 1.66 by the fuel consumption rate of 105 pounds per hour: 1.66 × 105 = 175 pounds.

12-134 CA.I.D.K3a, CA.VI.A.K1, 5
GIVEN:

True course...105°

True heading...085°

True airspeed...95 kts

Groundspeed...87 kts

Determine the approximate wind direction and speed.

A – 020° and 32 knots.

B – 030° and 38 knots.

C – 200° and 32 knots.

12-134. Answer A. GFDPP 12B, PHB
Consider this scenario. During a cross-country flight, your heading to maintain your course and groundspeed significantly vary from your original flight planning calculations. In this case, use your flight computer to determine what the actual wind direction and speed are at your altitude—019° at 33 knots.

This problem is easiest to solve by entering the given data into an electronic flight computer and solving for unknown wind. You can also work the problem in reverse on the wind side of your mechanical flight computer.

12-135 CA.I.D.K3a, CA.VI.A.K1, 5

GIVEN:

True course...345°

True heading...355°

True airspeed...85 kts

Groundspeed...95 kts

Determine the wind direction and speed.

A – 095° and 19 knots.

B – 113° and 19 knots.

C – 238° and 18 knots.

12-135. Answer B. GFDPP 12B, PHB

Consider this scenario. During a cross-country flight, your heading to maintain your course and groundspeed significantly vary from your original flight planning calculations. In this case, use your flight computer to determine what the actual wind direction and speed are at your altitude—112° at 19 knots.

This problem is easiest to solve by entering the given data into an electronic flight computer and solving for unknown wind. You can also work the problem in reverse on the wind side of your mechanical flight computer.

12-136 CA.I.F.K1, CA.I.F.K2a, d, CA.VI.A.K1, 5

An airplane descends under the following conditions:

Cruising altitude...6,500 ft MSL

Airport elevation...700 ft MSL

Descends to....800 ft AGL

Rate of decent...500 ft/m

Average true airspeed...110 kts

True course...335°

Average wind velocity...060° at 15 kts

Variation 3°W; Deviation...+2°

Average fuel consumption...8.5 gal/hr.

Find the approximate time, compass heading, distance, and fuel consumed.

A – 10 minutes, 348°, 18 NM, 1.4 gallons.

B – 10 minutes, 355°, 17 NM, 2.4 gallons.

C – 12 minutes, 346°, 18 NM, 1.6 gallons.

12-136. Answer A. GFDPP 12B, PHB

To determine the approximate time, compass heading, distance, and fuel consumed during the descent:

1. Determine the total height of the descent from the cruise altitude of 6,500 feet MSL to the the airport elevation of 700 feet MSL plus the traffic pattern altitude of 800 feet AGL: 6,500 feet – 1,500 feet = 5,000 feet.

2. Determine the time to descend by dividing the height of the descent by the rate of descent: 5,000 feet ÷ 500 feet/minute = **10 minutes**.

3. Enter the following given information into your flight computer to calculate a true heading and groundspeed.

- Wind: 060° at 15 knots

- True course: 335°

- True airspeed: 110 knots

True heading = 343°
Groundspeed = 108 knots

4. Determine the compass heading by adding the variation of 3°W and the deviation of +2° from the true heading: 343° + 3° +2° = **348°**.

5. Enter into a flight computer the time of 10 minutes and the groundspeed of 108 knots to determine a distance of **18 nautical miles**.

6. Enter into a flight computer the time of 10 minutes and a fuel flow of 8.5 gallons per hour to determine the fuel consumption of **1.4 gallons**.

SECTION B ■ **Predicting Performance**

12-137 CA.I.F.K1, CA.I.F.K2a, d, CA.VI.A.K1, 5
An airplane descends to an airport under the following conditions:

Cruising altitude...7,500 ft MSL

Airport elevation...1,300 ft MSL

Descends to...800 ft AGL

Rate of descent...300 ft/m

Average true airspeed...120 kts

True course...165°

Average wind velocity...240° at 20 kts

Variation...4°E

Deviation...-2°

Average fuel consumption...9.6 gal/hr

Determine the approximate time, compass heading, distance, and fuel consumed.

A – 16 minutes, 168°, 30 NM, 2.9 gallons.

B – 18 minutes, 164°, 34 NM, 3.2 gallons.

C – 18 minutes, 168°, 34 NM, 2.9 gallons.

12-137. Answer C. GFDPP 12B, PHB
To determine the approximate time, compass heading, distance, and fuel consumed during the descent:

1. Determine the total height of the descent from the cruise altitude of 7,500 feet MSL to the the airport elevation of 1,300 feet MSL plus the traffic pattern altitude of 800 feet AGL: 7,500 feet – 2,100 feet = 5,400 feet.

2. Determine the time to descend by dividing the height of the descent by the rate of descent: 5,400 feet ÷ 300 feet/minute = **18 minutes**.

3. Enter the following given information into your flight computer to calculate a true heading and groundspeed.

- Wind: 240° at 20 knots

- True course: 165°

- True airspeed: 120 knots

True heading = 174°
Groundspeed = 113 knots

4. Determine the compass heading by subtracting the variation of 3°W and the deviation of –2° from the true heading: 174° –4° –2° = 168°.

5. Enter into a flight computer the time of 18 minutes and the groundspeed of 113 knots to determine a distance of **34 nautical miles**.

6. Enter into a flight computer the time of 18 minutes and a fuel flow of 9.6 gallons per hour to determine the fuel consumption of **2.9 gallons**.

SECTION B ■ **Predicting Performance**

12-138 CA.I.F.K1, CA.I.F.K2a, d, CA.VI.A.K1, 5

An airplane descends to an airport under the following conditions:

Cruising altitude...10,500 ft MSL

Airport elevation...1,700 ft MSL

Descends to...1,000 ft AGL

Rate of descent...600 ft/m

Average true airspeed...135 kts

True course...263°

Average wind velocity...330° at 30 kts

Variation...7° E

Deviation...+3°

Average fuel consumption...11.5 gal/hr

Determine the approximate time, compass heading, distance, and fuel consumed.

A – 9 minutes, 274°, 26 NM, 2.8 gallons.

B – 13 minutes, 274°, 28 MN, 2.5 gallons.

C – 13 minutes, 271°, 26 NM, 2.5 gallons.

12-138. Answer C. GFDPP 12B, PHB

To determine the approximate time, compass heading, distance, and fuel consumed during the descent:

1. Determine the total height of the descent from the cruise altitude of 10,500 feet MSL to the the airport elevation of 1,700 feet MSL plus the traffic pattern altitude of 1,000 feet AGL: 10,500 feet – 2,700 feet = 7,800 feet.

2. Determine the time to descend by dividing the height of the descent by the rate of descent: 7,800 feet ÷ 600 feet/minute = 13 minutes.

3. Enter the following given information into your flight computer to calculate a true heading and groundspeed.

• Wind: 330° at 30 knots

• True course: 263°

• True airspeed: 135 knots

True heading = 275°
Groundspeed = 120 knots

4. Determine the compass heading by subracting the variation of 7°E from and adding the deviation of +3° to the true heading: 275° – 7° +3° = 271°.

5. Enter into a flight computer the time of 13 minutes and the groundspeed of 120 knots to determine a distance of 26 nautical miles.

6. Enter into a flight computer the time of 13 minutes and a fuel flow of 11.5 gallons per hour to determine the fuel consumption of 2.5 gallons.

12-139 CA.VI.A.K7

While flying enroute, you arrive at a checkpoint 15 minutes later than the time you calculated in your flight plan. What actions should you take next?

A – Recalculate your ETA and plan to use your fuel reserve as required.

B – Determine the reason for the deviation, add a fuel stop if needed, and notify Flight Service of your revised ETA.

C – Reduce power to increase fuel economy and notify Flight Service of your revised ETA.

12-139. Answer B. GFDPP 9A, PHB

After recognizing a change—the deviation from your ETA at the checkpoint—the next steps in the decision making process are to define the problem (determine the reason for the deviation) and choose a course of action based on your detemination.

For example if the actual winds aloft are substantially different than forecast, you must recalculate the estimated time enroute (ETE) and the fuel needed to reach your destination. Add a fuel stop if necessary and notify Flight Service of your revised ETA at the destination.

SECTION B ■ Predicting Performance

12-140 CA.VI.D.K1, 2, CA.III.A.K7, CA.IX.B.K6

Which is an action you should take in the event you become lost during a VFR cross-country flight?

A – Descend to a lower altitude so you can more easily identify landmarks.

B – Communicate with an ATC facility and receive radar vectors if available.

C – Immediately squawk 7700 on your transponder so ATC can locate you quickly.

12-140. Answer B. GFDPP 9A, PHB

If your aircraft is equipped with GPS or you have a portable GPS on board, use GPS to used to determine your position and the location of the nearest airport. In addition, the five Cs are guidelines to help you take positive action to establish your location: climb, communicate, confess, comply, and conserve.

Climb to a higher altitude to increase your chances of spotting an identifiable landmark and improve radio reception. Communicate with any available ATC facility, confess your situation, and comply with any of the controllers instructions, including radar vectors. Conserve fuel by reducing power and airspeed to the values for maximum endurance or range, whichever is most appropriate to your situation.

12-141 CA.I.D.K5

How should you close a VFR flight plan at the completion of the flight at a controlled airport?

A – The tower automatically closes the flight plan when the airplane turns off the runway.

B – You must close the flight plan by contacting Flight Service.

C – The tower relays the instructions to Flight Service when you contact the tower for landing.

12-141. Answer B. GFDPP 12B, PHB

After you arrive at your destination, close your flight plan by contacting Flight Service by phone or use the EasyCloseTM service. You can register to receive an EasyCloseTM text or email at 1800wxbrief.com.

SECTION C
CONTROLLING WEIGHT AND BALANCE

MAXIMUM WEIGHT LIMITS

- For light general aviation airplanes, the maximum weight limit is specified as maximum weight, maximum certificated weight, or maximum gross weight.

- Maximum ramp weight is what the airplane can weigh while on the ramp or during taxi. This weight is higher than maximum takeoff weight to allow for fuel used during engine start and taxi.

CENTER OF GRAVITY LIMITS

- The manufacturer establishes the CG range by designating the forward and aft CG limits, expressed as distances from the reference datum. The reference datum is an imaginary vertical plane from which longitudinal measurements are made.

- With the CG located near or in front of the forward CG limit, the tail-down force required to balance the airplane increases. This requires extra lift from the wings and a higher angle of attack. For this reason, forward loading increases stall speed and reduces cruise performance.

- If the CG is located near or aft of the center of pressure, the airplane is likely to be unstable in pitch (about the lateral axis). When the CG of an airplane is located at the aft limit:

    - the amount of tail-down force required decreases.

    - the horizontal control surface becomes more effective and you might have a tendency to over-control the airplane.

    - the airplane tends to pitch up more easily due to the aft CG position, which could cause an inadvertent stall.

- Loading beyond the aft of limits is dangerous. The airplane can become difficult to control and may not be able to recover from a stall or spin.

WEIGHT AND BALANCE DOCUMENTS

- Basic empty weight includes the standard airplane, optional equipment, unusable fuel, and full operating fluids including full engine oil.

- The useful load of the airplane includes usable fuel, pilot and crew, passengers, baggage or cargo, and engine oil if it is not already included in the empty weight. .

- When the installation or removal of equipment alters an airplane, the technician or agency conducting the alteration must revise the weight and balance report to reflect changes to the basic empty weight.

WEIGHT AND BALANCE COMPUTATIONS

- A moment is a twisting force calculated by multiplying a weight or other force by its distance from a specific reference.

- To simplify computations, most manufacturers use moment indexes—the actual moment value is divided by a standard reduction factor, such as 100, 1,000 or 10,000.

- To designate the position of an item as being ahead of or behind the reference datum, the arms are assigned positive or negative values. Items located ahead of the reference datum have negative values, and items located aft have positive values.

- To eliminate negative numbers in the arithmetic, some manufacturers locate the reference datum on the nose or at some point ahead of the airplane so that all arm values are positive.

- To compute the loaded center of gravity (CG) of an aircraft, add up the moments and weights of each item and divide the total moment by the total weight. To determine the moment of an individual item, use a loading graph, or multiply its weight by its arm.

WEIGHT AND BALANCE CONDITION CHECKS

Manufacturers provide various methods for determining weight and balance conditions, including the computation, table, and graph methods.

- To perform weight and balance condition checks, you can use a loading graph to locate the moment of all useful load items. After you compute the total weight and total moment, determine if the moment and weight are within allowable limits by using a center of gravity envelope graph.

- To determine the effects of fuel consumption on weight and balance, calculate the weight of fuel consumed for the specified period of time. Once the weight has been determined, deduct it from the original fuel weight and recompute the weight and balance for the airplane.

- The weight shift formula calculates the amount of weight that must be moved a specific distance or determines the distance a specific weight must be moved to bring the CG within limits:

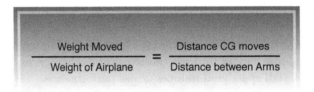

$$\frac{\text{Weight Moved}}{\text{Weight of Airplane}} = \frac{\text{Distance CG moves}}{\text{Distance between Arms}}$$

NOTE: *An asterisk appearing after an ACS code (i.e. CA.IV.A.K2*) indicates that the question subject appears more than one time in the ACS. The code shown corresponds to the first instance of the subject in the ACS.*

12-142　CA.I.F.K2e, f

If an airplane is loaded to the rear of its CG range, it will tend to be unstable about its

A– vertical axis.

B– lateral axis.

C– longitudinal axis.

12-142. Answer B. GFDIC 12C, PHB

If the CG is located near or aft of the center of pressure, the airplane is likely to be unstable in pitch (about the lateral axis). When the CG of an airplane is located at the aft limit:

- the amount of tail-down force required decreases.

- the horizontal control surface becomes more effective and you might have a tendency to over-control the airplane.

- the airplane tends to pitch up more easily due to the aft CG position, which could cause an

- inadvertent stall.

12-143 CA.I.F.K1, CA.I.F.K2e, f

If all moment index units are positive when computing weight and balance, the location of the datum would be at the

A – centerline of the main wheels.

B – nose, or out in front of the airplane.

C – centerline of the nose or tailwheel, depending on the type of airplane.

12-143. Answer B. GFDIC 12C, PHB

To simplify computations, most manufacturers use moment indexes—the actual moment value is divided by a standard reduction factor, such as 100, 1,000 or 10,000.

To designate the position of an item as being ahead of or behind the reference datum, the arms are assigned positive or negative values. Items located ahead of the reference datum have negative values, and items located aft have positive values. To eliminate negative numbers in the arithmetic, some manufacturers locate the reference datum on the nose or at some point ahead of the airplane so that all arm values are positive.

12-144 CA.I.F.K1, CA.I.F.K2f

When computing weight and balance, the basic empty weight includes the weight of the airframe, engine(s), and all installed optional equipment. Basic empty weight also includes

A – all usable fuel and oil, but does not include any radio equipment or instruments that were installed by someone other than the manufacturer.

B – all usable fuel, full oil, hydraulic fluid, but does not include the weight of pilot, passengers, or baggage.

C – the unusable fuel, full operating fluids, and full oil.

12-144. Answer C. GFDPP 12C, PHB

Basic empty weight includes the standard airplane, optional equipment, unusable fuel, and full operating fluids including full engine oil. The useful load of the airplane includes usable fuel, pilot and crew, passengers, baggage or cargo, and engine oil if it is not already included in the empty weight. .

The basic empty weight does not differentiate between manufacturer-installed equipment and equipment installed later. When the installation or removal of equipment alters an airplane, the technician or agency conducting the alteration must revise the weight and balance report to reflect changes to the basic empty weight.

12-145 CA.I.F.K1, CA.I.F.K2e, f

The CG of an aircraft can be determined by which of the following methods?

A – Dividing total arms by total moments.

B – Multiplying total arms by total weight.

C – Dividing total moments by total weight.

12-145. Answer C. GFDIC 12C, PHB

After you determine the moment of each item, you can locate the CG by adding up the weight of the items, totaling the moments, and dividing total moment by total weight. The result is the CG position in inches from the datum.

SECTION C ■ Controlling Weight and Balance

12-146 CA.I.F.K1, CA.I.F.K2e, f

GIVEN:

Weight A — 155 lb at 45 inches aft of datum

Weight B — 165 lb at 145 inches aft of datum

Weight C — 95 lb at 185 inches aft of datum

Based on this information, the CG would be located how far aft of datum?

A – 86.0 inches.

B – 116.8 inches.

C – 125.0 inches.

12-146. Answer B. GFDIC 12C, PHB

1. Fill in the table by multiplying each weight by the arm to find the moment.

2. Add the weights for a total of 415 lb.

3. Add the moments for a total of 48,475 lb-in.

4. Divide the total moment by the total weight to determine the CG: 48,475 ÷ 415 = 116.8 inches.

	WEIGHT (lb)	ARM (in)	MOMENT (lb-in)
Weight A	155	45	6,975
Weight B	165	145	23,925
Weight C	95	185	17,575
Totals	**415**		**48,475**

12-147 CA.I.F.K1, CA.I.F.K2e, f

GIVEN:

Total weight...4,137 lb

CG location station...67.8

Fuel consumption...13.7 GPH

Fuel CG station...68.0

After 1 hour 30 minutes of flight time, the CG would be located at station

A – 67.79.

B – 68.79.

C – 70.78.

12-147. Answer A. GFDIC 12C, PHB

1. Determine the amount fuel burned in 1.5 hours (1 hour and 30 minutes): 1.5 × 13.7 = 20.55 gallons.

2. Determine the weight of the fuel burned at 6 pounds per gallon: 20.55 × 6 = 123.3 pounds.

3. Multiply the weight of the fuel burned by the arm to determine the moment: 123.3 × 68 = 8,394.

4. Subtract the weight and moment of the fuel burned from the aircraft's total weight and moment. See table below.

5. Divide the total moment by the total weight to determine the CG: 272,104 ÷ 4,013.7 = 67.79 inches.

6. In 1:30:00, you will burn 20.55 gallons of fuel (1:30:00 × 13.7 = 20.55), or 123.3 lb (20.55 × 6 = 123.3)

	WEIGHT (lb)	ARM (in)	MOMENT (lb-in/100)
Total	4,137.0	67.8	2,804.88
Fuel 20.55 gal	– 123.3	68.0	– 83.84
	4,013.7		**2,721.04**

12-148   CA.I.F.K1, CA.I.F.K2e, f

GIVEN:

Total weight...3,037 lb

CG location...Station 68.8

Fuel consumption...12.7 gal/hr

Fuel CG...Station 68.0

After 1 hour 45 minutes of flight time, the CG would be located at station

A – 68.77.

B – 68.83.

C – 69.77.

12-148. Answer B. GFDIC 12C, PHB

1. Determine the amount fuel burned in 1.75 hours (1 hour and 45 minutes): 1.75 × 12.7 = 22.23 gallons.

2. Determine the weight of the fuel burned at 6 pounds per gallon: 22.23 × 6 = 133.38 pounds.

3. Multiply the weight of the fuel burned by the arm to determine the moment: 133.38 × 68.0 = 9,070.

4. Subtract the weight and moment of the fuel burned from the aircraft's total weight and moment. See table below.

5. Divide the total moment by the total weight to determine the CG: 199,876 ÷ 2,903.62 = 68.83 inches.

	WEIGHT (lb)	ARM (in)	MOMENT (lb-in/100)
Total	3,037.0	68.8	2,089.46
Fuel 22.23 gal	– 133.38	68.0	– 90.70
	2,903.62		1,998.76

12-149   CA.I.F.K2f

(Refer to Figure 38.) Given the following information, does the weight of the aircraft and center of gravity fall within allowable limits?

GIVEN:

Empty weight (oil is included) in-lb...1,275 lb

Empty weight moment (in-lb/1,000)...102.05

Pilot and copilot...390 lb

Rear seat passenger...145 lb

Cargo...95 lb

Fuel...35 gal

A – Yes, the weight and center of gravity is within allowable limits.

B – No, the weight exceeds the maximum allowable.

C – No, the weight is acceptable, but the center of gravity is aft of the allowable limits.

12-149. Answer A. GFDIC 12C, PHB

1. Convert fuel quantity to pounds at 6 pounds per gallon: 35 × 6 = 210 pounds.

2. Add the weights for a total of 2,111 pounds. Ensure the maximum weight is not exceeded by referring to the Center of Gravity Envelope.

3. Use the loading graph to find the moment for each weight. See table below.

4. Add the moments for a total of 188.05.

5. Locate the intersection of the total weight and total moment. The intersection falls within the upper right portion of the normal category within the envelope.

	WEIGHT (lb)	MOMENT (lb-in/100)
Empty Weight	1,275	102.05
Pilot/Co-Pilot	390	35.00
Rear Seat	145	18.50
Cargo	95	13.50
Fuel	210	19.00
Totals	**2,115**	**188.05**

SECTION C ■ Controlling Weight and Balance

12-150 CA.I.F.K1, CA.I.F.K2e, f

An aircraft is loaded with a ramp weight of 3,650 pounds and having a CG of 94.0. Approximately how much baggage would have to be moved from the rear baggage area at station 180 to the forward baggage area at station 40 in order to move the CG to 92.0?

A – 52.14 pounds.

B – 62.24 pounds.

C – 78.14 pounds.

12-150. Answer A. GFDIC 12C, PHB

To determine how much baggage must be moved use the weight shift formula:

$$\frac{\text{Weight Moved}}{\text{Airplane Weight}} = \frac{\text{Distance CG Moves}}{\text{Distance Between Arms}}$$

1. The weight of the baggage is represented by "X."

2. Determine the distance between arms: 180 – 40 = 140

3. Determine the distance you want to move CG: 94.0 – 92.0 = 2.0 inches.

4. Complete the weight shift formula:

$$\frac{X}{3,650} = \frac{2.0}{140}$$

3,650 ÷ X = 140 ÷ 2.0
X = 3,650 × 2.0 ÷ 140

5. You must move 52.14 pounds of baggage.

CHAPTER 13

Commercial Flight Considerations

SECTION A
EMERGENCY OPERATIONS

PILOT-IN-COMMAND RESPONSIBILITY

- FAR 91.3 describes the responsibility and authority of the pilot in command (PIC). As PIC, you:
    - Are directly responsible for, and are the final authority as to, the operation of that aircraft.
    - May deviate from any regulation to the extent required to meet an in-flight emergency requiring immediate action.
    - Must send a written report of a regulation deviation to meet an in-flight emergency to the Administrator (FAA) upon request.
- Always follow the specific procedures in your Aircraft Flight Manual (AFM)/Pilot's Operating Handbook (POH) for performing emergency procedures.
- Use a do-list to address a minor malfunction that does not require immediate action.
- Emergency checklists typically include tasks that you must perform from memory before referring to the checklist.
- In an emergency, divert promptly toward your alternate destination. Apply rule-of-thumb computations, estimates, and other appropriate shortcuts to divert to the new course as soon as possible. Use resources effectively, such as ATC vectors or the nearest airport feature of your GPS equipment.

PARTIAL POWER LOSS

- Depending on the airplane, causes for a partial power loss can include: carburetor or induction icing, partial failure of the engine driven fuel pump, fouled spark plugs, vapor in the fuel lines, and partial blockage of the intake air.
- To manage a partial power loss, decide how to proceed based on the cause of the power loss, the power available, airplane performance, and the flight environment.
- If the airplane can maintain altitude or climb, you might be able to continue the flight to a nearby airport in a reduced power condition. In this situation, maintain an airspeed that provides the best airplane performance available—approximately the best glide speed in many airplanes.
- If your airplane's performance with partial power is not sufficient to maintain altitude, or the cause of the power loss is severe enough that an engine failure is imminent, consider performing an off-airport precautionary landing.

SYSTEMS AND EQUIPMENT MALFUNCTIONS

ELECTRICAL SYSTEM MALFUNCTION
Consider these actions to manage an alternator failure:

- Shed electrical load to preserve battery power for essential equipment.
- Notify ATC of the situation and use ATC services.
- Be prepared to control the airplane and land without digital instruments, radio communication, lights, or flaps, and to perform a manual landing gear extension, if applicable.

GYROSCOPIC INSTRUMENT MALFUNCTION

- In an airplane with analog instruments, a vacuum/pressure system malfunction affects the attitude indicator and heading indicator.

- In IFR conditions, a failure of gyroscopic instruments is an emergency and you are trained to control the airplane by referring to a partial panel, which includes the pitot-static instruments (airspeed indicator, altimeter, and vertical speed indicator), the magnetic compass for heading information, and the turn coordinator for an indirect indication of bank.

- For an electronic flight display, an attitude and heading reference system (AHRS) failure causes red Xs to cover the attitude indicator and the HSI on a PFD. Use outside visual references, the backup analog attitude indicator, and the magnetic compass for reference.

PITOT-STATIC SYSTEM MALFUNCTION

- The errors displayed on analog pitot-static instruments vary based on whether the ram air source, drain hole, and/or static source is blocked. For example:
  - If the pitot ram air source and drain hold are blocked, the airspeed indicator displays an increase in altitude with altitude gain and a decrease with altitude loss.
  - If the static source is blocked, the airspeed decreases with altitude gain and increases with altitude loss. If both the static and pitot sources are blocked, the airspeed indication remains constant.

- If the static source is blocked, open the alternate static source. If the pitot tube is blocked, apply pitot heat.

- The air data computer (ADC) uses pitot-static and temperature inputs to determine the appropriate readings for the airspeed indicator, altimeter, and vertical speed indicator. If one or more of these sources stops providing input, or if the computer determines that its own internal operations are not correct, it typically places a red X over the display of the affected instrument.

ELECTRONIC FLIGHT DECK DISPLAY MALFUNCTION

- The PFD instruments should automatically display on the MFD in reversionary mode or you can manually switch to reversionary mode if necessary.

- Redundant power sources can continue to power the electronic flight display if your airplane experiences an electrical failure.

FLAP AND LANDING GEAR MALFUNCTIONS

- Consider these factors as you prepare to perform a no-flap approach and landing:
  - The glide path is not as steep as with flaps extended, so the higher nose attitude on final can cause errors in your judgment of height and distance.
  - Landing distance is substantially increased.
  - Floating during the flare is likely.

- If your airplane's landing gear fails to extend, follow the steps in the AFM/POH to manually extend the gear. If you cannot extend the gear, select an airport with crash and rescue facilities and request that emergency equipment be standing by.

- Use specific landing techniques if only one landing gear leg fails to extend or land with all the gear legs retracted.

LOSS OF ELEVATOR CONTROL AND INOPERATIVE TRIM

- If the linkage between the cabin and the elevator fails in flight—leaving the elevator free to weathervane in the wind—you typically can use trim to raise or lower the elevator within limits.

- An aural and/or visual warning normally signals you to an electric trim malfunction associated with either manual or autopilot trim. If you experience a trim malfunction, immediately grasp the control wheel to control the airplane. If you cannot correct the problem and are experiencing runaway trim, pull the applicable circuit breakers as recommended by the AFM/POH and land as soon as practical.

SECTION A ■ **Emergency Operations**

SMOKE AND FIRE

Managing smoke and fire in the cabin typically involves these actions:

1. Turn off the master switch to remove the possible source of the fire.

2. If flames exist, use the fire extinguisher to put out the fire.

3. After extinguishing the fire, open the air vents to clear the cabin of smoke and fumes.

4. Land as soon as possible.

DOOR OPENING IN FLIGHT

- Accidents have occurred on takeoff because pilots have stopped flying the airplane to concentrate on closing cabin or baggage doors.

- To manage an inadvertent door opening during flight:

  ○ Stay calm and maintain control of the airplane.

  ○ Do not release your shoulder harness in an attempt to reach the door.

  ○ Close the door safely on the ground after landing as soon as practical by performing a normal traffic pattern and landing.

DECOMPRESSION

- To decrease the risks of decompression hazards:

  ○ Be alert for visual and aural warnings.

  ○ Wear an oxygen mask when flying at 35,000 feet or higher.

  ○ Select the 100 percent oxygen setting if the airplane is equipped with a demand or pressure demand oxygen system.

  ○ Ensure individuals near openings wear safety harnesses or seatbelts at all times.

- To manage decompression:

  1. Immediately don an oxygen mask and ensure that the oxygen system is working.

  2. Start an emergency descent and declare an emergency.

  3. When you reach an altitude where oxygen is no longer required, proceed to the closest usable airport and seek medical attention.

  4. As a precaution in case of decompression sickness (DCS), seek medical attention for yourself and your passengers.

EMERGENCY DESCENT

- An emergency descent is a maneuver for descending to a lower altitude as rapidly as possible within the structural limitations of the airplane. You might need to perform an emergency descent due to an uncontrollable fire, smoke in the cockpit, a sudden loss of cabin pressurization, or any other situation that demands an immediate rapid descent.

- Steps to perform an emergency descent typically include:

  1. Configure the airplane to descend.

  2. Establish a descending turn at 30° to 45°.

  3. Maintain the bank angle and maximum allowable airspeed (VNE, VA, VFE or VLE).

  4. Return to straight-and-level flight.

- During an emergency descent, you typically maintain the maximum allowable airspeed for the situation:

  ○ V_{NE} for a clean aircraft, with no structural damage, in smooth air.

  ○ V_A for a clean aircraft, with no structural damage, in turbulent air.

  ○ V_{FE} or V_{LE}, whichever is more restrictive and applicable to the aircraft configuration recommended by the AFM/POH.

EMERGENCY APPROACH AND LANDING

- Steps to perform an emergency approach and landing typically include:

    1. Establish a glide—pitch for best glide speed. Attaining best glide speed is an immediate action item.

    2. Select a landing site within gliding distance.

    3. Turn toward the emergency landing site—prepare to dissipate any excess altitude near the field.

    4. Try to restart the engine.

    5. Set up the approach to the emergency landing site. If time permits, declare an emergency on 121.5 or the ATC frequency in use. Set your transponder to 7700.

    6. Configure the airplane for an emergency landing—perform the steps outlined in the AFM/POH checklist to configure the airplane and shut down systems to reduce the risk of a post-crash fire.

    7. Perform the landing.

- When selecting a field, you must consider the wind direction and speed, length of the field, obstructions, and surface condition.

- At night, if you are familiar with the area, consider planning the emergency approach and landing to an:

    ○ Unlighted area—lighted areas typically indicate structures that might obstruct the landing.

    ○ Area close to public access to facilitate rescue or help, if needed.

- Turning upwind reduces your groundspeed and glide distance. Conversely, turning downwind increases your groundspeed and glide distance. Because estimating glide distance is difficult, do not circle away from the landing site and then try to make a long straight-in glide to the field.

ENGINE FAILURE AFTER TAKEOFF

- Steps to manage an engine failure after takeoff typically include:

    1. Reduce the pitch attitude—lower the nose and pitch for best glide speed.

    2. If time permits, follow the steps on the emergency checklist.

    3. Land straight ahead—extend the flaps as necessary and make only small heading changes to avoid obstacles.

- An attempt to turn back to the runway greatly increases your risk of an accident. Specific risks include:

    ○ Performing a steep turn, which increases the descent rate and stall speed.

    ○ A cross-control stall situation.

    ○ Insufficient altitude to complete a turn considering the radius and rate of descent.

EMERGENCY EQUIPMENT AND SURVIVAL GEAR

- Designed to activate automatically if armed and subjected to crash-generated forces, emergency locator transmitters (ELTs) emit a distinctive audio tone on designated emergency frequencies. If necessary after a crash landing, you can manually activate the ELT—most aircraft have a remote ELT switch in the cockpit or are designed to provide pilot access to the ELT. The transmitters should operate continuously for at least 48 hours.

- Emergency locator transmitters (ELTs) should be tested in a screened room to prevent broadcast of signals, but when this cannot be done, you may test the ELT in your airplane only during the first five minutes after the hour, and for no longer than three audible sweeps. Airborne tests of ELTs are not allowed.

SECTION A ■ Emergency Operations

- You should be familiar with the emergency equipment and survival gear in each airplane you fly. Depending on the airplane, emergency equipment can include items such as a fire extinguisher, egress hammer, or a parachute system.

- According to FAR 91.205, your airplane is required to have an ELT, as well as flotation gear and a signaling device if operated for hire over water and beyond power-off gliding distance from shore.

- Although not required by regulation, to enhance safety, you should:

  ○ Pack your own gear or buy a commercial survival kit to keep in the airplane.

  ○ Ensure the survival gear is appropriate for the terrain and weather along your route.

  ○ Properly maintain and stow the equipment/gear.

  ○ Brief your passengers on the location and use of all emergency equipment and survival gear.

- The only survival gear required by the FARs are flotation gear and a signaling device if the aircraft is operated for hire over water and beyond power-off gliding distance from shore. However, any complete survival kit should contain a basic core of survival supplies around which you can assemble the additional items that are appropriate to the terrain and weather you would encounter in an emergency, such as:

  ○ Cold environments, including mountainous terrain—protective, warm clothing; a collapsible lightweight shelter.

  ○ Overwater operations—a personal flotation device for you and each passenger.

  ○ Hot desert conditions—sun block; clothing and a shelter for protection from the sand and sun.

NTSB PART 830

- Read NTSB 830.2 thoroughly for specific details. However, in general, 830.2 definitions include:

  ○ Aircraft accident—an occurrence associated with an aircraft operated for flight in which any person suffers death or serious injury, or in which the aircraft receives substantial damage.

  ○ Substantial damage—damage or failure that adversely affects the structural strength, performance, or flight characteristics of the aircraft, and which would normally require major repair or replacement of the affected component. The definition specifically states that, among other things, engine failure and damage limited to one engine or damage to landing gear are not considered substantial damage.

  ○ Serious injury—requires hospitalization for more than 48 hours within 7 days from the date of injury; a fracture of any bone (except simple fractures of fingers, toes, or nose); severe hemorrhages, nerve, muscle, or tendon damage; involves any internal organ; second- or third-degree burns, or any burns affecting more than 5 percent of the body surface.

- NTSB 830.5 states that as the aircraft operator, you must immediately notify the NTSB if an aircraft accident or serious incident occurs. You should read 830.5 thoroughly for specific details. However, in general, the regulation defines serious incidents as:

  ○ Flight control system malfunction or failure;

  ○ Inability of any required flight crewmember to perform normal flight duties as a result of injury or illness;

  ○ Failure of any internal turbine engine component that results in the escape of debris other than out the exhaust path;

  ○ In-flight fire;

  ○ Aircraft collision in flight;

  ○ Damage to property, other than the aircraft, estimated to exceed $25,000 for repair;

  ○ Release of all or a portion of a propeller blade from an aircraft;

  ○ A complete loss of information from more than 50 percent of an aircraft's electronic cockpit displays;

- Airborne collision and avoidance system (ACAS) resolution advisories issued either when an aircraft is being operated under IFR and compliance with the advisory is necessary to avert a substantial risk of collision between two or more aircraft;

- Additional incidents, which are specified for large multi-engine aircraft (more than 12,500 pounds maximum certificated takeoff weight).

- The operator of an aircraft that has been involved in an accident is required to file a report with the NTSB within 10 days or after 7 days if an overdue aircraft is still missing.

- The operator of an aircraft that is involved in an incident that requires immediate notification is required to file a report only as requested by an authorized NTSB representative.

- Aircraft wreckage may be moved prior to the time the NTSB takes custody only to protect the wreckage from further damage.

NOTE: An asterisk appearing after an ACS code (i.e. CA.IV.A.K2*) indicates that the question subject appears more than one time in the ACS. The code shown corresponds to the first instance of the subject in the ACS.

13-1   CA.IX.A.K2*

What action must be taken when a pilot in command deviates from any rule in 14 CFR Part 91?

A – Upon landing, report the deviation to the nearest FAA Flight Standards District Office.

B – Advise ATC of the pilot in command's intentions.

C – Upon the request of the Administrator, send a written report of that deviation to the Administrator.

13-1. Answer C. GFDIC 13A, FAR 91.3

FAR 91.3 describes the responsibility and authority of the pilot in command (PIC). As PIC, you:

- Are directly responsible for, and are the final authority as to, the operation of that aircraft.

- May deviate from any regulation to the extent required to meet an in-flight emergency requiring immediate action.

- Must send a written report of a regulation deviation to meet an in-flight emergency to the Administrator (FAA) upon request.

13-2   CA.VI.C.K1, 2, CA.IX.A.K2*

When diverting to an alternate airport because of an emergency, you should

A – rely upon radio as the primary method of navigation.

B – climb to a higher altitude because it will be easier to identify checkpoints.

C – apply rule-of-thumb computations, estimates, and other appropriate shortcuts to divert to the new course as soon as possible.

13-2. Answer C. GFDIC 13A, PHB

In an emergency, divert promptly toward your alternate destination. Apply rule-of-thumb computations, estimates, and other appropriate shortcuts to divert to the new course as soon as possible. Use resources effectively, such as ATC vectors or the nearest airport feature of your GPS equipment.

SECTION A ■ Emergency Operations

SECTION A ■ Emergency Operations

13-3   CA.I.G.K2, CA.VI.C.K1, 2, CA.IX.C.K1,

Your airplane suffers a partial power loss and you are unable to restore full power so you decide to divert to a nearby airport with maintenance services. What are the appropriate techniques to handle the diversion?

A – Perform precise measurements and calculations before turning toward your new destination to ensure that you do not miss it.

B – Prioritize tasks and avoid using the autopilot, so that you can maintain situational awareness enroute to the alternate airport.

C – Immediately turn the airplane in the general direction of the new landing point and then use rule-of-thumb computations, or the Nearest and Direct-To functions of your GPS, to navigate there.

13-3. Answer C. GFDIC 13A, PHB

In an emergency, divert promptly toward your alternate destination. Apply rule-of-thumb computations, estimates, and other appropriate shortcuts to divert to the new course as soon as possible. Use resources effectively, such as ATC vectors or the nearest airport feature of your GPS equipment.

13-4   CA.I.G.K2, CA.IX.C.K1

Which is true about experiencing a partial power loss?

A – You should immediately perform a precautionary landing.

B – Maintain cruise airspeed for best performance.

C – If the airplane can maintain altitude or climb, you might be able to continue to a nearby airport.

13-4. Answer C. GFDIC 13A, AFH

If the airplane can maintain altitude or climb, you might be able to continue the flight to a nearby airport in a reduced power condition. In this situation, maintain an airspeed that provides the best airplane performance available—approximately the best glide speed in many airplanes.

If your airplane's performance with partial power is not sufficient to maintain altitude or the cause of the power loss is severe enough that an engine failure is imminent, consider performing an off-airport precautionary landing.

13-5   CA.I.G.K2, CA.IX.C.K1

Which is not a likely cause of partial power loss?

A – Loss of oil pressure.

B – Carburetor or induction icing.

C – Alternator failure.

13-5. Answer C. GFDIC 13A, AFH

Depending on the airplane, causes for a partial power loss can include: carburetor or induction icing, partial failure of the engine driven fuel pump, fouled spark plugs, vapor in the fuel lines, and partial blockage of the intake air.

13-6   CA.I.G.K1f, K2, CA.IX.C.K2a

Which is an action to manage an alternator failure?

A – Shed electrical load to preserve battery power for essential equipment.

B – Prepare to perform an emergency approach and landing.

C – Turn off the master switch to avoid a fire and prepare to land without radio communication, lights, or flaps.

13-6. Answer A. GFDIC 13A, AFH

Consider these actions to manage an alternator failure:

- Shed electrical load to preserve battery power for essential equipment.

- Notify ATC of the situation and use ATC services.

- Be prepared to control the airplane and land without digital instruments, radio communication, lights, or flaps, and to perform a manual landing gear extension, if applicable.

13-7   CA.I.G.K2, CA.IX.C.K2b

You experience a vacuum/pressure system failure in IFR conditions in an airplane with analog instruments. You must fly the airplane with a partial panel that includes

A – the attitude indicator and airspeed indicator.

B – the magnetic compass and turn coordinator.

C – the heading indicator and turn coordinator.

13-7. Answer B. GFDIC 13A, AFH

In an airplane with analog instruments, a vacuum/pressure system malfunction affects the attitude indicator and heading indicator. In IFR conditions, a failure of these instruments is an emergency and you are trained to control the airplane by referring to a partial panel, which includes the pitot-static instruments (airspeed indicator, altimeter, and vertical speed indicator), the magnetic compass for heading information, and the turn coordinator for an indirect indication of bank.

13-8   CA.I.G.K2, CA.IX.C.K2c

The analog airspeed indicator shows an increase in airspeed with altitude gain and a decrease with altitude loss. You should

A – apply pitot heat.

B – open the alternate ram air source.

C – open the alternate static source.

13-8. Answer A. GFDIC 13A, AFH

If the pitot ram air source and drain hold are blocked, the airspeed indicator displays an increase in altitude with altitude gain and a decrease with altitude loss. In this case, apply pitot heat to attempt to unblock the pitot tube.

If the static source is blocked, the airspeed decreases with altitude gain and increases with altitude loss. If both the static and pitot sources are blocked, the airspeed indication remains constant.

13-9   CA.I.G.K2, CA.IX.C.K2d

You are flying an aircraft equipped with an electronic flight display and the air data computer fails. Which of the following instruments/equipment is affected?

A – ADS-B in capability.

B – Airspeed indicator.

C – Attitude indicator.

13-9. Answer B. GFDIC 13A, AFH

In an electronic flight display, the pitot tube, static source, and outside air temperature probe provide information to the air data computer (ADC). The ADC uses these pressure and temperature inputs to determine the appropriate readings for the airspeed indicator, altimeter, and vertical speed indicator. If one or more of these sources stops providing input, or if the computer determines that its own internal operations are not correct, it typically places a red X over the display of the affected instrument.

An attitude and heading reference system (AHRS) failure causes red Xs to cover the attitude indicator and the horizontal situation indicator (HSI).

13-10   CA.I.G.K1b, K2, CA.IX.C.K2e

If the flaps do not extend as you prepare for landing

A – the glide path is steeper and floating during the flare is likely.

B – landing distance is increased.

C – the glide path is not as steep so be alert for errors in your judgment of height and distance.

13-10. Answer A. GFDIC 13A, AFH

Consider these factors as you prepare to perform a no-flap approach and landing:

• The glide path is not as steep as with flaps extended, so the higher nose attitude on final can cause errors in your judgment of height and distance.

• Landing distance is substantially increased.

• Floating during the flare is likely.

SECTION A ■ Emergency Operations

SECTION A ■ Emergency Operations

13-11   CA.I.G.K1a, b, K2, CA.IX.C.K2f,

Immediately grasping the control wheel and pulling the applicable circuit breakers as recommended by the AFM/POH is an action to manage

A – runaway trim.

B – loss of elevator control due to linkage failure.

C – a flap malfunction.

13-11. Answer A. GFDIC 13A, AFH

An aural and/or visual warning normally signals you to an electric trim malfunction associated with either manual or autopilot trim. If you experience a trim malfunction, immediately grasp the control wheel to control the airplane. If you cannot correct the problem and are experiencing runaway trim, pull the applicable circuit breakers as recommended by the AFM/POH and land as soon as practical.

If the linkage between the cabin and the elevator fails in flight—leaving the elevator free to weathervane in the wind—you typically can use trim to raise or lower the elevator within limits.

13-12   CA.I.G.K2, CA.IX.C.K3

Turning off the master switch is an appropriate immediate action to take when

A – smoke or fire exists in the cabin.

B – the engine is running roughly.

C – you want to power only essential equipment after an alternator failure.

13-12. Answer A. GFDIC 13A, AFH

Managing smoke and fire in the cabin typically involves these actions:

1. Turn off the master switch to remove the possible source of the fire.

2. If flames exist, use the fire extinguisher to put out the fire.

3. After extinguishing the fire, open the air vents to clear the cabin of smoke and fumes.

4. Land as soon as possible.

13-13   CA.I.G.K2, CA.IX.C.K5

Which is an appropriate action to take to manage a cabin door opening after departure?

A – Immediately attempt to close the door.

B – Perform a normal traffic pattern and landing and close the door on the ground.

C – Decrease the airspeed to just above a stall speed to make it easier to close the door.

13-13. Answer B. GFDIC 13A, AFH

Accidents have occurred on takeoff because pilots have stopped flying the airplane to concentrate on closing cabin or baggage doors. To manage an inadvertent door opening during flight:

- Stay calm and maintain control of the airplane.

- Do not release your shoulder harness in an attempt to reach the door.

- Close the door safely on the ground after landing as soon as practical by performing a normal traffic pattern and landing.

13-14   CA.I.G.K2, CA.IX.A.K1, CA.IX.C.K4

Which are first two steps for managing decompression in order?

A – 1) Don an oxygen mask; 2) start an emergency descent.

B – 1) Declare an emergency; 2) start an emergency descent.

C – 1) Proceed toward the closest usable airport; 2) don an oxygen mask.

13-14. Answer C. GFDIC 13A, AFH

To manage decompression:

1. Immediately don an oxygen mask and ensure that the oxygen system is working.

2. Start an emergency descent and declare an emergency.

3. When you reach an altitude where oxygen is no longer required, proceed to the closest usable airport and seek medical attention.

4. As a precaution in case of decompression sickness (DCS), seek medical attention for yourself and your passengers.

13-15   CA.I.G.K2, CA.IX.A.K1

Which situations would require an emergency descent?

A – Loss of cabin pressurization; engine failure after takeoff; smoke on the flight deck.

B – Smoke on the flight deck; alternator failure; engine fire.

C – Loss of cabin pressurization; engine fire; smoke on the flight deck.

13-15. Answer C. GFDIC 13A, AFH

An emergency descent is a maneuver for descending to a lower altitude as rapidly as possible within the structural limitations of the airplane. You might need to perform an emergency descent due to an uncontrollable fire, smoke in the cockpit, a sudden loss of cabin pressurization, or any other situation that demands an immediate rapid descent.

13-16   CA.I.G.K2, CA.IX.A.K2

Steps for performing an emergency descent typically include to establish

A – best glide speed.

B – a standard-rate turn.

C – a descending turn at 30° to 45°.

13-16. Answer C. GFDIC 13A, AFH

Steps to perform an emergency descent typically include:

1. Configure the airplane to descend.

2. Establish a descending turn at 30° to 45°.

3. Maintain the bank angle and maximum allowable airspeed (V_{NE}, V_A, V_{FE} or V_{LE}).

4. Return to straight-and-level flight.

5. Return to cruise flight or prepare for landing.

13-17   CA.I.G.K2, CA.IX.A.K3

What airspeed should you maintain during an emergency descent for a clean aircraft, with no structural damage in turbulent air?

A – V_A.

B – V_{NE}.

C – V_{LE}.

13-17. Answer A. GFDIC 13A, AFH

During an emergency descent, you typically maintain the maximum allowable airspeed for the situation:

• V_{NE} for a clean aircraft, with no structural damage, in smooth air.

• V_A for a clean aircraft, with no structural damage, in turbulent air.

• V_{FE} or V_{LE} , whichever is more restrictive and applicable to the aircraft configuration recommended by the AFM/POH.

SECTION A ■ **Emergency Operations**

13-18   CA.I.G.K2, CA.IX.B.K1, CA.IX.C.K1

What is the first step and an immediate action item when you experience an engine failure and must perform an emergency approach and landing?

A – Turn toward the emergency landing site.

B – Establish best glide speed.

C – Try to restart the engine.

13-18. Answer B. GFDIC 13A, AFH

Steps to perform an emergency approach and landing typically include:

1. Establish a glide—pitch for best glide speed. Attaining best glide speed is an immediate action item.

2. Select a landing site within gliding distance.

3. Turn toward the emergency landing site—prepare to dissipate any excess altitude near the field.

4. Try to restart the engine.

5. Set up the approach to the emergency landing site. If time permits, declare an emergency on 121.5 or the ATC frequency in use. Set your transponder to 7700.

6. Configure the airplane for an emergency landing—perform the steps outlined in the AFM/POH checklist to configure the airplane and shut down systems to reduce the risk of a post-crash fire.

7. Perform the landing.

13-19   CA.I.G.K2, CA.IX.B.K2a, b, c, K3, 4

Which is true about your approach after an engine failure?

A – Flying upwind increases glide distance and flying downwind decreases glide distance.

B – A stabilized approach at best glide speed provides the least drag and maximum gliding distance.

C – Flying at minimum sink speed provides the same gliding distance as flying at best glide speed.

13-19. Answer B. GFDIC 13A, AFH

Attaining best glide speed is an immediate action item after an engine failure. Best glide speed provides the maximum gliding distance. Any speed other than the best glide speed creates more drag so it is critical that you fly a stabilized approach to the landing site and avoid making large pitch changes.

Turning upwind reduces your groundspeed and glide distance. Conversely, turning downwind increases your groundspeed and glide distance.

At minimum sink speed, the airplane loses altitude at the lowest rate. However, flying at this speed results in less distance traveled than when at best glide speed. Minimum sink speed is useful when time in flight is more important than distance flown, such as ditching an airplane at sea. This speed is not often published but generally is a few knots less than best glide speed.

13-20   CA.I.G.K2, CA.IX.B.K2, 4

Which is true about fly a stabilized approach at best glide speed after an engine failure?

A – Flying at best glide speed provides the maximum lift-to-drag ratio and the maximum gliding distance.

B – Flying faster than best glide speed increases induced drag.

C – Flying slower than best glide speed increases parasite drag.

13-20. Answer B. GFDIC 13A, AFH
The angle of attack that results in the least drag on the airplane, provides the maximum lift-to-drag ratio (L/Dmax), the best glide angle, and the maximum gliding distance corresponds to best glide speed.

Any speed other than the best glide speed creates more drag so it is critical that you fly a stabilized approach to the landing site and avoid making large pitch changes. If your airspeed is too high, parasite drag increases; and if you descend with too slow of an airspeed, induced drag increases.

13-21   CA.I.G.K2, CA.IV.A.R3b, CA.IX.B.K1, 2, 4

If you experience an engine failure in a single-engine aircraft after takeoff, you should

A – establish the proper glide attitude.

B – turn into the wind.

C – adjust the pitch to maintain V_Y.

13-21. Answer A. GFDIC 13A, AFH
Steps to manage an engine failure after takeoff typically include:

1. Reduce the pitch attitude—lower the nose and pitch for best glide speed.

2. If time permits, follow the steps on the emergency checklist.

3. Land straight ahead—extend the flaps as necessary and make only small heading changes to avoid obstacles.

13-22   CA.I.G.K2, CA.IV.A.R3b, CA.IX.B.K1, 2

Your most immediate and vital concern in the event of complete engine failure after becoming airborne on takeoff is

A – maintaining a safe airspeed.

B – landing directly into the wind.

C – turning back to the takeoff field.

13-22. Answer A. GFDIC 13A, AFH
Steps to manage an engine failure after takeoff typically include:

1. Reduce the pitch attitude—lower the nose and pitch for best glide speed.

2. If time permits, follow the steps on the emergency checklist.

3. Land straight ahead—extend the flaps as necessary and make only small heading changes to avoid obstacles.

An attempt to turn back to the runway greatly increases your risk of an accident. Specific risks include:

• Performing a steep turn, which increases the descent rate and stall speed.

• A cross-control stall situation.

• Insufficient altitude to complete a turn considering the radius and rate of descent.

SECTION A ■ Emergency Operations

13-23   CA.I.G.K2, CA.IX.B.K1

After experiencing a powerplant failure at night, one of the primary considerations should include

A – turning off all electrical switches to save battery power for landing.

B – planning the emergency approach and landing to an unlighted portion of an area.

C – maneuvering to, and landing on, a lighted highway or road.

13-23. Answer B. GFDIC 13A, AFH

When selecting an emergency landing site, you must consider the wind direction and speed, length of the field, obstructions, and surface condition. At night, if you are familiar with the area, consider planning the emergency approach and landing to

- An unlighted area—lighted areas typically indicate structures that might obstruct the landing.

- An area close to public access to facilitate rescue or help, if needed.

13-24   CA.I.G.K2, CA.IX.B.K1

When planning for an emergency landing at night, one of the primary considerations should include

A – selecting a landing area close to public access, if possible.

B – landing without flaps to ensure a nose-high landing attitude at touchdown.

C – turning off all electrical switches to save battery power for the landing.

13-24. Answer A. GFDIC 13A, AFH

When selecting an emergency landing site, you must consider the wind direction and speed, length of the field, obstructions, and surface condition. At night, if you are familiar with the area, consider planning the emergency approach and landing to

- An unlighted area—lighted areas typically indicate structures that might obstruct the landing.

- An area close to public access to facilitate rescue or help, if needed.

13-25   CA.IX.B.K5, CA.IX.D.K1

Which is true regarding the use of an emergency locator transmitter (ELT)?

A – You cannot manually activate the ELT after an emergency landing.

B – ELTs are designed to activate automatically if armed and subjected to crash-generated forces.

C – After activation, ELTs emit a distinctive automated tone on designated emergency frequencies continuously for up to an hour.

13-25. Answer B. GFDIC 13A, AIM

Designed to activate automatically if armed and subjected to crash-generated forces, emergency locator transmitters (ELTs) emit a distinctive audio tone on designated emergency frequencies. If necessary after a crash landing, you can manually activate the ELT—most aircraft have a remote ELT switch in the cockpit or are designed to provide pilot access to the ELT. The transmitters should operate continuously for at least 48 hours.

13-26   CA.IX.B.K5, CA.IX.D.K1

If an ELT cannot be tested in a screened room, you may test the ELT in your airplane

A – during the last five minutes of the hour.

B – for a maximum of 10 audible sweeps.

C – during the first five minutes after the hour.

13-26. Answer C. GFDIC 13A, AIM

Emergency locator transmitters (ELTs) should be tested in a screened room to prevent broadcast of signals, but when this cannot be done, you may test the ELT in your airplane only during the first five minutes after the hour, and for no longer than three audible sweeps. Airborne tests of ELTs are not allowed.

13-27   CA.IX.D.K2, 3

Which is true regarding emergency equipment and survival gear?

A – FAR 91.205 requires that a fire extinguisher, ELT, and a survival kit be on board the airplane.

B – Because items may vary depending on the airplane, you must be familiar with using the specific emergency emergency equipment and survival equipment on board each airplane you fly.

C – You are required by FAR Part 91 to brief your passengers on the location and use of all emergency equipment and survival gear.

13-27. Answer B. GFDIC 13A, PHB

You should be familiar with the emergency equipment and survival gear in each airplane you fly. Depending on the airplane, emergency equipment can include items such as a fire extinguisher, egress hammer, or a parachute system.

According to FAR 91.205, your airplane is required to have an ELT, as well as flotation gear and a signaling device if operated for hire over water and beyond power-off gliding distance from shore.

Although not required by regulation, to enhance safety, you should:

- Pack your own gear or buy a commercial survival kit to keep in the airplane.
- Ensure the survival gear is appropriate for the terrain and weather along your route.
- Properly maintain and stow the equipment/gear.
- Brief your passengers on the location and use of all emergency equipment and survival gear.

13-28   CA.IX.D.K3a, b, c

When packing a survival kit to have on board the airplane, you should include

A – only the items required by regulation.

B – equipment/gear needed for the specific terrain and weather along your route.

C – no more than a few core items to limit the weight in the baggage area.

13-28. Answer B. GFDIC 13A, PHB

The only survival gear required by the FARs are flotation gear and a signaling device if the aircraft is operated for hire over water and beyond power-off gliding distance from shore. However, any complete survival kit should contain a basic core of survival supplies around which you can assemble the additional items that are appropriate to the terrain and weather you would encounter in an emergency, such as:

- Cold environments, including mountainous terrain—protective, warm clothing; a collapsible lightweight shelter.
- Overwater operations—a personal flotation device for you and each passenger.
- Hot desert conditions—sun block; clothing and shelter for protection from the sand and sun.

13-29   CA.III.A.K8

Notification to the NTSB is required when there has been substantial damage

A – which requires repairs to landing gear.

B – to an engine caused by engine failure in flight.

C – which adversely affects structural strength or flight characteristics.

13-29. Answer C. NTSB 830.2

NTSB 830 defines substantial damage as damage or failure that adversely affects the structural strength, performance, or flight characteristics of the aircraft, and which would normally require major repair or replacement of the affected component.

The definition specifically states that, among other things, engine failure and damage limited to one engine or damage to landing gear are not considered substantial damage.

SECTION A ■ **Emergency Operations**

13-30   CA.III.A.K8

What period of time must a person be hospitalized before an injury may be defined by the NTSB as a "serious injury?"

A – 10 days; with no other extenuating circumstances.

B – 48 hours; commencing within 7 days after date of the injury.

C – 72 hours; commencing within 10 days after date of the injury.

13-30. Answer B. NTSB 830.2

NTSB defines a serious injury as an injury that requires hospitalization for more than 48 hours within 7 days from the date the injury; a fracture of any bone (except simple fractures of fingers, toes, or nose); severe hemorrhages, nerve, muscle, or tendon damage; involves any internal organ; second- or third-degree burns, or any burns affecting more than 5 percent of the body surface.

13-31   CA.III.A.K8, CA.XI.A.K1, 2

On a postflight inspection of your aircraft after an aborted takeoff due to an elevator malfunction, you find that the elevator control cable has broken. According to NTSB 830, you

A – must immediately notify the nearest NTSB office.

B – should notify the NTSB within 10 days.

C – must file a NASA report immediately.

13-31. Answer A. GFDIC 13B, NTSB 830.5

NTSB 830.5 states that you must immediately notify the NTSB if an aircraft accident or serious incident occurs. Serious incidents include occurrences such as flight control system malfunction or failure; inability of any required flight crewmember to perform normal flight duties as a result of injury or illness; and in-flight fire.

13-32   CA.III.A.K8

NTSB Part 830 requires an immediate notification as a result of which incident?

A – Engine failure for any reason during flight.

B – Damage to the landing gear as a result of a hard landing.

C – Any required flight crewmember being unable to perform flight duties because of illness.

13-32. Answer C. GFDIC 13B, NTSB 830.5

NTSB 830.5 states that the aircraft operator you must immediately notify the NTSB if an aircraft accident or serious incident occurs. Serious incidents include occurrences such as flight control system malfunction or failure; inability of any required flight crewmember to perform normal flight duties as a result of injury or illness; and in-flight fire.

13-33   CA.III.A.K8

Which incident would require that the nearest NTSB field office be notified immediately?

A – In-flight fire.

B – Ground fire resulting in fire equipment dispatch.

C – Fire of the primary aircraft while in a hanger which results in damage to other property of more than $25,000.

13-33. Answer A. GFDIC 13B, NTSB 830.5

NTSB 830.5 states that the aircraft operator you must immediately notify the NTSB if an aircraft accident or serious incident occurs. Serious incidents include occurrences such as flight control system malfunction or failure; inability of any required flight crewmember to perform normal flight duties as a result of injury or illness; and in-flight fire.

13-34   CA.III.A.K8

Which airborne incident would require that the nearest NTSB field office be notified immediately?

A – Flight control system malfunction or failure.

B – Cabin door opened in-flight.

C – Cargo compartment door malfunction or failure.

13-34. Answer A. GFDIC 13B, NTSB 830.5
NTSB 830.5 states that the aircraft operator you must immediately notify the NTSB if an aircraft accident or serious incident occurs. Serious incidents include occurrences such as flight control system malfunction or failure; inability of any required flight crewmember to perform normal flight duties as a result of injury or illness; and in-flight fire.

13-35   CA.III.A.K8

During flight, a fire, which was extinguished, burned the insulation from a transceiver wire. What action is required by regulations?

A – No notification or report is required.

B – A report must be filed with the avionics inspector at the nearest FAA Flight Standards District Office within 48 hours.

C – An immediate notification by the operator of the aircraft to the nearest NTSB field office.

13-35. Answer C. GFDIC 13B, NTSB 830.5
NTSB 830.5 states that the aircraft operator you must immediately notify the NTSB if an aircraft accident or serious incident occurs. Serious incidents include occurrences such as flight control system malfunction or failure; inability of any required flight crewmember to perform normal flight duties as a result of injury or illness; and in-flight fire.

13-36   CA.III.A.K8

When should notification of an aircraft accident be made to the NTSB if there was substantial damage and no injuries?

A – Immediately.

B – Within 10 days.

C – Within 30 days.

13-36. Answer A. GFDIC 13B, NTSB 830.5, 830.2
NTSB 830.5 states that the aircraft operator you must immediately notify the NTSB if an aircraft accident or serious incident occurs. In general, NTSB 830.2 defines an aircraft accident as an occurrence associated with an aircraft operated for flight in which any person suffers death or serious injury, or in which the aircraft receives substantial damage.

13-37   CA.III.A.K8

The operator of an aircraft that has been involved in an incident is required to submit a report to the nearest field office of the NTSB

A – within 7 days.

B – within 10 days.

C – only if requested to do so.

13-37. Answer C. GFDIC 13B, NTSB 830.15
The operator of an aircraft that is involved in an incident that requires immediate notification is required to file a report only as requested by an authorized NTSB representative.

The operator of an aircraft that has been involved in an accident is required to file a report with the NTSB within 10 days or after 7 days if an overdue aircraft is still missing.

13-38   CA.III.A.K8

How many days after an accident is a report required to be filed with the nearest NTSB field office?

A – 2.

B – 7.

C – 10 .

13-38. Answer C. GFDIC 13B, NTSB 830.15
The operator of an aircraft that has been involved in an accident is required to file a report with the NTSB within 10 days or after 7 days if an overdue aircraft is still missing.

SECTION A ■ **Emergency Operations**

SECTION B
COMMERCIAL PILOT SRM

Section 1D — SRM Concepts of the *Instrument/Commercial* textbook defines single-pilot resource management concepts that you should be aware of as you begin your instrument training. Chapter 13, Section B — Commercial Pilot SRM provides a more extensive examination of SRM as it applies to operating in the commercial flight environment. The FAA questions associated with SRM concepts, such as aeronautical decision making, risk, task and automation management, situational awareness, and controlled flight into terrain awareness are presented in this section of the test guide.

AERONAUTICAL DECISION MAKING

- The FAA defines aeronautical decision making (ADM) as a systematic approach to the mental process used by aircraft pilots to consistently determine the best course of action in response to a given set of circumstances.

- To make an analytical decision, you use the ADM process. The ADM process consists of the steps that you use to make effective decisions as pilot in command.

- Although the basic steps are the same, a variety of mnemonics are used by pilots to remember the steps in the decision-making process. The FAA uses the DECIDE model, which has six steps:

  1. Detect the fact that a change has occurred.

  2. Estimate the need to counter or react to the change.

  3. Choose a desirable outcome for the success of the flight.

  4. Identify actions that could successfully control the change.

  5. Do the necessary action to adapt to the change.

  6. Evaluate the effect of the action.

SELF ASSESSMENT

- The I'M SAFE checklist is an effective way to consider the factors that affect your fitness prior to flight in the commercial environment.

- Be aware of dangerous tendencies, referred to as operational pitfalls, that can develop as you gain experience, including:

  - Peer pressure
  - Mind set
  - Get-there-itis
  - Duck-under syndrome
  - Scud running
  - Continuing visual flight rules (VFR) into instrument conditions
  - Getting behind the aircraft
  - Loss of positional or situation awareness
  - Operating without adequate fuel reserves
  - Descent below the minimum enroute altitude
  - Flying outside the envelope
  - Neglect of flight planning, preflight inspections, checklists, etc.

HAZARDOUS ATTITUDES

Studies have identified five hazardous attitudes that can interfere with your ability to make effective decisions as a pilot. To neutralize a hazardous attitude, you must first recognize a thought as hazardous label the hazardous attitude, and then state the corresponding antidote. The five hazardous attitudes are:

- Anti-authority—don't tell me. You display this attitude if you resent having someone tell you what to do, or you regard rules and procedures as unnecessary.

  Antidote — Follow the rules. They are usually right.

- Impulsivity—do it quickly. If you feel the need to act immediately and do the first thing that comes to mind without considering the best solution to a problem, then you are exhibiting impulsivity.

  Antidote — Not so fast. Think first.

- Invulnerability—it won't happen to me. You are more likely to take chances and increase risk if you think accidents will not happen to you.

  Antidote — It could happen to me.

- Macho—I can do it. If you have this attitude, you might take risks trying to prove that you are better than anyone else.

  Antidote — Taking chances is foolish.

- Resignation—what's the use? You are experiencing resignation if you feel that no matter what you do it will have little effect on what happens to you. You may feel that when things go well, it is just good luck and when things go poorly, it is bad luck or someone else is responsible. This feeling can cause you to leave the action to others—for better or worse.

  Antidote — I'm not helpless. I can make a difference.

TASK MANAGEMENT

- A wide variety of resources both inside and outside the airplane can help you manage tasks and make effective decisions.

- You typically use one of these methods for following checklists:

    - Do-list—use do-lists for abnormal procedures, such as addressing an electrical malfunction. Read the checklist item and the associated action and then perform the action. Use a do-list when you have time and completing each step in the correct order is critical.

    - Flow pattern—use flow patterns to perform normal procedures when the checklist item sequence is not critical, such as configuring the airplane and the avionics for specific phases of flight. After completing the flow pattern, refer to the checklist and verify that you have accomplished each item.

    - Emergency checklists—perform critical tasks from memory and then refer to the checklist to manage specific emergencies, such as an engine failure.

SITUATIONAL AWARENESS

- Briefings are an effective tool to help you maintain situational awareness by preparing you for critical phases of flight.

- Regulations require that you explain to your passengers how to fasten and unfasten the safety belts and shoulder harnesses and when the safety belts must be fastened.

- The FAA also recommends that you cover certain safety considerations with passengers before flight. You can remember the elements of a passenger briefing by using the acronym SAFETY.

    - Safety belts—how to fasten and unfasten the safety belts and shoulder harnesses; when safety belts must be fastened—prior to movement on the surface, takeoff, and landing

    - Air vents—location and operation; operation of heating or air conditioning controls

    - Fire extinguisher—location and operation

- Egress and emergency—operation of doors and windows; location of the survival kit; use of onboard emergency equipment

- Traffic and talking—pointing out traffic; use of headsets; avoiding unnecessary conversation during critical phases of flight

- Your Questions—solicit questions from your passengers.

• Items in a takeoff briefing include:

- Wind direction and velocity;

- Runway length;

- Takeoff distance;

- Initial heading;

- Initial altitude;

- Takeoff and climb speeds;

- Departure procedures;

- Emergency plan in case of an engine failure after takeoff.

- Items in a before-landing briefing include:

- Airport information and weather conditions;

- Active runway;

- Terrain and obstacles;

- Airport elevation and pattern altitude;

- Traffic pattern entry.

NOTE: *An asterisk appearing after an ACS code (i.e. CA.IV.A.K2*) indicates that the question subject appears more than one time in the ACS. The code shown corresponds to the first instance of the subject in the ACS.*

13-39   CA.I.H.K4

Aeronautical decision making (ADM) is a

A – systematic approach to the mental process used by pilots to consistently determine the best course of action for a given set of circumstances.

B – decision making process which relies on good judgment to reduce risks associated with each flight.

C – mental process of analyzing all information in a particular situation and making a timely decision on what action to take.

13-39. Answer A. GFDIC 1D/13B, PHB

The FAA defines aeronautical decision making (ADM) as a systematic approach to the mental process used by aircraft pilots to consistently determine the best course of action in response to a given set of circumstances.

Managing risks and using the steps of the decision making process to analyze information and determine what action are some of the tools used to make effective decisions.

13-40   CA.I.H.K4

Which of the following is the final step of the DECIDE model for effective risk management and aeronautical decision making?

A – Estimate.

B – Evaluate.

C – Eliminate.

13-40. Answer B. GFDIC 1D/13B, PHB
The six steps of the DECIDE model are:

1. **D**etect the fact that a change has occurred.

2. **E**stimate the need to counter or react to the change.

3. **C**hoose a desirable outcome for the success of the flight.

4. **I**dentify actions that could successfully control the change.

5. **D**o the necessary action to adapt to the change.

6. **E**valuate the effect of the action.

13-41   CA.I.H.K4

Which of the following is the first step of the DECIDE model for effective risk management and aeronautical decision making?

A – Detect.

B – Identify.

C – Evaluate.

13-41. Answer A. GFDIC 1D/13B, PHB
The six steps of the DECIDE model are:

1. **D**etect the fact that a change has occurred.

2. **E**stimate the need to counter or react to the change.

3. **C**hoose a desirable outcome for the success of the flight.

4. **I**dentify actions that could successfully control the change.

5. **D**o the necessary action to adapt to the change.

6. **E**valuate the effect of the action.

13-42   CA.I.H.K4

The DECIDE model is comprised of a 6-step process to provide you with a logical way of approaching aeronautical decision making. These steps are:

A – Detect, estimate, choose, identify, do, and evaluate.

B – Determine, evaluate, choose, identify, do, and eliminate.

C – Determine, eliminate, choose, identify, detect, and evaluate.

13-42. Answer A. GFDIC 1D/13B, PHB
The six steps of the DECIDE model are:

1. **D**etect the fact that a change has occurred.

2. **E**stimate the need to counter or react to the change.

3. **C**hoose a desirable outcome for the success of the flight.

4. **I**dentify actions that could successfully control the change.

5. **D**o the necessary action to adapt to the change.

6. **E**valuate the effect of the action.

SECTION B ■ Commercial Pilot SRM

13-43   CA.II.B.K2

Select the true statement regarding the use of checklists.

A – Use do-lists to manage emergencies, such as an engine failure.

B – Use flow patterns for abnormal procedures, such as an equipment malfunction.

C – Use flow patterns to perform normal procedures, such as configuring the airplane and avionics.

13-43. Answer C. GFDIC 1D/13B, PHB

You typically use one of these methods for following checklists:

- Do-list—use do-lists for abnormal procedures, such as addressing an electrical malfunction. Read the checklist item and the associated action and then perform the action. Use a do-list when you have time and completing each step in the correct order is critical.

- Flow pattern—use flow patterns to perform normal procedures when the checklist item sequence is not critical, such as configuring the airplane and the avionics for specific phases of flight. After completing the flow pattern, refer to the checklist and verify that you have accomplished each item.

- Emergency checklists—perform critical tasks from memory and then refer to the checklist to manage specific emergencies, such as an engine failure.

13-44   CA.I.H.K4, CA.I.H.R2

Most pilots have fallen prey to dangerous tendencies or behavior problems at some time. Some of these dangerous tendencies or behavior patterns which must be identified and eliminated include:

A – Deficiencies in instrument skills and knowledge of aircraft systems or limitations.

B – Performance deficiencies from human factors such as, fatigue, illness or emotional problems.

C – Peer pressure, get-there-itis, loss of positional or situation awareness, and operating without adequate fuel reserves.

13-44. Answer C. GFDIC 13B, PHB

Be aware of dangerous tendencies, referred to as operational pitfalls, that can develop as you gain experience, including:

- Peer pressure
- Mind set
- Get-there-itis
- Duck-under syndrome
- Scud running
- Continuing visual flight rules (VFR) into instrument conditions
- Getting behind the aircraft
- Loss of positional or situation awareness
- Operating without adequate fuel reserves
- Descent below the minimum enroute altitude
- Flying outside the envelope
- Neglect of flight planning, preflight inspections, checklists, etc.

13-45   CA.I.H.K4, CA.I.H.R2, CA.II.A.K1

Which are hazardous attitudes that can interfere with your ability to make effective decisions as a pilot?

A – Anti-authority (don't tell me); impulsivity (do something quickly); macho (I can do it).

B – Risk management, stress management, and risk elements.

C – Poor decision making, situational awareness, and judgment.

13-45. Answer A. GFDIC 1D/13B, PHB

Studies have identified five hazardous attitudes that can interfere with your ability to make effective decisions as a pilot. To neutralize a hazardous attitude, you must recognize a thought as hazardous and state the corresponding attitude. The hazardous attitudes and their antidotes are:

- Anti-authority—don't tell me. Antidote: Follow the rules. They are usually right.

- Impulsivity—do something quickly. Antidote: Not so fast. Think first.

- Invulnerability—it won't happen to me. Antidote: It could happen to me.

- Macho—I can do it. Antidote: Taking chances is foolish.

- Resignation—what's the use? Antidote: I'm not helpless. I can make a difference.

13-46   CA.I.H.K4, CA.I.H.R2, CA.II.A.K1

What is the first step in neutralizing a hazardous attitude?

A – Recognition of invulnerability in the situation.

B – Dealing with improper judgment.

C – Recognition of hazardous thoughts.

13-46. Answer C. GFDIC 1D/13B, PHB

Studies have identified five hazardous attitudes that can interfere with your ability to make effective decisions as a pilot: anti-authority, impulsivity, invulnerability, macho, and resignation. To neutralize a hazardous attitude, you must first recognize a thought as hazardous label the hazardous attitude, and then state the corresponding antidote.

13-47   CA.I.H.K4, CA.I.H.R2, CA.II.A.K1

What should you do when recognizing a thought as hazardous?

A – Avoid developing this hazardous thought.

B – Develop this hazardous thought and follow through with modified action.

C – Label that thought as hazardous, then correct that thought by stating the corresponding learned antidote.

13-47. Answer C. GFDIC 1D/13B, PHB

Studies have identified five hazardous attitudes that can interfere with your ability to make effective decisions as a pilot: anti-authority, impulsivity, invulnerability, macho, and resignation. To neutralize a hazardous attitude, you must first recognize a thought as hazardous label the hazardous attitude, and then state the corresponding antidote.

SECTION B ■ **Commercial Pilot SRM**

13-48　CA.I.H.K4, CA.I.H.R2, CA.II.A.K1

When you recognize a hazardous thought, you should correct it by stating the corresponding antidote. Which of the following is the antidote for the macho hazardous attitude?

A – Follow the rules. They are usually right.

B – Not so fast. Think first.

C – Taking chances is foolish.

13-48. Answer C. GFDIC 1D/13B, PHB

Macho—I can do it. If you have this attitude, you might take risks trying to prove that you are better than anyone else.

Antidote — Taking chances is foolish.

13-49　CA.I.H.K4, CA.I.H.R, CA.II.A.K1

When you recognize a hazardous thought, you should correct it by applying the corresponding antidote. Which of the following is the antidote for the anti-authority attitude hazardous attitude?

A – Not so fast. Think first.

B – It won't happen to me. It could happen to me.

C – Follow the rules. They are usually right.

13-49. Answer C. GFDIC 1D/13B, PHB

Anti-authority—don't tell me. You display this attitude if you resent having someone tell you what to do, or you regard rules and procedures as unnecessary.

Antidote — Follow the rules. They are usually right.

13-50　CA.I.H.K4, CA.I.H.R2, CA.II.A.K1

The passengers for a charter flight have arrived almost an hour late for a flight that requires a reservation.

Which of the following reactions best illustrates the anti-authority attitude?

A – Those reservation rules do not apply to this flight.

B – If the pilot hurries, he or she may still make it on time.

C – The pilot can't help it that the passengers are late.

13-50. Answer A. GFDIC 1D/13B, PHB

Anti-authority—don't tell me. You display this attitude if you resent having someone tell you what to do, or you regard rules and procedures as unnecessary.

Antidote — Follow the rules. They are usually right.

13-51　CA.I.H.K4, CA.I.H.R2, CA.II.A.K1

While conducting an operational check of the cabin pressurization system, the pilot discovers that the rate control feature is inoperative. He knows that he can manually control the cabin pressure, so he elects to disregard the discrepancy. Which of the following reactions best illustrates the invulnerability attitude?

A – What is the worst that could happen?

B – He can handle a little problem like this.

C – It's too late to fix it now.

13-51. Answer A. GFDIC 1D/13B, PHB

Invulnerability—it won't happen to me. You are more likely to take chances and increase risk if you think accidents will not happen to you.

Antidote — It could happen to me.

13-52   CA.I.H.K4, CA.I.H.R2, CA.II.A.K1

The pilot and passengers are anxious to get to their destination for a business presentation. Level IV thunderstorms are reported to be in a line across their intended route of flight. Which of the following reactions best illustrates the impulsivity attitude?

A – They want to hurry and get going, before things get worse.

B – A thunderstorm won't stop them.

C – They can't change the weather, so they might as well go.

13-53   CA.I.H.K4, CA.I.H.R2, CA.II.A.K1

While on an IFR flight, a pilot emerges from a cloud to find himself within 300 feet of a helicopter. Which of the following reactions best illustrates the macho attitude?

A – He is not too concerned; everything will be alright.

B – He flies a little closer, just to show him.

C – He quickly turns away and dives, to avoid collision.

13-54   CA.I.H.K4, CA.I.H.R2, CA.II.A.K1

A pilot and friends are going to fly to an out-of-town football game. When the passengers arrive, the pilot determines that they will be over the maximum gross weight for takeoff with the existing fuel load. Which of the following reactions best illustrates the resignation attitude?

A – Well, nobody told him about the extra weight.

B – Weight and balance is a formality forced on pilots by the FAA.

C – He can't wait around to de-fuel, they have to get there on time.

13-52. Answer A. GFDIC 1D/13B, PHB

Impulsivity—do it quickly. If you feel the need to act immediately and do the first thing that comes to mind without considering the best solution to a problem, then you are exhibiting impulsivity.

Antidote — Not so fast. Think first.

13-53. Answer B. GFDIC 1D/13B, PHB

Macho—I can do it. If you have this attitude, you might take risks trying to prove that you are better than anyone else.

Antidote — Taking chances is foolish.

13-54. Answer A. GFDIC 1D/13B, PHB

Resignation—what's the use? You are experiencing resignation if you feel that no matter what you do it will have little effect on what happens to you. You may feel that when things go well, it is just good luck and when things go poorly, it is bad luck or someone else is responsible. This feeling can cause you to leave the action to others—for better or worse.

Antidote — I'm not helpless. I can make a difference.

SECTION B ■ Commercial Pilot SRM

13-55   CA.II.B.K1

Which items should you include in a passenger briefing?

A – Operations of doors and windows.

B – Location and operation of the fire extinguisher.

C – How to fasten and unfasten the safety belts and shoulder harnesses and when safety belts must be fastened

13-55. Answer C. GFDIC 1D/13B, PHB

Regulations require that you explain to your passengers how to fasten and unfasten the safety belts and shoulder harnesses and when the safety belts must be fastened. The FAA also recommends that you cover certain safety considerations with passengers before flight. You can remember the elements of a passenger briefing by using the acronym SAFETY.

- Safety belts—how to fasten and unfasten the safety belts and shoulder harnesses; when safety belts must be fastened—prior to movement on the surface, takeoff, and landing

- Air vents—location and operation; operation of heating or air conditioning controls

- Fire extinguisher—location and operation

- Egress and emergency—operation of doors and windows; location of the survival kit; use of onboard emergency equipment

- Traffic and talking—pointing out traffic; use of headsets; avoiding unnecessary conversation during critical phases of flight

- Your Questions—solicit questions from your passengers.

13-56   CA.III.B.K2, CA.II.D.K4

Which are items typically included in a takeoff briefing?

A – Weight and balance calculations, sky condition, enroute course.

B – Wind direction and velocity, runway length, and takeoff distance.

C – Frequencies for the destination airport, active runway, and traffic pattern entry.

13-56. Answer B. GFDIC 1D/13B, PHB

Items in a takeoff briefing include:

- Wind direction and velocity;
- Runway length;
- Takeoff distance;
- Initial heading;
- Initial altitude;
- Takeoff and climb speeds;
- Departure procedures;
- Emergency plan in case of an engine failure after takeoff.

CHAPTER 14

Commercial Maneuvers

SECTION A
COMMERCIAL MANEUVERS

Chapter 14 of the Instrument/Commercial textbook contains these sections:

- Section A—Accelerated Stalls
- Section B—Soft-Field and Short-Field Takeoffs and Landings
- Section C—Steep Turns
- Section D—Chandelles
- Section E—Lazy Eights
- Section F—Eights-on-Pylons
- Section G—Steep Spirals
- Section H—Power-Off 180° Accuracy Approach and Landing

Although the Commercial Pilot Airman Certification Standards (ACS) contains tasks, such as normal takeoff and landings and power-off and power-on stalls, these operations are not covered in detail in the textbook because, as a private pilot, you are familiar with the procedures to perform these tasks.

You might encounter knowledge test questions on the aerodynamics, airplane performance, and procedures that apply to takeoffs and landings, stalls, and maneuvers. Sample FAA questions on these subjects appear in this chapter of the test guide and in other chapters, such as Chapter 12 Aerodynamics and Performance Limitations.

ACCELERATED STALLS

- An accelerated stall occurs when an airplane stalls at a higher indicated airspeed when excessive maneuvering loads are imposed by steep turns, pull-ups, or other abrupt changes in its attitude.
- You increase the risk of experiencing an inadvertent accelerated stall during improperly performed turns, stall and spin recoveries, pullouts from steep dives, or when overshooting a base to final turn.
- At the first indication of an impending stall (for example, at the airplane buffet or sound of the stall warning horn), recover immediately by releasing back pressure and increasing power. Level the wings using coordinated aileron and rudder pressure.
- If the airplane is slipping toward the inside of the turn when a stall occurs, it tends to roll rapidly toward the outside of the turn at the onset of the stall because the outside wing stalls before the inside wing. If the airplane is skidding toward the outside of the turn, it has a tendency to roll to the inside of the turn because the inside wing stalls first.
- The indication of a full stall is typically an uncommanded nose-down pitch.

SOFT-FIELD AND SHORT-FIELD TAKEOFFS AND LANDINGS

- When performing a takeoff and climb, you must know V_X and V_Y for your airplane and when to use these speeds:
    - Best rate-of-climb speed (V_Y)—the most gain in altitude in the least amount of time. Use this speed during a normal takeoff to reach a safe maneuvering altitude quickly.
    - Best angle-of-climb speed (V_X)—the greatest altitude gain in the shortest distance. Use this speed to clear obstacles at the departure end of the runway.
- The objective of the soft-field takeoff is to transfer the weight of the airplane from the landing gear to the wings as quickly and smoothly as possible. To perform the takeoff, set the flaps as recommended by

the Aircraft Flight Manual (AFM)/Pilot's Operating Handbook (POH). Apply full elevator back pressure to reduce weight on the nosewheel, apply takeoff power, and initially, continue to maintain full back pressure. As the airplane accelerates, reduce elevator back pressure slightly to prevent the tail from hitting the runway,

- The high power setting with a high angle of attack increases the forces of torque, asymmetrical thrust, and spiraling slipstream, which cause left-turning tendency. In addition, when you lower the nose to accelerate in ground effect, gyroscopic precession causes a left-turning tendency.

- When performing an approach and landing, you must establish and maintain a stabilized approach—a constant angle glide path toward a predetermined point on the landing runway—by taking these actions:
    - Maintain a specified descent rate.
    - Maintain a specified airspeed.
    - Complete all briefings and checklists.
    - Configure the airplane for landing (gear, flaps, etc).
    - Be stabilized by 500 feet AGL.
    - Ensure only small changes in heading and pitch are necessary to maintain the correct flight path.

STEEP TURNS

- The objective of performing steep turns is to develop smoothness, coordination, orientation, division of attention, and control techniques. When entering a steep turn:
    - Roll into a 50° angle of bank turn at or below V_A.
    - Do not roll in too rapidly or you can have difficulty establishing the pitch attitude necessary to maintain altitude.
    - Coordinate the aileron and rudder to compensate for adverse yaw. Adverse yaw—the tendency for the airplane to yaw toward the outside of the turn—occurs because the lowered aileron on the outside wing increases the angle of attack, which produces more lift and therefore, more induced drag.

- When performing commercial maneuvers, ensure that you maintain coordinated flight throughout the chandelle. Be aware of and compensate for the effects of adverse yaw and overbanking tendency:
    - Adverse yaw—the tendency for the airplane to yaw toward the outside of the turn—occurs because the lowered aileron on the outside wing increases the angle of attack, which produces more lift and therefore, more induced drag.
    - Overbanking tendency—the tendency of the airplane to continue rolling into a steeper bank—occurs when the bank angle increases because the outside wing, which travels faster than the inside wing, produces more lift. Use a small amount of opposite aileron, away from the turn, to maintain your desired angle of bank.

- Design maneuvering speed (V_A) is the maximum speed at which you can use full, abrupt control movement without overstressing the airframe. If you exceed the maximum performance limit while maintaining your airspeed at or below V_A, the airplane will either stall or will lose altitude. With airspeed above V_A, it is possible to exceed the load limit. V_A increases with an increase in weight.

CHANDELLES

- A chandelle is a maximum performance 180° climbing turn that involves continual changes in pitch, bank, airspeed, and control pressures. During the maneuver, the airspeed gradually decreases from the entry speed to a few knots above stall speed at the completion of the 180° turn.

- Because you do not change the power setting throughout the chandelle, you must control airspeed by adjusting the pitch attitude of the airplane. Although altitude gain is not a criterion for the maneuver, the airplane should gain as much altitude as possible for the given bank angle and power setting without stalling.

SECTION A ■ Commercial Maneuvers

LAZY EIGHTS

- The lazy eight is basically two 180° turns in opposite directions, with each turn including a climb and a descent.
- Throughout the maneuver, airspeed, altitude, bank angle, and pitch attitude, as well as control pressures, are constantly changing.
- Because the power is set before you begin the maneuver, control airspeed by varying the pitch attitude.

EIGHTS ON PYLONS

- The pivotal altitude is the altitude at which, for a given groundspeed, the projection of the visual reference line to the pylon appears to pivot.
- Pivotal altitude increases as groundspeed increases and decreases as groundspeed decreases. As you proceed around the pylon, if the reference line
    - Moves ahead of the pylon, the pivotal altitude is too low. Climb to increase altitude.
    - Moves behind the pylon, the pivotal altitude is too high. Descend to decrease altitude.

STEEP SPIRALS

- The objective of the steep spiral to rapidly dissipate substantial amounts of altitude while remaining over a selected spot.
- A steep spiral consists of a minimum of three, uniform-radius, gliding 360° turns around a ground reference point. To maintain a constant radius, you vary the bank angle to adjust for wind effect.

POWER-OFF 180° ACCURACY APPROACH AND LANDING

- You perform power-off accuracy approaches and landings by gliding, with the engine idling, through a specific pattern to touch down on or beyond and within 200 feet of a specified point, typically a designated line or mark on the runway.

NOTE: *An asterisk appearing after an ACS code (i.e. CA.IV.A.K2*) indicates that the question subject appears more than one time in the ACS. The code shown corresponds to the first instance of the subject in the ACS.*

14-1   CA.VII.D.K3, CA.V.A.K2d, CA.V.C.K2d

An accelerated stall occurs when the airplane stalls

A – while accelerating immediately after takeoff in ground effect.

B – at a higher indicated airspeed due to excessive maneuvering loads.

C – at a lower indicated airspeed due to excessive maneuvering loads.

14-1. Answer B. GFDIC 14A, AFH

An accelerated stall occurs when an airplane stalls at a higher indicated airspeed when excessive maneuvering loads are imposed by steep turns, pull-ups, or other abrupt changes in its attitude.

14-2   CA.VII.D.K3, CA.V.A.K2d, CA.V.C.K2d

Which is a situation that could lead to an inadvertent accelerated stall?

A – Improperly performing a steep turn.

B – Leveling off too slowly from a steep descent.

C – Flying at too slow of an airspeed on final approach.

14-2. Answer A. GFDIC 14A, AFH

An accelerated stall occurs when an airplane stalls at a higher indicated airspeed when excessive maneuvering loads are imposed by steep turns, pull-ups, or other abrupt changes in its attitude. You increase the risk of experiencing an inadvertent accelerated stall during improperly performed turns, stall and spin recoveries, pullouts from steep dives, or when overshooting a base to final turn.

14-3   CA.VII.B.K2* CA.VII.D.K2, CA.V.A.K2d, CA.V.C.K2d

Which is true regarding accelerated stall indications?

A – An indication of an impending stall is an uncommanded nose-down pitch.

B – If the airplane is in a slipping turn when the stall occurs, it tends to roll rapidly toward the inside of the turn.

C – Buffeting of the airplane or the stall warning horn are both indications of an impending stall.

14-3. Answer C. GFDIC 14A, AFH

At the first indication of an impending stall (for example, at the airplane buffet or sound of the stall warning horn), recover immediately by releasing back pressure and increasing power.

If the airplane is slipping toward the inside of the turn when a stall occurs, it tends to roll rapidly toward the outside of the turn at the onset of the stall because the outside wing stalls before the inside wing. If the airplane is skidding toward the outside of the turn, it has a tendency to roll to the inside of the turn because the inside wing stalls first.

The indication of a full stall is typically an uncommanded nose-down pitch.

14-4   CA.VII.B.K2*, CA.VII.D.K2, CA.V.A.K2d, CA.V.C.K2d

To recover from an impending accelerated stall during a turn

A – increase back elevator pressure, increase power, and level the wings using coordinated aileron and rudder pressure.

B – release back elevator pressure, decrease power, and use coordinated aileron and rudder pressure to continue the turn.

C – release back elevator pressure, increase power, and level the wings using coordinated aileron and rudder pressure.

14-4. Answer C. GFDIC 14A, AFH

At the first indication of an impending stall (for example, at the airplane buffet or sound of the stall warning horn), recover immediately by releasing back pressure and increasing power. Level the wings using coordinated aileron and rudder pressure.

14-5   CA.IV.A.K2*

After takeoff, climb at V_Y to

A – gain the most altitude in the least amount of time.

B – gain the most altitude in the shortest distance.

C – clear obstacles at the departure end of the runway.

14-5. Answer A. GFDIC 14B, AFH

When performing a takeoff and climb, you must know V_X and V_Y for your airplane and when to use these speeds:

- Best rate-of-climb speed (V_Y)—the most gain in altitude in the least amount of time. Use this speed during a normal takeoff to reach a safe maneuvering altitude quickly.

- Best angle-of-climb speed (V_X)—the greatest altitude gain in the shortest distance. Use this speed to clear obstacles at the departure end of the runway.

14-6   CA.IV.A.K2*

After takeoff, climb at V_X to

A – gain the most altitude in the least amount of time.

B – gain the most altitude in the shortest distance.

C – reach a safe maneuvering altitude quickly when there are no obstacles at the departure end of the runway.

14-6. Answer B. GFDIC 14B, AFH

When performing a takeoff and climb, you must know V_X and V_Y for your airplane and when to use these speeds:

- Best rate-of-climb speed (V_Y)—the most gain in altitude in the least amount of time. Use this speed during a normal takeoff to reach a safe maneuvering altitude quickly.

- Best angle-of-climb speed (V_X)—the greatest altitude gain in the shortest distance. Use this speed to clear obstacles at the departure end of the runway.

14-7   CA.IV.A.K2*

14 CFR Part 1 defines V_Y as

A – speed for best rate of descent.

B – speed for best angle of climb.

C – speed for best rate of climb.

14-7. Answer C. GFDIC 14B, FAR 1.2, PHB

When performing a takeoff and climb, you must know V_X and V_Y for your airplane and when to use these speeds:

- Best rate-of-climb speed (V_Y)—the most gain in altitude in the least amount of time. Use this speed during a normal takeoff to reach a safe maneuvering altitude quickly.

- Best angle-of-climb speed (V_X)—the greatest altitude gain in the shortest distance. Use this speed to clear obstacles at the departure end of the runway.

14-8   CA.IV.C.K3, 4, 5, 6

When performing a soft-field takeoff, during the takeoff roll

A – apply less right rudder pressure due to decreased left turning tendency.

B – keep takeoff flaps retracted to prevent any damage due to loose dirt and gravel.

C – apply full elevator back pressure initially to transfer the weight of the airplane to the wings quickly and smoothly.

14-8. Answer C. GFDIC 14B, AFH

The objective of the soft-field takeoff is to transfer the weight of the airplane from the landing gear to the wings as quickly and smoothly as possible. To perform the takeoff, set the flaps as recommended by the AFM/POH. Apply full elevator back pressure to reduce weight on the nosewheel, apply takeoff power, and initially, continue to maintain full back pressure. As the airplane accelerates, reduce elevator back pressure slightly to prevent the tail from hitting the runway.

The high power setting with a high angle of attack increases the forces of torque, asymmetrical thrust, and spiraling slipstream, which cause left-turning tendency. In addition, when you lower the nose to accelerate in ground effect, gyroscopic precession causes a left-turning tendency.

14-9   CA.IV.B.K1*

To fly a stabilized approach to a landing

A – make large changes in heading and pitch to maintain the correct flight path.

B – maintain a constant angle glide path toward a predetermined point on the landing runway.

C – ensure your approach is stabilized by 1,000 feet AGL.

14-9. Answer B. GFDIC 14B, AFH

When performing an approach and landing, you must establish and maintain a stabilized approach—a constant angle glide path toward a predetermined point on the landing runway—by taking these actions:

- Maintain a specified descent rate.
- Maintain a specified airspeed.
- Complete all briefings and checklists.
- Configure the airplane for landing (gear, flaps, etc).
- Be stabilized by 500 feet AGL.
- Ensure only small changes in heading and pitch are necessary to maintain the correct flight path.

14-10   CA.V.A.K1, CA.V.A.K2a

When entering a steep turn

A – roll in rapidly to establish the necessary pitch attitude.

B – coordinate the aileron and rudder to compensate for adverse yaw.

C – use a bank angle of 60°.

14-10. Answer B. GFDIC 14C, AFH

The objective of performing steep turns is to develop smoothness, coordination, orientation, division of attention, and control techniques. When entering a steep turn:

- Roll into a 50° angle of bank turn at or below VA.
- Do not roll in too rapidly or you can have difficulty establishing the pitch attitude necessary to maintain altitude.
- Coordinate the aileron and rudder to compensate for adverse yaw. Adverse yaw—the tendency for the airplane to yaw toward the outside of the turn—occurs because the lowered aileron on the outside wing increases the angle of attack, which produces more lift and therefore, more induced drag.

14-11   CA.V.A.K2a*

What causes adverse yaw during a turn?

A – The outside wing, which travels faster than the inside wing, produces more lift.

B – The lowered aileron on the outside wing increases the angle of attack, which produces more induced drag.

C – The lowered aileron on the outside wing decreases the angle of attack, which produces more induced drag.

14-11. Answer B. GFDIC 14C, AFH

When performing commercial maneuvers, ensure that you maintain coordinated flight throughout the chandelle. Be aware of and compensate for the effects of adverse yaw and overbanking tendency:

- Adverse yaw—the tendency for the airplane to yaw toward the outside of the turn—occurs because the lowered aileron on the outside wing increases the angle of attack, which produces more lift and therefore, more induced drag.
- Overbanking tendency—the tendency of the airplane to continue rolling into a steeper bank—occurs when the bank angle increases because the outside wing, which travels faster than the inside wing, produces more lift. Use a small amount of opposite aileron, away from the turn, to maintain your desired angle of bank.

SECTION A ■ Commercial Maneuvers

14-12   CA.V.A.K2b*

What causes overbanking tendency in a turn?

A – The outside wing, which travels slower than the inside wing, produces less lift.

B – The lowered aileron on the outside wing increases the angle of attack, which produces more induced drag.

C – The outside wing, which travels faster than the inside wing, produces more lift.

14-12. Answer C. GFDIC 14C, AFH

When performing commercial maneuvers, ensure that you maintain coordinated flight throughout the chandelle. Be aware of and compensate for the effects of adverse yaw and overbanking tendency:

- Adverse yaw—the tendency for the airplane to yaw toward the outside of the turn—occurs because the lowered aileron on the outside wing increases the angle of attack, which produces more lift and therefore, more induced drag.

- Overbanking tendency—the tendency of the airplane to continue rolling into a steeper bank—occurs when the bank angle increases because the outside wing, which travels faster than the inside wing, produces more lift. Use a small amount of opposite aileron, away from the turn, to maintain your desired angle of bank.

14-13   CA.V.A.K2c*

Which is true regarding design maneuvering speed (V_A)?

A – V_A increases with an increase in weight.

B – V_A decreases with an increase in weight.

C – If you exceed the airplane's maximum performance limit at or below VA, the load limit will be exceeded.

14-13. Answer A. GFDIC 14C, AFH

Design maneuvering speed (V_A) is the maximum speed at which you can use full, abrupt control movement without overstressing the airframe. If you exceed the maximum performance limit while maintaining your airspeed at or below V_A, the airplane will either stall or will lose altitude. With airspeed above V_A, it is possible to exceed the load limit. V_A increases with an increase in weight.

14-14   CA.V.C.K1, 3, 4

When performing a chandelle

A – the airspeed gradually decreases from entry speed to a few knots above stall speed.

B – you must gain at least 1,000 feet in altitude during a high performance climb.

C – you must maintain the same pitch attitude and bank angle during a 180° turn.

14-14. Answer A. GFDIC 14D, AFH

A chandelle is a maximum performance 180° climbing turn that involves continual changes in pitch, bank, airspeed, and control pressures. During the maneuver, the airspeed gradually decreases from the entry speed to a few knots above stall speed at the completion of the 180° turn.

Because you do not change the power setting throughout the chandelle, you must control airspeed by adjusting the pitch attitude of the airplane. Although altitude gain is not a criterion for the maneuver, the airplane should gain as much altitude as possible for the given bank angle and power setting without stalling.

14-15   CA.V.D.K1, 3, 4

Which is true regarding a lazy eight?

A – You control the airspeed with power.

B – The objective is to must gain as much a altitude as possible for a given bank angle and power setting during a 180° turn.

C – The maneuver consists of two 180° turns— each with a climb and a descent—in opposite directions.

14-15. Answer C. GFDIC 14E, AFH

The lazy eight is basically two 180° turns in opposite directions, with each turn including a climb and a descent. Throughout the maneuver, airspeed, altitude, bank angle, and pitch attitude, as well as control pressures, are constantly changing. Because the power is set before you begin the maneuver, control airspeed by varying the pitch attitude.

14-16   CA.V.E.K1, 3, 4, 5

What is true regarding pivotal altitude when performing eights-on-pylons?

A – Pivotal altitude increases as groundspeed decreases and decreases as groundspeed increases.

B – You must decrease pivotal altitude when the airplane is heading downwind.

C – If the reference line moves ahead of the pylon, the pivotal altitude is too low.

14-16. Answer B. GFDIC 14F, AFH

The pivotal altitude is the altitude at which, for a given groundspeed, the projection of the visual reference line to the pylon appears to pivot. Pivotal altitude increases as groundspeed increases and decreases as groundspeed decreases. As you proceed around the pylon, if the reference line

- Moves ahead of the pylon, the pivotal altitude is too low. Climb to increase altitude.

- Moves behind the pylon, the pivotal altitude is too high. Descend to decrease altitude.

14-17   CA.V.B.K1, 2, 3

Select the true statement regarding steep spirals.

A – The maneuver consists of a minimum of four, uniform-radius, 360° turns around a ground reference point.

B – The objective is to rapidly dissipate substantial amounts of altitude while remaining over a selected spot.

C – To maintain a constant radius around the reference point, you must adjust the power to change your airspeed.

14-17. Answer B. GFDIC 14G, AFH

The objective of the steep spiral to rapidly dissipate substantial amounts of altitude while remaining over a selected spot. A steep spiral consists of a minimum of three, uniform-radius, gliding 360° turns around a ground reference point. To maintain a constant radius, you vary the bank angle to adjust for wind effect.

14-18   CA.IV.M.K4, CA.IV.M.R1*

When performing a power-off 180° accuracy approach and landing, you perform a glide

A – to touch down on or beyond and within 200 feet of a specified point on the runway.

B – to touch down on or beyond and within 400 feet of a specified point on the runway.

C – to rapidly dissipate substantial amounts of altitude while remaining over a selected spot.

14-18. Answer A. GFDIC 14H, AFH

You perform power-off accuracy approaches and landings by gliding, with the engine idling, through a specific pattern to touch down on or beyond and within 200 feet of a specified point, typically a designated line or mark on the runway.

SECTION A ■ **Commercial Maneuvers**

On the Commercial Pilot Airman Knowledge Test, you might be presented with basic maneuvers and flight operations questions that were introduced to you as a private pilot. Examples of these types of questions follow.

14-19   CA.IV.B.K2

What should be expected when making a downwind landing? The likelihood of

A – undershooting the intended landing spot and a faster airspeed at touchdown.

B – overshooting the intended landing spot and a faster groundspeed at touchdown.

C – undershooting the intended landing spot and a faster groundspeed at touchdown.

14-19. Answer A. PPM13, AFH
A tailwind increases the airplane's groundspeed and the landing distance. By landing downwind, you increase the risk of overshooting the intended landing spot and the airplane will have a faster groundspeed at touchdown.

14-20   CA.IV.B.R3a*

When conducting a go-around, you must be aware that

A – radio communications are key to alerting other aircraft in the pattern that a go-around maneuver is being conducted.

B – the airplane is trimmed for a power-off condition, and application of takeoff power will cause the nose to rise rapidly.

C – flaps should be raised as quickly as possible to reduce drag and increase airspeed for a successful go-around.

14-20. Answer B. PPM15, AFH
When performing a go-around, the first step is to apply takeoff power immediately and adjust the airplane's attitude to stop the descent. When you apply full power, you normally must hold a considerable amount of forward pressure on the control stick to prevent the nose from rising rapidly because the airplane was trimmed for approach.

After stopping the descent, partially retract the flaps (if applicable) as recommended by the manufacturer. Normally, you retract the flaps in small increments to allow the airplane to accelerate as the flaps are raised. Retracting the flaps prematurely causes a loss of lift that could result in the airplane settling back to the runway. Make the appropriate radio call only after you have reached a safe altitude,

14-21   CA.IV.N.K2

Which is true about airplane climb performance during a go-around?

A – A high density altitude increases climb performance.

B – When initiating a go-around close to the ground, you must be aware of the apparent increase in performance due to ground effect.

C – You should retract the landing gear immediately before the flaps to increase your climb performance.

14-21. Answer B. PPM15, AFH
When initiating a go-around close to the ground, be aware of the apparent increase in performance due to ground effect. Increasing the pitch too quickly could prevent the airplane from climbing or even maintaining altitude. Because full flaps produce more drag than extended landing gear, it is generally recommended that you partially retract the flaps before retracting the landing gear. This action also prevents damage if the airplane inadvertently touches down on the runway as you initiate the go-around.

For a given pressure altitude, density altitude increases when temperature increases. The density of the air directly influences the performance of your airplane by altering the lift of the airframe, as well as the ability of the engine to produce power. A high density altitude decreases climb performance.

14-22   CA.V.A.R2*

To scan properly for traffic, you should

A – use a series of short, regularly spaced eye movements that bring successive areas of the sky into the central visual field.

B – slowly sweep the field of vision from one side to the other at intervals.

C – concentrate on any peripheral movement detected.

14-22. Answer A. PP4A, AFH

Effective traffic scanning must be accomplished by using a series of short, regularly spaced eye movements that bring successive areas of the sky into the central, or foveal, area of vision. A series of 10-degree movements while pausing in between each for approximately 1 second is most effective.

14-23   CA.IV.A.K1*, CA.IV.A.K3*

With regard to the technique required for a crosswind correction on takeoff, you should use

A – aileron pressure into the wind and initiate the lift-off at a normal airspeed in both tailwheel- and nosewheel-type airplanes.

B – right rudder pressure, aileron pressure into the wind, and higher than normal lift-off airspeed in both tricycle- and conventional-gear airplanes.

C – rudder as required to maintain directional control, aileron pressure into the wind, and higher than normal lift-off airspeed in both conventional- and nosewheel-type airplanes.

14-23. Answer C. PPM11, AFH

During a crosswind takeoff, the rudder should be used to maintain directional control, the ailerons positioned into the wind, and lift off should be initiated at a slightly higher-than-normal speed.

14-24   CA.IV.B.K2, 3*

A proper crosswind landing on a runway requires that, at the moment of touchdown, the

A – direction of motion of the airplane and its lateral axis be perpendicular to the runway.

B – direction of motion of the airplane and its longitudinal axis be parallel to the runway.

C – downwind wing be lowered sufficiently to eliminate the tendency for the airplane to drift.

14-24. Answer B. PPM16, AFH

With either the crab or wing-low method of drift correction, the flight path and the aircraft's longitudinal axis must be parallel to the runway at touchdown.

14-25   CA.II.B.K1

Required flight crewmembers' safety belts must be fastened

A – only during takeoff and landing.

B – while the crewmembers are at their stations.

C – only during takeoff and landing when passengers are aboard the aircraft.

14-25. Answer B. FAR 91.105

During takeoffs and landings, and while enroute, each required flight crewmember shall keep their safety belt fastened while at the crewmember station.

SECTION A ■ Commercial Maneuvers

14-26　CA.II.B.K1

Each required flight crewmember is required to keep his or her shoulder harness fastened

A – during takeoff and landing only when passengers are aboard the aircraft.

B – during takeoff and landing, unless he or she is unable to perform required duties.

C – while the crewmembers are at their stations, unless he or she is unable to perform required duties.

14-26. Answer C. FAR 91.105

Each required flight crewmember of a U.S.-registered civil aircraft shall, during takeoff and landing, keep his or her shoulder harness fastened while at his or her assigned duty station, unless the crewmember would be unable to perform required duties with the shoulder harness fastened.

14-27　CA.II.B.K1

With U.S.-registered civil airplanes, the use of safety belts is required during movement on the surface, takeoffs, and landings for

A – safe operating practice, but not required by regulations.

B – each person over 2 years of age on board.

C – commercial passenger operations only.

14-27. Answer B. FAR 91.107, FAR 91.105

In addition to the required use of seat belts and shoulder harnesses for crewmembers, no pilot may cause to be moved on the surface, takeoff, or land a U.S.-registered civil aircraft unless the pilot in command of that aircraft ensures that each person on board has been notified to fasten his or her safety belt and, if installed, shoulder harness. In addition, the safety belt and shoulder harness must be properly secured about each person more than 2 years of age.

14-28　CA.I.B.K1

If an airplane category is listed as utility, it would mean that this airplane could be operated in which of the following maneuvers?

A – Any maneuver except acrobatics or spins.

B – Limited acrobatics, including spins (if approved).

C – Limited acrobatics, excluding spins.

14-28. Answer B. FAR 23.3

An airplane in the utility category can conduct limited acrobatics, including spins.

APPENDIX 1

FAA LEGENDS

The FAA Legends are a part of the Airman Knowledge Testing Supplement for Commercial Pilot designed by the Federal Aviation Administration (FAA) Flight Standards Service. These legends are an important resource for answering questions about charts and information included in the Chart Supplement. For example, if you do not know the answer to a chart-related question or how to interpret an Airport/Facility Directory excerpt, refer to the legends and remember that they are available during your test.

APPENDIX 1 ■ FAA Legends

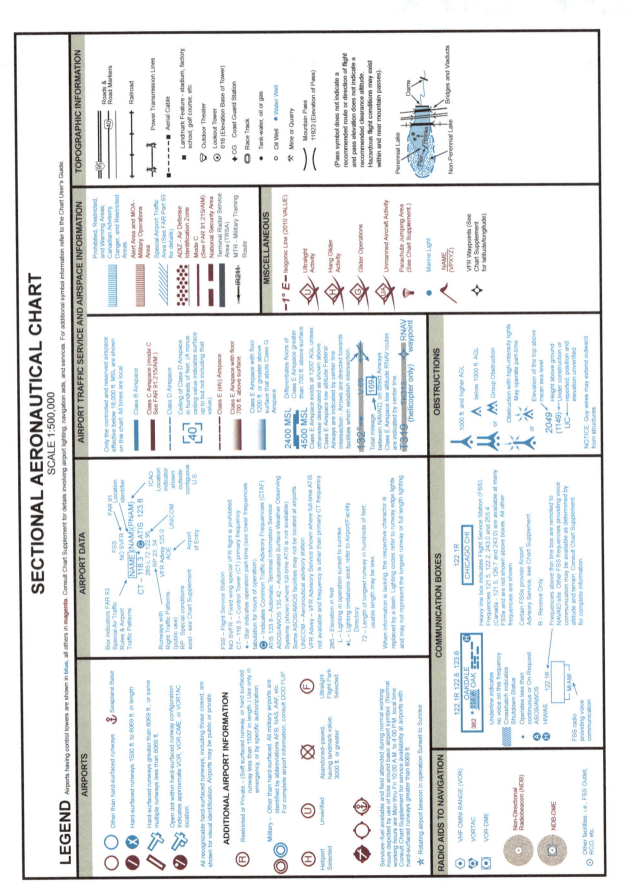

Legend 1. Sectional Aeronautical Chart.

12   **AIRPORT/FACILITY DIRECTORY LEGEND**

SAMPLE

① ② ③ ④ ⑤ ⑥ ⑦ ⑧

CITY NAME

AIRPORT NAME (ALTERNATE NAME) (LTS)(KLTS) CIV/MIL 3 N UTC–6(–5DT) N34°41.93´ W99°20.20´   JACKSONVILLE
   200   B   TPA—1000(800) AOE LRA Class IV, ARFF Index A NOTAM FILE ORL Not insp.   COPTER
⑪ ⑫   ⑬   ⑭   ⑮   ⑯   ⑰   H–4G, L–19C

IAP, DIAP, AD

⑱→ **RWY 18–36:** H12004X200 (ASPH–CONC–GRVD)
   S–90, D–160, 2D–300 PCN 80 R/B/W/T HIRL CL
   RWY 18: RLLS. MALSF. TDZL. REIL. PAPI(P2R)—GA 3.0° TCH 36´.
   RVR–TMR. Thld dsplcd 300´. Trees. Rgt tfc. 0.3% up.
   RWY 36: ALSF1. 0.4% down.
   RWY 09–27: H6000X150 (ASPH) MIRL
   RWY 173–353: H3515X150 (ASPH–PFC) AUW PCN 59 F/A/W/T
⑲→ **LAND AND HOLD–SHORT OPERATIONS**

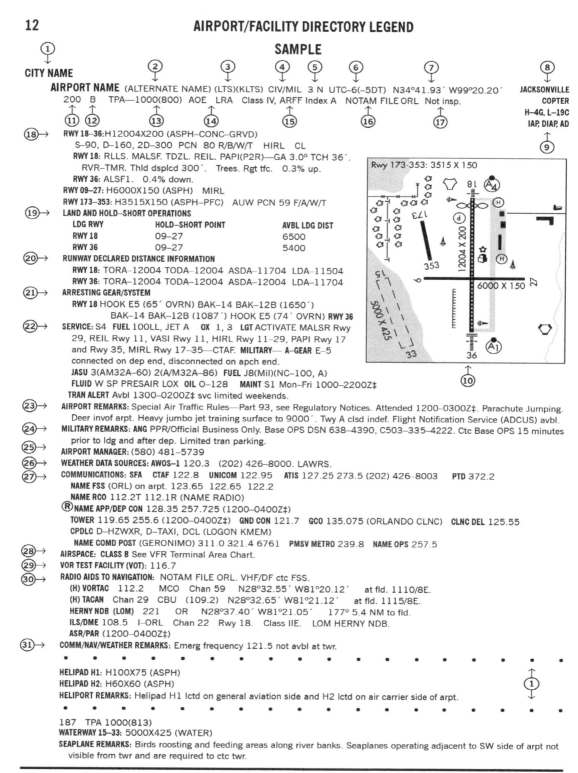

Rwy 173–353: 3515 X 150

LDG RWY	HOLD–SHORT POINT	AVBL LDG DIST
RWY 18	09–27	6500
RWY 36	09–27	5400

⑳→ **RUNWAY DECLARED DISTANCE INFORMATION**
   RWY 18: TORA–12004 TODA–12004 ASDA–11704 LDA–11504
   RWY 36: TORA–12004 TODA–12004 ASDA–12004 LDA–11704
㉑→ **ARRESTING GEAR/SYSTEM**
   RWY 18 HOOK E5 (65´ OVRN) BAK–14 BAK–12B (1650´)
        BAK–14 BAK–12B (1087´) HOOK E5 (74´ OVRN) **RWY 36**
㉒→ **SERVICE:** S4 **FUEL** 100LL, JET A **OX** 1, 3 **LGT** ACTIVATE MALSR Rwy
   29, REIL Rwy 11, VASI Rwy 11, HIRL Rwy 11–29, PAPI Rwy 17
   and Rwy 35, MIRL Rwy 17–35—CTAF. **MILITARY— A–GEAR** E–5
   connected on dep end, disconnected on apch end.
   JASU 3(AM32A–60) 2(A/M32A–86) **FUEL** J8(Mil)(NC–100, A)
   FLUID W SP PRESAIR LOX **OIL** O–128 **MAINT** S1 Mon–Fri 1000–2200Z‡
   TRAN ALERT Avbl 1300–0200Z‡ svc limited weekends.
㉓→ **AIRPORT REMARKS:** Special Air Traffic Rules—Part 93, see Regulatory Notices. Attended 1200–0300Z‡. Parachute Jumping.
   Deer invof arpt. Heavy jumbo jet training surface to 9000´. Twy A clsd indef. Flight Notification Service (ADCUS) avbl.
㉔→ **MILITARY REMARKS:** ANG PPR/Official Business Only. Base OPS DSN 638–4390, C503–335–4222. Ctc Base OPS 15 minutes
   prior to ldg and after dep. Limited tran parking.
㉕→ **AIRPORT MANAGER:** (580) 481–5739
㉖→ **WEATHER DATA SOURCES:** AWOS–1 120.3 (202) 426–8000. LAWRS.
㉗→ **COMMUNICATIONS: SFA CTAF** 122.8 **UNICOM** 122.95 **ATIS** 127.25 273.5 (202) 426–8003 **PTD** 372.2
   NAME **FSS** (ORL) on arpt. 123.65 122.65 122.2
   NAME **RCO** 112.2T 112.1R (NAME RADIO)
   ®NAME **APP/DEP CON** 128.35 257.725 (1200–0400Z‡)
   TOWER 119.65 255.6 (1200–0400Z‡) **GND CON** 121.7 **GCO** 135.075 (ORLANDO CLNC) **CLNC DEL** 125.55
   CPDLC D–HZWXR, D–TAXI, DCL (LOGON KMEM)
   NAME **COMD POST** (GERONIMO) 311.0 321.4 6761 **PMSV METRO** 239.8 **NAME OPS** 257.5
㉘→ **AIRSPACE: CLASS B** See VFR Terminal Area Chart.
㉙→ **VOR TEST FACILITY (VOT):** 116.7
㉚→ **RADIO AIDS TO NAVIGATION:** NOTAM FILE ORL. VHF/DF ctc FSS.
   (H) VORTAC 112.2 MCO Chan 59 N28°32.55´ W81°20.12´ at fld. 1110/8E.
   (H) TACAN Chan 29 CBU (109.2) N28°32.65´ W81°21.12´ at fld. 1115/8E.
   HERNY NDB (LOM) 221 OR N28°37.40´ W81°21.05´ 177° 5.4 NM to fld.
   ILS/DME 108.5 I–ORL Chan 22 Rwy 18. Class IIE. LOM HERNY NDB.
   ASR/PAR (1200–0400Z‡)
㉛→ **COMM/NAV/WEATHER REMARKS:** Emerg frequency 121.5 not avbl at twr.

• • • • • • • • • • • • • • • •

HELIPAD H1: H100X75 (ASPH)
HELIPAD H2: H60X60 (ASPH)
HELIPORT REMARKS: Helipad H1 lctd on general aviation side and H2 lctd on air carrier side of arpt.

• • • • • • • • • • • • • • • •

187 TPA 1000(813)
WATERWAY 15–33: 5000X425 (WATER)
SEAPLANE REMARKS: Birds roosting and feeding areas along river banks. Seaplanes operating adjacent to SW side of arpt not
   visible from twr and are required to ctc twr.

All bearings and radials are magnetic unless otherwise specified. All mileages are nautical unless otherwise noted.
All times are Coordinated Universal Time (UTC) except as noted. All elevations are in feet above/below Mean Sea Level (MSL) unless otherwise noted.
The horizontal reference datum of this publication is North American Datum of 1983 (NAD83), which for charting purposes is considered equivalent to World
Geodetic System 1984 (WGS 84).

SC, 1 FEB 20XX to 29 MAR 20XX

Legend 2. Chart Supplement.

18032

⑩   **SKETCH LEGEND**

RUNWAYS/LANDING AREAS

Hard Surfaced . . . .

Metal Surface . . . .

Sod, Gravel, etc. . . . .

Light Plane,
Ski Landing Area or Water . . . .

Under Construction . . . . .

Closed Rwy . . . .

Closed Pavement . . . .

Helicopter Landings Area . . . . (H)

Displaced Threshold . . . .

Taxiway, Apron and Stopways . .

RADIO AIDS TO NAVIGATION

VORTAC . . .   VOR . . . .

VOR/DME . .   NDB . . . .

TACAN . . . .   NDB/DME . . . .

DME . . . .

MISCELLANEOUS AERONAUTICAL FEATURES

Airport Beacon . . . .   ☆ ✪

Wind Cone . . . .

Landing Tee . . . .

Tetrahedron . . . .

Control Tower . . . .   or TWR

When control tower and rotating beacon
are co-located beacon symbol will be
used and further identified as TWR.

MISCELLANEOUS BASE AND CULTURAL FEATURES

Buildings . . . .

Power Lines . . . .   —T—T—

Fence . . . .

Towers . . . .

Wind Turbine . . . .

Tanks . . . .

Oil Well . . . .

Smoke Stack . . . .

Obstruction . . . .   5812 ⋀

Controlling Obstruction . . . .   +5812

Trees . . . .

Populated Places . . . .

Cuts and Fills . . . . . .   Cut   Fill

Cliffs and Depressions . .

Ditch . . . .

Hill . . . .

APPROACH LIGHTING SYSTEMS

A dot "•" portrayed with approach lighting
letter identifier indicates sequenced flashing
lights (F) installed with the approach lighting
system e.g. Ⓐ₁ Negative symbology, e.g., Ⓐ1
Ⓥ indicates Pilot Controlled Lighting (PCL).

Runway Centerline Lighting . . . . .

Ⓐ   Approach Lighting System ALSF-2 . .

Ⓐ₁   Approach Lighting System ALSF-1 . .

Ⓐ₂   Short Approach Lighting System
SALS/SALSF . . . .

Ⓐ₃   Simplified Short Approach Lighting
System (SSALR) with RAIL . . . . .

Ⓐ₄   Medium Intensity Approach Lighting System
(MALS and MALSF)/(SSALS
and SSALF) . . . .

Ⓐ₅   Medium Intensity Approach Lighting
System (MALSR) and RAIL . . . . . .

⊕   Omnidirectional Approach
Lighting System (ODALS) . . . .

Ⓓ   Navy Parallel Row and Cross Bar . . .

⊕   Air Force Overrun . . . .

Ⓥ   Visual Approach Slope Indicator with
Standard Threshold Clearance provided

Ⓥ₂   Pulsating Visual Approach Slope Indicator
(PVASI)

Ⓥ₃   Visual Approach Slope Indicator with a
threshold crossing height to accomodate
long bodied or jumbo aircraft

Ⓥ₄   Tri-color Visual Approach Slope Indicator
(TRCV)

Ⓥ₅   Approach Path Alignment Panel (APAP)

Ⓟ   Precision Approach Path Indicator (PAPI)

SC, 1 FEB 20XX to 29 MAR 20XX

Legend 3. Chart Supplement.

14   AIRPORT/FACILITY DIRECTORY LEGEND

LEGEND

This directory is a listing of data on record with the FAA on public–use airports, military airports and selected private–use airports specifically requested by the Department of Defense (DoD) for which a DoD Instrument Approach Procedure has been published in the U.S. Terminal Procedures Publication. Additionally this listing contains data for associated terminal control facilities, air route traffic control centers, and radio aids to navigation within the conterminous United States, Puerto Rico and the Virgin Islands. Civil airports and joint Civil/Military airports which are open to the public are listed alphabetically by state, associated city and airport name and cross–referenced by airport name. Military airports and private–use (limited civil access) joint Military/Civil airports are listed alphabetically by state and official airport name and cross–referenced by associated city name. Navaids, flight service stations and remote communication outlets that are associated with an airport, but with a different name, are listed alphabetically under their own name, as well as under the airport with which they are associated.

The listing of an airport as open to the public in this directory merely indicates the airport operator's willingness to accommodate transient aircraft, and does not represent that the airport conforms with any Federal or local standards, or that it has been approved for use on the part of the general public. Military airports, private–use airports, and private–use (limited civil access) joint Military/Civil airports are open to civil pilots only in an emergency or with prior permission. See Special Notice Section, Civil Use of Military Fields.

The information on obstructions is taken from reports submitted to the FAA. Obstruction data has not been verified in all cases. Pilots are cautioned that objects not indicated in this tabulation (or on the airports sketches and/or charts) may exist which can create a hazard to flight operation. Detailed specifics concerning services and facilities tabulated within this directory are contained in the Aeronautical Information Manual, Basic Flight Information and ATC Procedures.

The legend items that follow explain in detail the contents of this Directory and are keyed to the circled numbers on the sample on the preceding pages.

① CITY/AIRPORT NAME

Civil and joint Civil/Military airports which are open to the public are listed alphabetically by state and associated city. Where the city name is different from the airport name the city name will appear on the line above the airport name. Airports with the same associated city name will be listed alphabetically by airport name and will be separated by a dashed rule line. A solid rule line will separate all others. FAA approved helipads and seaplane landing areas associated with a land airport will be separated by a dotted line. Military airports and private–use (limited civil access) joint Military/Civil airports are listed alphabetically by state and official airport name.

② ALTERNATE NAME

Alternate names, if any, will be shown in parentheses.

③ LOCATION IDENTIFIER

The location identifier is a three or four character FAA code followed by a four–character ICAO code, when assigned, to airports. If two different military codes are assigned, both codes will be shown with the primary operating agency's code listed first. These identifiers are used by ATC in lieu of the airport name in flight plans, flight strips and other written records and computer operations. Zeros will appear with a slash to differentiate them from the letter "O".

④ OPERATING AGENCY

Airports within this directory are classified into two categories, Military/Federal Government and Civil airports open to the general public, plus selected private–use airports. The operating agency is shown for military, private–use and joint use airports. The operating agency is shown by an abbreviation as listed below. When an organization is a tenant, the abbreviation is enclosed in parenthesis. No classification indicates the airport is open to the general public with no military tenant.

A	US Army	MC	Marine Corps
AFRC	Air Force Reserve Command	MIL/CIV	Joint Use Military/Civil Limited Civil Access
AF	US Air Force	N	Navy
ANG	Air National Guard	NAF	Naval Air Facility
AR	US Army Reserve	NAS	Naval Air Station
ARNG	US Army National Guard	NASA	National Air and Space Administration
CG	US Coast Guard	P	US Civil Airport Wherein Permit Covers Use by Transient Military Aircraft
CIV/MIL	Joint Use Civil/Military Open to the Public		
DND	Department of National Defense Canada	PVT	Private Use Only (Closed to the Public)

⑤ AIRPORT LOCATION

Airport location is expressed as distance and direction from the center of the associated city in nautical miles and cardinal points, e.g., 4 NE.

⑥ TIME CONVERSION

Hours of operation of all facilities are expressed in Coordinated Universal Time (UTC) and shown as "Z" time. The directory indicates the number of hours to be subtracted from UTC to obtain local standard time and local daylight saving time UTC–5(–4DT). The symbol ‡ indicates that during periods of Daylight Saving Time (DST) effective hours will be one hour earlier than shown. In those areas where daylight saving time is not observed the (–4DT) and ‡ will not be shown. Daylight saving time is in effect from 0200 local time the second Sunday in March to 0200 local time the first Sunday in November. Canada and all U.S. Conterminous States observe daylight saving time except Arizona and Puerto Rico, and the Virgin Islands. If the state observes daylight saving time and the operating times are other than daylight saving times, the operating hours will include the dates, times and no ‡ symbol will be shown, i.e., April 15–Aug 31 0630–1700Z, Sep 1–Apr 14 0600–1700Z.

Legend 4. Chart Supplement.

AIRPORT/FACILITY DIRECTORY LEGEND   15

⑦ **GEOGRAPHIC POSITION OF AIRPORT—AIRPORT REFERENCE POINT (ARP)**
Positions are shown as hemisphere, degrees, minutes and hundredths of a minute and represent the approximate geometric center of all usable runway surfaces.

⑧ **CHARTS**
Charts refer to the Sectional Chart and Low and High Altitude Enroute Chart and panel on which the airport or facility is depicted. Helicopter Chart depictions will be indicated as COPTER. IFR Gulf of Mexico West and IFR Gulf of Mexico Central will be referenced as GOMW and GOMC.

⑨ **INSTRUMENT APPROACH PROCEDURES, AIRPORT DIAGRAMS**
IAP indicates an airport for which a prescribed (Public Use) FAA Instrument Approach Procedure has been published. DIAP indicates an airport for which a prescribed DoD Instrument Approach Procedure has been published in the U.S. Terminal Procedures. See the Special Notice Section of this directory, Civil Use of Military Fields and the Aeronautical Information Manual 5–4–5 Instrument Approach Procedure Charts for additional information. AD indicates an airport for which an airport diagram has been published. Airport diagrams are located in the back of each Chart Supplement volume alphabetically by associated city and airport name.

⑩ **AIRPORT SKETCH**
The airport sketch, when provided, depicts the airport and related topographical information as seen from the air and should be used in conjunction with the text. It is intended as a guide for pilots in VFR conditions. Symbology that is not self–explanatory will be reflected in the sketch legend. The airport sketch will be oriented with True North at the top. Airport sketches will be added incrementally.

⑪ **ELEVATION**
The highest point of an airport's usable runways measured in feet from mean sea level. When elevation is sea level it will be indicated as "00". When elevation is below sea level a minus "–" sign will precede the figure.

⑫ **ROTATING LIGHT BEACON**
B indicates rotating beacon is available. Rotating beacons operate sunset to sunrise unless otherwise indicated in the AIRPORT REMARKS or MILITARY REMARKS segment of the airport entry.

⑬ **TRAFFIC PATTERN ALTITUDE**
Traffic Pattern Altitude (TPA)—The first figure shown is TPA above mean sea level. The second figure in parentheses is TPA above airport elevation. Multiple TPA shall be shown as "TPA—See Remarks" and detailed information shall be shown in the Airport or Military Remarks Section. Traffic pattern data for USAF bases, USN facilities, and U.S. Army airports (including those on which ACC or U.S. Army is a tenant) that deviate from standard pattern altitudes shall be shown in Military Remarks.

⑭ **AIRPORT OF ENTRY, LANDING RIGHTS, AND CUSTOMS USER FEE AIRPORTS**
U.S. CUSTOMS USER FEE AIRPORT—Private Aircraft operators are frequently required to pay the costs associated with customs processing.
AOE—Airport of Entry. A customs Airport of Entry where permission from U.S. Customs is not required to land. However, at least one hour advance notice of arrival is required.
LRA—Landing Rights Airport. Application for permission to land must be submitted in advance to U.S. Customs. At least one hour advance notice of arrival is required.
NOTE: Advance notice of arrival at both an AOE and LRA airport may be included in the flight plan when filed in Canada or Mexico. Where Flight Notification Service (ADCUS) is available the airport remark will indicate this service. This notice will also be treated as an application for permission to land in the case of an LRA. Although advance notice of arrival may be relayed to Customs through Mexico, Canada, and U.S. Communications facilities by flight plan, the aircraft operator is solely responsible for ensuring that Customs receives the notification. (See Customs, Immigration and Naturalization, Public Health and Agriculture Department requirements in the International Flight Information Manual for further details.)

U.S. CUSTOMS AIR AND SEA PORTS, INSPECTORS AND AGENTS

Northeast Sector (New England and Atlantic States—ME to MD)	407–975–1740
Southeast Sector (Atlantic States—DC, WV, VA to FL)	407–975–1780
Central Sector (Interior of the US, including Gulf states—MS, AL, LA)	407–975–1760
Southwest East Sector (OK and eastern TX)	407–975–1840
Southwest West Sector (Western TX, NM and AZ)	407–975–1820
Pacific Sector (WA, OR, CA, HI and AK)	407–975–1800

⑮ **CERTIFICATED AIRPORT (14 CFR PART 139)**
Airports serving Department of Transportation certified carriers and certified under 14 CFR part 139 are indicated by the Class and the ARFF Index; e.g. Class I, ARFF Index A, which relates to the availability of crash, fire, rescue equipment. Class I airports can have an ARFF Index A through E, depending on the aircraft length and scheduled departures. Class II, III, and IV will always carry an Index A.

AIRPORT CLASSIFICATIONS

Type of Air Carrier Operation	Class I	Class II	Class III	Class IV
Scheduled Air Carrier Aircraft with 31 or more passenger seats	X			
Unscheduled Air Carrier Aircraft with 31 or more passengers seats	X	X		X
Scheduled Air Carrier Aircraft with 10 to 30 passenger seats	X	X	X	

SC, 1 FEB 20XX to 29 MAR 20XX

Legend 5. Chart Supplement.

16   **AIRPORT/FACILITY DIRECTORY LEGEND**

INDICES AND AIRCRAFT RESCUE AND FIRE FIGHTING EQUIPMENT REQUIREMENTS

Airport Index	Required No. Vehicles	Aircraft Length	Scheduled Departures	Agent + Water for Foam
A	1	<90′	≥1	500#DC or HALON 1211 or 450#DC + 100 gal H$_2$O
B	1 or 2	≥90′, <126′ ———— ≥126′, <159′	≥5 ———— <5	Index A + 1500 gal H$_2$O
C	2 or 3	≥126′, <159′ ———— ≥159′, <200′	≥5 ———— <5	Index A + 3000 gal H$_2$O
D	3	≥159′, <200′ ———— >200′	———— <5	Index A + 4000 gal H$_2$O
E	3	≥200′	≥5	Index A + 6000 gal H$_2$O

> Greater Than; < Less Than; ≥ Equal or Greater Than; ≤ Equal or Less Than;   H$_2$O–Water; DC–Dry Chemical.

NOTE: The listing of ARFF index does not necessarily assure coverage for non–air carrier operations or at other than prescribed times for air carrier. ARFF Index Ltd.—indicates ARFF coverage may or may not be available, for information contact airport manager prior to flight.

⑯ NOTAM SERVICE

All public use landing areas are provided NOTAM service. A NOTAM FILE identifier is shown for individual landing areas, e.g., "NOTAM FILE BNA". See the AIM, Basic Flight Information and ATC Procedures for a detailed description of NOTAMs. Current NOTAMs are available from flight service stations at 1–800–WX–BRIEF (992–7433) or online through the FAA PilotWeb at https://pilotweb.nas.faa.gov. Military NOTAMs are available using the Defense Internet NOTAM Service (DINS) at https://www.notams.faa.gov. Pilots flying to or from airports not available through the FAA PilotWeb or DINS can obtain assistance from Flight Service.

⑰ FAA INSPECTION

All airports not inspected by FAA will be identified by the note: Not insp. This indicates that the airport information has been provided by the owner or operator of the field.

⑱ RUNWAY DATA

Runway information is shown on two lines. That information common to the entire runway is shown on the first line while information concerning the runway ends is shown on the second or following line. Runway direction, surface, length, width, weight bearing capacity, lighting, and slope, when available are shown for each runway. Multiple runways are shown with the longest runway first. Direction, length, width, and lighting are shown for sea–lanes. The full dimensions of helipads are shown, e.g., 50X150. Runway data that requires clarification will be placed in the remarks section.

RUNWAY DESIGNATION

Runways are normally numbered in relation to their magnetic orientation rounded off to the nearest 10 degrees. Parallel runways can be designated L (left)/R (right)/C (center). Runways may be designated as Ultralight or assault strips. Assault strips are shown by magnetic bearing.

RUNWAY DIMENSIONS

Runway length and width are shown in feet. Length shown is runway end to end including displaced thresholds, but excluding those areas designed as overruns.

RUNWAY SURFACE AND SURFACE TREATMENT

Runway lengths prefixed by the letter "H" indicate that the runways are hard surfaced (concrete, asphalt, or part asphalt–concrete). If the runway length is not prefixed, the surface is sod, clay, etc. The runway surface composition is indicated in parentheses after runway length as follows:

(AFSC)—Aggregate friction seal coat   (GRVL)—Gravel, or cinders   (SAND)—Sand
(AM2)—Temporary metal planks coated   (MATS)—Pierced steel planking,   (TURF)—Turf
   with nonskid material   landing mats, membranes
(ASPH)—Asphalt   (PEM)—Part concrete, part asphalt   (TRTD)—Treated
(CONC)—Concrete   (PFC)—Porous friction courses   (WC)—Wire combed
(DIRT)—Dirt   (PSP)—Pierced steel plank
(GRVD)—Grooved   (RFSC)—Rubberized friction seal coat

Legend 6. Chart Supplement.

AIRPORT/FACILITY DIRECTORY LEGEND   17

RUNWAY WEIGHT BEARING CAPACITY

Runway strength data shown in this publication is derived from available information and is a realistic estimate of capability at an average level of activity. It is not intended as a maximum allowable weight or as an operating limitation. Many airport pavements are capable of supporting limited operations with gross weights in excess of the published figures. Permissible operating weights, insofar as runway strengths are concerned, are a matter of agreement between the owner and user. When desiring to operate into any airport at weights in excess of those published in the publication, users should contact the airport management for permission. Runway strength figures are shown in thousand of pounds, with the last three figures being omitted. Add 000 to figure following S, D, 2S, 2T, AUW, SWL, etc., for gross weight capacity. A blank space following the letter designator is used to indicate the runway can sustain aircraft with this type landing gear, although definite runway weight bearing capacity figures are not available, e.g., S, D. Applicable codes for typical gear configurations with S=Single, D=Dual, T=Triple and Q=Quadruple:

CURRENT	NEW	NEW DESCRIPTION
S	S	Single wheel type landing gear (DC3), (C47), (F15), etc.
D	D	Dual wheel type landing gear (BE1900), (B737), (A319), etc.
T	D	Dual wheel type landing gear (P3, C9).
ST	2S	Two single wheels in tandem type landing gear (C130).
TRT	2T	Two triple wheels in tandem type landing gear (C17), etc.
DT	2D	Two dual wheels in tandem type landing gear (B707), etc.
TT	2D	Two dual wheels in tandem type landing gear (B757, KC135).
SBTT	2D/D1	Two dual wheels in tandem/dual wheel body gear type landing gear (KC10).
None	2D/2D1	Two dual wheels in tandem/two dual wheels in tandem body gear type landing gear (A340–600).
DDT	2D/2D2	Two dual wheels in tandem/two dual wheels in double tandem body gear type landing gear (B747, E4).
TTT	3D	Three dual wheels in tandem type landing gear (B777), etc.
TT	D2	Dual wheel gear two struts per side main gear type landing gear (B52).
TDT	C5	Complex dual wheel and quadruple wheel combination landing gear (C5).

AUW—All up weight. Maximum weight bearing capacity for any aircraft irrespective of landing gear configuration.

SWL—Single Wheel Loading. (This includes information submitted in terms of Equivalent Single Wheel Loading (ESWL) and Single Isolated Wheel Loading).

PSI—Pounds per square inch. PSI is the actual figure expressing maximum pounds per square inch runway will support, e.g., (SWL 000/PSI 535).

Omission of weight bearing capacity indicates information unknown.

The ACN/PCN System is the ICAO standard method of reporting pavement strength for pavements with bearing strengths greater than 12,500 pounds. The Pavement Classification Number (PCN) is established by an engineering assessment of the runway. The PCN is for use in conjunction with an Aircraft Classification Number (ACN). Consult the Aircraft Flight Manual, Flight Information Handbook, or other appropriate source for ACN tables or charts. Currently, ACN data may not be available for all aircraft. If an ACN table or chart is available, the ACN can be calculated by taking into account the aircraft weight, the pavement type, and the subgrade category. For runways that have been evaluated under the ACN/PCN system, the PCN will be shown as a five–part code (e.g. PCN 80 R/B/W/T). Details of the coded format are as follows:

NOTE: Prior permission from the airport controlling authority is required when the ACN of the aircraft exceeds the published PCN or aircraft tire pressure exceeds the published limits.

(1) The PCN NUMBER—The reported PCN indicates that an aircraft with an ACN equal or less than the reported PCN can operate on the pavement subject to any limitation on the tire pressure.

(2) The type of pavement:
   R — Rigid
   F — Flexible

(3) The pavement subgrade category:
   A — High
   B — Medium
   C — Low
   D — Ultra–low

(4) The maximum tire pressure authorized for the pavement:
   W — Unlimited, no pressure limit
   X — High, limited to 254 psi (1.75 MPa)
   Y — Medium, limited to 181 psi (1.25 MPa)
   Z — Low, limited to 73 psi (0.50 MPa)

(5) Pavement evaluation method:
   T — Technical evaluation
   U — By experience of aircraft using the pavement

RUNWAY LIGHTING

Lights are in operation sunset to sunrise. Lighting available by prior arrangement only or operating part of the night and/or pilot controlled lighting with specific operating hours are indicated under airport or military remarks. At USN/USMC facilities lights are available only during airport hours of operation. Since obstructions are usually lighted, obstruction lighting is not included in this code. Unlighted obstructions on or surrounding an airport will be noted in airport or military remarks. Runway lights nonstandard (NSTD) are systems for which the light fixtures are not FAA approved L 800 series: color, intensity, or spacing does not meet FAA standards. Nonstandard runway lights, VASI, or any other system not listed below will be shown in airport remarks or military

SC, 1 FEB 20XX to 29 MAR 20XX

Legend 7. Chart Supplement.

18 **AIRPORT/FACILITY DIRECTORY LEGEND**

service. Temporary, emergency or limited runway edge lighting such as flares, smudge pots, lanterns or portable runway lights will also be shown in airport remarks or military service. Types of lighting are shown with the runway or runway end they serve.

NSTD—Light system fails to meet FAA standards.
LIRL—Low Intensity Runway Lights.
MIRL—Medium Intensity Runway Lights.
HIRL—High Intensity Runway Lights.
RAIL—Runway Alignment Indicator Lights.
REIL—Runway End Identifier Lights.
CL—Centerline Lights.
TDZL—Touchdown Zone Lights.
ODALS—Omni Directional Approach Lighting System.
AF OVRN—Air Force Overrun 1000′ Standard Approach Lighting System.
MALS—Medium Intensity Approach Lighting System.
MALSF—Medium Intensity Approach Lighting System with Sequenced Flashing Lights.
MALSR—Medium Intensity Approach Lighting System with Runway Alignment Indicator Lights.
RLLS—Runway Lead–in Light System

SALS—Short Approach Lighting System.
SALSF—Short Approach Lighting System with Sequenced Flashing Lights.
SSALS—Simplified Short Approach Lighting System.
SSALF—Simplified Short Approach Lighting System with Sequenced Flashing Lights.
SSALR—Simplified Short Approach Lighting System with Runway Alignment Indicator Lights.
ALSAF—High Intensity Approach Lighting System with Sequenced Flashing Lights.
ALSF1—High Intensity Approach Lighting System with Sequenced Flashing Lights, Category I, Configuration.
ALSF2—High Intensity Approach Lighting System with Sequenced Flashing Lights, Category II, Configuration.
SF—Sequenced Flashing Lights.
OLS—Optical Landing System.
WAVE–OFF.

NOTE: Civil ALSF2 may be operated as SSALR during favorable weather conditions. When runway edge lights are positioned more than 10 feet from the edge of the usable runway surface a remark will be added in the "Remarks" portion of the airport entry. This is applicable to Air Force, Air National Guard and Air Force Reserve Bases, and those joint use airfields on which they are tenants.

VISUAL GLIDESLOPE INDICATORS

APAP—A system of panels, which may or may not be lighted, used for alignment of approach path.
| PNIL | APAP on left side of runway | PNIR | APAP on right side of runway |

PAPI—Precision Approach Path Indicator
| P2L | 2–identical light units placed on left side of runway | P4L | 4–identical light units placed on left side of runway |
| P2R | 2–identical light units placed on right side of runway | P4R | 4–identical light units placed on right side of runway |

PVASI—Pulsating/steady burning visual approach slope indicator, normally a single light unit projecting two colors.
| PSIL | PVASI on left side of runway | PSIR | PVASI on right side of runway |

SAVASI—Simplified Abbreviated Visual Approach Slope Indicator
| S2L | 2–box SAVASI on left side of runway | S2R | 2–box SAVASI on right side of runway |

TRCV—Tri–color visual approach slope indicator, normally a single light unit projecting three colors.
| TRIL | TRCV on left side of runway | TRIR | TRCV on right side of runway |

VASI—Visual Approach Slope Indicator
V2L	2–box VASI on left side of runway	V6L	6–box VASI on left side of runway
V2R	2–box VASI on right side of runway	V6R	6–box VASI on right side of runway
V4L	4–box VASI on left side of runway	V12	12–box VASI on both sides of runway
V4R	4–box VASI on right side of runway	V16	16–box VASI on both sides of runway

NOTE: Approach slope angle and threshold crossing height will be shown when available; i.e., –GA 3.5° TCH 37′.

PILOT CONTROL OF AIRPORT LIGHTING

Key Mike	Function
7 times within 5 seconds	Highest intensity available
5 times within 5 seconds	Medium or lower intensity (Lower REIL or REIL–Off)
3 times within 5 seconds	Lowest intensity available (Lower REIL or REIL–Off)

Available systems will be indicated in the Service section, e.g., **LGT** ACTIVATE HIRL Rwy 07–25, MALSR Rwy 07, and VASI Rwy 07–122.8.

Where the airport is not served by an instrument approach procedure and/or has an independent type system of different specification installed by the airport sponsor, descriptions of the type lights, method of control, and operating frequency will be explained in clear text. See AIM, "Basic Flight Information and ATC Procedures," for detailed description of pilot control of airport lighting.

RUNWAY SLOPE

When available, runway slope data will be provided. Runway slope will be shown only when it is 0.3 percent or greater. On runways less than 8000 feet, the direction of the slope up will be indicated, e.g., 0.3% up NW. On runways 8000 feet or greater, the slope will be shown (up or down) on the runway end line, e.g., RWY 13: 0.3% up., RWY 31: Pole. Rgt tfc. 0.4% down.

SC, 1 FEB 20XX to 29 MAR 20XX

Legend 8. Chart Supplement.

AIRPORT/FACILITY DIRECTORY LEGEND   19

RUNWAY END DATA

Information pertaining to the runway approach end such as approach lights, touchdown zone lights, runway end identification lights, visual glideslope indicators, displaced thresholds, controlling obstruction, and right hand traffic pattern, will be shown on the specific runway end. "Rgt tfc"—Right traffic indicates right turns should be made on landing and takeoff for specified runway end. Runway Visual Range shall be shown as "RVR" appended with "T" for touchdown, "M" for midpoint, and "R" for rollout; e.g., RVR-TMR.

19 **LAND AND HOLD–SHORT OPERATIONS (LAHSO)**

LAHSO is an acronym for "Land and Hold–Short Operations" These operations include landing and holding short of an intersection runway, an intersecting taxiway, or other predetermined points on the runway other than a runway or taxiway. Measured distance represents the available landing distance on the landing runway, in feet.

Specific questions regarding these distances should be referred to the air traffic manager of the facility concerned. The Aeronautical Information Manual contains specific details on hold–short operations and markings.

20 **RUNWAY DECLARED DISTANCE INFORMATION**

TORA—Take–off Run Available. The length of runway declared available and suitable for the ground run of an aeroplane take–off.
TODA—Take–off Distance Available. The length of the take–off run available plus the length of the clearway, if provided.
ASDA—Accelerate–Stop Distance Available. The length of the take–off run available plus the length of the stopway, if provided.
LDA—Landing Distance Available. The length of runway which is declared available and suitable for the ground run of an aeroplane landing.

21 **ARRESTING GEAR/SYSTEMS**

Arresting gear is shown as it is located on the runway. The a–gear distance from the end of the appropriate runway (or into the overrun) is indicated in parentheses. A–Gear which has a bi–direction capability and can be utilized for emergency approach end engagement is indicated by a (B). Up to 15 minutes advance notice may be required for rigging A–Gear for approach and engagement. Airport listing may show availability of other than US Systems. This information is provided for emergency requirements only. Refer to current aircraft operating manuals for specific engagement weight and speed criteria based on aircraft structural restrictions and arresting system limitations.

Following is a list of current systems referenced in this publication identified by both Air Force and Navy terminology:

BI–DIRECTIONAL CABLE (B)

TYPE	DESCRIPTION
BAK–9	Rotary friction brake.
BAK–12A	Standard BAK–12 with 950 foot run out, 1–inch cable and 40,000 pound weight setting. Rotary friction brake.
BAK–12B	Extended BAK–12 with 1200 foot run, 1¼ inch Cable and 50,000 pounds weight setting. Rotary friction brake.
E28	Rotary Hydraulic (Water Brake).
M21	Rotary Hydraulic (Water Brake) Mobile.

The following device is used in conjunction with some aircraft arresting systems:

BAK–14	A device that raises a hook cable out of a slot in the runway surface and is remotely positioned for engagement by the tower on request. (In addition to personnel reaction time, the system requires up to five seconds to fully raise the cable.)
H	A device that raises a hook cable out of a slot in the runway surface and is remotely positioned for engagement by the tower on request. (In addition to personnel reaction time, the system requires up to one and one–half seconds to fully raise the cable.)

UNI–DIRECTIONAL CABLE

TYPE	DESCRIPTION
MB60	Textile brake—an emergency one–time use, modular braking system employing the tearing of specially woven textile straps to absorb the kinetic energy.
E5/E5–1/E5–3	Chain Type. At USN/USMC stations E-5 A–GEAR systems are rated, e.g., E–5 RATING–13R–1100 HW (DRY), 31L/R–1200 STD (WET). This rating is a function of the A–GEAR chain weight and length and is used to determine the maximum aircraft engaging speed. A dry rating applies to a stabilized surface (dry or wet) while a wet rating takes into account the amount (if any) of wet overrun that is not capable of withstanding the aircraft weight. These ratings are published under Service/Military/A-Gear in the entry.

FOREIGN CABLE

TYPE	DESCRIPTION	US EQUIVALENT
44B–3H	Rotary Hydraulic (Water Brake)	
CHAG	Chain	E–5

UNI–DIRECTIONAL BARRIER

TYPE	DESCRIPTION
MA–1A	Web barrier between stanchions attached to a chain energy absorber.
BAK–15	Web barrier between stanchions attached to an energy absorber (water squeezer, rotary friction, chain). Designed for wing engagement.

NOTE: Landing short of the runway threshold on a runway with a BAK–15 in the underrun is a significant hazard. The barrier in the down position still protrudes several inches above the underrun. Aircraft contact with the barrier short of the runway threshold can cause damage to the barrier and substantial damage to the aircraft.

OTHER

TYPE	DESCRIPTION
EMAS	Engineered Material Arresting System, located beyond the departure end of the runway, consisting of high energy absorbing materials which will crush under the weight of an aircraft.

SC, 1 FEB 20XX to 29 MAR 20XX

Legend 9. Chart Supplement.

20   **AIRPORT/FACILITY DIRECTORY LEGEND**

㉒ **SERVICE**

SERVICING—CIVIL

S1: Minor airframe repairs.	S5: Major airframe repairs.
S2: Minor airframe and minor powerplant repairs.	S6: Minor airframe and major powerplant repairs.
S3: Major airframe and minor powerplant repairs.	S7: Major powerplant repairs.
S4: Major airframe and major powerplant repairs.	S8: Minor powerplant repairs.

FUEL

CODE	FUEL	CODE	FUEL
80	Grade 80 gasoline (Red)	B	Jet B, Wide–cut, turbine fuel without FS–II*, FP** minus 50° C.
100	Grade 100 gasoline (Green)		
100LL	100LL gasoline (low lead) (Blue)	B+	Jet B, Wide–cut, turbine fuel with FS–II*, FP** minus 50° C
115	Grade 115 gasoline (115/145 military specification) (Purple)		
		J4 (JP4)	(JP–4 military specification) FP** minus 58° C.
A	Jet A, Kerosene, without FS–II*, FP** minus 40° C.	J5 (JP5)	(JP–5 military specification) Kerosene with FS–II, FP** minus 46°C.
A+	Jet A, Kerosene, with FS–II*, FP** minus 40°C.	J8 (JP8)	(JP–8 military specification) Jet A–1, Kerosene with FS–II*, CI/LI#, SDA##, FP** minus 47°C.
A++	Jet A, Kerosene, with FS–II*, CI/LI#, SDA##, FP** minus 40°C.		
A++100	Jet A, Kerosene, with FS–II*, CI/LI#, SDA##, FP** minus 40°C, with +100 fuel additive that improves thermal stability characteristics of kerosene jet fuels.	J8+100	(JP–8 military specification) Jet A–1, Kerosene with FS–II*, CI/LI#, SDA##,FP** minus 47°C, with +100 fuel additive that improves thermal stability characteristics of kerosene jet fuels.
		J	(Jet Fuel Type Unknown)
A1	Jet A–1, Kerosene, without FS–II*, FP** minus 47°C.	MOGAS	Automobile gasoline which is to be used as aircraft fuel.
A1+	Jet A–1, Kerosene with FS–II*, FP** minus 47° C.	UL91	Unleaded Grade 91 gasoline
		UL94	Unleaded Grade 94 gasoline

*(Fuel System Icing Inhibitor)   **(Freeze Point)   # (Corrosion Inhibitors/Lubricity Improvers)   ## (Static Dissipator Additive)

NOTE: Certain automobile gasoline may be used in specific aircraft engines if a FAA supplemental type certificate has been obtained. Automobile gasoline, which is to be used in aircraft engines, will be identified as "MOGAS", however, the grade/type and other octane rating will not be published.

Data shown on fuel availability represents the most recent information the publisher has been able to acquire. Because of a variety of factors, the fuel listed may not always be obtainable by transient civil pilots. Confirmation of availability of fuel should be made directly with fuel suppliers at locations where refueling is planned.

OXYGEN—CIVIL

OX 1	High Pressure	OX 3	High Pressure—Replacement Bottles
OX 2	Low Pressure	OX 4	Low Pressure—Replacement Bottles

SERVICE—MILITARY

Specific military services available at the airport are listed under this general heading. Remarks applicable to any military service are shown in the individual service listing.

JET AIRCRAFT STARTING UNITS (JASU)—MILITARY

The numeral preceding the type of unit indicates the number of units available. The absence of the numeral indicates ten or more units available. If the number of units is unknown, the number one will be shown. Absence of JASU designation indicates non–availability.

The following is a list of current JASU systems referenced in this publication:

USAF JASU (For variations in technical data, refer to T.O. 35–1–7.)

ELECTRICAL STARTING UNITS:

A/M32A–86	AC: 115/200v, 3 phase, 90 kva, 0.8 pf, 4 wire
	DC: 28v, 1500 amp, 72 kw (with TR pack)
MC–1A	AC: 115/208v, 400 cycle, 3 phase, 37.5 kva, 0.8 pf, 108 amp, 4 wire
	DC: 28v, 500 amp, 14 kw
MD–3	AC: 115/208v, 400 cycle, 3 phase, 60 kva, 0.75 pf, 4 wire
	DC: 28v, 1500 amp, 45 kw, split bus
MD–3A	AC: 115/208v, 400 cycle, 3 phase, 60 kva, 0.75 pf, 4 wire
	DC: 28v, 1500 amp, 45 kw, split bus
MD–3M	AC: 115/208v, 400 cycle, 3 phase, 60 kva, 0.75 pf, 4 wire
	DC: 28v, 500 amp, 15 kw
MD–4	AC: 120/208v, 400 cycle, 3 phase, 62.5 kva, 0.8 pf, 175 amp, "WYE" neutral ground, 4 wire, 120v, 400 cycle, 3 phase, 62.5 kva, 0.8 pf, 303 amp, "DELTA" 3 wire, 120v, 400 cycle, 1 phase, 62.5 kva, 0.8 pf, 520 amp, 2 wire

SC, 1 FEB 20XX to 29 MAR 20XX

Legend 10. Chart Supplement.

AIRPORT/FACILITY DIRECTORY LEGEND   21

AIR STARTING UNITS

AM32–95	150 +/– 5 lb/min (2055 +/– 68 cfm) at 51 +/– 2 psia
AM32A–95	150 +/– 5 lb/min @ 49 +/– 2 psia (35 +/– 2 psig)
LASS	150 +/– 5 lb/min @ 49 +/– 2 psia
MA–1A	82 lb/min (1123 cfm) at 130° air inlet temp, 45 psia (min) air outlet press
MC–1	15 cfm, 3500 psia
MC–1A	15 cfm, 3500 psia
MC–2A	15 cfm, 200 psia
MC–11	8,000 cu in cap, 4000 psig, 15 cfm

COMBINED AIR AND ELECTRICAL STARTING UNITS:

AGPU	AC: 115/200v, 400 cycle, 3 phase, 30 kw gen
	DC: 28v, 700 amp
	AIR: 60 lb/min @ 40 psig @ sea level
AM32A–60*	AIR: 120 +/– 4 lb/min (1644 +/– 55 cfm) at 49 +/– 2 psia
	AC: 120/208v, 400 cycle, 3 phase, 75 kva, 0.75 pf, 4 wire, 120v, 1 phase, 25 kva
	DC: 28v, 500 amp, 15 kw
AM32A–60A	AIR: 150 +/– 5 lb/min (2055 +/– 68 cfm at 51 +/– psia
	AC: 120/208v, 400 cycle, 3 phase, 75 kva, 0.75 pf, 4 wire
	DC: 28v, 200 amp, 5.6 kw
AM32A–60B*	AIR: 130 lb/min, 50 psia
	AC: 120/208v, 400 cycle, 3 phase, 75 kva, 0.75 pf, 4 wire
	DC: 28v, 200 amp, 5.6 kw

*NOTE: During combined air and electrical loads, the pneumatic circuitry takes preference and will limit the amount of electrical power available.

USN JASU

ELECTRICAL STARTING UNITS:

NC–8A/A1	DC: 500 amp constant, 750 amp intermittent, 28v;
	AC: 60 kva @ .8 pf, 115/200v, 3 phase, 400 Hz.
NC–10A/A1/B/C	DC: 750 amp constant, 1000 amp intermittent, 28v;
	AC: 90 kva, 115/200v, 3 phase, 400 Hz.

AIR STARTING UNITS:

GTC–85/GTE–85	120 lbs/min @ 45 psi.
MSU–200NAV/A/U47A–5	204 lbs/min @ 56 psia.
WELLS AIR START SYSTEM	180 lbs/min @ 75 psi or 120 lbs/min @ 45 psi. Simultaneous multiple start capability.

COMBINED AIR AND ELECTRICAL STARTING UNITS:

NCPP–105/RCPT	180 lbs/min @ 75 psi or 120 lbs/min @ 45 psi. 700 amp, 28v DC. 120/208v, 400 Hz AC, 30 kva.

ARMY JASU

59B2–1B	28v, 7.5 kw, 280 amp.

OTHER JASU

ELECTRICAL STARTING UNITS (DND):

CE12	AC 115/200v, 140 kva, 400 Hz, 3 phase
CE13	AC 115/200v, 60 kva, 400 Hz, 3 phase
CE14	AC/DC 115/200v, 140 kva, 400 Hz, 3 phase, 28vDC, 1500 amp
CE15	DC 22–35v, 500 amp continuous 1100 amp intermittent
CE16	DC 22–35v, 500 amp continuous 1100 amp intermittent soft start

AIR STARTING UNITS (DND):

CA2	ASA 45.5 psig, 116.4 lb/min

COMBINED AIR AND ELECTRICAL STARTING UNITS (DND)

CEA1	AC 120/208v, 60 kva, 400 Hz, 3 phase DC 28v, 75 amp
	AIR 112.5 lb/min, 47 psig

ELECTRICAL STARTING UNITS (OTHER)

C–26	28v 45kw 115–200v 15kw 380–800 Hz 1 phase 2 wire
C–26–B, C–26–C	28v 45kw: Split Bus: 115–200v 15kw 380–800 Hz 1 phase 2 wire
E3	DC 28v/10kw

AIR STARTING UNITS (OTHER):

A4	40 psi/2 lb/sec (LPAS Mk12, Mk12L, Mk12A, Mk1, Mk2B)
MA–1	150 Air HP, 115 lb/min 50 psia
MA–2	250 Air HP, 150 lb/min 75 psia

CARTRIDGE:

MXU–4A	USAF

SC, 1 FEB 20XX to 29 MAR 20XX

Legend 11. Chart Supplement.

A1-12

22 AIRPORT/FACILITY DIRECTORY LEGEND

FUEL—MILITARY

Fuel available through US Military Base supply, DESC Into–Plane Contracts and/or reciprocal agreement is listed first and is followed by (Mil). At commercial airports where Into–Plane contracts are in place, the name of the refueling agent is shown. Military fuel should be used first if it is available. When military fuel cannot be obtained but Into–Plane contract fuel is available, Government aircraft must refuel with the contract fuel and applicable refueling agent to avoid any breach in contract terms and conditions. Fuel not available through the above is shown preceded by NC (no contract). When fuel is obtained from NC sources, local purchase procedures must be followed. The US Military Aircraft Identaplates DD Form 1896 (Jet Fuel), DD Form 1897 (Avgas) and AF Form 1245 (Avgas) are used at military installations only. The US Government Aviation Into–Plane Reimbursement (AIR) Card (currently issued by AVCARD) is the instrument to be used to obtain fuel under a DESC Into–Plane Contract and for NC purchases if the refueling agent at the commercial airport accepts the AVCARD. A current list of contract fuel locations is available online at https://cis.energy.dla.mil/ip_cis/. See legend item 14 for fuel code and description.

SUPPORTING FLUIDS AND SYSTEMS—MILITARY

CODE	
ADI	Anti–Detonation Injection Fluid—Reciprocating Engine Aircraft.
W	Water Thrust Augmentation—Jet Aircraft.
WAI	Water–Alcohol Injection Type, Thrust Augmentation—Jet Aircraft.
SP	Single Point Refueling.
PRESAIR	Air Compressors rated 3,000 PSI or more.
De–Ice	Anti–icing/De–icing/Defrosting Fluid (MIL–A–8243).

OXYGEN:

LPOX	Low pressure oxygen servicing.
HPOX	High pressure oxygen servicing.
LHOX	Low and high pressure oxygen servicing.
LOX	Liquid oxygen servicing.
OXRB	Oxygen replacement bottles. (Maintained primarily at Naval stations for use in acft where oxygen can be replenished only by replacement of cylinders.)
OX	Indicates oxygen servicing when type of servicing is unknown.

NOTE: Combinations of above items is used to indicate complete oxygen servicing available;

LHOXRB	Low and high pressure oxygen servicing and replacement bottles;
LPOXRB	Low pressure oxygen replacement bottles only, etc.

NOTE: Aircraft will be serviced with oxygen procured under military specifications only. Aircraft will not be serviced with medical oxygen.

NITROGEN:

LPNIT — Low pressure nitrogen servicing.

HPNIT — High pressure nitrogen servicing.

LHNIT — Low and high pressure nitrogen servicing.

OIL—MILITARY

US AVIATION OILS (MIL SPECS):

CODE	GRADE, TYPE
O–113	1065, Reciprocating Engine Oil (MIL–L–6082)
O–117	1100, Reciprocating Engine Oil (MIL–L–6082)
O–117+	1100, O–117 plus cyclohexanone (MIL–L–6082)
O–123	1065, (Dispersant), Reciprocating Engine Oil (MIL–L–22851 Type III)
O–128	1100, (Dispersant), Reciprocating Engine Oil (MIL–L–22851 Type II)
O–132	1005, Jet Engine Oil (MIL–L–6081)
O–133	1010, Jet Engine Oil (MIL–L–6081)
O–147	None, MIL–L–6085A Lubricating Oil, Instrument, Synthetic
O–148	None, MIL–L–7808 (Synthetic Base) Turbine Engine Oil
O–149	None, Aircraft Turbine Engine Synthetic, 7.5c St
O–155	None, MIL–L–6086C, Aircraft, Medium Grade
O–156	None, MIL–L–23699 (Synthetic Base), Turboprop and Turboshaft Engines
JOAP/SOAP	Joint Oil Analysis Program. JOAP support is furnished during normal duty hours, other times on request. (JOAP and SOAP programs provide essentially the same service, JOAP is now the standard joint service supported program.)

TRANSIENT ALERT (TRAN ALERT)—MILITARY

Tran Alert service is considered to include all services required for normal aircraft turn–around, e.g., servicing (fuel, oil, oxygen, etc.), debriefing to determine requirements for maintenance, minor maintenance, inspection and parking assistance of transient aircraft. Drag chute repack, specialized maintenance, or extensive repairs will be provided within the capabilities and priorities of the base. Delays can be anticipated after normal duty hours/holidays/weekends regardless of the hours of transient maintenance operation. Pilots should not expect aircraft to be serviced for TURN–AROUNDS during time periods when servicing or maintenance manpower is not available. In the case of airports not operated exclusively by US military, the servicing indicated by the remarks will not always be available for US military aircraft. When transient alert services are not shown, facilities are unknown. NO PRIORITY BASIS—means that transient alert services will be provided only after all the requirements for mission/tactical assigned aircraft have been accomplished.

SC, 1 FEB 20XX to 29 MAR 20XX

Legend 12. Chart Supplement.

AIRPORT/FACILITY DIRECTORY LEGEND   23

㉓ AIRPORT REMARKS

The Attendance Schedule is the months, days and hours the airport is actually attended. Airport attendance does not mean watchman duties or telephone accessibility, but rather an attendant or operator on duty to provide at least minimum services (e.g., repairs, fuel, transportation).

Airport Remarks have been grouped in order of applicability. Airport remarks are limited to those items of information that are determined essential for operational use, i.e., conditions of a permanent or indefinite nature and conditions that will remain in effect for more than 30 days concerning aeronautical facilities, services, maintenance available, procedures or hazards, knowledge of which is essential for safe and efficient operation of aircraft. Information concerning permanent closing of a runway or taxiway will not be shown. A note "See Special Notices" shall be applied within this remarks section when a special notice applicable to the entry is contained in the Special Notices section of this publication.

Parachute Jumping indicates parachute jumping areas associated with the airport. See Parachute Jumping Area section of this publication for additional Information.

Landing Fee indicates landing charges for private or non–revenue producing aircraft. In addition, fees may be charged for planes that remain over a couple of hours and buy no services, or at major airline terminals for all aircraft.

Note: Unless otherwise stated, remarks including runway ends refer to the runway's approach end.

㉔ MILITARY REMARKS

Joint Civil/Military airports contain both Airport Remarks and Military Remarks. Military Remarks published for these airports are applicable only to the military. Military and joint Military/Civil airports contain only Military Remarks. Remarks contained in this section may not be applicable to civil users. When both sets of remarks exist, the first set is applicable to the primary operator of the airport. Remarks applicable to a tenant on the airport are shown preceded by the tenant organization, i.e., (A) (AF) (N) (ANG), etc. Military airports operate 24 hours unless otherwise specified. Airport operating hours are listed first (airport operating hours will only be listed if they are different than the airport attended hours or if the attended hours are unavailable) followed by pertinent remarks in order of applicability. Remarks will include information on restrictions, hazards, traffic pattern, noise abatement, customs/agriculture/immigration, and miscellaneous information applicable to the Military.

Type of restrictions:

CLOSED: When designated closed, the airport is restricted from use by all aircraft unless stated otherwise. Any closure applying to specific type of aircraft or operation will be so stated. USN/USMC/USAF airports are considered closed during non–operating hours. Closed airports may be utilized during an emergency provided there is a safe landing area.

OFFICIAL BUSINESS ONLY: The airfield is closed to all transient military aircraft for obtaining routine services such as fueling, passenger drop off or pickup, practice approaches, parking, etc. The airfield may be used by aircrews and aircraft if official government business (including civilian) must be conducted on or near the airfield and prior permission is received from the airfield manager.

AF OFFICIAL BUSINESS ONLY OR NAVY OFFICIAL BUSINESS ONLY: Indicates that the restriction applies only to service indicated.

PRIOR PERMISSION REQUIRED (PPR): Airport is closed to transient aircraft unless approval for operation is obtained from the appropriate commander through Chief, Airfield Management or Airfield Operations Officer. Official Business or PPR does not preclude the use of US Military airports as an alternate for IFR flights. If a non–US military airport is used as a weather alternate and requires a PPR, the PPR must be requested and confirmed before the flight departs. The purpose of PPR is to control volume and flow of traffic rather than to prohibit it. Prior permission is required for all aircraft requiring transient alert service outside the published transient alert duty hours. All aircraft carrying hazardous materials must obtain prior permission as outlined in AFJI 11–204, AR 95–27, OPNAVINST 3710.7.

Note: OFFICIAL BUSINESS ONLY AND PPR restrictions are not applicable to Special Air Mission (SAM) or Special Air Resource (SPAR) aircraft providing person or persons on aboard are designated Code 6 or higher as explained in AFJMAN 11–213, AR 95–11, OPNAVINST 3722–8J. Official Business Only or PPR do not preclude the use of the airport as an alternate for IFR flights.

㉕ AIRPORT MANAGER

The phone number of the airport manager.

㉖ WEATHER DATA SOURCES

Weather data sources will be listed alphabetically followed by their assigned frequencies and/or telephone number and hours of operation.

ASOS—Automated Surface Observing System. Reports the same as an AWOS–3 plus precipitation identification and intensity, and freezing rain occurrence;

    AWOS—Automated Weather Observing System

    AWOS–A—reports altimeter setting (all other information is advisory only).

    AWOS–AV—reports altimeter and visibility.

    AWOS–1—reports altimeter setting, wind data and usually temperature, dew point and density altitude.

    AWOS–2—reports the same as AWOS–1 plus visibility.

    AWOS–3—reports the same as AWOS–1 plus visibility and cloud/ceiling data.

    AWOS–3P reports the same as the AWOS–3 system, plus a precipitation identification sensor.

    AWOS–3PT reports the same as the AWOS–3 system, plus precipitation identification sensor and a thunderstorm/lightning reporting capability.

SC, 1 FEB 20XX to 29 MAR 20XX

Legend 13. Chart Supplement.

24   **AIRPORT/FACILITY DIRECTORY LEGEND**

AWOS–3T reports the same as AWOS–3 system and includes a thunderstorm/lightning reporting capability.

See AIM, Basic Flight Information and ATC Procedures for detailed description of Weather Data Sources.

AWOS–4—reports same as AWOS–3 system, plus precipitation occurrence, type and accumulation, freezing rain, thunderstorm and runway surface sensors.

HIWAS—See RADIO AIDS TO NAVIGATION

LAWRS—Limited Aviation Weather Reporting Station where observers report cloud height, weather, obstructions to vision, temperature and dewpoint (in most cases), surface wind, altimeter and pertinent remarks.

LLWAS—indicates a Low Level Wind Shear Alert System consisting of a center field and several field perimeter anemometers.

SAWRS—identifies airports that have a Supplemental Aviation Weather Reporting Station available to pilots for current weather information.

SWSL—Supplemental Weather Service Location providing current local weather information via radio and telephone.

TDWR—indicates airports that have Terminal Doppler Weather Radar.

WSP—indicates airports that have Weather System Processor.

When the automated weather source is broadcast over an associated airport NAVAID frequency (see NAVAID line), it shall be indicated by a bold ASOS, AWOS, or HIWAS followed by the frequency, identifier and phone number, if available.

㉗ **COMMUNICATIONS**

Airport terminal control facilities and radio communications associated with the airport shall be shown. When the call sign is not the same as the airport name the call sign will be shown. Frequencies shall normally be shown in descending order with the primary frequency listed first. Frequencies will be listed, together with sectorization indicated by outbound radials, and hours of operation. Communications will be listed in sequence as follows:

Single Frequency Approach (SFA), Common Traffic Advisory Frequency (CTAF), Aeronautical Advisory Stations (UNICOM) or (AUNICOM), and Automatic Terminal Information Service (ATIS) along with their frequency is shown, where available, on the line following the heading "COMMUNICATIONS." When the CTAF and UNICOM frequencies are the same, the frequency will be shown as CTAF/UNICOM 122.8.

The FSS telephone nationwide is toll free 1–800–WX–BRIEF (1–800–992–7433). When the FSS is located on the field it will be indicated as "on arpt". Frequencies available at the FSS will follow in descending order. Remote Communications Outlet (RCO) providing service to the airport followed by the frequency and FSS RADIO name will be shown when available. FSS's provide information on airport conditions, radio aids and other facilities, and process flight plans. Airport Advisory Service (AAS) is provided on the CTAF by FSS's for select non–tower airports or airports where the tower is not in operation. (See AIM, Para 4–1–9 Traffic Advisory Practices at Airports Without Operating Control Towers or AC 90–42C.)

Aviation weather briefing service is provided by FSS specialists. Flight and weather briefing services are also available by calling the telephone numbers listed.

Remote Communications Outlet (RCO)—An unmanned air/ground communications facility that is remotely controlled and provides UHF or VHF communications capability to extend the service range of an FSS.

Civil Communications Frequencies–Civil communications frequencies used in the FSS air/ground system are operated on 122.0, 122.2, 123.6; emergency 121.5; plus receive–only on 122.1.

    a.   122.0 is assigned as the Enroute Flight Advisory Service frequency at selected FSS RADIO outlets.

    b.   122.2 is assigned as a common enroute frequency.

    c.   123.6 is assigned as the airport advisory frequency at select non–tower locations. At airports with a tower, FSS may provide airport advisories on the tower frequency when tower is closed.

    d.   122.1 is the primary receive–only frequency at VOR's.

    e.   Some FSS's are assigned 50 kHz frequencies in the 122–126 MHz band (eg. 122.45). Pilots using the FSS A/G system should refer to this directory or appropriate charts to determine frequencies available at the FSS or remoted facility through which they wish to communicate.

Emergency frequency 121.5 and 243.0 are available at all Flight Service Stations, most Towers, Approach Control and RADAR facilities.

Frequencies published followed by the letter "T" or "R", indicate that the facility will only transmit or receive respectively on that frequency. All radio aids to navigation (NAVAID) frequencies are transmit only. In cases where communications frequencies are annotated with (R) or (E), (R) indicates Radar Capability and (E) indicates Emergency Frequency.

TERMINAL SERVICES

SFA—Single Frequency Approach.

CTAF—A program designed to get all vehicles and aircraft at airports without an operating control tower on a common frequency.

ATIS—A continuous broadcast of recorded non–control information in selected terminal areas.

D–ATIS—Digital ATIS provides ATIS information in text form outside the standard reception range of conventional ATIS via landline & data link communications and voice message within range of existing transmitters.

AUNICOM—Automated UNICOM is a computerized, command response system that provides automated weather, radio check capability and airport advisory information selected from an automated menu by microphone clicks.

UNICOM—A non–government air/ground radio communications facility which may provide airport information.

PTD—Pilot to Dispatcher.

APP CON—Approach Control. The symbol Ⓡ indicates radar approach control.

TOWER—Control tower.

GCA—Ground Control Approach System.

GND CON—Ground Control.

SC, 1 FEB 20XX to 29 MAR 20XX

Legend 14. Chart Supplement.

AIRPORT/FACILITY DIRECTORY LEGEND   25

GCO—Ground Communication Outlet—An unstaffed, remotely controlled, ground/ground communications facility. Pilots at uncontrolled airports may contact ATC and FSS via VHF to a telephone connection to obtain an instrument clearance or close a VFR or IFR flight plan. They may also get an updated weather briefing prior to takeoff. Pilots will use four "key clicks" on the VHF radio to contact the appropriate ATC facility or six "key clicks" to contact the FSS. The GCO system is intended to be used only on the ground.

DEP CON—Departure Control. The symbol ® indicates radar departure control.

CLNC DEL—Clearance Delivery.

CPDLC—Controller Pilot Data Link Communication. FANS ATC data communication capability from the aircraft to the ATC Data Link system.

PRE TAXI CLNC—Pre taxi clearance.

VFR ADVSY SVC—VFR Advisory Service. Service provided by Non–Radar Approach Control.
  Advisory Service for VFR aircraft (upon a workload basis) ctc APP CON.

COMD POST—Command Post followed by the operator call sign in parenthesis.

PMSV—Pilot–to–Metro Service call sign, frequency and hours of operation, when full service is other than continuous. PMSV installations at which weather observation service is available shall be indicated, following the frequency and/or hours of operation as "Wx obsn svc 1900–0000Z‡" or "other times" may be used when no specific time is given. PMSV facilities manned by forecasters are considered "Full Service". PMSV facilities manned by weather observers are listed as "Limited Service".

OPS—Operations followed by the operator call sign in parenthesis.

CON

RANGE

FLT FLW—Flight Following

MEDIVAC

NOTE: Communication frequencies followed by the letter "X" indicate frequency available on request.

㉘ AIRSPACE

Information concerning Class B, C, and part–time D and E surface area airspace shall be published with effective times, if available.

CLASS B—Radar Sequencing and Separation Service for all aircraft in CLASS B airspace.

CLASS C—Separation between IFR and VFR aircraft and sequencing of VFR arrivals to the primary airport.

TRSA—Radar Sequencing and Separation Service for participating VFR Aircraft within a Terminal Radar Service Area.

Class C, D, and E airspace described in this publication is that airspace usually consisting of a 5 NM radius core surface area that begins at the surface and extends upward to an altitude above the airport elevation (charted in MSL for Class C and Class D). Class E surface airspace normally extends from the surface up to but not including the overlying controlled airspace.

When part–time Class C or Class D airspace defaults to Class E, the core surface area becomes Class E. This will be formatted as:
AIRSPACE: CLASS C svc "times" ctc **APP CON** other times CLASS E:
or
AIRSPACE: CLASS D svc "times" other times CLASS E.

When a part–time Class C, Class D or Class E surface area defaults to Class G, the core surface area becomes Class G up to, but not including, the overlying controlled airspace. Normally, the overlying controlled airspace is Class E airspace beginning at either 700´ or 1200´ AGL and may be determined by consulting the relevant VFR Sectional or Terminal Area Charts. This will be formatted as:
AIRSPACE: CLASS C svc "times" ctc **APP CON** other times CLASS G, with CLASS E 700´ (or 1200´) AGL & abv:
or
AIRSPACE: CLASS D svc "times" other times CLASS G with CLASS E 700´ (or 1200´) AGL & abv:
or
AIRSPACE: CLASS E svc "times" other times CLASS G with CLASS E 700´ (or 1200´) AGL & abv.

NOTE: AIRSPACE SVC "TIMES" INCLUDE ALL ASSOCIATED ARRIVAL EXTENSIONS. Surface area arrival extensions for instrument approach procedures become part of the primary core surface area. These extensions may be either Class D or Class E airspace and are effective concurrent with the times of the primary core surface area. For example, when a part–time Class C, Class D or Class E surface area defaults to Class G, the associated arrival extensions will default to Class G at the same time. When a part–time Class C or Class D surface area defaults to Class E, the arrival extensions will remain in effect as Class E airspace.

NOTE: CLASS E AIRSPACE EXTENDING UPWARD FROM 700 FEET OR MORE ABOVE THE SURFACE, DESIGNATED IN CONJUNCTION WITH AN AIRPORT WITH AN APPROVED INSTRUMENT PROCEDURE.
Class E 700´ AGL (shown as magenta vignette on sectional charts) and 1200´ AGL (blue vignette) areas are designated when necessary to provide controlled airspace for transitioning to/from the terminal and enroute environments. Unless otherwise specified, these 700´/1200´ AGL Class E airspace areas remain in effect continuously, regardless of airport operating hours or surface area status. These transition areas should not be confused with surface areas or arrival extensions.

(See Chapter 3, AIRSPACE, in the Aeronautical Information Manual for further details)

SC, 1 FEB 20XX to 29 MAR 20XX

Legend 15. Chart Supplement.

26   **AIRPORT/FACILITY DIRECTORY LEGEND**

㉙ **VOR TEST FACILITY (VOT)**

The VOT transmits a signal which provided users a convenient means to determine the operational status and accuracy of an aircraft VOR receiver while on the ground. Ground based VOTs and the associated frequency shall be shown when available. VOTs are also shown with identifier, frequency and referenced remarks in the VOR Receiver Check section in the back of this publication.

㉚ **RADIO AIDS TO NAVIGATION**

The Airport/Facility Directory section of the Chart Supplement lists, by facility name, all Radio Aids to Navigation that appear on FAA, Aeronautical Information Services Visual or IFR Aeronautical Charts and those upon which the FAA has approved an Instrument Approach Procedure, with exception of selected TACANs. All VOR, VORTAC, TACAN and ILS equipment in the National Airspace System has an automatic monitoring and shutdown feature in the event of malfunction. Unmonitored, as used in this publication, for any navigational aid, means that monitoring personnel cannot observe the malfunction or shutdown signal. The NAVAID NOTAM file identifier will be shown as "NOTAM FILE IAD" and will be listed on the Radio Aids to Navigation line. When two or more NAVAIDS are listed and the NOTAM file identifier is different from that shown on the Radio Aids to Navigation line, it will be shown with the NAVAID listing. NOTAM file identifiers for ILSs and its components (e.g., NDB (LOM) are the same as the associated airports and are not repeated. Automated Surface Observing System (ASOS), Automated Weather Observing System (AWOS), and Hazardous Inflight Weather Advisory Service (HIWAS) will be shown when this service is broadcast over selected NAVAIDs.

NAVAID information is tabulated as indicated in the following sample:

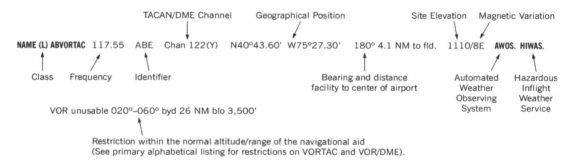

Note: Those DME channel numbers with a (Y) suffix require TACAN to be placed in the "Y" mode to receive distance information.

HIWAS—Hazardous Inflight Weather Advisory Service is a continuous broadcast of inflight weather advisories including summarized SIGMETs, convective SIGMETs, AIRMETs and urgent PIREPs. HIWAS is presently broadcast over selected VOR's throughout the U.S.

ASR/PAR—Indicates that Surveillance (ASR) or Precision (PAR) radar instrument approach minimums are published in the U.S. Terminal Procedures. Only part–time hours of operation will be shown.

APPENDIX 1 ■ FAA Legends

Legend 16. Chart Supplement.

APPENDIX 2

FAA FIGURES

The FAA Figures are a part of the Airman Knowledge Testing Supplement for Commercial Pilot designed by the FAA Flight Standards Service. The FAA deletes figures as they become obsolete and this appendix only includes figures that apply to airplanes. For example, figures that correspond to test questions regarding gliders, airships, rotorcraft, and balloons have been removed. Therefore, in some cases, the figure numbers are not continuous. Refer to these figures when required to answer questions about information in a figure. A copy of this supplement is available during your test.

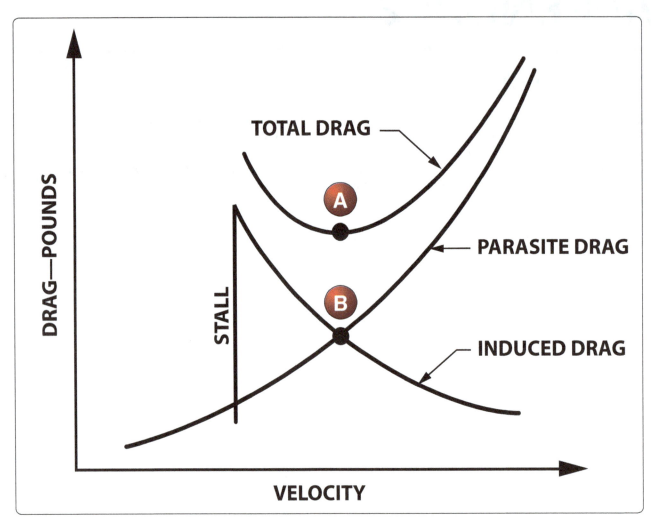

Figure 1. Drag vs. Velocity.

GROSS WEIGHT 2,750 LB			ANGLE OF BANK			
			LEVEL	30°	45°	60°
POWER			GEAR AND FLAPS UP			
ON		MPH	62	67	74	88
		KTS	54	58	64	76
OFF		MPH	75	81	89	106
		KTS	65	70	77	92
			GEAR AND FLAPS DOWN			
ON		MPH	54	58	64	76
		KTS	47	50	56	66
OFF		MPH	66	71	78	93
		KTS	57	62	68	81

Figure 2. Stall Speeds.

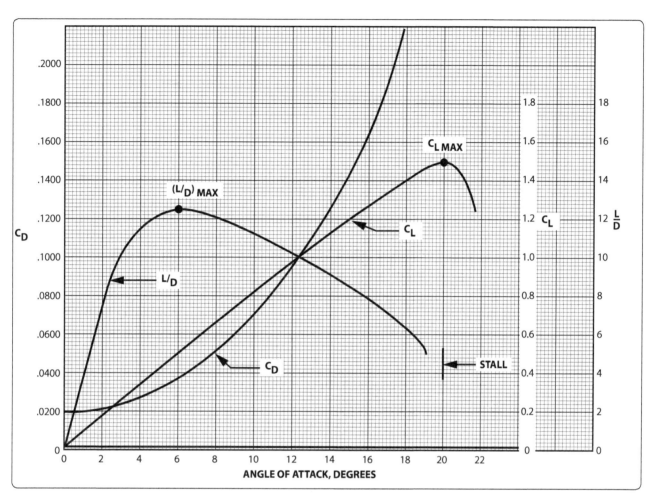

Figure 3. Angle of Attack vs. Lift.

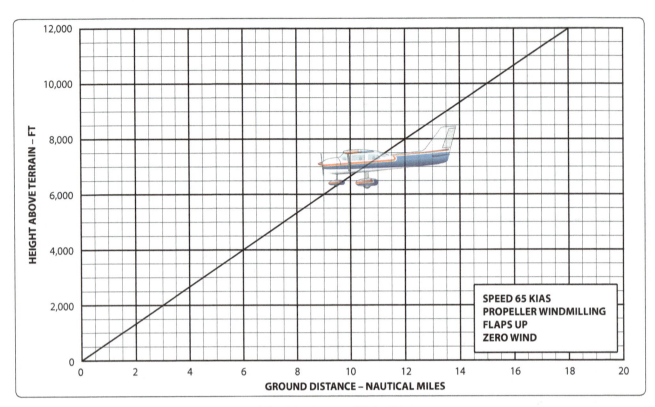

Figure 3A. Maximum Glide Distance.

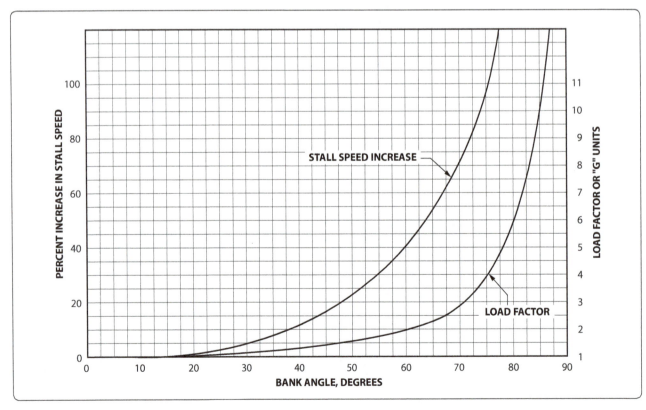

Figure 4. Stall Speed vs. Load Factor.

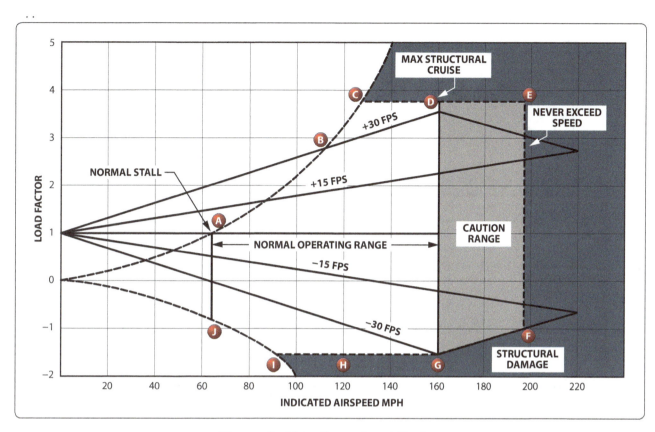

Figure 5. Velocity vs. Load Factor.

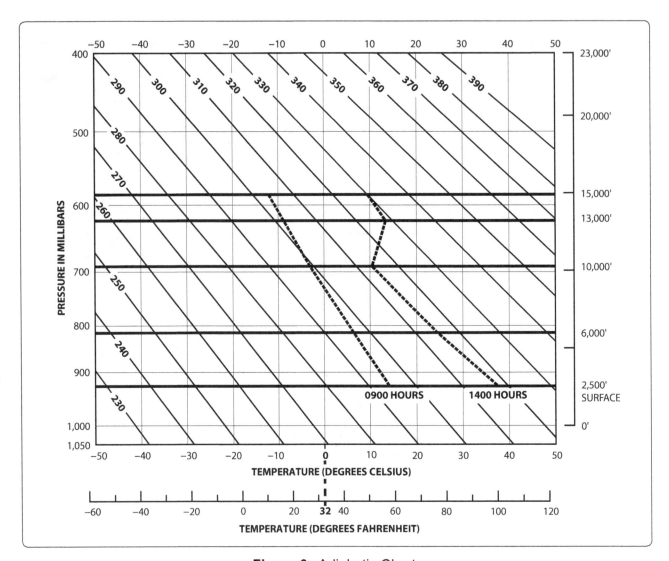

Figure 6. Adiabatic Chart.

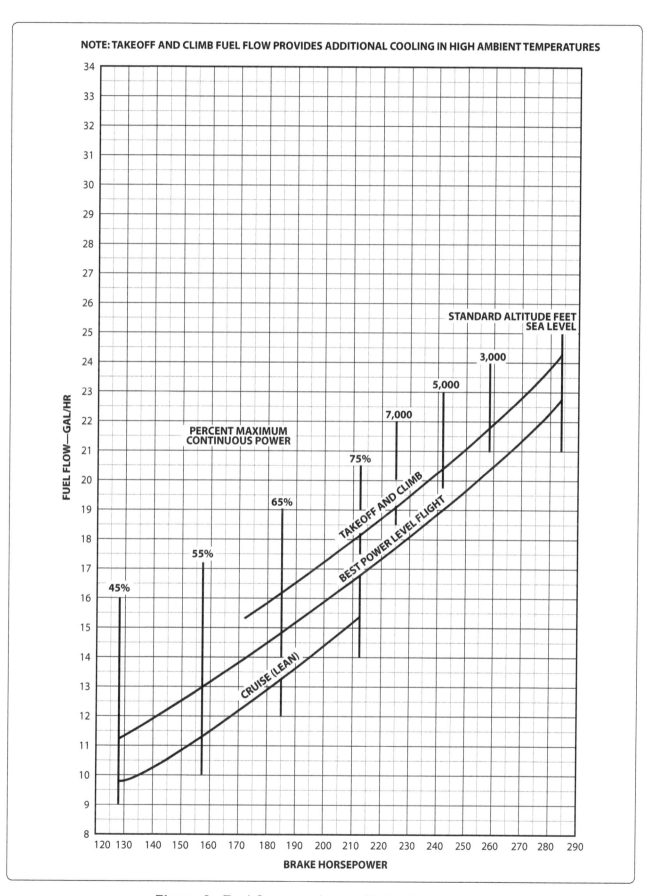

Figure 8. Fuel Consumption vs. Brake Horsepower.

NORMAL CLIMB—100 KIAS

CONDITIONS:
FLAPS UP
GEAR UP
2,550 RPM
25 INCHES MP OR FULL THROTTLE
COWL FLAPS OPEN
STANDARD TEMPERATURE

MIXTURE SETTING	
PRESS ALT	PPH
S.L. to 4,000	108
8,000	96
12,000	84

NOTES:
1. INCREASE TIME, FUEL, AND DISTANCE BY 10% FOR EACH 10 °C ABOVE STANDARD TEMPERATURE.
2. ADD 12 POUNDS OF FUEL FOR ENGINE START, TAXI, AND TAKEOFF ALLOWANCE.
3. DISTANCES SHOWN ARE BASED ON ZERO WIND.

WEIGHT (LB)	PRESS ALT (FT)	RATE OF CLIMB (FPM)	FROM SEA LEVEL		
			TIME (MIN)	FUEL USED (LB)	DISTANCE (NM)
3,800	S.L.	580	0	0	0
	2,000	580	3	6	6
	4,000	570	7	12	12
	6,000	470	11	19	19
	8,000	365	16	27	28
	10,000	265	22	37	40
	12,000	165	32	51	59
3,500	S.L.	685	0	0	0
	2,000	685	3	5	5
	4,000	675	6	11	10
	6,000	565	9	16	16
	8,000	455	13	23	23
	10,000	350	18	31	33
	12,000	240	25	41	46
3,200	S.L.	800	0	0	0
	2,000	800	2	4	4
	4,000	795	5	9	8
	6,000	675	8	14	13
	8,000	560	11	19	19
	10,000	445	15	25	27
	12,000	325	20	33	37

Figure 9. Fuel, Time, and Distance to Climb.

MAXIMUM RATE OF CLIMB

CONDITIONS:
FLAPS UP
GEAR UP
2,700 RPM
FULL THROTTLE
MIXTURE SET AT PLACARD FUEL FLOW
COWL FLAPS OPEN
STANDARD TEMPERATURE

MIXTURE SETTING	
PRESS ALT	PPH
S.L.	138
4,000	126
8,000	114
12,000	102

NOTES:
1. ADD 12 POUNDS OF FUEL FOR ENGINE START, TAXI, AND TAKEOFF ALLOWANCE.
2. INCREASE TIME, FUEL, AND DISTANCE BY 10% FOR EACH 10 °C ABOVE STANDARD TEMPERATURE.
3. DISTANCES SHOWN ARE BASED ON ZERO WIND.

WEIGHT (LB)	PRESS ALT (FT)	CLIMB SPEED (KIAS)	RATE OF CLIMB (FPM)	FROM SEA LEVEL		
				TIME (MIN)	FUEL USED (LB)	DISTANCE (NM)
3,800	S.L.	97	860	0	0	0
	2,000	95	760	2	6	4
	4,000	94	660	5	12	9
	6,000	93	565	9	18	14
	8,000	91	465	13	26	21
	10,000	90	365	18	35	29
	12,000	89	265	24	47	41
3,500	S.L.	95	990	0	0	0
	2,000	94	885	2	5	3
	4,000	93	780	5	10	7
	6,000	91	675	7	16	12
	8,000	90	570	11	22	17
	10,000	89	465	15	29	24
	12,000	87	360	20	38	32
3,200	S.L.	94	1,135	0	0	0
	2,000	92	1,020	2	4	3
	4,000	91	910	4	9	6
	6,000	90	800	6	14	10
	8,000	88	685	9	19	14
	10,000	87	575	12	25	20
	12,000	86	465	16	32	26

Figure 10. Fuel, Time, and Distance to Climb.

GROSS WEIGHT – 2,300 LB
STANDARD CONDITIONS
ZERO WIND LEAN MIXTURE

NOTE: MAXIMUM CRUISE IS NORMALLY LIMITED TO 75% POWER.

ALT.	RPM	% BHP	TAS MPH	GAL/ HOUR	38 GAL (NO RESERVE)		48 GAL (NO RESERVE)	
					ENDR (HOURS)	RANGE (MILES)	ENDR (HOURS)	RANGE (MILES)
2,500	2,700	86	134	9.7	3.9	525	4.9	660
	2,600	79	129	8.6	4.4	570	5.6	720
	2,500	72	123	7.8	4.9	600	6.2	760
	2,400	65	117	7.2	5.3	620	6.7	780
	2,300	58	111	6.7	5.7	630	7.2	795
	2,200	52	103	6.3	6.1	625	7.7	790
5,000	2,700	82	134	9.0	4.2	565	5.3	710
	2,600	75	128	8.1	4.7	600	5.9	760
	2,500	68	122	7.4	5.1	625	6.4	790
	2,400	61	116	6.9	5.5	635	6.9	805
	2,300	55	108	6.5	5.9	635	7.4	805
	2,200	49	100	6.0	6.3	630	7.9	795
7,500	2,700	78	133	8.4	4.5	600	5.7	755
	2,600	71	127	7.7	4.9	625	6.2	790
	2,500	64	121	7.1	5.3	645	6.7	810
	2,400	58	113	6.7	5.7	645	7.2	820
	2,300	52	105	6.2	6.1	640	7.7	810
10,000	2,650	70	129	7.6	5.0	640	6.3	810
	2,600	67	125	7.3	5.2	650	6.5	820
	2,500	61	118	6.9	5.5	655	7.0	830
	2,400	55	110	6.4	5.9	650	7.5	825
	2,300	49	100	6.0	6.3	635	8.0	800

Figure 11. Cruise and Range Performance.

PRESSURE ALTITUDE – 18,000 FEET

CONDITIONS:
4,000 POUNDS
RECOMMENDED LEAN MIXTURE
COWL FLAPS CLOSED

NOTES:
FOR BEST FUEL ECONOMY AT 70% POWER OR LESS, OPERATE AT 6 PPH LEANER THAN SHOWN IN THIS CHART OR AT PEAK EGT.

RPM	MP	20 °C BELOW STANDARD TEMPERATURE −41 °C			STANDARD TEMPERATURE −21 °C			20 °C ABOVE STANDARD TEMP −1 °C		
		% BHP	KTAS	PPH	% BHP	KTAS	PPH	% BHP	KTAS	PPH
2,500	30	---	---	---	81	188	106	76	185	100
	28	80	184	105	76	182	99	71	178	93
	26	75	178	99	71	176	93	67	172	88
	24	70	171	91	66	168	86	62	164	81
	22	63	162	84	60	159	79	56	155	75
2,400	30	81	185	107	77	183	101	72	180	94
	28	76	179	100	72	177	94	67	173	88
	26	71	172	93	67	170	88	63	166	83
	24	66	165	87	62	163	82	58	159	77
	22	61	158	80	57	155	76	54	150	72
2,300	30	79	182	103	74	180	97	70	176	91
	28	74	176	97	70	174	91	65	170	86
	26	69	170	91	65	167	86	61	163	81
	24	64	162	84	60	159	79	56	155	75
	22	58	154	77	55	150	73	51	145	65
2,200	26	66	166	87	62	163	82	58	159	77
	24	61	158	80	57	154	76	54	150	72
	22	55	148	73	51	144	69	48	138	66
	20	49	136	66	46	131	63	43	124	59

Figure 12. Cruise Performance.

MAXIMUM RATE OF CLIMB

CONDITIONS:
FLAPS UP
GEAR UP
2,600 RPM
COWL FLAPS OPEN
STANDARD TEMPERATURE

MIXTURE SETTING		
PRESS ALT	MP	PPH
S.L. TO 17,000	35	162
18,000	34	156
20,000	32	144
22,000	30	132
24,000	28	120

NOTES:
1. ADD 16 POUNDS OF FUEL FOR ENGINE START, TAXI, AND TAKEOFF ALLOWANCE.
2. INCREASE TIME, FUEL, AND DISTANCE BY 10% FOR EACH 10 °C ABOVE STANDARD TEMPERATURE.
3. DISTANCES SHOWN ARE BASED ON ZERO WIND.

WEIGHT (LB)	PRESS ALT (FT)	CLIMB SPEED (KIAS)	RATE OF CLIMB (FPM)	FROM SEA LEVEL		
				TIME (MIN)	FUEL USED (LB)	DISTANCE (NM)
4,000	S.L.	100	930	0	0	0
	4,000	100	890	4	12	7
	8,000	100	845	9	24	16
	12,000	100	790	14	38	25
	16,000	100	720	19	52	36
	20,000	99	515	26	69	50
	24,000	97	270	37	92	74
3,700	S.L.	99	1,060	0	0	0
	4,000	99	1,020	4	10	6
	8,000	99	975	8	21	13
	12,000	99	915	12	33	21
	16,000	99	845	17	45	30
	20,000	97	630	22	59	42
	24,000	95	370	30	77	60
3,400	S.L.	97	1,205	0	0	0
	4,000	97	1,165	3	9	5
	8,000	97	1,120	7	19	12
	12,000	97	1,060	11	29	18
	16,000	97	985	15	39	26
	20,000	96	760	19	51	36
	24,000	94	485	26	65	50

Figure 13. Fuel, Time, and Distance to Climb.

NORMAL CLIMB – 110 KIAS

CONDITIONS:
FLAPS UP
GEAR UP
2,500 RPM
30 INCHES HG
120 PPH FUEL FLOW
COWL FLAPS OPEN
STANDARD TEMPERATURE

NOTES:
1. ADD 16 POUNDS OF FUEL FOR ENGINE START, TAXI, AND TAKEOFF ALLOWANCE.
2. INCREASE TIME, FUEL, AND DISTANCE BY 10% FOR EACH 7 °C ABOVE STANDARD TEMPERATURE.
3. DISTANCES SHOWN ARE BASED ON ZERO WIND.

WEIGHT (LB)	PRESS ALT (FT)	RATE OF CLIMB (FPM)	FROM SEA LEVEL		
			TIME (MIN)	FUEL USED (LB)	DISTANCE (NM)
4,000	S.L.	605	0	0	0
	4,000	570	7	14	13
	8,000	530	14	28	27
	12,000	485	22	44	43
	16,000	430	31	62	63
	20,000	365	41	82	87
3,700	S.L.	700	0	0	0
	4,000	665	6	12	11
	8,000	625	12	24	23
	12,000	580	19	37	37
	16,000	525	26	52	53
	20,000	460	34	68	72
3,400	S.L.	810	0	0	0
	4,000	775	5	10	9
	8,000	735	10	21	20
	12,000	690	16	32	31
	16,000	635	22	44	45
	20,000	565	29	57	61

Figure 14. Fuel, Time, and Distance to Climb.

APPENDIX 2 ■ **FAA Figures**

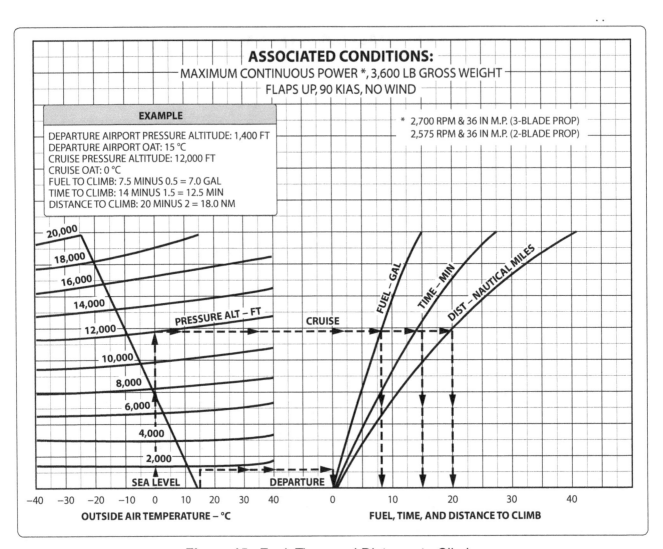

Figure 15. Fuel, Time, and Distance to Climb.

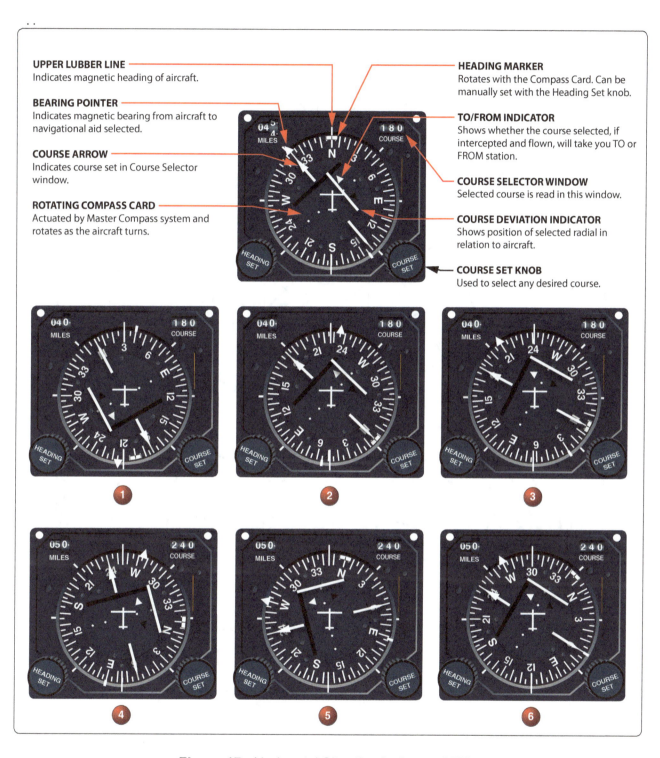

UPPER LUBBER LINE
Indicates magnetic heading of aircraft.

BEARING POINTER
Indicates magnetic bearing from aircraft to navigational aid selected.

COURSE ARROW
Indicates course set in Course Selector window.

ROTATING COMPASS CARD
Actuated by Master Compass system and rotates as the aircraft turns.

HEADING MARKER
Rotates with the Compass Card. Can be manually set with the Heading Set knob.

TO/FROM INDICATOR
Shows whether the course selected, if intercepted and flown, will take you TO or FROM station.

COURSE SELECTOR WINDOW
Selected course is read in this window.

COURSE DEVIATION INDICATOR
Shows position of selected radial in relation to aircraft.

COURSE SET KNOB
Used to select any desired course.

Figure 17. Horizontal Situation Indicator (HSI).

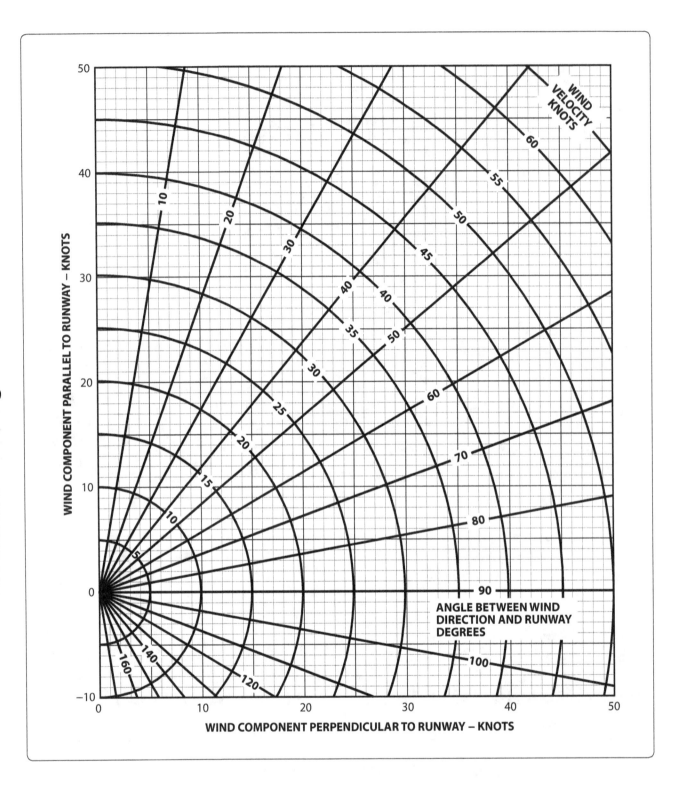

Figure 31. Wind Component Chart.

ASSOCIATED CONDITIONS:

POWER   TAKEOFF POWER
SET BEFORE
BRAKE RELEASE
FLAPS   20°
RUNWAY   PAVED, LEVEL, DRY SURFACE
TAKEOFF SPEED IAS AS TABULATED

NOTE: GROUND ROLL IS APPROX 73% OF TOTAL TAKEOFF
DISTANCE OVER A 50 FT OBSTACLE

EXAMPLE:

OAT	75 °F
PRESSURE ALTITUDE	4,000 FT
TAKEOFF WEIGHT	3,100 LB
HEADWIND	20 KNOTS

TOTAL TAKEOFF DISTANCE	
OVER A 50 FT OBSTACLE	1,350 FT
GROUND ROLL (73% OF 1,350)	986 FT
IAS TAKEOFF SPEED	
LIFT-OFF	74 MPH
AT 50 FT	74 MPH

WEIGHT (LB)	IAS TAKEOFF SPEED (ASSUMES ZERO INSTR ERROR)			
	LIFT-OFF		50 FEET	
	MPH	KNOTS	MPH	KNOTS
3,400	77	67	77	67
3,200	75	65	75	65
3,000	72	63	72	63
2,800	69	60	69	60
2,600	66	57	66	57
2,400	63	55	63	55

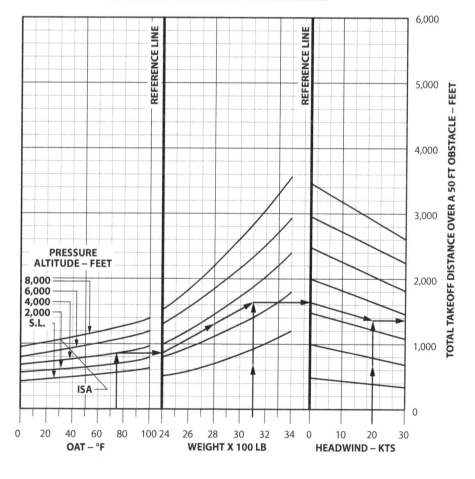

Figure 32. Obstacle Take-off Chart.

CONDITIONS:
FLAPS UP
GEAR UP
2,600 RPM
COWL FLAPS OPEN

PRESS ALT	MP	PPH
S.L. TO 17,000	35	162
18,000	34	156
20,000	32	144
22,000	30	132
24,000	28	120

WEIGHT (LB)	PRESS ALT (FT)	CLIMB SPEED (KIAS)	RATE OF CLIMB (FPM)			
			−20 °C	0 °C	20 °C	40 °C
4,000	S.L.	100	1,170	1,035	895	755
	4,000	100	1,080	940	800	655
	8,000	100	980	840	695	555
	12,000	100	870	730	590	---
	16,000	100	740	605	470	---
	20,000	99	485	355	---	---
	24,000	97	190	70	---	---
3,700	S.L.	99	1,310	1,165	1,020	875
	4,000	99	1,215	1,070	925	775
	8,000	99	1,115	965	815	670
	12,000	99	1,000	855	710	---
	16,000	99	865	730	590	---
	20,000	97	600	470	---	---
	24,000	95	295	170	---	---
3,400	S.L.	97	1,465	1,320	1,165	1,015
	4,000	97	1,370	1,220	1,065	910
	8,000	97	1,265	1,110	955	795
	12,000	97	1,150	995	845	---
	16,000	97	1,010	865	725	---
	20,000	96	730	595	---	---
	24,000	94	405	275	---	---

Figure 33. Maximum Rate of Climb Chart.

PRESSURE ALTITUDE 6,000 FEET

CONDITIONS:
3,800 POUNDS
RECOMMENDED LEAN MIXTURE
COWL FLAPS CLOSED

RPM	MP	20 °C BELOW STANDARD TEMPERATURE −17 °C			STANDARD TEMPERATURE 3 °C			20 °C ABOVE STANDARD TEMPERATURE 23 °C		
		% BHP	KTAS	PPH	% BHP	KTAS	PPH	% BHP	KTAS	PPH
2,550	24	---	---	---	78	173	97	75	174	94
	23	76	167	96	74	169	92	71	171	89
	22	72	164	90	69	166	87	67	167	84
	21	68	160	85	65	162	82	63	163	80
2,500	24	78	169	98	75	171	95	73	172	91
	23	74	166	93	71	167	90	69	169	87
	22	70	162	88	67	164	85	65	165	82
	21	66	158	83	63	160	80	61	160	77
2,400	24	73	165	91	70	166	88	68	167	85
	23	69	161	87	67	163	84	64	164	81
	22	65	158	82	63	159	79	61	160	77
	21	61	154	77	59	155	75	57	155	73
2,300	24	68	161	86	66	162	83	64	163	80
	23	65	158	82	62	159	79	60	159	76
	22	61	154	77	59	155	75	57	155	72
	21	57	150	73	55	150	71	53	150	68
2,200	24	63	156	80	61	157	77	59	158	75
	23	60	152	76	58	153	73	56	154	71
	22	57	149	72	54	149	70	53	149	67
	21	53	144	68	51	144	66	49	143	64
	20	50	139	64	48	138	62	46	137	60
	19	46	133	60	44	132	58	43	131	57

Figure 34. Cruise Performance Chart.

ASSOCIATED CONDITIONS:

POWER	AS REQUIRED TO MAINTAIN 800 FT/MIN DESCENT ON APPROACH
FLAPS	DOWN
RUNWAY	PAVED, LEVEL, DRY SURFACE
APPROACH SPEED	IAS AS TABULATED

NOTE: GROUND ROLL IS APPROX 53% OF TOTAL LANDING DISTANCE OVER A 50 FT OBSTACLE.

EXAMPLE:

OAT	75 °F
PRESSURE ALTITUDE	4,000 FT
LANDING WEIGHT	3,200 LB
HEADWIND	10 KNOTS

TOTAL LANDING DISTANCE OVER A 50 FT OBSTACLE	1,475 FT
GROUND ROLL (53% OF 1,475)	782 FT
IAS TAKEOFF SPEED	87 MPH IAS

WEIGHT (LB)	IAS APPROACH SPEED (ASSUMES ZERO INSTR ERROR)	
	MPH	KNOTS
3,400	90	78
3,200	87	76
3,000	84	73
2,800	81	70
2,600	78	68
2,400	75	65

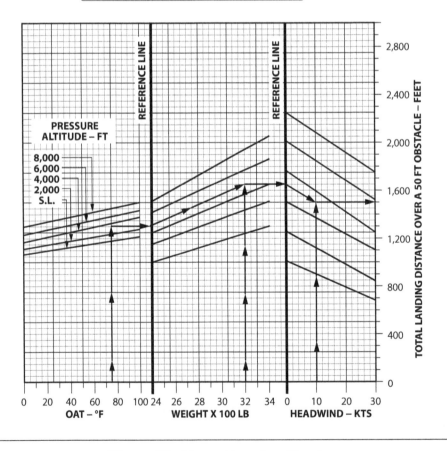

Figure 35. Normal Landing Chart.

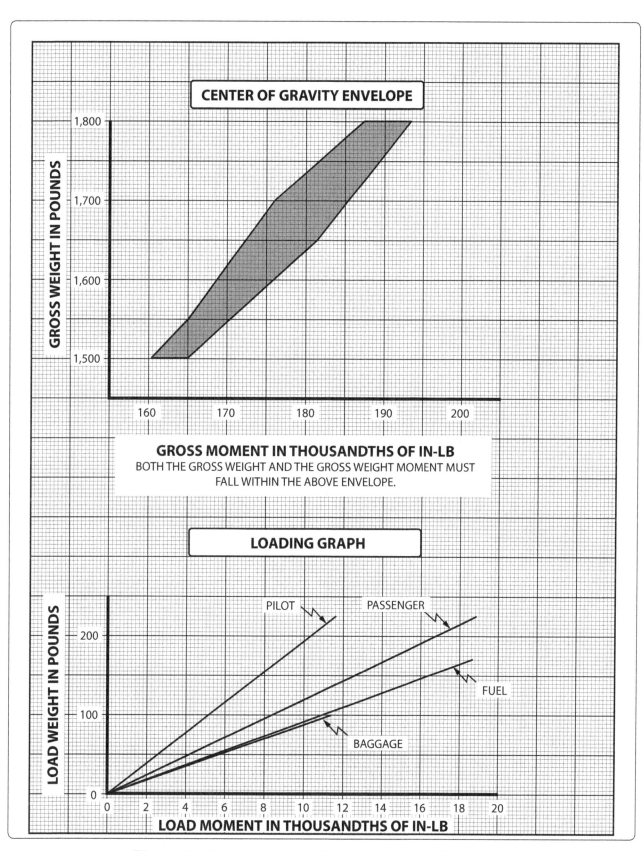

Figure 37. Center of Gravity Envelope and Loading Graph.

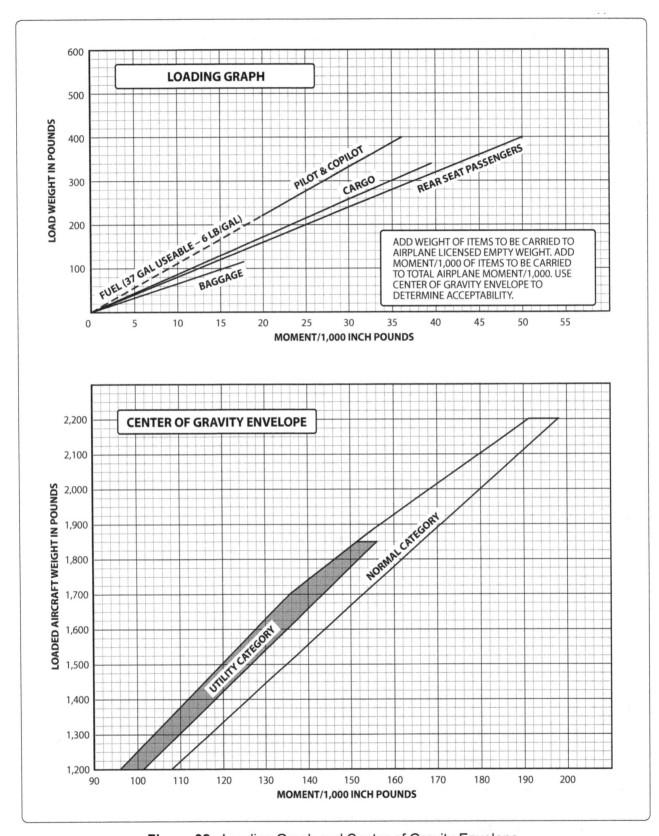

Figure 38. Loading Graph and Center of Gravity Envelope.

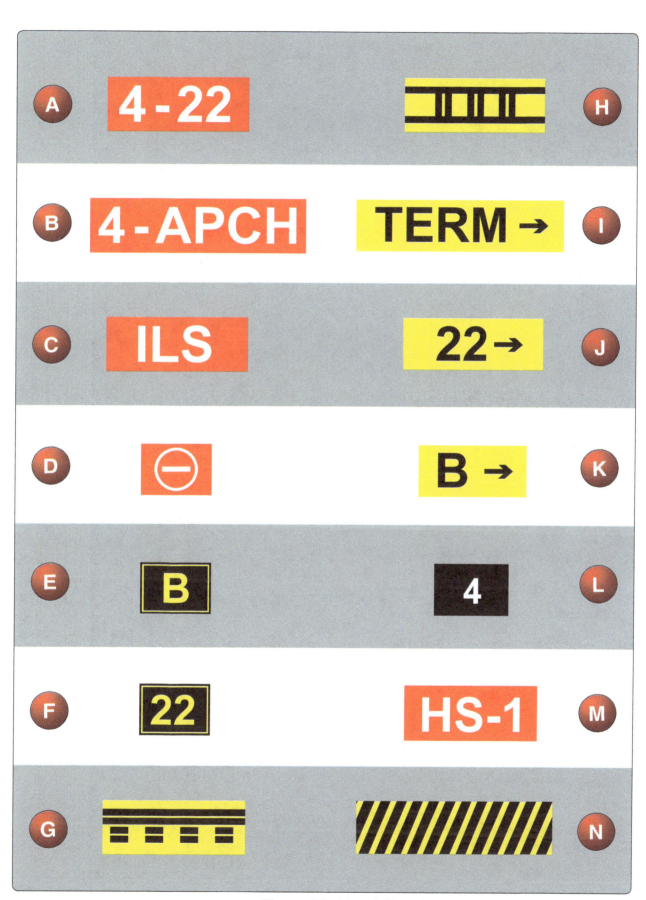

Figure 51. Airport Signs.

APPENDIX 2 ■ FAA Figures

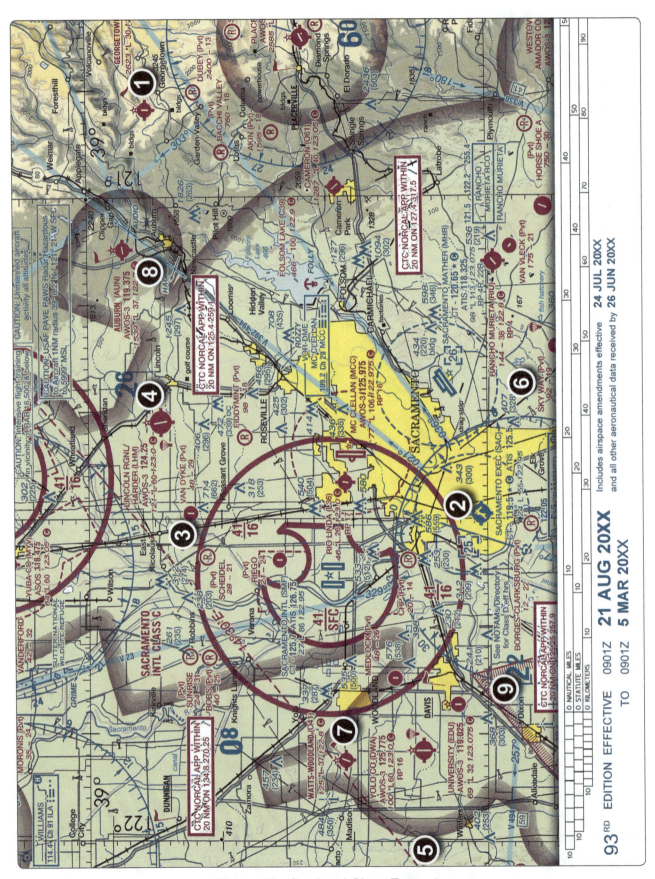

Figure 52. Sectional Chart Excerpt.

Note: *Chart is not to scale and should not be used for navigation. Chart is for testing purposes only.*

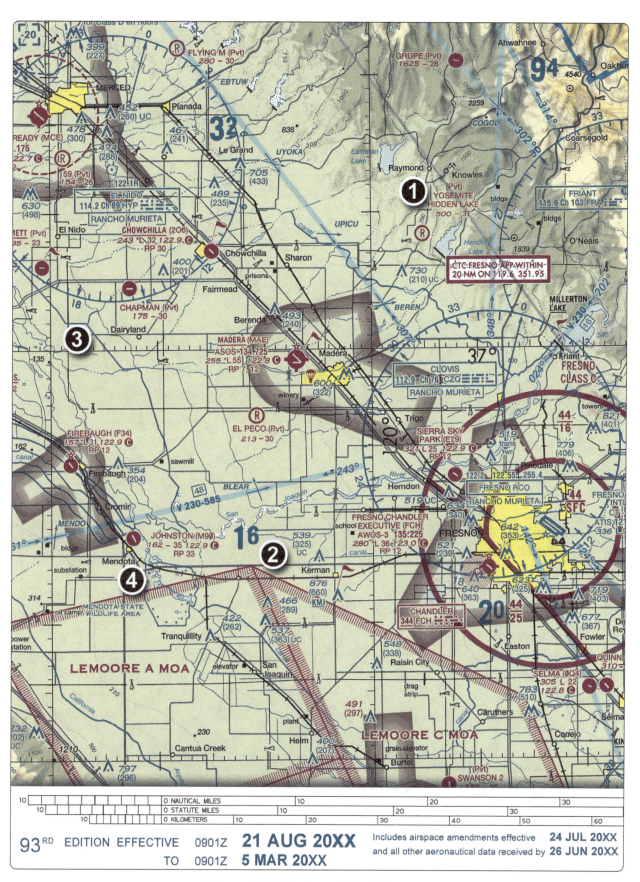

Figure 53. Sectional Chart Excerpt.

Note: Chart is not to scale and should not be used for navigation. Chart is for testing purposes only.

APPENDIX 2 ■ FAA Figures

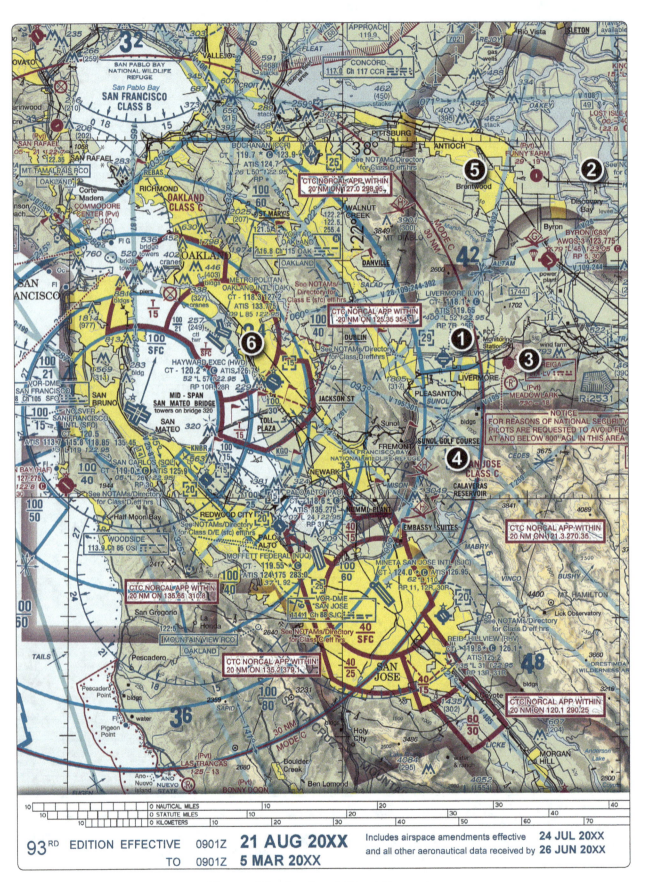

Figure 54. Sectional Chart Excerpt.

Note: Chart is not to scale and should not be used for navigation. Chart is for testing purposes only.

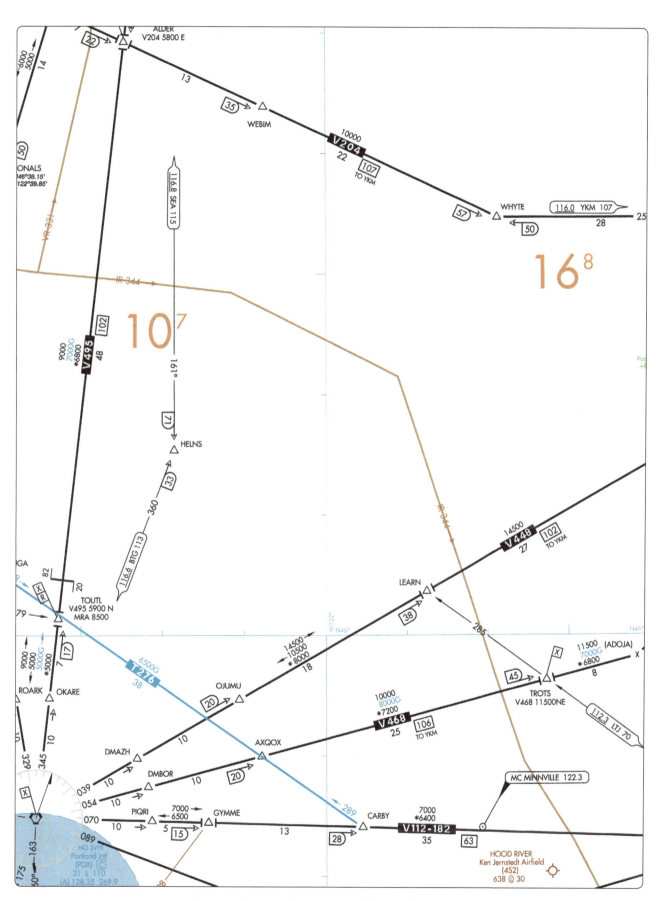

Figure 55. En Route Low Altitude Segment.

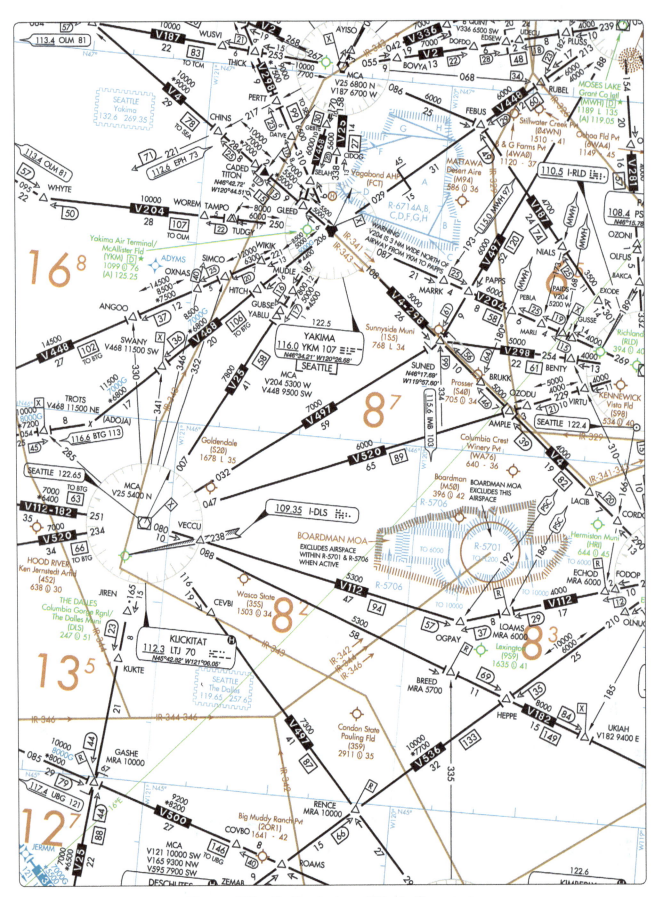

Figure 55A. En Route Low Altitude Segment.

Figure 56. Two signs.

Figure 57. Sign.

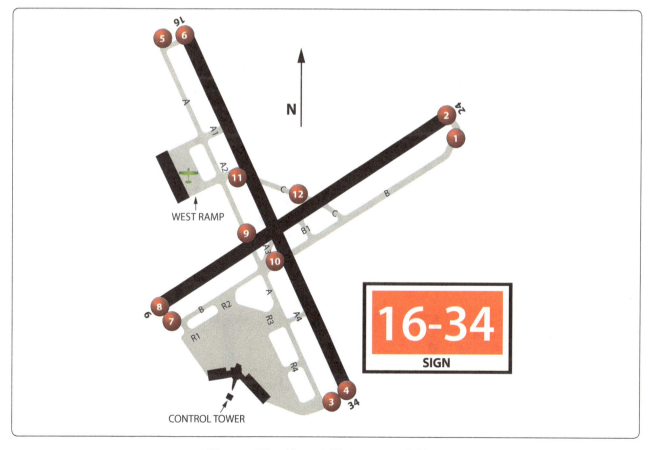

Figure 58. Airport Diagram and Sign.

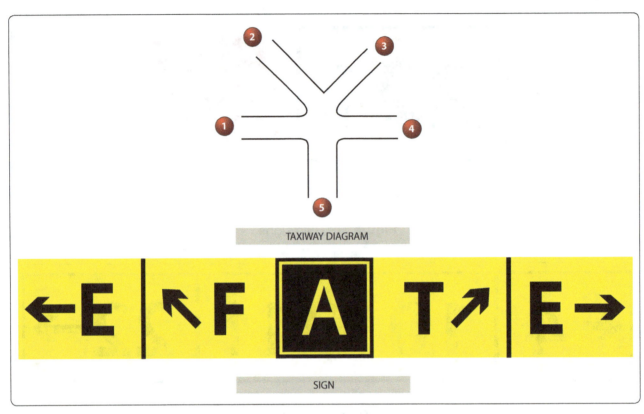

Figure 59. Taxiway Diagram and Sign.

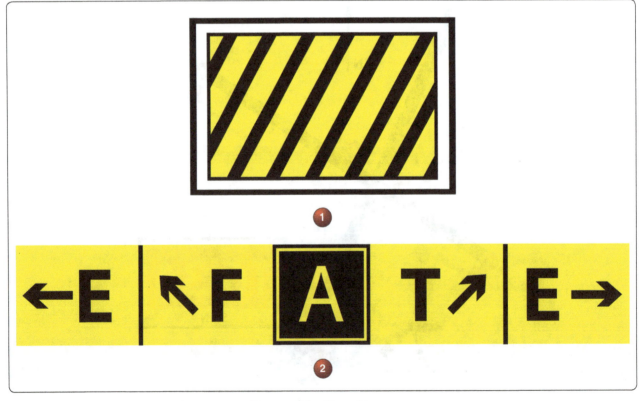

Figure 60. Two Signs.

Figure 61. Sign.

Figure 62. Sign.

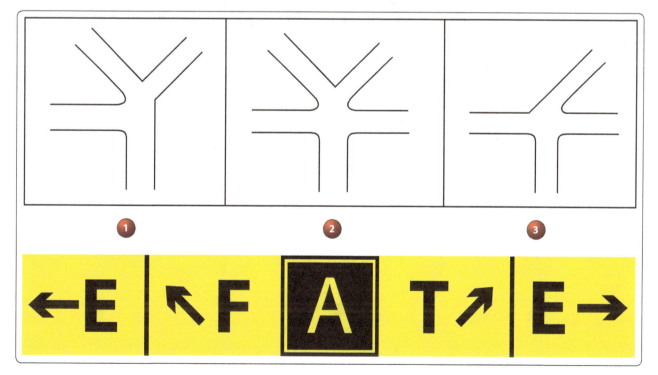

Figure 63. Sign and Intersection Diagram.

Figure 64. Sign.

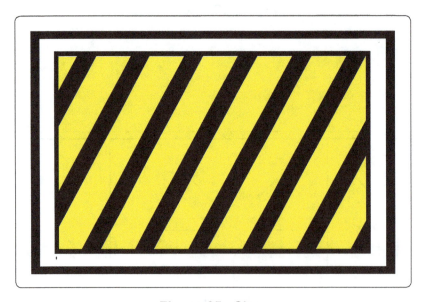

Figure 65. Sign.

200   **OKLAHOMA**

- -

WILEY POST (PWA)(KPWA)   7 NW   UTC–6(–5DT)   N35°32.05´ W97°38.82´   DALLAS–FT WORTH
  1300   B   TPA—See Remarks   NOTAM FILE PWA   H–6H, L–15D
  RWY 17L–35R: H7199X150 (CONC) S–35, D–50, 2D–90 HIRL   IAP, AD
    RWY 17L: MALSR. PAPI(P4L)—GA 3.0° TCH 54´. Rgt tfc.
    RWY 35R: MALSR. PAPI(P4L)—GA 3.0° TCH 54´. Thld dsplcd 355´.
    Trees.
  RWY 17R–35L: H5002X75 (ASPH–CONC) S–26, D–45   MIRL
    RWY 17R: REIL. PAPI(P4L)—GA 3.0° TCH 43´. Tree. Rgt tfc.
    RWY 35L: REIL. PAPI(P4L)—GA 3.0° TCH 42´.
  RWY 13–31: H4214X100 (CONC) S–35, D–50, 2D–90   MIRL
    0.6% up SE
    RWY 13: Rgt tfc. 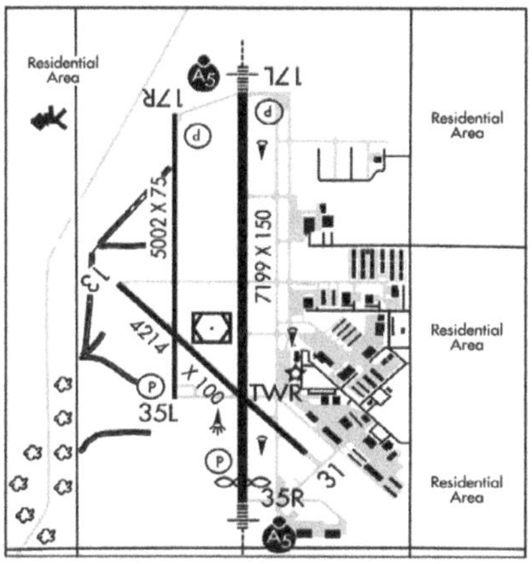
  RUNWAY DECLARED DISTANCE INFORMATION
    RWY 13: TORA–4214   TODA–4214   ASDA–4214   LDA–4214
    RWY 17L: TORA–7199   TODA–7199   ASDA–6844   LDA–6844
    RWY 17R: TORA–5002   TODA–5002   ASDA–5002   LDA–5002
    RWY 31: TORA–4214   TODA–4214   ASDA–4214   LDA–4214
    RWY 35L: TORA–5001   TODA–5001   ASDA–5001   LDA–5001
    RWY 35R: TORA–7198   TODA–7198   ASDA–7198   LDA–6844
  SERVICE: S4   FUEL 100LL, JET A   **OX** 1, 2, 3, 4   **LGT** Dusk–Dawn. When
    twr clsd ACTIVATE HIRL Rwy 17L–35R and MALSR Rwy 17L and Rwy
    35R—CTAF.
  AIRPORT REMARKS: Attended continuously. 100LL fuel avbl 24 hrs self serve with credit card. Surface conditions reported
    Mon–Fri 1400–2300Z‡. Rwy 13–31 CLOSED 0400–1300Z‡. Rwy 13–31 CLOSED to tkof and Rwy 31 CLOSED to acft
    over 12,500 lbs gross weight. Flocks of birds on and invof arpt all quadrants. Noise abatement procedure: Acft in excess
    of 12,500 pounds departing Rwy 17L–35R climb at a maximum rate consistent with safety to an altitude of 1500´ AGL
    then reduce power setting and climb rate to 3000´ AGL or 2 NM from arpt depending on air traffic control and safety
    conditions. TPA for Rwy 17R/35L 1900(600) 2300(1000) all other rwys. Rwy 13–31 unlighted 0400–1300Z‡. Touch
    & go or stop & go ldgs not authorized Rwy 13–31.
  AIRPORT MANAGER: 405-316-4061
  WEATHER DATA SOURCES: ASOS (405) 798–2013
  COMMUNICATIONS: CTAF 126.9 **ATIS** 128.725 **UNICOM** 122.95
    RCO 122.65 (MC ALESTER RADIO)
Ⓡ **OKE CITY APP/DEP CON** 124.6 (171°–360°) 120.45 (081°–170°) 124.2 (001°–080°)
    TOWER 126.9 (1300–0400Z‡) **GND CON** 121.7
  AIRSPACE: CLASS D svc 1300–0400Z‡ other times **CLASS E.**
  RADIO AIDS TO NAVIGATION: NOTAM FILE PWA.
    (T) VORW/DME 113.4   PWA   Chan 81   N35°31.98´ W97°38.83´   at fld. 1271/8E.
    ILS 110.15 I–PWA   Rwy 17L.   Unmonitored when ATCT clsd. DME also serves Rwy 35R.
    ILS/DME 110.15 I–TFM   Chan 38(Y)   Rwy 35R.   Class IT.   DME also serves Rwy 17L.

- -

Figure 66. Chart Supplement.

APPENDIX 2 ■ FAA Figures

LUBBOCK

LUBBOCK EXECUTIVE AIRPARK (F82)   5 S   UTC–6(–5DT)   N33°29.14′ W101°48.76′   **DALLAS–FT WORTH**
    3200   B   TPA—4200(1000)   NOTAM FILE FTW   **L–6H**
    RWY 17–35: H3500X70 (ASPH)   S–13   HIRL
    RWY 07–25: 1500X110 (TURF)
      RWY 07: P–line.
    SERVICE: S4   **FUEL** 100LL, JET A
    AIRPORT REMARKS: Attended 1400–0000Z‡. After hrs 806–789–6437, 806–589–8143. Fuel avbl 24 hrs with major credit
      card. Rwy 17 road located at thld. Farm equipment ops AER 17, Rwy 25 and Rwy 35.
    AIRPORT MANAGER: 806–789–6437
    COMMUNICATIONS: CTAF/UNICOM 122.8
    RADIO AIDS TO NAVIGATION: NOTAM FILE LBB.
      (L) VORTACW 109.2   LBB   Chan 29   N33°42.30′ W101°54.84′   148° 14.1 NM to fld. 3310/11E.   **HIWAS.**
      VOR portion unusable:
        140°–190° byd 20 NM blo 5,100′

- -

LUBBOCK PRESTON SMITH INTL (LBB)(KLBB)   4 N   UTC–6(–5DT)   N33°39.82′ W101°49.23′   **DALLAS–FT WORTH**
    3282   B   LRA   Class I, ARFF Index C   NOTAM FILE LBB   **H–6G, L–6H**
    RWY 17R–35L: H11500X150 (CONC–GRVD)   S–100, D–170, 2S–175,   **IAP, AD**
      2D–350 PCN 65 R/B/W/T   HIRL
      RWY 17R: MALSR. PAPI(P4R)—GA 3.0° TCH 69′. RVR–T Rgt tfc.
      0.4% down.
      RWY 35L: ODALS. VASI(V4L)—GA 3.0° TCH 54′. RVR–R 0.3% up.
    RWY 08–26: H8003X150 (CONC–GRVD)   S–100, D–170, 2S–175,
      2D–350 PCN 71 R/B/W/T   HIRL
      RWY 08: REIL. PAPI(P4L)—GA 3.0° TCH 50′. RVR–R Rgt tfc.
      RWY 26: MALSR. PAPI(P4L)—GA 3.0° TCH 50′. RVR–T
    RWY 17L–35R: H2891X74 (ASPH)   S–12.5
      RWY 35R: Road. Rgt tfc. 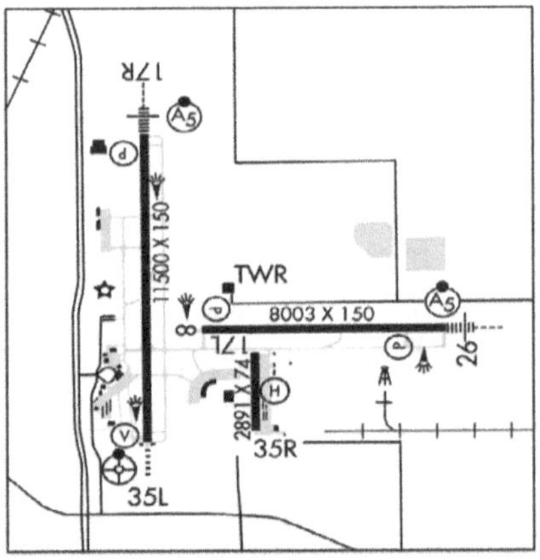
    RUNWAY DECLARED DISTANCE INFORMATION
      RWY 08: TORA–8003   TODA–8003   ASDA–8003   LDA–8003
      RWY 17L: TORA–2891   TODA–2891   ASDA–2891   LDA–2891
      RWY 17R: TORA–11500 TODA–11500 ASDA–11500 LDA–11500
      RWY 26: TORA–8003   TODA–8003   ASDA–8003   LDA–8003
      RWY 35L: TORA–11500 TODA–11500 ASDA–11500 LDA–11500
      RWY 35R: TORA–2891   TODA–2891   ASDA–2891   LDA–2891
    SERVICE: S4   **FUEL** 100LL, JET A, A1+   **OX** 1, 2, 3, 4
    AIRPORT REMARKS: Attended continuously. Numerous birds on and invof
    arpt. PAEW adjacent Rwy 08–26 and Rwy 17R–35L. Passenger terminal ramp access rstd to air carriers and others with
    prior permission call 806–775–2044. Rwy 17L–35R rstd to general aviation acft 12,500 lbs or less. Rwy 17L–35R, Twy
    B, Twy D, and Twy E not avbl for air carrier acft with over 9 psgr seats. Twy B, Twy D, and Twy E rstd to acft weighing
    less than 50,000 lbs. Twy L between Twy F and Twy J clsd to more than 120,001 lbs. East ramp delineated taxilane and
    apron area rstd to 120,000 lbs dual tandem acft, 89,000 lbs dual single wheel acft and 60,000 lbs single wheel acft.
    All other east ramp pavements rstd to acft less than 12,500 lbs single wheel acft. Flight Notification Service (ADCUS)
    available.
    AIRPORT MANAGER: 806–775–3126
    WEATHER DATA SOURCES: ASOS 125.3 (806) 766–6432. **HIWAS** 109.2 LBB. WSP.
    COMMUNICATIONS: ATIS 125.3 **UNICOM** 122.95
      RCO 122.55 (FORT WORTH RADIO)
  Ⓡ **APP/DEP CON** 119.2 119.9
      TOWER 120.5 **GND CON** 121.9 **CLNC DEL** 125.8
    AIRSPACE: CLASS C svc ctc **APP CON**
    RADIO AIDS TO NAVIGATION: NOTAM FILE LBB.
      (L) VORTACW 109.2   LBB   Chan 29   N33°42.30′ W101°54.84′   107° 5.3 NM to fld. 3310/11E.   **HIWAS.**
      VOR portion unusable:
        140°–190° byd 20 NM blo 5,100′
      LUBBI NDB (LOMW) 272   LD   N33°39.76′ W101°43.39′   265° 4.9 NM to fld. 3198/6E.
      POLLO NDB (LOM) 219   LB   N33°44.26′ W101°49.76′ 168° 4.5 NM to fld.
      ILS/DME 111.7   I–LBB   Chan 54   Rwy 17R.   Class IA.   LOM POLLO NDB.
      ILS 111.9   I–LDT   Rwy 26.   Class IA.   LOM LUBBI NDB.

Figure 67. Chart Supplement.

DALLAS

ADDISON (ADS)(KADS) 9 N UTC–6(–5DT) N32°58.11´ W96°50.19´

645 B TPA—See Remarks LRA NOTAM FILE ADS

RWY 15–33: H7203X100 (ASPH–GRVD) S–60, D–120 HIRL

RWY 15: MALSR. PAPI(P4R)—GA 3.0° TCH 60´. Thld dsplcd 979´.
Tree.

RWY 33: REIL. PAPI(P4L)—GA 3.0° TCH 60´. Thld dsplcd 772´. Bldg.

RUNWAY DECLARED DISTANCE INFORMATION

RWY 15: TORA–7203 TODA–7203 ASDA–7203 LDA–6224

RWY 33: TORA–7203 TODA–7203 ASDA–7203 LDA–6431

ARRESTING GEAR/SYSTEM

RWY 15: EMAS

SERVICE: S4 **FUEL** 100LL, JET A **OX** 2, 3 **LGT** ACTIVATE HIRL Rwy
15–33 and MALSR Rwy 15—CTAF.

AIRPORT REMARKS: Attended continuously. Birds on and invof arpt. No
touch and go ldgs without arpt mgr apvl. Numerous 200´ bldgs within
1 mile east, and south of arpt, transmission twrs and water tanks west
of arpt. Noise sensitive areas surround arpt. Pilots req to use NBAA std
noise procedures. TPA—1601 (956) for light acft, 2001 (1356) for
large acft. Be alert, rwy holding position markings lctd at the west
edge of Twy A. Flight Notification Service (ADCUS) available.

AIRPORT MANAGER: 972-392-4850

WEATHER DATA SOURCES: AWOS–3 (972) 386–4855 LAWRS.

COMMUNICATIONS: CTAF 126.0 ATIS 133.4 972–628–2439

UNICOM 122.95

®REGIONAL APP/DEP CON 124.3

TOWER 126.0 (1200–0400Z‡) **GND CON** 121.6 **CLNC DEL** 119.55

AIRSPACE: CLASS D svc 1200–0400Z‡, other times CLASS G.

RADIO AIDS TO NAVIGATION: NOTAM FILE FTW.

MAVERICK (H) VORW/DME 113.1 TTT Chan 78 N32°52.15´ W97°02.43´ 054° 11.9 NM to fld. 540/6E.
All acft arriving DFW are requested to turn DME off until departure due to traffic overload of Maverick DME
DME unusable:
180°–190°

ILS/DME 110.1 I–ADS Chan 38 Rwy 15. Class IT. Unmonitored when ATCT closed. DME also serves Rwy 33.

ILS/DME 110.1 I–TBQ Chan 38 Rwy 33. Class IB. Localizer unmonitored when ATCT closed. DME also serves
Rwy 15.

- -

AIR PARK–DALLAS (F69) 16 NE UTC–6(–5DT) N33°01.41´ W96°50.22´

695 TPA—1890(1195) NOTAM FILE FTW

RWY 16–34: H3080X30 (ASPH) LIRL(NSTD)

RWY 16: Thld dsplcd 300´. Pole.

RWY 34: Tree. Rgt tfc.

SERVICE: S4 **FUEL** 100LL **LGT** ACTIVATE LIRL Rwy 16–34—CTAF. Rwy 16–34 NSTD LIRL; 2780´ of rwy lgtd. Thld and
dsplcd thld not lighted.

AIRPORT REMARKS: Uattended. For fuel call 972–248–4265 prior to arr. Rwy 16–34 pavement cracking, loose stones on rwy.
Rwy 34 NSTD cntrln marking incorrect size and spacing. Rwy numbers 25´ tall, markings faded. Rwy number 34 not
located at rwy end.

AIRPORT MANAGER: 972–248–4265

COMMUNICATIONS: CTAF 122.9

RADIO AIDS TO NAVIGATION: NOTAM FILE FTW.

MAVERICK (H) VORW/DME 113.1 TTT Chan 78 N32°52.15´ W97°02.43´ 042° 13.8 NM to fld. 540/6E.
All acft arriving DFW are requested to turn DME off until departure due to traffic overload of Maverick DME
DME unusable:
180°–190°

COMM/NAV/WEATHER REMARKS: For Clnc Del ctc Regional Apch at 972–615–2799.

- -

DALLAS–FT WORTH
COPTER
H–6H, L–17C, A
IAP, AD

DALLAS–FT WORTH
COPTER
L–17C, A

SC, 1 FEB 20XX to 29 MAR 20XX

Figure 68. Chart Supplement.

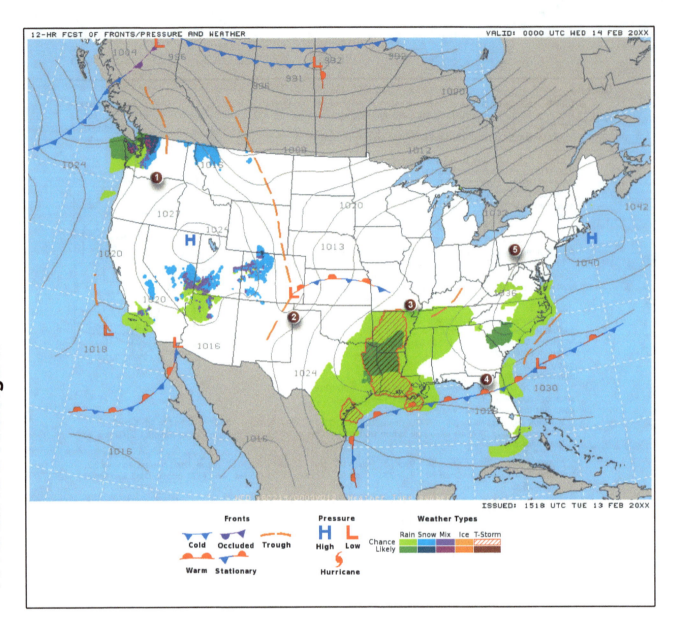

Figure 69. Weather Prediction Center (WPC) Surface Prog Chart.

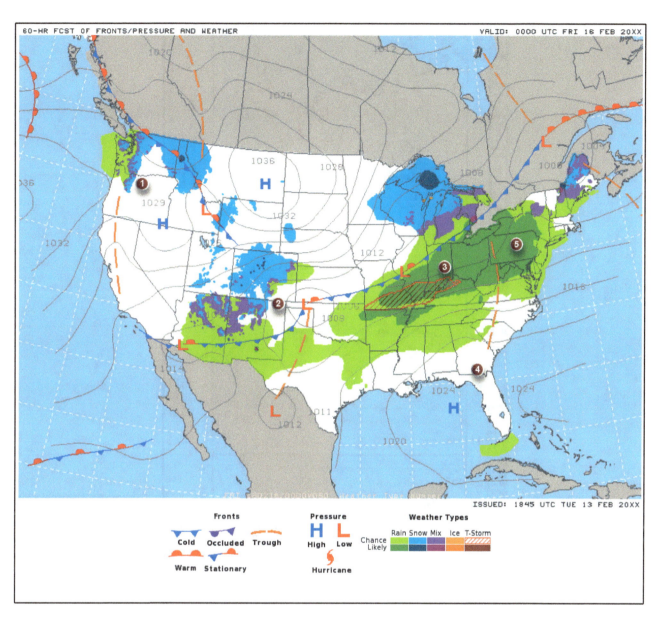

Figure 70. Weather Prediction Center (WPC) Surface Prog Chart.

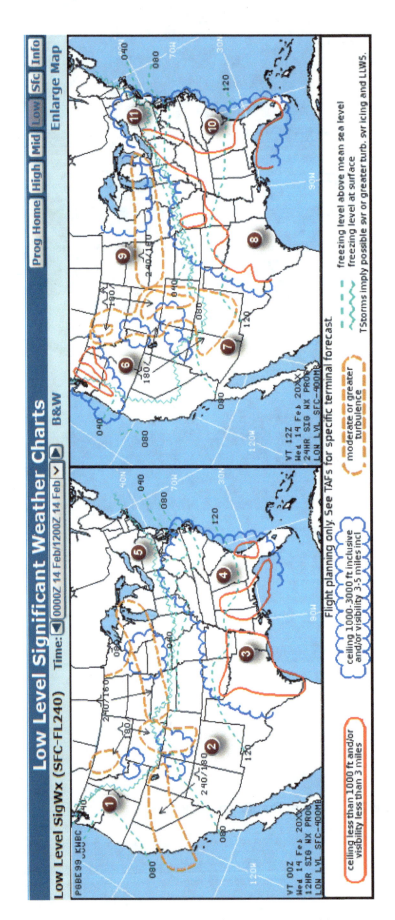

Figure 71. Low-level Significant Weather Chart.